SCHOOL OF ADVANCED STUDY UNIVERSITY OF LONDON
Institute of Languages, Cultures and Societies

A Critical Encounter
Bataille and Blanchot
Exploring the Literary Real

imlr books

Established by the Institute of Languages, Cultures and Societies, this series (formerly known as igrs books) aims to bring to the public monographs and collections of essays in the field of modern foreign languages. Proposals for publication are selected by the Institute's editorial board, which is advised by a peer review committee of some fifty senior academics in the field. To make titles as accessible as possible to an English-speaking and multi-lingual readership, volumes are written in English and quotations given in English translation.

For further details, visit:
https://ilcs.sas.ac.uk/search-publications/imlr-books

Editorial Board

Professor Charles Burdett (Italian)
Professor Catherine Davies (Hispanic)
Dr Joseph Ford (French)
Dr Naomi Wells (Italian)
Professor Godela Weiss-Sussex (Germanic)

imlr books Volume 17

Volume Editor
Dr Anne Simon

A Critical Encounter
Bataille and Blanchot
Exploring the Literary Real

Zoe Angeli

SCHOOL OF ADVANCED STUDY UNIVERSITY OF LONDON

Institute of Languages, Cultures and Societies

2022

Published by the

Institute of Languages, Cultures and Societies
School of Advanced Study, University of London
Senate House, Malet Street, London WC1E 7HU
https://ilcs.sas.ac.uk

© Zoe Angeli, 2022

The author has asserted her rights under the Copyright, Designs and Patents Act 1988 to be identified as the author of this work.

All rights reserved. No part of this publication may be reproduced, stored in a retrieval system, or transmitted, in any form or by any means, electronic, mechanical, photocopying, recording or otherwise, without the prior permission of the author and the publisher.

Cover image
Elegant Man Looking at a Book with Blank Pages
Detail from photograph by Stokkete
Shutterstock ID 134607065

First published 2022

ISBN 978 0 85457 282 3
ISSN 2632-9573 (Print)

Contents

Acknowledgements	vii
Note to the Reader	ix
Introduction	1

Part I Double Dissymmetries — 15

1. Bataille: The Passion of the Real — 17
2. Blanchot: The Passion of Literature — 39
3. The Value of Annexes: *Coïncidences et Correspondences* — 57

Part II Confusions — 69

4. The Imaginary: The Real of Literature — 71
5. The Instant: The Ethics of Literature — 93
6. The Speech of Analysis — 131

Part III (Re)turns — 159

7. Blanchot: Turning and Reveiling — 161
8. Bataille: Returning and Masking — 193

Conclusion	231
Bibliography	237
Index	255

Acknowledgements

I would like to offer my warm thanks to all those who have helped with the production of this work in 'imlr books'. Special thanks are due to the anonymous readers of the manuscript, whose reviews paved the way for the subsequent versions; to Jane Lewin, who made the editing of this book seem effortless; and to Anne Simon, whose attentive reading and comments contributed invaluably to the accessibility, clarity and flow of the final version. As this book draws on my PhD thesis at the University of Cambridge, I am grateful to my supervisor, Ian James, for his thoroughness and lucidity and for always being there to read and comment on my work. I am also thankful to have had the opportunity to conduct my research at the University of Cambridge, which offered a challenging and stimulating academic environment. There I met exceptional researchers and gave presentations which would eventually turn into the chapters of this book. In particular, I would like to thank Martin Crowley, who exposed us to his *pensées sensibles* during the various sessions of the Modern French Research Seminar. Additional thanks are due to Ian Maclahlan, my thesis examiner, who provided valuable feedback for my work. My gratitude also goes to my friend Blake Gutt for, on many occasions, showing me the way; to Helena Chadderton for being the first to foresee the prospect of publication; and to Pierre Bayard for urging me to radicalize the comparison between the two thinkers into unthought-of ways. Finally, I cannot thank my mother and brother, Ioanna and Georgios, enough: they have always been at my side and made everything possible.

Note to the Reader

Throughout this book reference is made to both the original French editions and their published English translations. In quotations the French text comes first and the English translation follows. Where no published English translation is given, the translations are by the author. In the Bibliography English translations are listed directly beneath the original, except for translations of works by Georges Bataille and Maurice Blanchot, which are listed in separate sections.

Introduction

[C]e qui est dit une fois d'un côté, est redit une deuxième fois de l'autre côté et non pas seulement réaffirmé mais (parce que il y a reprise) élevé à une forme d'affirmation nouvelle où, changeant de place, la chose dite entre en rapport avec sa différence, devient plus aiguë, plus tragique, non pas plus unifiée, mais au contraire suspendue tragiquement entre deux poles d'attraction.

[[W]hat is said a first time on one side is said again a second time on the other and is not only reaffirmed but also (because there is repetition) raised to a new form of affirmation whereby, changing place, the thing that is said enters into relation with its difference and becomes sharper, more tragic: not more unified, but, on the contrary, tragically suspended between two poles of attraction.][1]

The aim of this book is to examine the encounter of the real and literature – as thematically crystallized in the contrivance of the literary real – in terms of an irreducible tension. The encounter of literature and the real (their co-existence and inseparability) is examined conjointly with the encounter (the meeting and interlinking) of Georges Bataille and Maurice Blanchot. The encounter between the two thinkers is thus reflected in the structure of the book, as in all three parts the two thinkers are examined in comparison. The investigation into the literary real revolves around two strands which are constantly entwined: the first deals with the question of the way in which literature (writing) engages with and contemplates human reality, perceives and depicts, transforms, renounces or neglects worldly existence, while the second focuses on the question of the

---

1 Maurice Blanchot, 'L'Expérience-limite', in Maurice Blanchot, *L'Entretien infini* (Paris: Gallimard, 1969), pp. 300–42 (p. 318); Maurice Blanchot, 'The Limit-Experience', in Maurice Blanchot, *The Infinite Conversation*, trans. by Susan Hanson (Minneapolis, MN and London: University of Minnesota Press, 1993), pp. 202–29 (p. 214).

reality of writing itself, of the particular mode of being of the literary, as posed in the old but persistent inquiry, 'What *is* literature?'. Briefly, the literary real addresses both the question of what kind of 'real' is involved and disclosed in writing (and how that might differ from reality in its more traditional sense – or, more precisely, from more conventional representations of reality) and the question of writing's own 'being' – that is, the particularity of its mode of being, its peculiar reality/unreality.

The focus of the book is how Bataille and Blanchot – the first through an exposure to the violent disorder of life, the second through a passionate meditation on literature and language – reconfigure our common understanding of the terms 'being', 'existence' and 'real', as well as 'literature' and writing; and, more importantly, how they radically alter the way we usually think about their relationship. Both thinkers bring out a radical notion of writing, one which breaks with all representational logic since it does not reflect a pre-given reality and which entails an understanding of the real, of being, as inappropriable and ungraspable. In so doing, they make of writing an encounter with a dimension of existence which is excessive, outside phenomenological disclosure and ontological discerning and otherworldly, beyond the logic (itself worldly) of transcendence and immanence. Thus, the real of literature is a strange and paradoxical suspension of the representation (or the presentation) of worldly existence and literature is an exposure to (and an imbrication with) a 'real' which exceeds (and is anterior to) all appearance and manifestation as such. It is in this sense that one can speak of a 'literary real'.

Bataille and Blanchot conceive of writing as a sovereign realm, not subordinate to worldly (social) causes and, by its very disengagement, as deeply engaged with the world (in its more fundamental sense, in its more hidden aspects). In that respect, their account of writing is suspended between the Hegelian dismissal of the literary intellectual, who in a mere display of his natural, inherent talent remains completely detached from the world, and the Sartrean praise of the writer, whose writing incarnates the highest form of worldly commitment and therefore remains wedded to positivistic values and goals.

Bataille's writing revolves around an excessive experience which touches upon the limit(lessness) of the self and affirms the whole of existence. Blanchot privileges writing, since it emanates from an experience of the world which slips from the appropriative grasp of the subject, an experience of radical exteriority that he calls *le dehors*. However, and this is a key claim, since for Bataille and Blanchot writing involves an encounter with what is excessive and inappropriable, they both insinuate an asymmetrical and asymptotic relation between the two, namely a relation which diverges from the conventional meaning of the term (a relation without relation, as Blanchot says – but one which is thereby the condition of any and all relationality *per se*).[2] As a result, writing for both becomes bound to loss, expenditure, withdrawal and absence and is willingly described in terms of failure, imposture, privation, incompleteness and, more importantly, impossibility. In that regard, this study examines how the referential capacity of language is undermined in their works, derisively in Bataille, serenely in Blanchot, and how what is written gestures towards an outside which is suggested but not fully contained within writing. This volume demonstrates throughout how the demands of the real (meant in terms of both resistance and corporeality) are already operative in Blanchot's and Bataille's conception of the literary; additionally, it shows how writing both addresses and questions what counts as real. As writing is suspended between an affirmative (setting up) and a questioning (upsetting) attitude, it distances itself from both the pole of autonomy (relishing its own logic and in its separate place) and the pole of subversion (being reduced to a critical tool), thereby offering a radical rethinking of the key question of relation, a question as old as thought itself.

Relations and modes of relating have been, in various ways, the central preoccupation of thought. In this respect, a number of influential concepts which have decisively – and to a certain extent irrevocably – marked the trajectory of thought bear on the broader question of relation. The constitutive distinction of metaphysics between the sensible and the intelligible, the apparent and the essential, what we perceive (see, hear, grasp) and what truly (really?) 'is' is introduced in the Platonic theory of ideal forms. In Plato's *Republic* the opposites are not only designated in the hierarchical terms of the fundamental and the derivative but also in terms of visual semblance or, more broadly, of participation. The relation between ideas and material forms, thought and matter, human freedom and natural constraints, is also at the heart of the Kantian notion of presentation, inasmuch as the latter consists precisely in the problem of co-ordination (co-articulation) between sensible forms

---

2   Maurice Blanchot, 'Le Rapport du troisième genre (homme sans horizon)', in Blanchot, *L'Entretien infini*, pp. 94–105 (p. 104); Maurice Blanchot, 'The Relation of the Third Kind', in Blanchot, *The Infinite Conversation*, pp. 66–74 (p. 73).

and ideas. The Kantian category of the aesthetic in the *Third Critique* aims at uniting the sensuous and intelligible, inasmuch as a rose, in its beauty, stands in and presents or, in terms closer to the Kantian lexicon, is the sensibilization of the idea of freedom in nature – an idea which would otherwise not be present within the domain of the sensible.[3] From a worldlier and more historical perspective and in an attempt to remodel reality as a dynamic process, the intersection (the inter-action) between freedom and nature, between the subject and the given, is glossed by Georg Wilhelm Friedrich Hegel in terms of negation. Hegelian negation becomes synonymous with reality, as the human world consists precisely in – and emerges through – interaction.[4]

The spatial and cognitive distinction between an intending subject (here, within) and an intended object (there, outside) is suspended by the phenomenological insistence on phenomena and appearances (rather than real things in themselves). More broadly, after the Nietzschean attack on metaphysics the problem of sensible experience displaces the Kantian problem of the sensibilization of ideas. In this regard, in the post-Nietzschean context the problem of presentation is subsequently recast, most notably by Heidegger, not in the technical and epistemological terms of co-ordination between ideas and sensible forms but in the ontological terms of 'originary' experience.[5] The problem of the world with which we are left is raised by Nietzsche in the final lines of 'How the True World Finally became a Fable': 'The true world – we have abolished. What world has remained? The apparent one perhaps? But no! With the true

---

[3] For an outline of the stakes of the Third Critique, see Alison Ross, *The Aesthetic Paths of Philosophy: Presentation in Kant, Heidegger, Lacoue-Labarthe and Nancy* (Stanford, CA: Stanford University Press, 2007), pp. 38–47. The Kantian category of the aesthetic and the key term of aesthetic judgement are neither synonymous nor reducible to the realm of art and artworks but refer primarily to the beauty of nature. In Romantic thought, in which presentation becomes an ontological (rather than an epistemological, technical) problem (as it was for Kant) which relates to (and affects) human existence, the work of art becomes both a realization and an activation of human freedom.

[4] Subsequently Hegelian negativity becomes unbound from the realm of action. Once the force of negation – in its capacity critically to engage with the world – is freed to move into the realm of art, it informs various theorizations of modern art and literature.

[5] Here 'originary' means originating. It refers to an experience that is an origin or a source, gives rise to and causes the existence of something new.

world we have also abolished the apparent one'.[6] The question of presentation subsequently becomes that of making sense of – and relating to – worldly existence (being, the sensible, that which is), while avoiding the binary structure of opposition (which opposes the sensible to the intelligible) or phenomenological reduction (which privileges the apparent against the real and dissolves reality by reducing it to an image of our consciousness).

The intellectual world from which Bataille's and Blanchot's works derive is described by Foucault, who often brings the two writers together and is influenced by both, as marked by the passage from the limit of the limitless (God) to the limitless reign of the limit (our intrinsic finitude).[7] However, as Foucault underlines, this is not to be considered 'un monde limité et positif' [a limited and positivistic world], but rather 'un monde qui *se dénoue* dans l'expérience de la limite' [a world *exposed* by the experience of its limits].[8] Drawing on the implications for literature of such a philosophical outlook, Simon Critchley remarks that literature becomes 'the name of the place where the issue of religious disappointment is thought through'.[9] According to Critchley, 'it is *in* and *as* literature that the issue of life's possible redemption is played out' (more precisely, the 'redemption from redemption', as he adds).[10] Similarly, the task of future thought – now, contemporary thought – is articulated by Susan Sontag in the following terms: 'to try to make a fresh way of talking at the most serious, ardent, and enthusiastic level, heading off the religious encapsulation'.[11] The following discussion demonstrates how Bataille (un-working the Nietzschean and Hegelian/Kojevian legacy) and Blanchot (cross-fertilizing Heidegger and Levinas) respond to the challenges of

---

6   Friedrich Nietzsche, *Twilight of the Idols*, in *The Portable Nietzsche*, ed. and trans. by Walter Kaufmann (London; New York: Penguin, 1982 [1954]), pp. 463–564 (p. 485).

7   Michel Foucault, 'Préface à la transgression', *Critique*, 195/196 (1963), 751–69 (p. 754); Michel Foucault, 'A Preface to Transgression', in *Bataille. A Critical Reader*, ed. by Fred Botting and Scott Wilson (Oxford: Blackwell, 1998), pp. 24–40 (p. 26).

8   Foucault, 'Preface to Transgression', p. 26 (my emphasis).

9   Simon Critchley, 'Preface to the Second Edition: As my father I have already died', in Simon Critchley, *Very Little ... Almost Nothing*, 2nd edn (London and New York: Routledge, 2004 [1997]), pp. xv–xxviii (pp. xx, xxiii) (my emphasis).

10 Critchley, 'Preface to the Second Edition', pp. xx, xxiii.

11 Susan Sontag, 'The Pornographic Imagination', in Susan Sontag, *Styles of Radical Will* (London: Penguin, 1966), pp. 35–73 (p. 69).

their time, which are still ours, and displace the transcendental 'beyond' of religion in the intensity of the experience of writing. For both it is in writing, both within and outside it, both presented and withdrawn in the same movement, that a (non-transcendental) beyond appears where meaning is not guaranteed but shudders. Blanchot's confident allegiance to literature might be seen as lending itself at times to a conception of literature along the lines of negative transcendence (inasmuch as it bears the longing for an absolute which always, somehow, slips away), while Bataille's turbulent relation with writing engenders a tragic vision in which redemption is always already scattered and parodied. Nonetheless, what is crucial for both Bataille and Blanchot is that the logic (and attempt) of representation are undermined without being replaced by the logic (and temptation) of grounding and originality, since the primal scene of writing is conceived as a failure of discourse and as an encounter with an overriding alterity.

The comparative angle of the project, rather than tracing influence, aims to underline aspects of both thinkers which would otherwise remain unobserved. It shows how we sense Bataille and Blanchot differently through their exposure to each other. Without aspiring to promote Bataille as a theorist of literature and Blanchot as a theorist of the real, this reading focuses primarily on the representational and literary stakes of the Bataillean 'operations' and on the way in which Blanchot's several definitions of literature redefine existence.[12] Directing attention to how Bataille's uncompromising commitment to the experience of the real (and the real of experience), which can be for the moment defined as that which is beyond the order of representation, *exerts pressure on* (upsets) writing and literature, this reading differs decisively from the approach adopted by the theorists of *écriture*, namely *Tel Quel*, Jacques Derrida and, more recently, Patrick ffrench, who enclose and consider the Bataillean operations – of excess, expenditure, sacrifice (or exposure) – *in and as writing*. Additionally, and conversely, since in the case of Blanchot the existence of literature makes demands on and challenges existence, this work explores how the Blanchotian fervent allegiance to literature and writing offers precious insights into the theorization (setting up) of the real. In this respect the chronological unfolding of the sections on Blanchot does not provide a historical narrative of

---

12   The term 'operations' is widely used in Bataillean scholarship. It stands for an act, a practice, a process, a way of working (amongst which the act of writing) which goes beyond the usual, necessary or proper limit and introduces a new mode of knowledge.

Blanchot's several definitions of literature as they develop from the 1940s onwards, but rather examines, from a synchronic perspective, how they offer a reconfiguration of existence in terms of extreme affirmation (in the case of the *il y a*), concealment and obscurity (in the case of the *other night*), doubleness, impersonality and indeterminacy (in the case of the *neuter*).

One cannot make the claim that not much has been written on Bataille and Blanchot. Nonetheless, in the substantial body of monographs, commentaries and comparative studies the question of relation emerges more strongly with respect to the intricate interplay between two modes of writing and discourse as revealed and activated in their hybrid, unclassified work. Eleanor Kaufman's original book *The Delirium of Praise* devotes one chapter to the textual inscription of the Blanchot-Bataille friendship as reflected in their praise for each other.[13] However, as the title indicates, it is a genre study meditating upon the laudatory essay as a singular, excessive mode of writing which contradicts standard critical, measured discourse. Similarly, Leslie Hill's discerning study on Blanchot and Bataille, *Writing at the Limit*, focuses on the intersection of literary practice with philosophical discourse and the redefinition of the latter through its contaminative interaction with the former and provides a powerful defence of literary writing as a relation to the limit(less).[14] Other studies are devoted to central themes within the work of Bataille and Blanchot and how they need to be worked though (ffrench's *After Bataille. Sacrifice, Exposure, Community* is indicative in this respect, as it centres on the motif of 'sacrifice' and its recasting in terms of exposure rather than in terms of a structure).[15] This study differentiates itself from existing scholarship in that it moves away from the consideration of writing as a different, renewed way of thinking and brings it together with the question (and questioning) of the real. It thereby insists on the fact that writing might offer critical and resourceful insights on the theorization of the real, in the case of Blanchot, and that the demands of the real reinsert and revitalize

---

13 Eleanor Kaufman, 'Chattering Silences: Bataille and Blanchot on Louis-René des Forêts's *Le Bavard*', in Eleanor Kaufman, *The Delirium of Praise: Bataille, Blanchot, Deleuze, Foucault, Klossowski* (Baltimore, MD: Johns Hopkins University Press, 2002), pp. 18–36.

14 Leslie Hill, *Bataille, Klossowski, Blanchot: Writing at the Limit* (Oxford: Oxford University Press, 2001).

15 Patrick ffrench, *After Bataille: Sacrifice, Exposure, Community* (Oxford: Legenda, 2007).

questions of representation, referentiality and figuration, in the case of Bataille. In this sense, this study develops out of, and contributes to, a recent emergence within French thought which, in the wake of deconstruction, turns away from the linguistic paradigm and its emphasis on discourse in order to address materiality, worldly existence and the concreteness of the real.

Here the conception of the 'literary real' steers a more nuanced middle path between the anti-postmodern readings of Bataille, which celebrate his incitement of an unmediated experience of the real, and more textualist readings, which insist on the self-referentiality of the Bataillean 'operations' and the impossibility of reference. Similarly, in respect to Blanchot the understanding of the 'literary real' in this study counters readings of him as aristocratically distanced from real existence. The present analysis shows how Blanchot offers us a conception of the literary that is not disconnected from the concerns of lived (real) existence; and outlines how Bataille's and Blanchot's conception of the real/'being'/existence in terms of the excessive and the inappropriable is a cross-fertilization of the philosophy of their predecessors (Georg Wilhelm Friedrich Hegel/Alexandre Kojève, Friedrich Nietzsche), a radicalization of the philosophy of their contemporaries (most notably, Jean-Paul Sartre and Martin Heidegger) and a forerunner of the post-modern attraction to unmastered negativity and the impossibility of closure.[16] Bringing into focus Bataille's and Blanchot's engagement with the sensory and sense, the discussion situates them both within the current context of the material/affective turn. In so doing, it aims to provide not a historical – linear – narrative but a renewed reading of both thinkers as situated at the crossroads of post-deconstructionism (welcoming the real, experience) and anti-realism (differentiating the real from – its equation and reduction to – empirical reality and the current state of affairs). In parallel, and more broadly, the book uses Bataille and Blanchot to recast the key terms of the literary and aesthetic tradition (such as creation and inspiration, autonomy and mimesis), but also

---

16 Alexandre Kojève (1902–1968) was a Russian-born, German-educated, Marxist political philosopher who introduced Hegel into twentieth-century French thought through a series of lectures he gave during the years 1933 to 1939. Kojève read Hegel through the lenses of materialism and ontology. His lectures on Hegel were attended by, and had a profound influence on, André Breton, Georges Bataille, Raymond Aron, Jean-Paul Sartre, Maurice Merleau-Ponty, Jacques Lacan and Raymond Queneau. Queneau collected, edited and published the lectures in 1947 under the title *Introduction à la lecture de Hegel* (Paris: Gallimard, 1947).

concepts relevant to wider current debates (such as space, inside and outside, time, experience and the event, visibility and invisibility, intimacy and distance).

Part I is constructed around the first encounter (both real and textual) between the two thinkers. It shows how Georges Bataille and Maurice Blanchot manifest some crucial differences, alongside a strong affinity for fostering writing as a heteronomic practice in which something 'other' can affirm itself. To some extent these differences appear, along with their common preoccupations, in the thread of their works from the 1930s and the 1940s which precede *La Littérature et le mal* (Bataille, 1957) and *L'Espace littéraire* (Blanchot, 1955), their major works from the 1950s devoted to literature.[17] Schematically, Bataille's early works draw on the demand made on writing by the exposure, his exposure, to the chaotic reality of the world and man (due to his engagement with the findings of other disciplines – anthropology, sociology, ethnology – and his own turbulent life). In an inverse movement Blanchot addresses in his works the question posed to being by the existence of literature, by the peculiar mode of being of the literary (due to his exposure and his fervent devotion to writing as a writer and a literary critic).

Juxtaposing the Bataillean privileging of embodied experience and the Blanchotian literary, Part I examines the reconfiguration of experience in terms of the impossible and the inappropriable. More specifically, it explores how, for Blanchot, a paradoxical non-knowledge of (a relation without relation with) being emerges through a passionate attraction to writing, while for Bataille it is rather a desire to embrace life in its totality that drives him towards writing and marks it (Chapters 1 and 2). For the purpose of this discussion, this section turns first to some of Bataille's influential pre-war essays which led to *L'Expérience intérieure*, the first part of the *Somme athéologique* trilogy.[18] It then focuses on Bataille's treatise on experience, as this both comes out of and fosters the first encounter

---

17 Georges Bataille, *La Littérature et le mal*, in *Œuvres complètes*, 12 vols (Paris: Gallimard, 1970–88), IX (1979), pp. 171–315; Georges Bataille, *Literature and Evil*, trans. by Alastair Hamilton (London; New York: Marion Boyars, 1973); Maurice Blanchot, *L'Espace littéraire* (Paris: Gallimard, 1955); Maurice Blanchot, *The Space of Literature*, intro. and trans. by Ann Smock (Lincoln, NE; London: University of Nebraska Press, 1982).

18 Georges Bataille, *L'Expérience intérieure*, in *Œuvres complètes*, 12 vols (Paris: Gallimard, 1970–88), V: *La Somme athéologique. Tome I* (1973), pp. 7–189; Georges Bataille, *The Inner Experience*, trans. by Leslie Anne-Boldt (Albany, NY: State University of New York Press, 1988).

(which would become a life-long friendship), the mutual influence and the two-way relationship between Bataille and Blanchot. The analysis subsequently turns to Blanchot's review of the book, passes through 'Comment la littérature est-elle possible?' and concludes by looking at his seminal essay 'La Littérature et le droit à la mort'.[19] Part I frames the work of the two thinkers historically, within the intellectual milieu from which it comes, showing how the re-conceptualization of the real, 'being', existence as excessive and inappropriable though the Bataillean notion of 'unemployed negativity' and the Blanchotian *il y a*, is a cross-fertilization and radicalization of Hegel (Kojève) and Heidegger. In parallel, it relates both Bataille and Blanchot to the recent trend within French thought, as exposed most notably in the work of Jean-Luc Nancy and his concepts of *excrit* and *regard*.[20] Finally, a third chapter adopts the focal point of autobiography and unravels how both Bataille and Blanchot unsettle the link between 'life' and 'writing'.

Part II, the core of this book, provides an analysis of Blanchot's and Bataille's major critical texts from the 1950s, *L'Espace littéraire* and *La Littérature et le mal*, and tackles more directly the question of how literature becomes a privileged way of relating to the world. It inscribes both writers within the Modernist heritage, an approach which brings in a subjectivist perspective on worldly reality and at times aspires to cast out the presence of worldly reality from the domain of literature and art. Flaubert's desire to write a book about nothing and Manet's paintings, both of which are admirable in, and precisely due to, their thematic insignificance, are indicative of the aims of Modernism: the subject of the work is insignificant, nothing but a pretext, since the true subject of the work is itself. In the case of the literary work, language becomes its content and, more specifically,

---

19   Maurice Blanchot, 'La Littérature et le droit à la mort', in Maurice Blanchot, *La Part du feu* (Paris: Gallimard, 1949), pp. 291–331; Maurice Blanchot, 'Literature and the Right to Death', in Maurice Blanchot, *The Work of Fire*, trans. by Charlotte Mandell (Stanford, CA: Stanford University Press, 1995), pp. 300–44.

20   The term *excrit* is coined by Nancy with reference to Bataille. The term *regard* is not directly applied by Nancy with reference to Blanchot but with reference to the Iranian film director Abbas Kiarostami. See Jean-Luc Nancy, 'L'excrit', in Jean-Luc Nancy, *Une pensée finie* (Paris: Galilée, 1990), pp. 54–65; Jean-Luc Nancy, 'Exscription', trans. by Katherine Lydon, *Yale French Studies*, 78 (1990), 47–65; Jean-Luc Nancy, 'L'Évidence du Film. Abbas Kiarostami / The Evidence of Film. Abbas Kiarostami', in Jean-Luc Nancy, *L'Évidence du Film. Abbas Kiarostami / The Evidence of Film. Abbas Kiarostami*, trans. by Christine Irizarry and Verena Andermatt Conley (Brussels: Gaevert, 2001), pp. 8–79.

language in its non-communicative and intransitive dimension, that is, language outside communicative and instrumental use.

Both Georges Bataille and Maurice Blanchot adhere and pay homage to the tradition of literary Modernism. Blanchot dedicates an essay to Flaubert and considers, in principle, the experience of writing as the direct opposite of being in the world. Similarly, Bataille not only dedicates a book to Manet but, transferring the attributes of inner experience to literature, designates as the object of the latter nothing but itself. Additionally, Bataille and Blanchot radicalize Modernism, since they move beyond subjectivist presentation and conceive writing in terms of a (non-)relation to a pre-subjective and pre-objective real. Bringing together (in a confrontational – both agonistic and intimate – manner) Blanchot's account of the spatiality of the literary work with Bataille's account of its temporality, Part II aspires to fill a gap not only in existing scholarship but also, more crucially, in the dialogue between the two writers. In this respect the Blanchotian paradigm of writing, which counteracts the logic of creation and creativity, is accompanied and complemented by Bataillean a-teleological logic, which runs against salvation and redemption. Drawing on the sensory and tactile aspect of the Blanchotian image (as opposed to the common conception of it as a form of mediation) as well as on the transient and fleeting character of the Bataillean present (as opposed to its positing in terms of presence), Part II insists on the problematization of presence, origin and *telos* (Chapters 4 and 5). While Part I (by way of the tropes of the *il y a* and *négativé sans emploi*) focuses on the impossibility of negation and of not-being, Part II (through a detailed analysis of the notions of the 'image' and the 'instant') revolves around the impossibility of being. In this respect the irreducibility of presence, as attested in Part I, is joined to an account of the entanglement of the non-existent with the existent and of disappearance in appearance. Here, Bataille's and Blanchot's thought is elaborated not only in dialogue and discussion with their usual interlocutors, such as Emmanuel Levinas and Friedrich Nietzsche, but also in relation to Susan Sontag, Judith Butler, Simone Weil and Paul Ricœur. Finally, psychoanalytic discourse is introduced as a third pole, a critical stance which reframes the Blanchotian Imaginary from the viewpoint of the Lacanian Real and repositions psychoanalytic theory from the viewpoint of writing (Chapter 6).

Part III expands on the spectral logic of the double, which intersects the argument of the study as a whole. Throughout, the book addresses this in different ways, most notably in Blanchot's several spatial accounts of literature (in terms of two sides – one that moves towards the negation/absence of things, one that concerns itself with the reality/presence of things – but also in terms of spacing and passage) and in Bataille's economic account of existence (in terms of excess, waste, expenditure rather than exchange). In order to show how Bataille's and Blanchot's central concerns might be seen as the problematization of the idea of the 'One', under its different configurations of origin, unity, identity, totality and end, this study puts forward the problematic of the *neutre*, with reference to Blanchot, as a figure from which one can address the question of irreducible doubleness (which undoes both sameness and radical alterity) (Chapter 7). With reference to Bataille, the key term of the 'mask' is employed as a concept which reconfigures mimesis in terms of incongruity and separation (Chapter 8). This last part, by way of the trope of the 'mask' in the case of Bataille and the *neutre* in the case of Blanchot, will show how writing is governed (that is, bound to and overridden) by a fundamental duplicity which denounces both dualism and the logic of the 'one'. Nonetheless, as the terms chosen indicate, in their common fight against oneness and duality Bataille opts for the striking, the flagrant, whereas Blanchot directs his attention to the unremarkable, the featureless.

This spectral, yet fundamental, logic of the double gives the discussion both its thematic content and its structure: each part, as indicated by its title – 'Double Dissymmetries', 'Confusions' and '(Re)turns' – points to a revolt against, and calls into question, identity and presence; correspondingly, each part is divided and doubled, treated conjointly and differently, by a chapter devoted to Bataille and a chapter devoted to Blanchot. The first two parts are further composed of a third chapter which brings a distinct angle and a further critical perspective – through the genre of autobiography and psychanalytic theory – on the matters previously discussed. As the comparative perspective of the ensuing chapters will show, the concept of the literary real emerges more forcefully when *not* treated in isolation.

As demonstrated throughout this study, encounter is that which undoes the logic of harmonious coexistence and coherence (being at one) as well as the logic of identity (being or becoming oneself) in its various constellations of origin, autonomy, (self-)authorship and (self-)productivity. The logic of encounter is put forth as that of double (rather than one-sided) dissymmetries, confusions (which run counter to all fusional and unitary logic) and (re)turns (where re-turning is not meant as a re-turn *to* but as that which erases the point of departure). The impossibility of negation (the excess of presence as signalled in the *il y a* and in *negativité sans emploi*), the impossibility of presence (the absenting of presence as brought forth by the image and the instant) and, finally, the impossibility of properly relating (in the case of the *neutre* and the mask) – namely, the impossibility of not-being (in Part I), the impossibility of being (in Part II) and, finally, the impossibility of being oneself (in Part III) – all attest to a double logic.

Part I
Double Dissymmetries

1. Bataille: The Passion of the Real

S'il fallait me donner une place dans l'histoire de la pensée, ce serait je crois pour avoir discerné les effets, dans notre vie humaine, de l' 'évanouissement du réel discursif', et pour avoir tiré de la description de ces effets une lumière évanouissante.

[If it were necessary to be given a place in intellectual history, it would be, I think, for having discerned in our human life the effects of the 'fading of the discursive real' and having drawn from these effects an evanescent light.][1]

Writing as the Pursuit of the Outside

In the early 1930s Bataille was briefly involved in the editorial board of the Surrealist journal *Documents*, to which he contributed a series of articles which bring forth his intellectual obsessions. The title of the journal, as Denis Hollier mentions and as Bataille himself suggested, is, in its anti-aesthetic (and anti-literary) connotation, indicative of what Bataille would come to pursue in his writing.[2] Unlike the Surrealists he does not search for the imaginary, the oneiric, the dreamlike, but, in a documentary-like endeavour, seeks to embrace human and material life in its entirety (which for him does not coincide with reality in its depiction by realist representation). Bataille saw his contribution to *Documents* as an excellent occasion on which to attack

---

1 Georges Bataille, 'Post-scriptum. 1953', in *Œuvres Complètes*, v: *La Somme athéologique. Tome I*, pp. 229–34 (p. 231); Georges Bataille, 'Post-Scriptum 1953', in Georges Bataille, *Inner Experience*, trans. by Stuart Kendall (New York: State University of New York Press, 2014), pp. 203–07 (p. 203).

2 Denis Hollier, 'La Valeur d'usage de l'impossible', in Denis Hollier, *Les Dépossédés (Bataille, Caillois, Leiris, Malraux, Sartre)* (Paris: Minuit, 1993), pp. 153–78 (p. 153).

André Breton and the Surrealist Movement's uplifting, idealistic considerations (as indicated by the prefix *sur*).³ André Masson, recounting his first encounter with Bataille, notes that Bataille also disliked the Dadaist Movement, the Surrealists' predecessors.⁴ As Masson recalls, Bataille's charge against Dada is that, despite its attack on conventional art and rational thought, it shows a considerable lack of foolishness: '"*Dada*? – pas assez idiot", c'est en ces termes que Georges Bataille conclut notre premier entretien. [...] Oui, *Dada* pas assez idiot, et le surréalisme beaucoup trop "mental"' ['Dada? – not stupid enough'; this is how Georges Bataille concluded our first interview. [...] Yes, Dada is not stupid enough and Surrealism is far too 'mental'].⁵ In light of this account, the *Documents* endeavour can be seen as an impulse towards documentation which records and demonstrates the deficiency of the intellect.

In 'Le Gros orteil', the parodic praising of the big toe as the most human (and lowly) part of the body, Bataille sketches out the 'retour à la réalité' [return to reality] for which he strives as directly opposed to poetic haze, which is dismissed as synonymous with idealistic (ethereal) diversion.⁶ Echoing Deleuze, for whom to write is neither to draw on reality⁷ nor to have recourse to the imagination,⁸ the Bataillean

---

3   Michel Surya describes Bataille's contributions in *Documents* as 'une machine de guerre contre le surréalisme' [a war machine against Surrealism]. See Michel Surya, *Georges Bataille. La mort à l'œuvre* (Paris: Gallimard, 2012 [1992]), p. 143; Michel Surya, *Georges Bataille: An Intellectual Biography*, trans. by Krzysztof Fijalkowski and Michael Richardson (London; New York: Verso, 2002), p. 118.

4   In this respect, one might recall that Tristan Tzara famously designates disgust as the beginning of Dada.

5   André Masson, 'Le Soc de la charrue', *Critique*, 195/196 (1963), 701–05 (pp. 704–05).

6   Georges Bataille, 'Le Gros orteil', in *Œuvres Complètes*, I (1970): *Premiers écrits. 1922–1940*, pp. 200–04 (p. 204); Georges Bataille, 'The Big Toe', in Georges Bataille, *Visions of Excess: Selected Writings, 1927–1939*, ed. by Allan Stoekl, trans. by Allan Stoekl with Carl R. Lovitt and Donald M. Leslie, Jr. (Minneapolis, MN: University of Minnesota Press, 1985), pp. 20–23 (p. 23).

7   According to Deleuze, 'écrire n'est certainement pas imposer une forme (d'expréssion) à une matière vécue' [to write is certainly not to impose a form (of expression) on the matter of lived experience] (Gilles Deleuze, 'La Littérature et la vie', in Gilles Deleuze, *Critique et Clinique* (Paris: Minuit, 1993), pp. 11–17 (p. 12); Gilles Deleuze, 'Literature and Life', trans. by Daniel W. Smith and Michael A. Greco, *Critical Inquiry*, 23 (1997), 225–30 (p. 225)).

8   Deleuze claims that 'écrire n'est pas raconter [...] ses rêves et phantasmes' [to write is not to recount [...] one's dreams and phantasms] (Deleuze, 'La Littérature et la vie', p. 11; Deleuze, 'Literature and Life', p. 227).

return to reality is depicted as a spasmodic convulsion: 'jusqu' à en crier, en écarquillant les yeux [...] devant un gros orteil' [to the point of screaming, opening his eyes wide [...] before a big toe].[9] As Deleuze notes in his essay 'La Littérature et la vie', 'c'est la même chose de pécher par excès de réalité, ou d'imagination' [it is the same thing to sin through an excess of reality as through an excess of imagination], since both belong to the realm of the possible, of artistic/subjective expression.[10] In this respect, Bataille's writing, rejecting both surrealism (due to its underlying idealism in its pretention to accede to a superior reality) and representational (mimetic, conventional) realism (due to its inability to depict reality in its fullness), can be seen, paraphrasing Deleuze, to be entangled with the excess *in* reality, an excessive reality which persistently remains outside all attempts at seizure.

In an attempt to decipher the ambiguous nature of the entanglement between writing and reality, we might refer to Nancy's term 'exscription'. Nancy employs the term with particular reference to the Bataillean act of writing and offers a response to the question of, as he puts it, 'how to accede to this excess'.[11] The sound of the term exscription resonates with Bataillean vocabulary, which is, in Denis Hollier's observation, 'une célébration du préfixe *ex*' [a celebration of the prefix *ex*] (as the recurrence of the words 'excess', 'experience' and 'expenditure' documents).[12] More significantly, the prefix of ex-scription, having the meaning 'out, out of, outside' (as opposed to that of in-scription, which denotes an enclosure, an inside, a within), gestures towards something outside textual enclosure. Nancy has shown that this conception of writing in terms of an opening and an exposure dis-locates existence (the existence of everything that is in question 'in' the text and 'about' which the text writes) outside the text:

> Elle [l'écriture] excrit le sens, c'est-à-dire qu'elle montre que ce dont il s'agit, *la chose même*, la 'vie' de Bataille ou le 'cri', et pour finir l'existence de toute chose dont il 'est question' dans le texte

---

9   Bataille, 'Le Gros orteil', p. 204; Bataille, 'The Big Toe', p. 23.

10   Deleuze, 'La Littérature et la vie', p. 12; Deleuze, 'Literature and Life', p. 227.

11   Jean-Luc Nancy, *Multiple Arts: The Muses II*, ed. by Simon Sparks (Stanford, CA: Stanford University Press: 2006), p. 7.

12   Denis Hollier, 'De l'équivoque entre littérature et politique', in Hollier, *Les Dépossédés*, pp. 109–30 (p. 118). While Hollier makes this remark with regard to Bataille's *erotics*, it can arguably be extended and refer to the whole body of Bataille's work.

(y compris [...] l'existence de l'écriture elle-même) est hors du texte, a lieu hors de l'écriture.

[It [writing] exscribes meaning, that is to say, it shows that what it is about, the thing itself, Bataille's 'life' or 'cry', and finally the existence of everything 'under discussion' in the text (including [...] the existence of writing itself) is outside the text, takes place outside writing.][13]

The fabrication of writing as exscription, or, more particularly, as an intricate play of inscription and exscription, denotes that writing's access to the real of the world is far from being a straightforward path but is, in fact, rather difficult. However, as Nancy puts it, 'that difficulty makes access occur'.[14]

Bataille's unconventional understanding of the real and the pressure exerted by it on discourse (and subsequently on his own writing) emerges in 'Le Bas matérialisme et la gnose'. In this essay, in which matter takes a central role, Bataille engages in a materialist decomposition of Surrealist elevations and of the Hegelian system. Materialism is defined as 'avant tout la négation obstinée de l'idéalisme, ce qui revient à dire en dernier lieu de la base même de *toute* philosophie' [above all the obstinate negation of idealism, which amounts to saying, finally, of the basis of *all* philosophy].[15] In the dualistic nature of Gnosticism, with its duck-headed, monstrous *archontes*, matter is found 'comme un *leitmotiv* [...], comme un principe *actif* ayant son existence éternelle autonome' [as a *leitmotiv* [...] as an *active* principle having its own eternal autonomous existence].[16] Bataille's interest in Gnosticism and base Materialism lies in the intellectual implications of their postulates, since 'la matière basse est *extérieure* et *étrangère* aux aspirations idéales humaines' [base matter

---

13 Nancy, 'L'excrit', p. 61; Nancy, 'Exscription', p. 63.

14 Nancy, *Multiple Arts*, p. 4.

15 Georges Bataille, 'Le Bas matérialisme et la gnose', in *Œuvres complètes*, I: *Premiers écrits. 1922–1940*, pp. 220–26 (p. 220); Georges Bataille, 'Base Materialism and Gnosticism', in Bataille, *Visions of Excess*, ed. by Stoekl, pp. 45–52 (p. 45). Bataille adds that materialism is also a critique of ontological materialism, 'impliquant que la matière est la chose en soi' [implying that matter is the thing-in-itself] (Bataille, 'Le Bas matérialisme et la gnose', p. 225; Bataille, 'Base Materialism and Gnosticism', p. 49).

16 Bataille, 'Le Bas matérialisme et la gnose', p. 223; Bataille, 'Base Materialism and Gnosticism', p. 47.

is *external* and *foreign* to ideal human aspirations].[17] Revealing what is at stake, Bataille notes:

> Il s'agit avant tout de ne pas se soumettre à quoi que ce soit de plus élevé, qui puisse donner à l'être que je suis, à la raison qui arme cet être, une autorité d'emprunt. Cet être et sa raison ne peuvent se soumettre qu'à ce qui est plus *bas*, à ce qui ne peut servir en aucun cas à singer une autorité quelconque.

> [For it is a question above all of not submitting oneself, and with oneself one's reason, to whatever is more elevated, to whatever can give a borrowed authority to the being that I am, and to the reason that arms this being. This being and its reason can in fact only submit to what is *lower*, to what can never serve in any case to ape a given authority.][18]

It is in this early text that the ideas which will haunt Bataille's thought are introduced: sovereign action (not serving any goal, any value) versus servile attitude (a subjection to ends outside oneself), base matter (low) versus idealized spirit and human aspirations (high). However, what is highly original in Bataille's approach is that in his praise of base matter and 'the low' he does not assign them a place alongside, or as substitutes for, old values in an attempt to elevate them.[19] As Denis Hollier observes, Bataille privileges dualism not as a system of thought but rather as an 'attitude of thought', since for him dualism is precisely a 'resistance to system and homogeneity'.[20] Put differently, what Bataille emphasizes in the low and the base

---

17 Bataille, 'Le Bas matérialisme et la gnose', p. 225; Bataille, 'Base Materialism and Gnosticism', p. 51 (my emphasis).

18 Bataille, 'Le Bas matérialisme et la gnose', p. 225; Bataille, 'Base Materialism and Gnosticism', p. 50.

19 The fact that Bataille does not postulate a simple inversion of the high/low paradigm marks his break with the ethnographers and, to some extent, with Nietzsche. With regard to the ethnographers, Denis Hollier remarks that in their inclusion of the low and the everyday they looked for continuity and classification, while Bataille wanted rupture and to put things out of order. With regard to Nietzsche, Surya notes that his battle against the world is conducted from the elevated viewpoint of the *Übermensch*, whilst the Bataillean war is conducted from below (Hollier, 'La Valeur d'usage de l'impossible', pp. 169, 172; Surya, *Georges Bataille*, p. 169; Surya, *Georges Bataille: An Intellectual Biography*, pp. 141–42).

20 Denis Hollier, 'The Dualist Materialism of Georges Bataille', in *Bataille: A Critical Reader*, ed. by Fred Botting and Scott Wilson (Oxford: Blackwell, 1998), pp. 59–73 (p. 62).

is precisely their baseness and unworthiness as disruptive forces which resist, and remain outside of, any attempt at codification, thus destabilizing idealized aspirations.

Henceforth Bataille will constantly turn his attention to the low and the filthy. Many of his fictions draw largely on debauchery, as he seeks in it, in Surya's words, 'de l'existence l'ininterprétable verité' [the uninterpretable truth of existence].[21] Bataille engages with the low and the obscene, joyfully submitting to and writing on it, not in a fetishistic compulsion with filth *per se*, but in a total affirmation of life, an unreserved consent, a Nietzschean 'yes' to the world to the point of its upsetting of one's stomach (or, as Surya puts it, 'un amour témoigné jusqu'à la honte' [a love bearing witness to the point of shame]).[22] Nonetheless, the importance of this early essay lies in the fact that it does not simply unveil the insufficiency of existing, homogenizing discourses that repress and disregard matter, turning it into concepts and ideas. By designating the low, the base, precisely as what cannot be incorporated into signifying systems (as it is in-significant, un-worthy), this early essay announces what is at stake for Bataille in writing itself. Bataille does not mean to compensate for the exclusion of base matter by embracing it in his writings. Though the low might become the obsessive theme of his own writing (equally embraced and not disregarded by him), it will still not (and cannot) be captured in his writing (which is precisely what draws him to it). Therefore, writing on the debased, on the vile and dirty, amounts to writing on the impossible. Besides, the ob-scene, that is, the off-stage, refers etymologically to what takes place behind – hidden from – the scene, including the scene of writing. In this regard, this early essay displays how, for Bataille, writing is crucially related to the (its) outside and how his writing will aim at what cannot be grasped, namely the impossible.

Excess as Extra-Textual

Associating writing with the outside and the impossible, Bataille is attracted to the Marquis de Sade, since the latter's texts give an aberrant access to a heterogeneous world, namely, to what is radically other, excluded and silenced by systems of thought and by the social body.

---

21 Surya, *Georges Bataille*, p. 149; Surya, *Georges Bataille: An Intellectual Biography*, p. 124.

22 Surya, *Georges Bataille*, p. 149; Surya, *Georges Bataille: An Intellectual Biography*, p. 124.

Critical of the Surrealists' sublimation (aestheticization) of de Sade's work, which results in the disregard of the odious and excremental forces at play within it, Bataille, in his essay 'La Valeur d'usage de D. A. F. de Sade' (1929), does not exile the Sadean undertaking in the unreality of fiction ('en dehors et au-dessus de toute réalité' [outside of and above all reality]), but extracts the actual implications of the outrageous reality it triggers, both hideous and hidden.[23] De Sade's importance for Bataille lies, amongst other things, in the fact that he inaugurates writing as a hetero-logous practice, as the speech (*logos*) of the wholly other (*heteros*). In his definition of '*le corps étranger (das ganz Anderes* [sic])' [a foreign body (*das ganz Anderes*)] as what society tries to repress under the elaboration of taboos, prohibitions or rituals, Bataille, in a daring equivalence, subsumes what is frequently considered to be excremental (faeces, sperm, menstrual blood) into the sacred and the divine.[24] The significance of Bataille's essay on de Sade lies in the fact that it does not simply favour the excessive dimension of human existence, attributing a quasi-ontological priority to it, but instead elaborates a complex relation between the primordial excess of human life and all social and rational constructions intrinsically bound up with it (in the sense of both stemming from and striving – in vain – to delimit it). Bringing forth this intricate interrelation, the essay unveils the insufficiency of all attempts at enclosure (including the attempt at linguistic and textual codification). In this respect, Bataille proclaims the paradox of writing as a heterological project due to the resistance of heterogeneous elements (sacred or/and excremental), as excessive and immoderate, to any attempt at objectification and definition. As he remarks, 'il faut même ajouter qu'*il n'existe aucun moyen* de placer de tels éléments dans le domaine objectif humain immédiat' [it must even be added *there is no way* of placing such elements in the immediate objective human domain].[25]

This first encounter with the challenging nature of de Sade's venture foreshadows Bataille's ambiguous disposition towards writing. The fact that the Sadean texts call for an alertness to excess,

---

23   Georges Bataille, 'La Valeur d'usage de D. A. F. de Sade', in *Œuvres complètes*, II: *Écrits posthumes. 1922–1940* (1970), pp. 54–69 (p. 56); Georges Bataille, 'The Use Value of D. A. F. de Sade', in Bataille, *Visions of Excess*, ed. by Stoekl, pp. 91–104 (p. 93).

24   Bataille, 'La Valeur d'usage de D. A. F. de Sade', p. 58; Bataille, 'The Use Value of D. A. F. de Sade', p. 94.

25   Bataille, 'La Valeur d'usage de D. A. F. de Sade', p. 63; Bataille, 'The Use Value of D. A. F. de Sade', p. 98 (my emphasis).

which at the same time cannot be incorporated into any discursive modality (including de Sade's – and Bataille's – own texts), triggers and determines Bataille's ongoing, perplexed relationship to language. In this respect, excess is crucially moulded by Bataille as extra-textual, as what cannot be successfully attained and sustained by any means, including by means of writing. In an attempt to accede to excess, de Sade's long books, the 'Wagnerian music dramas' of pornographic literature, as Susan Sontag describes them, opt for a repetitive, detailed, linear writing style which, forcing the symbolic order to encompass everything, *ultimately* results in its overburdening and disintegration. On the contrary, Bataille's short compositions of 'chamber music', as Sontag defines them, present a writing practice that is more *immediately* (hurriedly) exposed to (that is, contaminated, undone by) excess in its yearning to enter into an intimacy with it.[26]

The uniqueness of Bataille's texts lies in the fact that, despite their extreme, violent, excessive concerns, in their desire to confront the whole of existence they do not aspire, in a Barthesian mode, to be correspondingly excessive, orgasmic, explosive. They claim for themselves, and are confined to, the status of an inadequate residue; they merely are, and present themselves as, residual remainders, leftovers of an uncontained-by-them excess (an excess which is designated by them precisely as extra-textual). In an attempt to approach the ambiguity in which the Bataillean texts are caught up, Pierre Klossowski employs the contrivance of the 'simulacrum', thereby cutting them off from all claims to truth, originality and authenticity and stressing the element of performativity, simulation and misrepresentation (rather than representation) which prevails in them. The simulacrum, as opposed to notional language which presupposes and subsequently addresses 'closed beings', has the advantage, according to Klossowski, 'de ne pas prétendre fixer ce qu'il présente d'une expérience et ce qu'il en dit' [of not claiming to stabilize what it presents of an experience and what it says of it], since it portrays, as Ian James points out, 'in its very structure' 'the *movement* of Being, as heterogeneity and expenditure'.[27] The simulacrum brings forth a form of contact inflected with separation

---

26 Sontag, 'The Pornographic Imagination', pp. 60, 62.
27 Pierre Klossowski, 'Le simulacre dans la communication de Georges Bataille', *Critique*, 195/196 (1963), 742–51 (p. 743); Pierre Klossowski, 'Of the Simulacrum in Georges Bataille's Communication', in *On Bataille: Critical Essays*, ed. by Leslie Anne Boldt-Irons (Albany, NY: State University of New York Press, 1995), pp. 147–56 (p. 148) (my emphasis); Ian James, 'From Recuperation to Simulacrum', in *The Beast at Heaven's Gate: Georges Bataille and the Art of*

in as much as it presents itself as a *residue* of what it says. To the degree that it 'mimics' the incommunicable, it displays itself as a simulation and an absence rather than as a representation and a presence.[28] In so doing, it reveals, as Klossowski acknowledges, that it will not account for what has happened ('en parler ne rendra compte d'aucune manière de ce qui s'est alors passé' [to speak of it will not in any way account for what has thus happened]).[29] It is precisely in admitting its betrayal and failure that it is complicit with, and faithful to, what it recounts, as in the order of simulation (unlike the order of conceptualization) there is no substantive being or originary ground. Briefly, the simulacrum has a logic similar to that of exscription, but, apart from a play of inside / outside, it is further constructed around a tension (thereby undermining a firm distinction) between originality and simulation. Emanating from such a tension, simulacra, as Deleuze emphasizes, differ radically from 'copies' to the extent that the latter are, in a long Platonic tradition, considered as degraded or secondary in their relation to an original. In Deleuze's phrasing: 'Les *copies* sont possesseurs en second, prétendants bien fondés, garantis par la ressemblance; les *simulacres* sont comme les faux prétendants, construits sur une dissimilitude, impliquant une perversion, un détournement essentiels' [Copies are secondary possessors, well-founded pretenders, guaranteed by resemblance; *simulacra* are like false pretenders, built on dissimilarity, implying a perversion, an essential diversion].[30] Hence the simulacrum, laying no claims of truth or resemblance, but exposing its dissimilarity (in introducing itself as a relic), becomes a privileged trope in an attempt to address the question of how excess can be accessed.

The Bataillean excess, as depicted above, unseizable (excreted by social life and human thought) and useless (serving no ends, what

---

Transgression, ed. by Andrew Hussey (Amsterdam: Rodopi, 2006), pp. 91–100 (p. 98).

28 Briefly, the mimetic gesture, which is constitutive of the simulacrum and which sets it apart from notions and concepts, is not to be considered in terms of mimesis, imitation or identification, but rather in terms of non-sameness, of difference, echoing the way in which Benjamin defines the mimetic faculty as becoming or behaving *'like something else'* (Walter Benjamin, 'On the Mimetic Faculty', in Walter Benjamin, *Reflections: Essays, Aphorisms, Autobiographical Writings*, ed. by Peter Demetz (New York: Schocken, 1986), pp. 333–36 (p. 333)) (my emphasis).

29 Klossowski, 'Le simulacre', p. 743; Klossowski, 'Of the Simulacrum', p. 148.

30 Gilles Deleuze, 'Simulacre et philosophie antique', in Gilles Deleuze, *Logique du sens* (Paris: Minuit, 1969), pp. 292–324 (pp. 295–96).

Bataille would later designate as 'sovereign'), has the particularity of being conceived in terms of irrecoverable loss and waste. In that sense, it deviates from the common use of the term 'excess' inasmuch as it *is*, is constituted as, unproductive (sovereign) expenditure. These distinguishing features become more obvious in the essay 'La Notion de dépense', in which, attacking all representations linked to an impoverished view of existence, Bataille unveils, beside the world of production, necessity and utility (the reproduction and conservation of goods and human life), the world of non-productive expenditure.[31] Subsuming the realm of luxury, mourning, war, cults, games and perverse sexuality under non-productive expenditure, he focuses on the dimension of loss as constitutive when he writes: '[D]ans chaque cas l'accent est placé sur la *perte* [...] qui doit être la plus grande possible pour que l'activité prenne son véritable sens' [[I]n each case the accent is placed on a *loss* that must be as great as possible in order for that activity to take on its true meaning].[32] Further, Bataille provides this economy of expenditure with an anthropological basis, drawing on the archaic practice of potlatch, as described by Mauss. In this ceremonial feast, American tribes give or destroy an important part of their wealth in order to oblige and humiliate their rivals (who would then have to respond by giving or destroying a greater part of their wealth). What intrigues Bataille in this antagonistic confrontation is that power amounts to the power to lose and wealth is constituted through, and is directed towards, loss. The practice of potlatch might be about wealth and luxury, prestige and hierarchy and, ultimately, power, but it demands the radical reconfiguration of all of the above, since what confers wealth and respect are the contempt for and disrespecting of wealth, as it is loss that counts as gain. In other words, it becomes evident that excess, in Bataille's cosmological vision (as also condensed in his favoured figure of the sun, whose existence *is* – is bound to – an incessant loss of heat and light), does not have the fixed, solid character of the acquired, accumulated surpluses of capitalism, but a rather fluid character which is presented in and as the fleeting movement of extravagant and useless expenditure.

In this respect, the Bataillean reconfiguration of excess in terms of expenditure is still relevant in as much as it challenges not only the

---

31 Georges Bataille, 'La Notion de dépense', in *Œuvres complètes*, ɪ: *Premiers écrits. 1922–1940*, pp. 302–20 (p. 303); Georges Bataille, 'The Notion of Expenditure', in *Visions of Excess*, ed. by Stoekl, pp. 116–29 (p. 118).

32 Bataille, 'La Notion de dépense', p. 305; Bataille, 'The Notion of Expenditure', p. 119.

workings of early capitalism and its principle of effectiveness and utility but also those of late capitalism and its inclination towards excessive accumulation. Bataille's (anti-)economy of boundless wastage is starkly different from the excessive undertakings of capitalism, in which huge losses suffered (by some) are exchanged and regained as gross profits (for others). The continuing relevance of Bataille lies in the fact that he conceives the human subject and human life as what eludes and persistently un-works organization and systemic order as well as deriding every attempt to encode it. In so doing, he demonstrates – and keeps reminding us – that to celebrate human life as luxurious and prodigal in itself, to consider ourselves as a material and existential exaggeration, superfluous, unseizable, ungraspable and overflowing, is not the same as conceding and glorifying a system which offers – or rather promises – prodigality (in its diminished and impoverished version of limitless wealth) to the appropriative and greedy grasp of a subject.

Over all forms of writing Bataille privileges poetry, since he sees it as being animated by the fundamental principle of expenditure which governs human life. Moving away from his earlier dismissal of poetry as synonymous with idealization and refinement, Bataille now renders poetry (and favours it as) a site of expenditure, both symbolic and real, as he notes: 'Le terme de poésie [...] peut être considéré comme synonyme de dépense: il signifie en effet, de la façon la plus précise, création au moyen de la perte' [The term poetry [...] can be considered synonymous with expenditure; it in fact signifies, in the most precise way, creation by means of loss].[33] Referring in 'La Notion de dépense' to the fate of the *poètes maudits*, Bataille sees poetry as a mode of real expenditure in which the life of the poet is actually spent (sacrificed) and words originate from and cause the poet's own (real) loss: '[L]a dépense poétique cesse d'être symbolique dans ses conséquences' [[P]oetic expenditure ceases to be symbolic in its consequences].[34] The poet's life is consumed and ruined, while poetry offers no compensation, since, far from contributing to the poet's glory and immortality, it cuts him off from the world, confining him to misery and sealing him with the destiny of a reprobate. The definition of poetry as primarily a symbolic expenditure, as the words' power to undo themselves (and the fixity

---

33 Bataille, 'La Notion de dépense', p. 307; Bataille, 'The Notion of Expenditure', p. 120.

34 Bataille, 'La Notion de dépense', p. 307; Bataille, 'The Notion of Expenditure', p. 120.

of meaning), is given in a brief passage in *Méthode de méditation*, where it is noted: '[E]lle [la poésie] exprime dans l'ordre des mots les grands gaspillages d'énergie; elle est le pouvoir qu'ont les mots d'évoquer l'effusion, la dépense immodérée de ses propres forces' [In the order of words it [poetry] expresses the great waste of energy; it is the power of words to evoke effusion, the immoderate expenditure of one's own strength].[35] Bataille ascribes a sacrificial structure to poetry, as he sees in it, in Nancy's expression, 'un sacrifice de l'écriture, par l'écriture' [a sacrifice of writing by writing], due to its acting as an interruption of articulated language through the capacity of the words to consume their own power by destabilizing their usual (useful) meaning.[36] Poetry, the very form of writing dismissed by Sartre, is, for Bataille, sacrificial (sacrifice being linked, as its etymology suggests, to the sacred), since it is freed from the secular production and closure of meaning. In this sense, Bataille's poetic sacrifice, as radically distinct from meaning-producing, signifying discourses, is not to be strictly confined to the genre of poetry, but rather denotes, in a broader sense, a writing practice which would eventually become his own and that of his epigones. Derrida, in his essay on Bataille, calls for a recasting of the poetic as a process of writing, of Derridean *écriture* (without, however, escaping an oblique allusion to Mallarméan poetry): 'La poétique ou l'extatique est ce qui *dans tout discours* peut s'ouvrir à la perte absolu de son sens, [...], à la perte de connaissance dont il se réveille par un coup de dés' [The poetic or the ecstatic is that *in every discourse* which can open itself to the absolute loss of its sense [...] to the swoon from which it is reawakened by a throw of the dice].[37]

Inner Experience: The Breakdown of the Discursive Real

The awakening swooning and the sacrifice of writing by writing, reported by Derrida and Nancy respectively, both take place in the main text of *L'Expérience intérieure*, in which Bataille launches a practice of writing as poetic outpouring. Striving to break with life's

---

35 Georges Bataille, 'Méthode de méditation', in *Œuvres Complètes*, v: *La Somme athéologique. Tome I*, pp. 191–227 (p. 220).

36 Nancy, 'L'excrit', p. 57; Nancy, 'Exscription', p. 60.

37 Jacques Derrida, 'De l'économie restreinte à l'économie générale. Un hégélianisme sans réserve', *L'Arc*, 32 (1967), 24–45 (pp. 31–32); Jacques Derrida, 'From Restricted to General Economy: A Hegelianism without Reserve', in *Bataille: A Critical Reader*, ed. by Botting and Wilson, pp. 102–38 (p. 113).

consoling illusions (as fabricated by prevalent discourses), Bataille puts forth a dis-intoxicated vision of life, access to which is offered through vertiginous moments of intoxication (profound laughter, violent eroticism and poetic sacrifice) in which both intentionality and the ability to express (and comprehend) fade out. On that basis, *L'Expérience intérieure* unfolds as a discordant pact between writing and the experience of the outside, inasmuch as it is a written account of something impossible for language to reach and account for. In a celebrated passage from the text, experience is rendered as a desperate yearning for an intimacy with the world and words are designated as both deficient and an impediment: '[D]ans l'expérience, l'enoncé n'est rien, sinon un moyen et même, autant qu'un moyen, un obstacle; ce qui compte n'est plus l'enoncé du vent, c'est le vent' [[I]n experience, what is stated is nothing, if not a means and even, as much as a means, an obstacle; what counts is no longer the statement of the wind, but the wind].[38] In that sense, the text of *L'Expérience intérieure* becomes the stage of the encounter, the battle, between what cannot be written of and (its) writing. Pointing out the tension that marks the text, Julia Kristeva concludes: '[I]l s'agit d'une expérience "non-discursive" mais qui suppose le discours et s'en sert' [[I]t is a matter of 'non-discursive' experience but one which assumes discourse and makes use of it]. As Kristeva notes: 'Et c'est seulement lorque d'autres "operations" passent à travers le "réel discursive", que celui-ci cesse d'être un réel discursif seulement et témoigne de la réalité hétérogène' [It is only when the other 'operations' pass through 'the discursive real' that the latter ceases to be simply a discursive real, and witnesses heterogeneous reality].[39] In this respect, the text of *L'Expérience intérieure*, alongside a written record of the experience of the outside, unfolds as a parallel record of the experience of (its) writing, which takes place as a sacrifice of language through language. In it, as language is challenged and relentlessly called into question due to its deficiency, the texture of the text is elusive, fissured, composed of paratactic, frenzied, unfinished sentences. It is through this broken texture that the text points to something outside it, to an excess of signification, which is concurrently exposed but withheld, presented in the text (inscribed), yet uncontained by it

---

38   Bataille, *L'Expérience intérieure*, p. 25; Bataille, *The Inner Experience*, p. 13.
39   Julia Kristeva, 'Bataille, l'expérience, et la pratique', in *Bataille*, ed. by Philippe Sollers (Paris: Union Générale d'Éditions, 1973), pp. 267–301 (p. 272); Julia Kristeva, 'Bataille, Experience and Practice', in *On Bataille: Critical Essays*, ed. by Boldt-Irons, pp. 237–64 (p. 241).

(absent, exscribed); access to something outside is given and, at the same time, by the same gesture, taken away, blocked.

Set against the historical background from which it emerged – the German occupation of Paris and the increasing number of killings taking place in the autumn of 1941 – *L'Expérience intérieure* can be read not, as Suleiman suggests, as an '*inward* turn in Bataille's thought' juxtaposed with, and dissociated from, the violence of the '*outward* events around him', but rather as an erratic register of the surrounding turbulence and void in a world where everything stable is shaken.[40] In this respect, despite its characterization as 'inner', the Bataillean experience is not an esoteric, introspective turn, but a disquieting and opening experience which implicates an encounter between the self and its outside since in it the distinction between interiority and exteriority crumbles. Additionally, against all semantic connotations, experience does not lead to knowledge (but to non-knowledge), nor does it foster subjectivity (but brings about its dissolution; and yet, as the experience is impossible, the subject always returns from – and persists in – its dissolution, in a series of repeated failures, endlessly, until the end). Bataille nevertheless employs the term 'inner', willing to challenge the savant's external standpoint of objectivity and detachment, and, correspondingly, the term 'experience' (as synonymous to life, as something *we go through*), willing further to oppose the realm of thought, which firmly *separates* subjects from objects. As he notes: '[E]lle [l'expérience] apparaît unissant ce que la pensée discursive doit séparer' [[I]t appears to unify that which discursive thought must separate].[41] Put differently, the Bataillean experience exceeds the phenomenological tradition from which it derives, since the self, as Martin Crowley elucidates, is not the subject of this excessive and uncontainable experience, but 'its shattered locus'.[42] As Bataille puts it: '"Soi-même", ce n'est pas le sujet s'isolant du monde, mais *un lieu de communication*' [Oneself is not the subject isolating itself from the world, but *a place of communication*].[43] Moreover, the Bataillean 'communication'

---

40 Susan Rubin Suleiman, 'Bataille in the Street: The Search for Virility in the 1930s', in *Bataille: Writing the Sacred*, ed. by Carolyn Bailey Gill (London: Routledge, 1995), pp. 26–45 (p. 40) (my emphasis). This essay was first published in *Critical Inquiry*, 21 (1994), 61–79.

41 Bataille, *L'Expérience intérieure*, p. 21; Bataille, *Inner Experience*, p. 9.

42 Martin Crowley, 'Bataille's Tacky Touch', *MLN*, 119 (2004), 766–80 (p. 771).

43 Bataille, *L'Expérience intérieure*, p. 21; Bataille, *Inner Experience*, p. 9 (my emphasis).

is construed not as a (Hegelian) mutual recognition, nor as a (Habermasian) rational act of exchange between two solid entities, but as a moment of surrendering. Calling for a reconfiguration of the communicative process, Bataille notes: '[I]l y a *passage, communication* mais non de l'un à l'autre: l'un et l'autre ont perdu l'existence distincte' [[T]here is *passage, communication* but not from one to the other: the one and the other have lost their separate existence].[44] For Bataille, communication occurs precisely in and as passing, in gaps and breaches (of the self and of language), in openings and wounds (as hypostasized in the crater of Mount Etna, this earthy crack the ascent of which plunged him and his lover Laure into an experience of – shared – terror). As becomes evident, Bataillean communication, far from being an interchange in and through language, occurs in and as an excess of the order of signification and meaning which approximates the incommunicable. Its governing logic is close to that of exscription, since it denotes an excess that is not amenable to expression or figuration. In its affective dimension, it is also close to another central figure in Nancy's thought, that of touch, which is conceived not as a confident grasp, but as a contact in (and as) separation. Thus, the poetic becomes a privileged trope of communication, since, in its acting as an interruption (a sacrifice) of articulated language and meaning, it touches upon (opens to) the excess of signification. The poetic, as activated in the very writing of *L'Expérience intérieure*, is signifying discourse (relying upon the discursive) which, exceeding the order of signification (opposing and sacrificing the discursive positions on which it relies), shows that sense cannot be summed up in any discursive structure. Put differently, communication for Bataille (defined as poetic sacrifice and brought forth in the structure of *L'Expérience intérieure*) is constructed around a tension between meaning and non-meaning which is neither an inclination towards the nonsensical (since in this case his communicatory operation – apart from being unreadable – would be irrelevant) nor a transformation of this non-meaning into something meaningful (as the Existentialist postulate of the absurd of existence does).[45] Communication accedes, poetically, to (and poetry communicates) 'a dawning of sense', as Nancy puts it, since in its

---

44 Bataille, *L'Expérience intérieure*, p. 74; Bataille, *Inner Experience*, p. 59 (my emphasis).

45 For a critique of Existential philosophy on this point, see Critchley, *Very Little ... Almost Nothing*, pp. 172–73.

exhaustion meaning emerges anew, inexhaustible, as the infinity, or the dawning, of sense.[46]

Inner experience, as sketched out above, shares with mysticism the state of rapture and ecstasy, but lacks the reassuring presence of God and redemption, which channel mysticism and ultimately guarantee its meaning. Leading towards 'non-savoir' (non-knowledge, un-knowing),[47] it is meaningless, horror laid bare, which is why Bataille chooses, as a personal object of adoration, the photograph of 'The Torture of the 100 Pieces', an image of irredeemable pain and abandonment, over the image of the Crucifixion.[48] Gratefully attributing to Blanchot the much-quoted guiding principle of inner experience, Bataille defines experience as an end in itself. Rejecting every attempt to justify experience (being, life) from the outside and, by the same token, affirming its lack of self-identity, he notes: '[L]'expérience elle-même est l'autorité (mais l'autorité s'expie)' [[E]xperience itself is authority (but authority expiates itself)].[49] In Hegelian, or anti-Hegelian terms, what Bataille looks for when he remarks, 'Je vis d'expérience sensible et non d'explication logique' [I live by tangible experience and not by logical explanation] is a lived (un-mediated) experience of radical negativity, impossible to recuperate in a synthetic, positive, comforting result (be it work, knowledge or salvation).[50] The conception of existence in terms of an

46 Nancy, *Multiple Arts*, p. 3.

47 Bataille, *L'Expérience intérieure*, p. 15; Bataille, *Inner Experience*, p. 3. Not-knowing and non-knowledge are different from the unknown, since they enact a different kind of knowing and knowledge rather than lying on the other side. Not-knowing and non-knowledge highlight a movement of expenditure and slippage as well as a process of undoing and relentless contestation, which constantly expose (deconstruct) knowledge in the usual sense and lead nowhere. The unknown, on the contrary, is a sharply delimited area which relishes the certitude of established conceptuality and contributes to the construction of knowledge as its outer edge. While 'non-knowledge' is the more commonly used term in English, 'un-knowing' is more precise because it brings out the dynamic dimension of the process (rather than its outcome).

48 The extreme penalty, torture and execution known as *lingchi* and called by Western observers 'death by a thousand cuts' or 'death by slicing' were reserved for the worst crimes in China from the tenth century until the abolition of *lingchi* in 1905. From his analyst Adrien Borel Bataille received a photograph depicting the 'death by a thousand cuts'. Bataille referred to the photograph as the 'Torture of the Hundred Pieces' and was obsessed by this image of pain, since he considered it both ecstatic and repulsive.

49 Bataille, *L'Expérience intérieure*, p. 19; Bataille, *Inner Experience*, p. 7.

50 Bataille, *L'Expérience intérieure*, p. 45; Bataille, *Inner Experience*, p. 33.

excessive negativity has already been announced in Bataille's famous letter to Kojève, 'Lettre à X' (1937), in which he asks what becomes of the motor of history (Hegelian negativity) once history arrives at its end: '[L]a question se pose alors de savoir si la négativité de qui n'a "plus rien à faire" disparaît ou subsiste à l'état de "negativité sans emploi"' [The question which then arises is whether the negativity of someone who has 'nothing left to do' disappears or remains in the state of 'unemployed negativity'].[51] Bataille goes on defining himself as that 'négativité sans emploi', stating: '[J]e ne pourrais me définir de façon plus précise' [I could not define myself more precisely].[52] In light of this letter, *L'Expérience intérieure* can be read as a frenzied response to, an exhaustion and overturning of, the *Phenomenology of the Spirit*. Where Hegel's *'Bildungsroman'*, 'an optimistic narrative of adventure and edification', as Butler eloquently describes it, envisions the outcome of the process (establishing the triumph of the appropriative spirit), Bataille focuses on the non-discursive moments that forerun it (discerning the failure, the impossibility of writing to bring them within reach).[53] Butler's critique of Kojève and Hegel is that in their work subjects are disembodied agents lacking a 'corporeal life'.[54] In his letter to Kojève, Bataille, relentlessly responsive to bodily existence, utters an objection very similar to Butler's: 'J'imagine que ma vie – [...] la *blessure ouverte* qu'est ma vie – à elle seule constitue la réfutation du *système fermé* de Hegel' [I imagine that my life – [...] the *open wound* that my life is – in and of itself alone constitutes the refutation of Hegel's *closed system*].[55] In this respect, '*the existence* of the knower', as Baugh puts it, in a state of open being presents itself as a blind spot to absolute knowledge and resists the Hegelian project of completion (be it of work or of meaning).[56]

51 Georges Bataille, 'Lettre à X', in *Œuvres complètes*, v: *La Somme athéologique. Tome I*, pp. 361–71 (p. 369).

52 Bataille, 'Lettre à X', p. 369.

53 Judith Butler, *Subjects of Desire: Hegelian Reflections in Twentieth Century France* (New York: Columbia University Press, 1987), p. 17.

54 Butler, *Subjects of Desire*, p. 78.

55 Bataille, 'Lettre à X', pp. 369–70 (my emphasis).

56 Bruce Baugh, *French Hegel* (London: Routledge, 2003), p. 84 (my emphasis). It is important to underline that, when endorsing non-knowledge, Bataille does not dismiss but rather *exposes* knowledge, refusing to see existence as reducible to it. As Bataille himself expresses his divergence from Hegel: 'Le seul achoppement de cette manière de voir [...] est ce qui dans l'homme irréductible au projet: l'existence non-discursive, le rire, l'exstase' [The only obstacle in this way of seeing [...] is what, in man, is irreducible to project: non-discursive

The destruction of the structure of being as closed and completed (understood in terms of unity, identity and solidity) is the main task of inner experience. As Bataille proclaims: 'L'expérience est la mise en question (à l'épreuve), dans la fièvre et l'angoisse, de ce qu'un homme sait du fait d'être' [Experience is, in fever and anguish, the putting into question (to the test) of that which a man knows of being].[57] The role of 'anguish' in Bataille is both in alignment with and in aberration from Heideggerian thought. Echoing Heidegger, Bataille designates being as open and unknown: 'L'être est insaisissable; il n'est jamais saisi que par erreur' [Being is 'ungraspable'. It is only 'grasped' in error].[58] Being, for Bataille, cannot be located: 'L'être n'est nulle part' [Being is nowhere], as he puts it.[59] It exists only in and as passage and as such is ungraspable: 'La vie n'est jamais située en un point particulier: elle passe rapidement d'un point à l'autre [...]. Ainsi, où tu voudrais saisir ta substance intemporelle, tu ne rencontres *qu'un glissement*' [Life is never situated at a particular point: it passes rapidly from one point to another [...]. Thus, where you would like to grasp your timeless substance, you encounter *only slipping*].[60] In this consideration of being in and as slippage – and, more crucially, in the laughter which arises from it – Bataille directly inverts Heideggerian ontology (as the latter remains tied up in a tradition that envisions being as presence). Attributing a revelatory force to laughter, Bataille remarks in L'Expérience intérieure: 'Le rire pressent que [...] notre volonté de fixer l'être est maudite' [Laughter intuits [...] that our will to arrest being is damned].[61] As he more clearly states in Méthode de méditation, with regard to his attitude towards the slipping away (the absenting) of being: '[J]e suis parti du rire et non, comme le fait Heidegger, de l'angoisse' [My point of departure was laughter and not, as in the case of Heidegger, anguish].[62] Bringing out the overlooked, yet immensely significant, element of laughter in Bataille's thought, Mikkel Borch-Jacobsen underlines its communicative and disruptive force, as it does not arise from a dominant and solid position of the

---

existence, laughter, ecstasy] (Bataille, *L'Expérience intérieure*, p. 96; Bataille, *Inner Experience*, p. 80).

57 Bataille, *L'Expérience intérieure*, p. 16; Bataille, *Inner Experience*, p. 4.
58 Bataille, *L'Expérience intérieure*, p. 98; Bataille, *Inner Experience*, p. 82.
59 Bataille, *L'Expérience intérieure*, p. 98; Bataille, *Inner Experience*, p. 82.
60 Bataille, *L'Expérience intérieure*, p. 111; Bataille, *Inner Experience*, p. 94 (my emphasis).
61 Bataille, *L'Expérience intérieure*, p. 107; Bataille, *Inner Experience*, p. 91.
62 Bataille, 'Méthode de méditation', p. 217.

one who laughs, but out of a communicative passion with the 'other' who falls ('other' both to himself as self-contained and to us).[63] The Bataillean tragic laughter (caused, as Jacobsen clarifies, by a passer-by who, amidst a carefully arranged, busy daily schedule, slips on a banana peel and abruptly falls, as well as by the tragic downfall of Oedipus) approximates tears, as we laugh *with* the other, at the slippage (the passing) of the world as stable and within our control to its unexpected revelation as unknown and out of reach.[64]

Due to his vision of being as a 'glissement' [slippage], Bataille directs his attention to what he terms 'mots glissants' [slipping words], words which precisely fail to capture what they supposedly denote, appointing as exemplary in this respect two loaded words from the religious and monastic tradition: 'God' and 'silence'. As George Steiner remarks with regard to silence, the holy man, in his retreat in a cell, withdraws not only from action but, most importantly, from audibly articulated, oral communication, due to a suspicion of 'the *veil of language*' and to a desire 'to break through it to the more real'.[65] In his resorting to the slipping words, bringing about the paradox of their enunciation, Bataille *unveils* the tension (the gap), *within language*, between signifiers and their (non-)corresponding signifieds. In the tension which makes them, the slipping words ultimately bring about their explosion and result in their own ruin (sacrifice). As Bataille notes: 'Le silence est un mot qui n'est pas un mot' [Silence is a word which is not a word]. He continues: '[I]l est déjà [...] l'abolition du bruit qu'est le mot; entre tous les mots c'est le plus pervers, ou le plus poétique: il est lui-même gage de sa mort' [[I]t is already [...] the abolition of the sound which the word is; among all words it is the most perverse, or the most poetic: it is the token of its own death].[66] Indeed, not only is silence betrayed by the utterance of the word 'silence', but the word 'silence' is nullified by its reference. Similarly, in the preface to his disturbing narrative *Madame Edwarda*, which he entitles 'the lubricious key' to *L'Expérience Intérieure*, we read: 'Nous ne pouvons pas ajouter au langage impunément le mot qui dépasse les mots, le mot *Dieu*; ce mot se dépassant lui-même détruit vertigineusement ses limites'

---

63 Mikkel Borch-Jacobsen, 'The Laughter of Being', in *Bataille: A Critical Reader*, ed. by Botting and Wilson, pp. 146–66 (pp. 158–59).

64 Borch-Jacobsen, 'The Laughter of Being', pp. 158–59.

65 George Steiner, *Language and Silence: Essays on Language, Literature, and the Inhuman* (New Haven, CT: Yale University Press, 1998), p. 13.

66 Bataille, *L'Expérience intérieure*, pp. 28, 29; Bataille, *Inner Experience*, p. 16.

[We cannot with impunity incorporate the very word in our speech which surpasses words, the word *God*; directly we do so, this word, surpassing itself, explodes past its defining, restrictive limits].[67] The explosion of the word 'God' as surpassing itself is brought into play in *Madame Edwarda*, inasmuch as a public whore, Edwarda (impure, terrifying, cadaverous) is appointed God.

The slipping words, in the tension that constitutes them, or, more precisely, that tears them apart, bring forth paradigmatically the paradoxical status that Bataille attributes to writing and his own ambiguous (tumultuous) relationship with it. This tension within (and with regard to) writing, which animates *L'Expérience intérieure* and many of his other works, has given rise to different and conflicting readings of the Bataillean corpus, which Suleiman classifies under the two opposing categories of the 'textual' and the 'ultrathematic'. As one might expect, Barthes, Sollers and Derrida, who read the Bataillean texts as 'a discursive practice which exceeds the boundaries of meaning, unity, representation', are gathered in the first group.[68] For them, the openness of Bataille's texts towards the body, the obscene, the corporeal, serves as an apt metaphor for the opening and dispersal of the signifying process towards multiplicity, non-meaning, incompleteness. As a result, as Suleiman observes, the textual critics transpose many of Bataille's key concepts (i.e., expenditure, excess, heterogeneity) from the realm of experience to that of writing.[69] Conversely, the second group, within which Suleiman subsumes the feminist readings of Bataille (but we might also include Bataille's contemporaries and rivals Breton and Sartre and, more recently, Zizek), pays no attention to the textual status, the 'framing', as Suleiman puts it, of Bataille's writings and, overemphasizing their content, 'gets to their core'.[70] Zizek's account of the Bataillean endeavour as 'the act of forcing one's way into the raw heart of the Real, of its palpitating flesh' is indicative of such a

---

67   Georges Bataille, *Madame Edwarda*, in *Œuvres complètes*, III: *Œuvres littéraires* (1974), pp. 7–31 (p. 12); Georges Bataille, *Madame Edwarda*, in Georges Bataille, *My Mother, Madame Edwarda, The Dead Man*, trans. by Austryn Wainhouse (London: Penguin, 2012), pp. 121–44 (p. 127).

68   Susan Suleiman, 'Transgression and the Avant-Garde: Bataille's *Histoire de l'œil*', in *On Bataille: Critical Essays*, ed. by Boldt-Irons, pp. 313–34 (p. 317).

69   Suleiman, 'Transgression and the Avant-Garde', p. 318.

70   Suleiman, 'Transgression and the Avant-Garde', p. 322.

reading.⁷¹ Ignoring, as Suleiman observes, the fact that what is written is filtered through a specific medium, namely that it is 'a text rather than life itself', the ultra-thematic readings reduce Bataille's writings to a chronicle of 'male desire' (in the case of Dworkin), or dismiss Bataille as an excremental philosopher or a mystic (in the case of Breton and Sartre, respectively).⁷² In brief, what the ultra-thematic reading misses is *the fact* that Bataille nevertheless *writes* about experience. As Patrick ffrench remarks, by choosing, or rather surrendering, to write, Bataille defies an account of him as an 'apologist of unmediated experience' 'at the expense of thought and writing'.⁷³ On the other hand, the textual reading ignores the haunting dimension of the real (existence) in Bataille's work and of his striving to posit, as Allen Weiss mentions, 'life itself as interpretation'.⁷⁴ Nevertheless, while exposing the deficiencies in the prevalent reception of Bataille's work, Suleiman does not step out of them but rather softens the edges of the ultra-thematic by offering what she terms her 'thematic' reading. It is Klossowski and Nancy, in their figures of the 'simulacrum' and 'exscription', who advance a reading of the Bataillean work which draws precisely on the tensional and *asymmetrical relationship* between his writings and what is written of. The above terms bring into focus, and dwell on, the paradoxical status of Bataille's writings, showing how he works out a language which points towards something uncontained by it, outside it. Nancy's 'exscription' (as indicated by its prefix) and Klossowski's 'simulacrum' (in its self-exposure as a relic) reveal that Bataille, *in* and *when* writing, points towards an existence *outside* his texts rather than merely inscribing (incorporating) it in them. In this way, the above terms show the ambiguity which lies at the heart of the Bataillean act of writing, as it is precisely in pointing towards the excess of what makes it – from which it originates – that writing points simultaneously towards its own exigency, in order to speak – albeit deficiently – of it.

71 Slavoj Zizek, 'Ideology III: To Read Too Many Books is Harmful' <http://www.lacan.com/zizchemicalbeats.html> [accessed 18 February 2022].
72 Suleiman, 'Transgression and the Avant-Garde', pp. 320, 322.
73 Patrick ffrench, 'Georges Bataille', in *Encyclopedia of Modern French Thought*, ed. by Christopher John Murray (New York and London: Routledge, 2004), pp. 55–59 (p. 57).
74 Alen S. Weiss, 'Impossible Sovereignty: Between *The Will to Power* and *The Will to Chance*', October 102, 36 (1986), 128–46 (p. 138).

2. Blanchot: The Passion of Literature

[A]ucune situation littéraire n'est définitivement réglée. La littérature est faite de mots, ces mots opèrent une transmutation continuelle du réel en irréel et de l'irréel en réel.

[[N]o literary situation is definitively settled. Literature is made of words, and these words work a continuous transmutation from the real to the unreal and from the unreal to the real.]¹

The Literary Experience: Writing Outside Language

In his review of Bataille's book *L'Expérience intérieure*, also entitled 'L'Expérience intérieure', Blanchot embraces and thoroughly comprehends the Bataillean passion for the negative, writing of the vital necessity to 'aller au délà' and 'dire non à tout' [go beyond and say no to everything].² Similarly, in a much later essay devoted to Bataille under the title 'L'Expérience-limite' and included in *L'Entretien infini*, Blanchot, in accordance with Bataille's sketch of experience as a descent into 'non-savoir' [non-knowledge, unknowing], construes experience (in its excess, its strange surplus) as a movement towards the inaccessible and the unknown: 'L'expérience-limite est l'expérience de ce qu'il y a hors de tout [...]: l'inaccessible même, l'inconnu même' [The limit-experience is the experience of what is outside the whole [...]: the inaccessible, the unknown

---

1 Maurice Blanchot, 'Les Romans de Sartre', in Blanchot, *La Part du feu*, pp. 188–203 (p. 190); Maurice Blanchot, 'The Novels of Sartre', in Blanchot, *The Work of Fire*, pp. 188–203 (p. 190).
2 Maurice Blanchot, 'L'Expérience intérieure', in Maurice Blanchot, *Faux pas* (Paris: Gallimard, 1971 [1943]), pp. 47–52 (pp. 48–49).

itself].³ In 'L'Expérience intérieure' Blanchot provides a definition of inner experience close to the one he offered as the main interlocutor in the conversations out of which Bataille's work finally emerged: in its infinite putting into question, inner experience is its own authority, as it has no reference (no meaning, value, justification, end or response) outside itself. In Blanchot's words, 'l'expérience intérieure est *la réponse qui attend l'homme lorsqu'il a décidé de n'être que question*' [inner experience is *the answer* that awaits man when he has decided to be nothing but a question].⁴ Thus we see that Blanchot conceptualizes experience as an exposition of absence. Inner experience, as the experience of the limit, cannot be delimited but rather imposes itself as an exposure to limitlessness. Joining Bataille in his unending questioning, Blanchot, in very Nietzschean terms, adds: 'Si [l'homme] s'arrête, c'est dans le malaise du mensonge et pour avoir fait de sa fatigue une vérité' [If [man] stops, it is in the discomfort of the lie and for having turned his fatigue into a truth].⁵ In accordance with Bataille, Blanchot further mentions that this radical contestation, this restless, never-ending negation, this excess which makes every *arrêt* (stop, ending, conclusion, but also judgement) impossible, is twofold:⁶ in its violence it turns against all knowledge but against subjectivity as well, its decisive trait being that, due to its intensity, the one who undergoes it finds it incomprehensible, uncomfortable, overwhelming and is, therefore, no longer 'there' fully to assimilate it or properly to experience it. For Blanchot, such an experience is an *hasard* in the sense that it cannot be mastered or willingly attained.⁷ Such an experience, not experienced, is the paradox of non-experience.⁸

---

3   Blanchot, 'L'Expérience-limite', p. 305; Blanchot, 'The Limit-Experience', p. 205. The title of Blanchot's essay 'L'Expérience-limite' denotes more distinctly what is at stake in the Bataillean inner experience, which is, after all, an experience of the limit, that is, of limitlessness.

4   Blanchot, 'L'Expérience intérieure', p. 47 (my emphasis).

5   Blanchot, 'L'Expérience intérieure', p. 47.

6   Bataille's key notion of *négativité sans emploi* denotes that the end is impossible and the negation is never-ending, since it is not sublimated in a dialectical synthesis.

7   Blanchot, 'L'Expérience intérieure', p. 58.

8   In 'L'Expérience-limite' Blanchot uses the paradoxical yet illuminating formula of the experience of non-experience ('expérience de la non-expérience') (p. 311).

Blanchot's dense, six-page article 'L'Expérience intérieure' is a poised, serene synopsis of Bataille's long, disordered book of the same title. In that sense, despite its consonance with Bataille's major preoccupations, as briefly sketched out above, it displays, in Bident's description, 'la passivité de Bataille (sa part d'apaisement, de retrait, de réserve)' [Bataille's passivity (his appeasement, withdrawal, reserve)] and 'la passion de Blanchot (sa violence intérieure, son désordre mental) [Blanchot's passion (his inner violence, his mental disorder)].[9] As already mentioned, it was Blanchot who gave to inner experience its essential attribute (of an authority which nevertheless expiates itself) and, as Bataille recounts, comparing himself again to a wound (long in closing), this answer calmed him: 'Dès le moment cette réponse m'apaisa, me laissant à peine (comme la cicatrice longue à se fermer d'une blessure) un résidu d'angoisse' [From that moment, this answer calmed me, barely leaving me (like the scar of a wound long in closing) a residue of anguish].[10] Nevertheless, juxtaposing Blanchot's 'L'Expérience intérieure' with that of Bataille does not reveal two different idiosyncrasies or two writing styles, each idiosyncratic in its own way, but two different ways of engaging with language in its relation to what both Blanchot and Bataille denote as inner experience. More specifically, Blanchot shares with Bataille the concern (and imperative) to reconfigure the question of being and existence and think them anew in terms of absence, inappropriable excess and constant ungrounding and not in terms of presence, fixed essence, solidity and ground. Nevertheless, their different writing styles (the one serene and calming, the other disordered and violent) invite comparison, as two different attitudes towards language and writing emerge. The different textual character, the form and syntax of the texts (crafted and orderly in the case of Blanchot; unfinished and broken, intense and paroxysmal in the case of Bataille) call for our attention in as much as *what* is said (around the theme of inner experience) is bound to the *way* in which it is said (which is the way language relates to inner experience).[11] In other words, Blanchot more readily acclaims language as an accommodating space for the abysmal experience of limitlessness.

---

9 Christophe Bident, *Maurice Blanchot. Partenaire Invisible. Essai Biographique* (Seyssel: Champ Vallon, 1998), p. 168.

10 Bataille, *L'Expérience intérieure*, p. 19; Bataille, *Inner Experience*, p. 8.

11 In doing so, both Bataille's and Blanchot's theoretical texts on inner experience, although they are – typically – critical essays, testify to their entanglement with, and their partaking in, the literary.

Blanchot's article 'L'Expérience intérieure' recognizes that, in its extremity, experience involves a passage from the discursive to another plane (where 'l'action, le discours, les formes intelligibles et exprimables de la vie n'ont plus leur place' [action, discourse, the intelligible and expressible forms of life no longer have their place]). However, it nonetheless affirms, towards its end, that discourse bears and bears witness to, responds to and takes responsibility for, the non-discursive: '[C]ependant, il n'est pas interdit au discours d'essayer de *prendre à son compte* ce qui échappe au discours; cela est même necessaire' [[H]owever, it is not forbidden to discourse to try to take over what escapes discourse; it is even a necessary attempt].[12] In this respect, when he classes Bataille's book as 'an authentic translation' of the experience around which it revolves, Blanchot speaks less of Bataille's venture and more of his own confident alliance to literature.[13]

As a step towards emphasizing Blanchot's trustful bond with literature, one should stress that he confers on writing the demands of inner experience, since for him it is precisely *in* and *as* writing that an experience of the impossible and the incommunicable, of the other as the other, emerges. Indeed, while in Bataille's *L'Expérience intérieure* writing, or at least a certain practice of writing, is placed alongside other privileged moments (i.e., violent eroticism, explosive laughter), Blanchot insistently posits the question of language as unreservedly essential, not as an obstacle but as a point of departure. In this regard, Nancy's term exscription, which captures Bataille's writing so well and testifies to his struggling relationship with language, fails to account for the vigilance which Blanchot bestows upon writing (in its relation to the outside). Slightly displacing the Bataillean alertness to life and existence by an impassioned attraction to language and literature, Blanchot gives prominence to what Christopher Fynsk calls the fundamental, albeit eluding, *fact* 'that there is language'.[14] In so doing, he renders writing the inner experience *par excellence* and portrays the mode of being of literary words in terms of the *négativité sans emploi* under which Bataille defined the lavishness and the vulnerability of his own (and, subsequently, of the human) condition. In this respect, if Blanchot's unsurpassed contribution consists of driving us constantly back, as Fynsk points out, 'to the

---

12   Blanchot, 'L'Expérience intérieure', p. 52 (my emphasis).
13   Blanchot, 'L'Expérience intérieure', p. 52.
14   Christopher Fynsk, 'Introduction', in *Language and Relation ... that there is language* (Stanford, CA: Stanford University Press, 1996), pp. 1–11 (p. 1).

"fact" of language', Bataille's determinative influence (an influence that both Leslie Hill and Bident, two ardent, deeply attached readers of Blanchot, acknowledge) lies in Blanchot's conception of writing in terms of a radical contestation.[15] It is throughout his conversations with Bataille that Blanchot moves, as Christophe Bident asserts, 'from a classical conception of literature as *revelation* to a modern conception of writing as *contestation*'.[16] In this contestation, writing turns, first, against itself and, subsequently, against the world – or, from a more holistic viewpoint, it attacks the world both in its materiality and as a word-clogged reality.

The Negative Force of Literature

Blanchot unravels writing in terms of the contestatory force of inner experience in an early essay (which precedes Blanchot's review 'L'Expérience intérieure' but overlaps with and bears the mark of his conversations with Bataille) with the telling title, 'Comment la littérature est-elle possible?'. In it language turns upon itself in order to question the conditions of its own possibility. Similarly, literature is no longer considered a *site* of human and spiritual values but a *space* withdrawn from the social (actual) world or, rather, as a *spacing* in which language reflects and relates to itself. Put differently, Blanchot here sets up his view of literature, not in the Sartrean sense of a useful project which *serves* concrete values, including revolutionary goals, but as an inherently negating (revolutionary) force which posits *itself as* violent. In this essay, an oblique critique of Paulhan's *Les Fleurs de Tarbes*, Blanchot examines a literary attitude which he, like Paulhan, calls 'Terror', equating all literature, or at least its very soul, with Terror.[17] For Blanchot, authentic literature is synonymous with Terror in that it consists of a contestation of both language and pre-existing

---

15 Fynsk, 'Introduction', p. 1.

16 Christophe Bident, 'The Movements of the Neuter', trans. by Michael FitzGerald and Leslie Hill, in *After Blanchot: Literature, Criticism, Philosophy*, ed. by Leslie Hill, Brian Nelson and Dimitris Vardoulakis (Newark, DE: University of Delaware Press, 2006), pp. 13–34 (p. 26).

17 The essay also exposes Blanchot's idiosyncratic literary practice, which Christophe Bident describes as an appropriation and expansion of the original text that finally open it to a questioning and a consummation of itself. In that respect, Paulhan himself says of Blanchot's article: '[U]n article [...] qui me passion[e], [qui] les [*Les Fleurs*] compren[d] bien mieux que moi, qui vraiment il me les révèl[e]' [[I]t fascinates me, it understands them [*Les Fleurs*] much better than I do, it really reveals them to me] (Lettre de Jean Paulhan à Monique

works of literature, rhetorical commonplaces, linguistic clichés and established literary conventions. However, in this contestatory undertaking the question which inevitably arises, and which Blanchot himself raises, is the following:

> Comment dans ces conditions la littérature peut-elle exister? Comment l'écrivain, qui se distingue des autres hommes par ce seul fait qu'il conteste la validité du langage, et dont le travail devrait être d'empêcher la formation d'une œuvre écrite, finit-il par créer quelque ouvrage littéraire?[18]

> [How, under these conditions, can literature exist? How does the writer, who distinguishes himself from other men only by the fact that he contests the validity of language and whose work should be to prevent the formation of a written work, end up creating a sort of literary work?]

For Blanchot, literature, in its mistrust of worn-out words and its dismissal of previous literary texts, ultimately realizes that the conditions of its own possibility lie precisely in pre-existing words and texts: to them it owes its existence. Thus one fights language with the weapons provided by language and a work cannot claim to be original except by exposing its fundamental unoriginality, hence its impostor status. In other words, literature for Blanchot becomes possible insofar as it is, and faces itself as, impossible.

This constitutional impossibility that makes literature possible is expanded in Blanchot's essay 'Kafka et la littérature', in which the impossibility of writing is pronounced in its relationship, not only to the always already eroded words, but also to the reality it supposedly expresses. Speaking of the strange and scandalous possibility of literature, Blanchot unveils the hiatus which constitutes and enacts writing:

> Je suis malheureux, je m'assieds à ma table et j'écris: 'Je suis malheureux.' Comment est-ce possible? [...] Mon état de malheur signifie épuisement de mes forces; l'expression de mon malheur, surcroît de forces. Du côté de la douleur, il y a impossibilité de tout, vivre, être, penser; du côté de l'écriture, possibilité de tout, mots harmonieux, développements justes, images heureuses.

Saint-Hélier, no 11, 22 novembre 1941, in Jean Paulhan and Monique Saint-Hélier, *Correspondence, 1941–1955* (Paris: Gallimard, 1995), pp. 47–48).

18 Maurice Blanchot, 'Comment la littérature est-elle possible?', in Blanchot, *Faux pas*, pp. 92–101 (p. 97).

[I am unhappy, so I sit down at my table and write 'I am unhappy'. How is this possible? [...] My state of unhappiness signifies an exhaustion of my forces; the expression of my unhappiness an increase in my forces. From the side of sadness, there is the impossibility of everything – living, existing, thinking; from the side of writing, the possibility of everything – harmonious words, accurate exposition, felicitous images.][19]

He goes on, adding: 'C'est comme si la possibilité que représente mon écriture avait pour essence de *porter sa propre impossibilité* – l'impossibilité d'écrire qu'est ma douleur' [It is as if the possibility that my writing represents essentially exists to express *its own impossibility* – the impossibility of writing that constitutes my sadness].[20] Leslie Hill deciphers the impossibility of literature as an aporetic moment, in which the term aporia is to be understood in its double sense (both as a puzzlement, a doubting, and as a destitution, a lack of resources). As Hill argues, 'literature's essence does not lie in the foundational purity of the work but rather *in the aporia* that turns the act of its foundational purity into the impossibility of a possibility'.[21]

Blanchot's conception of literature in terms of a foundational impossibility, in the sense that, in its aporia, it founds nothing and rests on nothing, is historically determined and significant. In the book *Les Dépossédés* Denis Hollier focuses on the historical context out of which the destitution of literature emerges. The naming of the book, in a way analogous to Gertrude Stein's 'Lost Generation', includes a whole generation of post-war writers. The introductory chapter, entitled 'La littérature *doit*-elle être possible', refers to the opening scene of *La douleur,* in which Duras, sketching herself as seated at a table during the Liberation of Paris, interviewing refugees and taking notes, recounts the moment when an officer told her: 'On vous permet de travailler debout, mais je ne veux *plus* voir cette table ici' [You are allowed to work standing up, but I don't want to see this table here *anymore*].[22] As Hollier emphasizes, attributing an

---

19 Maurice Blanchot, 'Kafka et la littérature', in Blanchot, *La Part du feu*, pp. 20–34 (p. 27); Maurice Blanchot, 'Kafka and Literature', in Blanchot, *The Work of Fire*, pp. 19–20.

20 Blanchot, 'Kafka et la littérature', p. 27; Blanchot, 'Kafka and Literature', p. 20 (my emphasis).

21 Leslie Hill, *Blanchot: Extreme Contemporary* (London: Routledge, 1997), p. 74 (my emphasis).

22 Denis Hollier, 'La Littérature doit-elle être possible?', in Hollier, *Les Dépossédés*, pp. 7–22 (p. 10) (my emphasis).

allegorical value to the scene, the writer has nothing to cling on to any longer. In that sense Blanchot complies with and fosters, throughout the French post-war years, a view of literature which chooses as its theme, and recounts the impossibility of, its proper writing. In this way, Blanchot's writing carries within it the Adornean aesthetic (and ethical) imperative imposed by the Holocaust.[23] Blanchot discerns the ethical implications of writing, depicting it, and its self-reflexive capacity, as an attempt to formulate a just relation to the world. He notes:

> Écrire comme question d'écrire, question qui porte l'écriture qui porte la question, ne te permet plus ce rapport à l'être – entendu d'abord comme tradition, ordre, certitude, vérité, toute forme d'enracinement – que tu as reçu un jour du passé du monde.

> [Writing as a question of writing, a question that carries the writing that carries the question, allows you no longer a relationship to being – understood primarily as tradition, order, certainty, truth, any form of rootedness – that you once received from the world's past.][24]

To the extent that it bears both the trace of his pre-war attachment to rootedness (nationhood) and his subsequent turning away from it, this slightly autobiographical phrase crystallizes and illuminates, in a quite straightforward way, that for Blanchot it is through writing that a renewed way of thinking 'being' emerges. In this respect, Leslie Hill connects Blanchot's pre-war attachment to homogeneity, nation and tradition to his subsequent devotion to (re)thinking the question of 'being' and existence in terms of an ontological groundlessness, exteriority and alterity, outside topologies of sameness, identity or substance. Blanchot's post-war works strongly attest that 'being' can never be gathered, reducible within an order, be it philosophical or political.

The Ontological Peculiarity of Literature[25]

The ontological peculiarity with which Blanchot endows literature finds its more striking account in his essay 'La Littérature et le

---

23 Christophe Bident suggests such a reading (Bident, *Maurice Blanchot*, p. 285).
24 Maurice Blanchot, *Le Pas au-delà* (Paris: Gallimard, 1973), pp. 8–9; Hill, *Blanchot: Extreme Contemporary*, pp. 43–44.
25 It is Gerard L. Bruns who employs the term 'ontological peculiarity' for Blanchot's conception of the artwork to indicate how writing, for Blanchot, is bound with impossibility and thereby incompatible with being in the world

droit à la mort'. In this major essay, literature is outlined in quasi-ontological terms not as a form or a genre but as a mode of being. More importantly, in the Heideggerian resonance that marks the essay, the mode of being of the literary offers a way to revitalize and rethink the question of being (beings). It is this essay that first puts forward the fundamental entanglement, constantly highlighted in many of Blanchot's works, of literature and being (both in the sense of literature as a peculiar mode of being and in the sense of its relation with beings). Blanchot himself articulates the question: 'Qu'est-ce qui est en jeu par ce fait que quelque chose comme l'art ou la littérature existerait?' [What would be at stake in the fact that something like art or literature exists?].[26] It therefore becomes explicit that literature's self-referentiality, the infinite questioning of its essence and its origin, does not result in and is not driven by a narcissistic, hermetic debate on artistic creativity and inspiration (despite the fact that Blanchot was at first, and is still, read by those exposed to and dealing with the process of creation). Blanchot postulates the question of literature as essential and contemplates it in a highly original (*insoupçonné*, in Foucault's expression) way, both drawing on and moving away from Heidegger, since its existence as such poses a question to being.[27] In this respect, the essay 'La Littérature et le droit à la mort', which Leslie Hill characterizes as the 'most programmatic philosophical account of literature', starkly shows that for Blanchot, in contrast to Bataille, who provocatively pronounces himself to be an anti-philosopher, literature cannot do without philosophy.[28] However, conversely, as this essay reveals, literary writing opposes, exceeds and in a way supersedes philosophical thought.

At the beginning of the essay Blanchot suggests: 'Admettons que la littérature commence au moment où la littérature devient une question' [Let us suppose that literature begins when literature

---

(Gerard L. Bruns, 'Anarchic Temporality: Writing, Friendship, and the Ontology of the Work of Art in Maurice Blanchot's Poetics', in *The Power of Contestation: Perspectives on Maurice Blanchot*, ed. by Kevin Kart and Geoffrey H. Hartman (Baltimore, MD and London: Johns Hopkins University Press, 2004), pp. 121–40 (p. 122)).

26   Maurice Blanchot, 'Note', in Blanchot, *L'Entretien infini*, pp. vi–viii (p. vi); Maurice Blanchot, 'Note', in Blanchot, *The Infinite Conversation*, pp. xi–xii (p. xi).

27   Michel Foucault, 'Sur les façons d'écrire l'histoire' (entretien avec R. Bellour), *Les Lettres françaises*, 1187 (1967), 6–9 (p. 8).

28   Hill, *Blanchot: Extreme Contemporary*, p. 103.

becomes a question].²⁹ However, as he immediately adds, this question is not to be reduced, as we might be tempted to think, to the writer's doubts: it is a more fundamental question, a question which lies silent within the work. Subsequently, the analogy of literature and Terror reappears, acquiring, as the title of the essay indicates, a more radical, a more violent meaning. The negative force of literature is pushed to its limits, as here literary Terror does not merely turn against literary conventions but tends towards a worldly life in a desire to negate 'quelque chose de réel, de plus réel que les mots' [something real, more real than words].³⁰ Using Hegel against Sartre, Blanchot attacks the statement that literature should be considered as, and identified with, action in the world, as developed in Sartre's *Qu'est-ce que la littérature?*. According to Blanchot, literary activity differs radically from worldly action, to the extent that literature negates the totality of the world. For Blanchot, the *specificity* of writing lies in its absolute negation of the world; therefore, of all worldly action, literature can only be analogous to revolutionary action, in which everything pre-existing (God, other people, the state, laws) is totally negated.³¹ As Critchley points out, literature's right to death consists in 'its absolute freedom, its right to the total negation of reality, as realized *in* and *as* language'.³² Blanchot here sees in a writer's activity the highest form of radical negation and hence de Sade, who partakes of the fate of the revolutionary, as the writer *par excellence*.

However, the Hegelian conception of language as murder – since language deprives things of their being – takes an interesting twist in Blanchot, since for him language indeed kills, but also appears as a bearer of death.³³ Taking as his starting point Hegel's position that in the word 'cat' the cat loses its singular reality and becomes an idea in which the real cat is absent, Blanchot replaces the 'cat' by a 'woman', emphasizing that the ideal negation performed in language (the

---

29 Maurice Blanchot, 'La Littérature et le droit à la mort', in Blanchot, *La Part du feu*, pp. 291–331 (p. 293); Maurice Blanchot, 'Literature and the Right to Death', in Blanchot, *The Work of Fire*, pp. 300–44 (p. 300). The essay was initially published in two parts in Bataille's review, *Critique*.

30 Blanchot, 'La Littérature et le droit à la mort', p. 308; Blanchot, 'Literature and the Right to Death', p. 318.

31 Blanchot, 'La Littérature et le droit à la mort', p. 308; Blanchot, 'Literature and the Right to Death', p. 318.

32 Critchley, *Very Little … Almost Nothing*, p. 63 (my emphasis).

33 Blanchot asserts: '[Q]uand je parle, la mort parle en moi' [[W]hen I speak, death speaks in me] (Blanchot, 'La Littérature et le droit à la mort', p. 313; Blanchot, 'Literature and the Right to Death', p. 323).

ease with which we say 'a woman', detaching her from her existing reality) would not be possible 'si cette femme n'était pas réellement capable de mourir' [if this woman were not really capable of dying].³⁴ By indicating that language, in retaining nothing but an absence, is a constant allusion to real death, Blanchot makes what Christopher Fynsk calls an 'ontological claim about language'.³⁵ Moreover, as Blanchot underlines, it is, in particular, literary language which designates (and makes us encounter) the void, 'ce vide qu'il ne peut pas ni combler ni représenter' [this void which they can neither fill nor represent]. Meanwhile, common language, in its search for peace, accepts that the reality of the existent comes to life fully and certainly in the form of its idea.³⁶ As Timothy Clark points out, for Blanchot the language of literature is constituted not in the familiar context of everyday life but in a context of ignorance, since it is the literary work that first discloses and elucidates what is written in it. This context of ignorance, which constitutes the world of a novel in the sense that this world emerges for the first time in that particular novel (since there is no pre-existing source of information which enlightens us about what occurs in a book), echoes Bataille's notion of non-knowledge (as it appears in *L'Expérience intérieure*). Clark further argues that in a literary world words are not *signs*; words are not 'about' something, 'disappearing before what they represent', but rather words take place in a vacuum (which is the novel) and simply 'are'. In this respect, literary words are not a *useful* means of communication but exist in the way of what Bataille termed an *unemployed* (useless) negativity.³⁷

Nevertheless, while placing the Bataillean experience of non-knowledge (the void) in the world of literature, Blanchot does not disregard the bodily dimension of this experience as expressed in the Bataillean moments of laughter, tears and the erotic. For Blanchot, literary language, in its questioning of itself, searches for that moment

---

34   Blanchot, 'La Littérature et le droit à la mort', p. 313; Blanchot, 'Literature and the Right to Death', p. 323.

35   Christopher Fynsk, 'Crossing the Threshold: On "Literature and the Right to Death"', in Fynsk, *Language and Relation*, pp. 227–44 (p. 230).

36   Blanchot, 'La Littérature et le droit à la mort', p. 315; Blanchot, 'Literature and the Right to Death', p. 326.

37   Timothy Clark, 'Blanchot and the Literary', in Timothy Clark, *Derrida, Heidegger, Blanchot: Sources of Derrida's Notion and Practice of Literature* (Cambridge: Cambridge University Press, 1992), pp. 64–107 (pp. 75–76).

of existence, of being, prior to its negation by language; it seeks to recover the pre-linguistic materiality of things:

> Dans la parole meurt ce qui donne vie à la parole. [...] Admirable puissance. Mais quelque chose était là, qui n'y est plus. Quelque chose a disparu. Comment le retrouver, comment me retourner vers ce qui était *avant*, si tout mon pouvoir consiste à en faire ce qui est *après*? Le langage de la littérature est la recherche de ce moment qui la précède.
>
> [In speech what dies is what gives life to speech. [...] What wonderful power. But something was there and is no longer there. Something has disappeared. How can I recover it, how can I turn around and look at what exists *before*, if all my power consists in making it into what exists *after*? The language of literature is a search for this moment which precedes literature.][38]

In its endeavour to reach the lost materiality of things, literature is assisted by the materiality of language as manifested paradigmatically in poetry. Words, instead of being an obstacle, are now a precious ally. Here, the influence of Heidegger and of what he considers the 'thingly' character of a poem (the physicality of rhythm, shape) is manifest. Unlike Bataille, Blanchot does not consider poetry in terms of a writing practice of outpouring (which operates beyond, and thereby contests, the order of signified and meaning), but as a condensed materiality which partakes, by analogy, in the materiality of the world.

Having divided literature into two 'slopes', the de Sadean total negation of things and the poetic salvation of things, Blanchot faces the impossibility of both and the inevitable passing from one slope to the other.[39] Literature, in its infinite power immediately to negate everything, in its global negation negates nothing in the end. Writing, outstepping the Hegelian dialectics, has the peculiar status of being, in Leslie Hill's formulation, 'an absolute negation and affirmation'.[40] In that respect the case of de Sade, who spent his whole life as a writer isolated in his cell, is exemplary. Similarly, in its concern for the reality of things the second slope described above also inevitably fails, since, in Critchley's depiction, it has 'the Midas touch' and

---

38   Blanchot, 'La Littérature et le droit à la mort', p. 316; Blanchot, 'Literature and the Right to Death', p. 327.

39   The term 'slopes' is the translation of the French term used by Blanchot, i.e., 'versants'. 'Versants' can also be translated as 'sides' but the inclined surface of the slope better captures the process and the challenge involved.

40   Hill, *Blanchot: Extreme Contemporary*, p. 107.

conceals (with words) that which was meant to be revealed (being).⁴¹ It is in this intermediary space, never coinciding with either of its two slopes, constantly divided and suspended between them, between negation and what cannot be negated, between revelation and what precisely resists being revealed, that Blanchot locates the fate and struggle of literature. However, despite – or precisely because of – the Heideggerian resonance of such a struggle (as explored in 'The Origin of the Work of Art', in which the artwork is defined in terms of a tension between the world, which reveals itself, and the earth, which hides), one should note that for Blanchot literature provides no Heideggerian disclosure of truth. Rather, he depicts it as a space that leads, as Levinas writes, 'pas à la vérité de l'être [mais] à l'erreur de l'être – à l'être comme lieu de l'errance' [not to the truth of being [but] to a mistake of being – to being as a place of wandering].⁴² This conception of being as place of wandering (*errance*) is close to the Deleuzian motif of 'becoming' and to the Nietzschean view of existence in terms of an eternal return, namely, of existence alone in its nakedness (without ground, aim or meaning) recurring infinitely. In this way, in opposition to Heidegger's view of poetry as a foundation (a revelation) of truth and his final depiction of the origin of the artwork in terms of an *enracinement*, Blanchot describes this origin in terms of a never-reached (and appropriated) longing.⁴³ Committed in his radical conception of literature as unfoundational and impossible, as already asserted in his earlier essays, he asks: 'Mais, au départ, que s'est-il perdu? Le tourment du langage est ce qu'il manque par la nécessité où il est d'en être le manque. Il ne peut même pas le nommer' [But in the beginning, what was lost? The torment of language is what it lacks because of the necessity that it be the lack of precisely this. It cannot even name it].⁴⁴ Nevertheless, ultimately Blanchot finds a name for language in the paradoxical status of the Levinasian *il y a*, a name which nevertheless defies language as it presents itself as the unfathomable pre-conceptual materiality for which literature longs (but cannot reach). While the reference to the *il y a* is brief and

---

41 Critchley, *Very Little ... Almost Nothing*, p. 71.

42 Emmanuel Levinas, *Sur Maurice Blanchot* (Montpellier: Fata Morgana, 2004 [1975]), p. 19.

43 Martin Heidegger, 'The Origin of the Work of Art', in Martin Heidegger, *Poetry, Language, Thought*, trans. by Albert Hofstadter (New York: Harper & Row, 1971), pp. 15–88 (p. 75).

44 Blanchot, 'La Littérature et le droit à la mort', p. 316; Blanchot, 'Literature and the Right to Death', p. 327.

marginal in 'La Littérature et le droit à la mort' in its status as always already there, it signposts all of Blanchot's subsequent attempts not to sidestep the question of origin but to think of it otherwise, untying it from any foundational logic as well as from a melancholic resurrection of origin in terms of loss. In parallel, the *il y a* signposts Blanchot's subsequent attempts to recase 'being' as 'otherwise than being', that is, in excess of ontological possibility.

Levinas describes the *il y a* in terms of an otherworldly absence which, in the disappearance of everything, would be experienced as a sort of presence. This 'otherworldliness', which cannot be qualified in terms of transcendence or immanence, as it exceeds this dichotomy and opposition, is depicted by Levinas as a rumbling silence, 'un silence bruissant': it is 'quelque chose qui ressemble à ce que l'on entend quand on approche un coquillage vide de l'oreille, comme si le vide était plein, comme si le silence était un bruit' [it is something resembling what one hears when one puts an empty shell close to the ear, as if the emptiness were full, as if the silence were a noise].[45] The attempt of literary language to address the preconceptual singularity of things, things in their singular existence, as explored above, touches on the broader question of how thought approaches (and relates to) what is beyond and outside thought. In this respect, the *il y a*, posited as logically prior, as what is outside – before and after – every worldly formation, is a passive (yet persistent and fundamental) resistance to every attempt at construction or destruction; it is, one might say, an irreducible remnant that ruins every possibility of ruination or of construction.

To frame the above in/against the lexicon of contemporary debates of object-oriented ontology, the *il y a*, in its outsideness, designates the anonymous, impersonal murmur of being in excess of phenomenal thingness rather than a realm of things as such. Whereas object-oriented philosophy, in its emphasis on the existence of objects as independent and in its rejection of the privileging of human existence, attempts to posit the world of objects as autonomous – *as equal in its autonomy to* the human world, the *il y a* is, rather, the constant *objection to* every attempt to construct a world in terms of autonomy

---

45   Emmanuel Levinas, *Éthique et infini* (Paris: Fayard, 1982), p. 38; Emmanuel Levinas, *Ethics and Infinity: Conversations with Philippe Nemo*, trans. by Richard A. Cohen (Pittsburgh, PA: Duquesne University Press, 1985), p. 48. The first reference to the *il y a* as the density of the void, the presence of absence with explicit reference to Maurice Blanchot's novel *Thomas l'obscur* appears in Levinas's work *De l'existence à l'existant* in 1947 (Emmanuel Levinas, *De l'existence à l'existant* (Paris: Vrin, 1993 [Fontaine, 1947]), p. 103 n. 1).

and stability. While object-oriented philosophy, in its defence of the autonomy of objects, refuses absolutely their reduction to any relation (be it with humans or with other objects), as it considers every relation distortive for the related object, the Blanchotian *il y a* (as the unity of being) calls for an absolute relation of extreme affirmation. In this respect, as will be made clear in the next chapter on Blanchot, the significance of the *il y a* lies neither in the substantiation nor in the provision of a name for preconceptual absolute singularity (or difference as such), but in its call for an entirely different kind of relation.

Object-oriented ontology, asserting the primacy of ontology to which its name testifies, renders objects its focal point, against the Heideggerian idea of a pre-eminently human way of being and being-in-the world. Overthrowing the Kantian transcendent subject as the ground of, and that which constitutes, objective reality, object-oriented ontology disengages and liberates objects from human perception and posits them as autonomous substances. The anti-Kantian endeavour of object-oriented ontology can be described in Kantian terms as follows: objects are dissociated from human cognition and perception (cease to be phenomena) and are reconsidered as autonomous (become noumena which exist independently). In this context, the contrivance of the *il y a*, rather than introducing a world of objects (in its independence and solidity), indicates the dizzying absence of any world whatsoever, as in Blanchot's thought there is no room for anything of substance and all there is *is* an experience of voiding and emptiness. In other words, the *il y a*, rather than complementing and radicalizing ontology by institutionalizing another ontological state (that of objects and substance), points to a state prior to – and more 'primal' than – ontology (that of non-being).

In his recourse to, and in his *naming* of, the *il y a*, which is 'neither nothingness, nor being' (and whose status is close to the Bataillean 'unemployed negativity', an indestructible negativity which pre-exists and would still remain at the end of history, when there is nothing more to do), Blanchot, in his trustful bond with literature, sees language as opening a space and providing a distinct name (a pre- or a pseudo-concept, in Leslie Hill's expression) for precisely what cannot be said in language.[46] In that respect, Blanchot renders mythical Orpheus as the emblematic figure of the writer and his experience (in its longing for the inaccessible, his gaze at what resists being looked at, Eurydice in the Underworld, and her instant

---

46 Hill, *Blanchot: Extreme Contemporary*, p. 110.

disappearance) as the experience, the fate and torture of writing, its double bind. For Blanchot, what literature can (and cannot) attain is crystallized in Orpheus's gaze, in Eurydice's image: a presence not sustained but given in its withdrawal.

The above features of the 'gaze' and the 'image', which acquire a central place in Blanchot's *L'Espace littéraire,* can be understood by Nancy's untying of the term *regard*. Though the term is not directly applied by Nancy with reference to Blanchot (but with reference to Abbas Kiarostami, a director whose ethics of discretion vis-à-vis the infinite alterity of existence can be compared to that of Blanchot), it elucidates (especially in its juxtaposition to exscription) the relation of Blanchot's writing to the real. As Nancy notes, by again directing his attention to the prefix of the term, the *re-gard* is an intensification of vigilance, of care (*garde*).[47] As he further emphasizes, the regard is also an *égard*, a respect, a consideration (not penetrating or appropriating) and an attentive observation. In this respect, for Blanchot writing, as a *regard* is a taking care, and a respecting, of existence in its alterity. As becomes evident, the virility of the gaze and the appropriative force usually attributed to the act of seeing are undermined. For Blanchot, writing (much like looking) is to be exposed to a sense that is outside one's reach. This outside is the *il y a* [*there is*], which exists (is there) before the coming of words and concepts (as well as before the phenomenalization of being as beings or things) and still remains (persists) as the presence of the absence of being, as the inescapability and indestructability of being after the coming of language (as well as after the world of beings and things). The *il y a* designates 'being' as a preconceptual singularity, anonymity and materiality and can be thought of as an indivisible – or radical – immanence, prior to the phenomenological division of the terms 'immanence' and 'transcendence'. This exposure to existence as the *il y a* happens in and as literature, since philosophy cannot account for it. In this respect, while Bataille's writing might be seen as an attempt to silence the oppressive power of discourse, Blanchot's attempt might be seen as offering a voice to silence in writing.[48]

---

47 Nancy, *L'Évidence du Film*, p. 39.

48 In the final lines of 'Méthode de méditation' Bataille writes: '… des mots! qui sans répit m'épuisent: j'irais toutefois au bout de la possibilité misérable des mots. J'en veux trouver qui réintroduisent – en un point – le souverain silence qu'interrompt le langage articulé' [… words! which tirelessly exhaust me: I would, however, go to the end of the miserable possibility of words. I want to find some of them that reintroduce – at one point – the sovereign silence interrupted by articulated language] (Bataille, 'Méthode de méditation', p. 210).

More irreparably (irredeemably) marked by the Hegelian desire to be and say everything, and keener on excess than Blanchot, Bataille adopts Hegel's all-encompassing strategy and excessively accumulates (puts everything in) language, making it finally crash down. Blanchot's endeavour, on the contrary, can be thought of as the flipside to the Hegelian strategy of negation, as language (after negating worldly objects) turns against itself (against itself as the negation of objects). Whereas in Bataille language becomes the tool through which language is broken apart – since, in its attempt to say everything, it finally becomes used up and consumed – language in Blanchot proceeds through the logic of negation in which language negates itself and points towards that which lies beyond ('beyond' here understood as the antecedence or precedence of a singularity of existing prior to being, world, thought or manifestation). One might say that the inadequacy of language is better expressed by Bataille, while the unsayable is better expressed by Blanchot.

Nonetheless, what is urgent in our inquiry into both Bataille and Blanchot is how the non-identical can be secured without adopting (or reintroducing) a transcendent position and without substantiating difference as such (difference in itself). To put it another way, it is crucial *not* to consider the Bataillean moments of laughter or ec-stasy as moments of 'being' and the Blanchotian 'il y a' in terms of the incarnation of radical alterity as such. The next chapter, through a critical analysis of Blanchot's conception of the image (as the absenting of presence) and of Bataille's conception of the instant (as the absenting of the present), focuses on how presence is tied up with absence and the present with retreat and disappearance. Additionally, it shows how the usual pairing of transcendence with the beyond (what is out of reach, above the ordinary and the contingent) and of immanence with presence (what is here, now) is reworked in Blanchot and Bataille.

3. The Value of Annexes:
Coïncidences et Correspondences

This chapter, which concludes the opening section of the book, critically examines Bataille and Blanchot's singular attitudes towards annexes. Annexes raise the question of form, a question that has been in the background and to some extent touched upon in our previous discussion on Bataille and Blanchot. One can trace a metamorphosis of form in their writings (both fictional and critical) throughout the 1950s, as we see in the chapters that follow. Bataille moves away from his short and bold pre-war essays, passes through the hybrid form of *Somme athéologique* and ultimately opts for more rigorous and systematic forms in his post-war writings. In parallel, Blanchot shifts from short *compte rendus* of literary texts to extended literary-philosophical essays and from novels to *récits*.

As additional, secondary parts, annexes relate to form. They raise the question of what is counted (or miscounted) as essential and what is added as extra (as well as whether this addition is to be taken as an extension or as a subordinate). Thus, at the heart of the issue of the annex are questions of appropriation, incorporation, continuity, discontinuity and wholeness. Annexes question what belongs or does not belong to a whole, as well as whether there is a whole. As Bataille and Blanchot's stances on annexing relate to and bring forth the issue of autobiographical writing, these liminal additions call into question the relation between literature and life. Thus, the term 'real' is used in this section to refer to its more conventional meaning of real events that have taken place in the lives of Bataille and Blanchot.

The question – and questioning – of appendices show how writing, for both Bataille and Blanchot, is neither privileged as that which gives form and coherence to life nor undermined as that which is overthrown by life's vital force. In this respect, appendices illuminate how the relation between life and literature (and, more broadly, the relation between the real and the aesthetic) is reworked by Bataille and Blanchot in terms of a double dissymmetry, as neither pole is privileged at the expense of the other. Writing and life neither oppose each other (according to the formula: writing, *unlike* life, is X), nor are equivalent to each other (according to the formula: writing, *like* life, is X), but endlessly confront each other – without entering into a harmonious composition or merely rejoicing in an internal coherence.

In their respective biographies of Bataille and Blanchot, Surya and Bident emphasize how Bataille's and Blanchot's work (both fictional and theoretical) resists and, concurrently, calls for a biographical reading, thereby establishing an asymptotic, incommensurable relation between life (their life) and literature (their works). As Surya notes with reference to Bataille's stories, although they evidently bear the mark of his disturbed life, they are largely fictitious, as their material, while heavily drawn from (and drawing on) his life, goes through 'un savant travail de décentrement et de metamorphose' [a deliberate work of decentering and metamorphosis].[1] Therefore, though there are recognizable traces of Bataille's life and obsessions in his fictions, there is no exact, measurable correspondence between the two.[2] Nevertheless, Surya, identifying Bataille as 'un-literary' and 'un-abstract', insists on the capital significance of a biographical approach in order to understand his work (both fictional and critical), as 'il [Bataille] n'a jamais rien pensé qu'il ne voulût vivre, et rien imaginé dont il ne voulût, sur lui-même, seul, ou avec quelques autres, faire l'expérience' [he [Bataille] never thought about anything he did not also wish to live out, never imagined anything he did not – alone or in the company of others – also wish to experience].[3]

In a reverse movement, Blanchot's fragmentary narratives include scarce, barely noticeable, autobiographical elements, while large periods of his life, since it was lived in isolation, remain unknown. In his *récits* it is often uncertain who is speaking, as language is not distinctly enunciated by and attributed to a specific subject. Despite this one might argue that the impersonal tone of Blanchot's narratives bears exactly the mark of, and testifies to, his own immersion in literature (as Blanchot renders writing synonymous with the

---

1 Surya, *Georges Bataille*, p. 122; Surya, *Georges Bataille: An Intellectual Biography*, p. 98.

2 Surya, *Georges Bataille*, pp. 450–51; Surya, *Georges Bataille: An Intellectual Biography*, p. 390.

3 Surya, *Georges Bataille*, p. 293; Surya, *Georges Bataille: An Intellectual Biography*, p. 253.

effacement of the writer and recasts literature as the passage from the author-itative 'I' to the 's/he' – what he calls *le neutre*).

When it comes to Blanchot's critical work biographical questions are, on the contrary, at the centre, since his literary essays extensively engage, in a conversational, intimate tone, with the experience of other writers. As Bident mentions, with reference to Blanchot's approach to Maupassant: 'De Maupassant? Il interroge moins son art que sa folie' [Of Maupassant? He questions his art less than his madness].[4] As he adds, '[c]ette tendance marquera toute son œuvre critique. Blanchot commente moins l'œuvre que l'expérience qui la précède et l'accompagne' [[t]his tendency will mark all his critical work. Blanchot comments less on the work than on the experience that precedes and accompanies it].[5] However, while it is in the inseparable mingling of life and creation that Blanchot attributes an importance to experience (since his attention is directed to the genesis of the work, the unfolding of the creative process, the conditions which both enable it and torture it), it cannot be said that he is interested in the life of the work or the intellectual life of the creator rather than the latter's 'ordinary' life. More precisely, while Blanchot begins by privileging the intellectual life of the author (the life of the spirit, in Hegelian terms; artistic genius, in Romantic terms) – echoing and subscribing to Mallarmé's credo that a writer has no biography – he ends up embracing, while commenting on Baudelaire, the more human, contingent and vulnerable aspects of a life. Posing as well the question of what the 'life' of writing is, and how it needs to be recast, he writes:

> [L']hypothèse qui sépare définitivement l'homme et l'auteur […] pour plus proche qu'elle soit de la vérité poétique […] fait de la création un absolu prodigieusement à l'abri des hasards et des accidents contre lesquels aucun homme, fût-il divin, n'a jamais été protégé.[6]
>
> [[T]he hypothesis which definitively separates the man from the author […] in order to stay as close as possible to poetic truth […] turns creation into an absolute, tremendously sheltered from chance and accidents, against which no man, even if he be divine, has ever been protected.]

---

4   Bident, *Maurice Blanchot*, p. 197.
5   Bident, *Maurice Blanchot*, p. 197.
6   Maurice Blanchot, 'Une édition des Fleurs du mal', in Blanchot, *Faux pas*, pp. 180–88 (p. 181).

Written Reminiscences and Personal Correspondence

Bataille's handling of (and stance towards) annexes arises in (and with regard to) the celebrated and extensively commented-upon section 'Coïncidences' in his first novel, *Histoire de l'œil*, published under the pseudonym Lord Auch.[7] The 'Coïncidences' section (later named 'Réminiscences') offers an over-self-conscious acknowledgement of the unconscious impulses which have already asserted themselves in the narrative and, as signalled by its title, attests to a strong correspondence between the story (a frenzied initiation of two adolescents into eroticism and death) and the author's own turbulent life. However, as many critics have argued, since this appended section is included in the novel as its second part, its value as testimonial evidence (as biographical truth) is undermined by the very gesture which fosters its creation.[8] Therefore, because the section 'Coïncidences' overturns the clear-cut division between a life and a written account of it, as well as the conventional differentiation between a narrator and an author, *Histoire de l'œil* refuses to be subsumed under either autobiography or fiction.

Blanchot brings in the question of annexing in his literary essay dedicated to Antonin Artaud. Referring to Artaud's famous correspondence with Jacques Rivière, Blanchot directs his attention to the anomaly that characterizes the publication of the letters. Artaud, Blanchot reminds us, sends his first poems to the *Nouvelle Revue Française*; these are rejected by the director of the journal, Jacques Rivière. Since an exchange between the two follows, the correspondence acquires literary value and is eventually published in the *Nouvelle Revue Française*, while some of the poems are published as complementary to the letters, 'comme exemples et

---

7 Georges Bataille, *L'Histoire de l'œil*, in *Œuvres complètes*, I: *Premiers écrits. 1922–1940*, pp. 9–77. The novel consists of a first long section entitled 'Récit' and of following shorter section entitled 'Coïncidences'.

8 Patrick ffrench glosses the problematic and paradoxical status of the 'Coïncidences' in terms of the 'multiplication of the frame', as the framing of the fiction by the real occurs 'from within' (Patrick ffrench, *The Cut: Reading Bataille's Histoire de l'œil* (Oxford: Oxford University Press, 1999), pp. 82–85). Leslie Hill underlines the (impossible) dialectics the epilogue enacts between legibility and (un)interpretability, since, while the narrator attempts to bring interpretation to an end, he finally opens the text to further reading (Hill, *Bataille, Klossowski, Blanchot*, pp. 29–30).

témoignage' [as examples and evidence].[9] Because the letters are published in place of the poems, the correspondence (in which the young Artaud expresses his suffering, which is amplified due to the fact that his poetic attempt offered no relief or appeasement to his tormented existence) is endowed with literary merit, while the poems end up being published as mere anecdotes that throw light on the letters. As Blanchot writes with reference to the deficiency of the poems: 'Comme si ce qui leur manquait, leur défaut, devenait plénitude et achèvement par l'expression ouverte de ce manque et l'approfondissement de sa nécessité' [As if what they lacked, their defect, became fullness and completion through the honest expression of this lack and the deepening of its necessity]. Moreover, as he adds, referring to Rivière's (but mainly Blanchot's own) preference and interest in the experience which leads to the work rather than the work itself: 'Plus qu'à l'œuvre elle-même, c'est assurément à l'expérience de l'œuvre, au mouvement qui conduit jusqu'à elle, que Jacques Rivière s'intéresse' [More than the work itself, it is certainly the experience of the work, the movement which leads to it, that interests Jacques Rivière].[10]

The Reality of Fiction – Pseudonymity

The critical reception of the Bataillean 'Coïncidences' is grouped by Martin Crowley under the terms of the explanatory and the parodic: the explanatory approach considers the section as separate from the main text (the first part, explicitly entitled 'Récit') and thereby undermines the value of the annex – inasmuch as a literary work can never be reduced to its explanatory account (even if it is provided by the author and especially if, as in this case, what is offered by the author is autobiographical exegesis).[11] On the contrary, the parodic approach considers the section indistinguishable from the main text (the 'Récit') and thereby insists on the value of the annex – in so far as, in its inseparability from the first section, it accounts for the indivisible textuality of the story (*Histoire de l'œil*) as a whole.

---

9   Maurice Blanchot, 'Artaud', in Maurice Blanchot, *Le Livre à venir* (Paris: Gallimard, 1959), pp. 50–58 (p. 50); Maurice Blanchot, 'Artaud', in Maurice Blanchot, *The Book to Come*, trans. by Charlotte Mandell (Stanford, CA: Stanford University Press, 2003), pp. 34–40 (p. 34).
10 Blanchot, 'Artaud', p. 50.
11 Crowley, 'Bataille's Tacky Touch', pp. 772–73.

This polarity, as Martin Crowley further shows, has been problematized more recently by an attempt to reconsider the value of the section 'Coïncidences' while untying it (liberating it) from a textual reading (and from its labelling as parodic).[12] The attempt to take the section *à la lettre*, or at face value, is an attempt to read it as a trustworthy document which accounts for and records the unavoidable interference of the real – an interference which turns out to be both invasive and evasive. In this respect, Patrick ffrench insists on the two-sided framing of the fictional by the real as well as of the real by the fictional. As ffrench argues, the section 'Coïncidences' triggers a framing of the fictional (the 'Récit') by the real, inasmuch as it alludes primarily to the writing process, which is real indeed.[13] Accordingly, the term 'une fiction réelle' [a real fiction] is coined by Surya to underline the idea that although the story might be fictional, the book is real.[14] Additionally, since 'Coïncidences' alludes to the real event of the direct blow to Manuel Granero's eye during a bullfight, a blow which resulted in his instantaneous death (on 7 May 1922 in Madrid), as well as to more personal episodes in Bataille's life (such as the incident of the white of the syphilitic's father eyes), it results in a second framing of the fictional by the real.[15] Nonetheless, as ffrench has noted, because this framing of fiction happens from within (since it is the text of 'Coïncidences' which informs us about the real events which gave rise to the 'Récit'), the display of the traumatic origins of the story, however real, cannot be considered determinant.[16]

Bringing in the broader issue of the use of the first person in all Bataille's narratives, Surya remarks that although it might be naïve to take the narratives as strictly autobiographical (as veracious accounts corresponding to the author's real life), it is equally unwise (or probably too prudent and prudish) to dismiss them as simply imaginary (invented).[17] In this respect, in *Histoire de l'œil* both the real and the fictional find themselves constantly undermined and

---

12   Crowley, 'Bataille's Tacky Touch', pp. 773–74.

13   ffrench, *The Cut*, p. 83.

14   Surya, *Georges Bataille*, p. 112; Surya, *Georges Bataille: An Intellectual Biography*, p. 88.

15   Bataille's blind father would open wide his white, sightless eyes while urinating. In Bataille's imagery, the whites of eyes, linked to the whites of eggs, are associated with urination.

16   ffrench, *The Cut*, pp. 84, 131.

17   Surya, *Georges Bataille*, p. 123; Surya, *Georges Bataille: An Intellectual Biography*, p. 100.

mutually contaminated: the reality of the events is undermined inasmuch as they are added as complementary to the *récit* and are thereby implicated in fiction, while the fictive status of the *récit* is undermined by the occurrence of the events, which dissuade us from not believing what is recounted.

This resistance of the real, the impossibility of sidestepping and sublimating it though fiction, is further highlighted in the case of *Histoire de l'œil* by the pseudonym under which both sections are signed. 'Lord Auch', in all his apparent unreality, far from providing the author of the story with a self-owned identity (thereby fulfilling a fantasy of self-origination) results in the reintroducing, intensifying and vitalizing of the presence of the father.[18] Commenting on the paradox of the pseudonym, Surya notes that rather than achieving a movement away from reality, it brings about a violent initiation of the real (in its social and civil dimension of a name and in its personal and psychic dimension of an over-traumatizing memory).[19] The father becomes at once magnified (recast as Lord, God), corporeal and horrific (as Auch stands for the abbreviated form of *aux chiottes* [to the toilet] and God reveals Himself in His corporeality and monstrosity (relieving Himself). Focusing on the German resonance of the term *auch* [also], Martin Crowley adds alongside the authorial presence of Lord Auch the residual presence of Georges Bataille.[20] Hence, next to (not behind) Lord Auch there is also (*auch*) Bataille himself.

---

18   As Leslie Hill notes, Bataille's several pseudonyms (Lord Auch, Louis Trente, Pierre Angélique) do not, as pseudonyms commonly do, establish another (a literary) identity, but indicate, in their implausibility, the sacrifice of identity as such. According to Leslie Hill, the Bataillean pseudonyms, provocative and irreal, from which his writings originate, 'advertise the fact that it is a false and assumed name' (Hill, *Bataille, Klossowski, Blanchot*, p. 94). Nevertheless, in their implausibility they bear witness to Bataille's singular attitude with regard to writing. They both register and point to the fact that for Bataille writing becomes the stage on which identity is put at play, a place where the self, rather than re-presenting itself, is presented in its explosion, in its downfall.

19   As Surya informs us, Bataille appears to have said that he wrote in order to erase his name. In this respect, Surya notes, the recourse to a pseudonym is not simply an act of dissimulation but a sovereign act that aspires to break with the paternal name and the family heritage, which have been imposed (a fate more complex than that of Oedipus, at least in its psychoanalytical appropriation, as Bataille's syphilitic father was already blind). However, as Surya shows, the name of the father bursts violently into the name invented by the son (Surya, *Georges Bataille*, pp. 112–13; Surya, *Georges Bataille: An Intellectual Biography*, p. 89).

20   Crowley, 'Bataille's Tacky Touch', p. 774.

In light of these remarks, *Histoire de l'œil*, Bataille's first work of fiction, which wavers undecidedly between fiction and autobiography, can *also* be read as Bataille's literary manifesto, alongside 'Le Gros orteil' and *L'Expérience intérieure*, inasmuch as it announces – in perfect, absolute honesty – all of Bataille's subsequent endeavours. It proclaims how his work thereon will turn against the primacy of vision, that is, in metaphysical terms, the primacy of the present and presence, or, in architectural terms, what Denis Hollier refers to as 'prétensions édifiantes' [enlightening claims], without nonetheless succumbing, through an exaltation of blindness, to the Romantic imagery of the nocturnal and darkness.[21] In erotic terms, this first narrative shows how Eros will be recast not as life-affirming but as inextricably bound to death.

The Lived Experience of Writing – Anonymity

The issue of autobiography is tackled by Blanchot in his critical essay on Antonin Artaud, in which, as already mentioned, predominance is given to Artaud's confessional letters rather than to his first poems. In so doing, Blanchot devalues the literary work (as it offers no frame or appeasement to one's tortured existence) and endows with literary value the record of the lived experience from which the work emanates. This displacement of the centre of gravity from the literary work (which becomes secondary) to the experience of (its) writing is glossed by Blanchot in Artaud's case in terms of writing *despite* the void (admitting one's impotence to get rid of it) rather than *against* it (hoping that one might get rid of it). With reference to the poems, Blanchot remarks, 'Artaud écrivait contre le vide et pour s'y dérober' [Artaud wrote against the void, to escape it]. He adds with reference to the letters: 'Il écrit maintenant en s'y exposant et en essayant de l'exprimer et d'en tirer expression' [He now writes exposing himself to it, trying to express it, to draw expression from it].[22] Finally,

21 Denis Hollier, 'La Prise de la Concorde', in Denis Hollier, *La Prise de la Concorde, suivi de Les Dimanches de la Vie. Essais sur Georges Bataille* (Paris: Gallimard, 1993), pp. 11–298 (p. 52). Commenting on how Bataille introduces the play of writing against all hierarchical structure, Hollier notes: 'L'écriture en ce sens serait un geste profondément anti-architectural, geste non pas constructif, mais qui mine et qui ruine au contraire tout ce qui vit de prétensions édifiantes' [Writing in this sense would be a profoundly anti-architectural gesture, a gesture which is not constructive, but rather undermines and ruins everything that lives by edifying claims] (p. 52). There is a pun here between the term édifiantes/edifying, which is related to knowledge, and the architectural term édifice/edifice.

22 Blanchot, 'Artaud', p. 56.

Blanchot concludes by endorsing the culminating inseparability between life and thought in Artaud because, as he points out, 'jamais Artaud n'acceptera le scandale d'une pensée separée de la vie' [Artaud will never accept the scandal of a thought separated from life].[23]

Nevertheless, while Artaud and Blanchot share the view that intellectual activity needs to be infused with life (Artaud himself proclaimed that 'on ne sépare pas le corps de l'esprit, ni le sens de l'intelligence' [one does not separate the body from the mind, nor sense from intelligence]), their views radically diverge with regard to what counts and needs to be re-introduced as life.[24] In the case of Artaud, life is thought of in terms of intensity and of a sensual (bodily) experience that implicates one's nervous sensibility; in the case of Blanchot, life amounts to the dedication of one's life to writing, an act which renders the experience of writing a 'lived experience' in its own right.[25] In this respect, the value of Blanchot's essay on Artaud is neither that it fosters literary criticism as a mode of autobiography nor that it brings in the conception of the autobiography of the work (in a way that parallels the approach of *critique génétique* in its interest in the genesis of the work and broader questions of creation), but that it challenges received notions of autobiography by redrawing the boundaries between life and writing.

In the inseparability of life and writing as comprehended and put forward by Blanchot, the term and process of 'autobiography' can be reconfigured and realized in its strictest and most literal sense: the life (*bios*) of writing (*graphy*) recounted by writing itself (*auto*). In parallel, his writings also prove to be the most appropriate (impossible) autobiography of Blanchot (himself), the most exact and (im)personal account of Blanchot's life – of a life dedicated to and eroded by the question of writing.

In his discussion of autobiography, when commenting on the subject (subjectivity) that is its subject matter (its theme) Philippe Lacoue-Labarthe notices, against the semantic connotation of the

---

23 Blanchot, 'Artaud', p. 57.

24 Antonin Artaud, *Le Théâtre et son double* (Paris: Gallimard, 1964), pp. 134–35.

25 Artaud's major work *Le Théâtre et son double* calls for a theatre that addresses and speaks to the viewer's *sensual experience*. Theatre's double is life and life needs to come to the forefront and occupy the theatrical scene as a combination of gestures, sounds and lighting which will shock and address the body of the spectator and overthrow written language and of theatrical dialogues which address the mind of the audience.

prefix 'auto', a double lack: a lack of substance (selfhood) and of consistency (sameness).[26] Additionally, Lacoue-Labarthe marks out the fragment '(Une Scène primitive?)' of *L'Ecriture du désastre* and the short narrative *L'Instant de ma mort* as Blanchot's two autobiographical texts. These two texts, as signalled by their title, are a childhood scene and a death scene, a childhood memory and a death memory. Lacoue-Labarthe ponders the fact that in both texts Blanchot speaks (of himself) in the third person. Differentiating autobiographical enunciation from the general question of the enunciation of the subject (which results in the constitution of the thinking subject as split), as well as from classical enunciation of the narrative (in its firm distinction between an author and a narrator), Lacoue-Labarthe finally deduces from the Blanchotian use of the third person the founding rule of autobiography: to write itself, the subject of autobiography must somehow absent itself; it must already somehow be dead in order to write itself – as another.[27] In light of this account, autobiography is glossed by Lacoue-Labarthe both as *autothanatographie* and as *allobiographie*.

Autobiography is additionally recast by Lacoue-Labarthe in terms of a process, a process not simply in the sense that it is the procedure, the activity (rather than the object, the product, the result, the argument as such or the argument in its veracity) that counts, but in the judicial and legal sense of the term, which is 'engager un procès' [to bring proceedings], to put on trial, in brief, to come together to dispute.[28] In this respect, what is put on trial in the autobiographical process is not merely subjectivity but, more broadly and more crucially, attestation. Autobiography shows, for Lacoue-Labarthe, how to attest is always to con-test, as con-testation – in its strictest sense, that is *cum-testari* (bearing witness with) – is always implicated in attestation (bearing witness).

Finally, slightly modifying the Nietzschean remark that attributes to Plato the invention of the novel of antiquity (rather than the invention

---

26 Philippe Lacoue-Labarthe, 'La Contestation de la mort', *Le Nouveau Magazine Littéraire*, 424 (2003), 58–60 (p. 58); Philippe Lacoue-Labarthe, 'The Contestation of Death', in *The Power of Contestation*, ed. by Hart and Hartmann, pp. 141–55 (p. 148). A fuller version of this article, also entitled 'La contestation de la mort', appears in Philippe Lacoue-Labarthe, *Agonie terminée, agonie interminable. Sur Maurice Blanchot* (Paris: Galilée, 2004), pp. 91–117.

27 Lacoue-Labarthe, 'La Contestation de la mort', p. 58; Lacoue-Labarthe, 'The Contestation of Death', p. 150.

28 Lacoue-Labarthe, 'La Contestation de la mort', p. 59; Lacoue-Labarthe, 'The Contestation of Death', p. 154.

of philosophy), Lacoue-Labarthe suggests that if an invention needed to be attributed to Plato, it would be that of autobiography (rather than that of the novel). With particular reference to the Platonic *Phaedo*, Lacoue-Labarthe declares that it should be re-read as 'l'impossible autobiographie de Socrate, "celui qui n'écrivait pas"' [the impossible autobiography of Socrates, of 'the one who did not write'] – the autobiography of one who did not write and himself left no trace of his existence (i.e., Socrates), composed by the one who could not write, especially his thoughts about death, as himself (Plato).[29]

Elaborating on Lacoue-Labarthe's insights, one can undertake to read Blanchot's *L'Entretien infini*, in its both rigorous and conversational tone, as Blanchot's oblique homage to both Plato and Socrates, as his impossible autobiography. *L'Entretien infini* can be read as Blanchot's allo-biography, which records his post-war obsessive immersion in (and dispossession due to) the question of writing, as well as his devotion to the question of the other (*allos*). As the Blanchot of *L'Entretien infini* draws on and addresses, empties out and exhausts the itinerary of writing (its audacious and uneventful life – whose audacity and uneventfulness consist precisely in the fact that it is recounting itself, its lack), he also, by the same token, offers an account of his life – a life not dedicated simply to the question of writing but also to the relentless questioning which the existence of writing poses to one's own existence.

Nevertheless, what is at stake in the above suggestions of requalification, tentative as they are, are not genre specification and classification or genre hybridity. What is at stake is to show how truth and fiction, the real and the unreal (from a Bataillean standpoint), literature and reality, life and work (from a Blanchotian standpoint) are mutually exposed to (and implicated within) one another – in a series of displacements without the possibility of localization, in a series of reduplications which can neither be brought to conclusion within the stable site of writing nor attributed to a life, one's life, as their originating point of reference. The mutual exposure between the 'life' of writing and the 'worldly' life we know points towards their interrelatedness, despite the suspension of the former and dispersal of the latter. The motif of mutual exposure, which is a revolt against the authority of presence and identity of whatever kind, is pursued and intensified in Part II by the confusion between 'what is' and 'what is not' – a confusion which relates to both the literary and the real.

29 Lacoue-Labarthe, 'La Contestation de la mort', p. 60; Lacoue-Labarthe, 'The Contestation of Death', p. 155.

Part II
Confusions

4. The Imaginary: The Real of Literature

> Mais qu'arrive-t-il quand ce qu'on voit, quoique à distance, semble vous toucher par un contact saisissant, quand la manière de voir est une sorte de touche, quand voir est un *contact* à distance?
>
> [But what happens when what you see, although at a distance, seems to touch you with a gripping contact, when the manner of seeing is a kind of touch, when seeing is contact at a distance?][1]

In the famous final line of her essay 'Against Interpretation', published in 1964, Susan Sontag attacks the hermeneutic approach in its constant search for meaning, announcing: 'In place of a hermeneutics, we need an erotics of art'.[2] The essay 'Against Interpretation' alludes to and deplores the transition from an experience of art in which art is considered a ritual and affects one's life, to a theory of art, first posited by Plato, in which art is thought of in terms of mimesis and representation and is installed on a remote pedestal. Sontag examines the persistence of the mimetic theory of art, tracing it not only through the opponents but, most notably, through the defenders of art, who, overemphasizing the content of an artwork (as opposed to its form), assume and argue that a work of art always 'says something' and hence calls for interpretation. Sontag criticizes this modern hegemony of content since in her view it attests to an enduring Platonic dualism, to the extent that apart from, behind, beneath the manifest, the appearance, there lies – hidden – the latent,

---

1 Maurice Blanchot, 'La Solitude essentielle', in Blanchot, *L'Espace littéraire*, pp. 11–32 (p. 28); Maurice Blanchot, 'The Essential Solitude', in Blanchot, *The Space of Literature*, pp. 19–34 (p. 32).

2 Susan Sontag, 'Against Interpretation', in Susan Sontag, *Against Interpretation and Other Essays* (London: Penguin, 2009), pp. 3–14 (p. 14).

i.e., the truth.[3] In her arguing against this Platonic posture she allies herself with Oscar Wilde's praise of appearance, as fashioned in his epigraph which opens the essay: 'The mystery of the world is the visible, not the invisible'.

Sontag goes on to observe that it is literature that has particularly suffered from the overemphasis on the idea of content and gives the example of Kafka, whose puzzling work has been interpreted as all kinds of allegory: social, psychoanalytic and religious. Of course, in her polemic against criticism, or at least its prevailing tendency, Sontag, a critic herself, asserts its exigency. She therefore asks: 'What kind of criticism, of commentary on the arts, is desirable today? […] What would criticism look like that would serve the work of art, not usurp its place?'.[4] Thus she calls for a transparent criticism which would allow us to see 'the thing in itself', 'things being what they are', and which would sharpen our deadened sensory experience, enabling us 'to *see* more, to *hear* more, to *feel* more'.[5] As she declares in a concluding remark: 'The function of criticism should be to show *how it* [the work of art] *is what it is,* even *that it is what it is,* rather than to show *what it means*'.[6]

In *L'Espace littéraire*, his collection of critical essays written in the early 1950s, a decade before Sontag's article, Maurice Blanchot both anticipates and endorses the anti-interpretative stance of literature and art celebrated by Sontag. Blanchot shares Kafka's absolute belonging to literature: 'Je ne suis que littérature et je ne peux ni je veux être rien d'autre' [All I am is literature, and I am not able or willing to be anything else].[7] Ann Smock, in her introduction to the *Space of Literature*, observes that Blanchot is not interested in Kafka's *work*, in the actual *object* produced by the writer, but rather in the torturing *experience* of the young man who seems unable to write.[8] This inability, this impossibility of writing, particularly attracts Blanchot since for him therein lies the 'mystery' of literature. In its

---

3 While Plato himself condemned the mimetic function of art as a degraded copy of a copy and hence rendered art synonymous with untruth.

4 Sontag, 'Against Interpretation', p. 12.

5 Sontag, 'Against Interpretation', p. 14.

6 Sontag, 'Against Interpretation', p. 14.

7 As quoted by Blanchot in Blanchot, 'Kafka et la littérature', p. 20; Blanchot, 'Kafka and Literature', p. 12. The original source is not specified and has not proved possible to trace.

8 Ann Smock, 'Translator's Introduction', in Blanchot, *The Space of Literature*, pp. 1–15 (p. 9).

impossibility the literary work (*œuvre*) is radically different from the work as productive activity and effective action (*travail*); being ineffective, unproductive, the *œuvre* for Blanchot becomes almost synonymous with *désœuvrement*.

Blanchot's marking out of literature as a special realm which revolves around a fundamental tension, as analysed in the previous chapter, is further developed in his major work dedicated to literature, *L'Espace littéraire*. The artwork (and by the same token, fiction, in which speech is the artist's material) rests outside the world, the world of action – and yet this does not, in any way, mean that art exists for art's sake (as a certain tradition of Aestheticism might suggest); moreover, art is anti-mimetic, non-representational – and yet this does not indicate that a literary work exists as an artefact which, representing nothing, presents merely itself, enclosed in a narcissistic self-referentiality (as a tradition of Formalism or Hermeticism might contend). It is precisely this tensional third space, in defiance of the persistently recurring dichotomies, that is designated by Blanchot the constituent space of art and literature.

A spatial account of literature in terms of a third space is already given in 'La Littérature et le droit à la mort', examined in the previous section. As already mentioned, literature's right to death is its absolute freedom, its right to the total negation of reality as realized in and as language; yet literature's right to death is also the poetic attempt to recover, through the materiality of language, the pre-linguistic materiality of things that dies in everyday language. The essay sketches literature as an intermediary space in the sense that it never coincides with either of its two slopes, remaining constantly divided and suspended between them, between negation and what cannot be negated, between revelation and what resists being revealed. The conception of literature as a tensional third space in *L'Espace littéraire* arises though a more insistent and detailed questioning of the origin of the artwork. Problematizing both the dependency of art on the realm of the world as well as the autonomy of art as world-disclosing and self-originating, the Blanchot of *L'Espace littéraire* succeeds in putting forth literature as both anti-realist and anti-foundationalist as well as in reconfiguring, via literature, a new way of relating to the world. Therefore, space (the space of literature), one might argue, is where the question of relationality is radically reconfigured. Space is neither a boundless, all-encompassing entity in its own right nor an a priori that structures and makes possible sensible experience. Literary space is, rather, an opening which occurs due to the process of writing and, more broadly, of composition. Nonetheless, the spatial opening involved here is a venue of discordant and missed encounters rather than a site of inauguration or emergence; and spatiality is rethought in terms of a lived experiential order in which oppositions between distance and proximity, separation and contact, remoteness and immediacy become inoperative.

The following discussion unfolds and critically examines the ways in which Blanchot's idiosyncratic conception of literature does not comply with the prevailing philosophical, aesthetic and literary tradition. First, through an inquiry into the central notion of the *image* and with particular reference to 'Les Deux versions de l'imaginaire' and 'Le Regard d'Orphée' of *L'Espace littéraire*, it examines how the crucial distinction between 'what is' and its representation is called into question. This distinction goes hand-in-hand with the mimetic theory of art which, albeit disguisedly, still persists. Then, with particular reference to the 'Le Chant de Sirènes. La Rencontre de l'imaginaire' of *Le Livre à venir* and an inquiry into the key term of the *event*, the analysis will show how the postulate of presentation and its counterpart in the anti-mimetic theory of art are also challenged. This will reveal how Blanchot's vision of art and literature, while in principle aligning with Sontag's claims, questions and mistrusts her call, which is an ongoing call and demand on art to compel us to 'see more, hear more, feel more'. Despite the presence of sensory elements in Blanchot's key essays (the gaze, the song, the voice), the two main encounters which are staged, that of Orpheus with Eurydice and that of Ulysses with the Sirens, revolve around numbness and stupor rather than the sharpening of the senses, to the degree that the image proves blinding rather than eye-opening and the song requests deafness rather than hearing. To paraphrase Oscar Wilde's maxim slightly, for Blanchot the mystery of the world lies at the turning point where the visible opens up to the invisible.

Emmanuel Levinas, Blanchot's lifelong friend and companion (in Blanchot's words, 'mon plus ancien ami, le seul qui m'autorise d'un tutoiement' [my oldest friend, the only one I address using the familiar form of the second person singular]),[9] alludes to the unparalleled significance of art in Blanchot's thinking:

> Déjà pour Heidegger l'art, au-delà de toute signification esthétique, faisait luire la vérité de l'être, mais il avait cela en commun avec d'autres formes d'existence. Pour Blanchot la vocation de l'art est hors pair. Mais

---

9   This phrase is used by Blanchot in a letter written in 1988 to Salomon Malka, Levinas's friend and disciple. The opening line of the letter is: 'Je crois qu'il est connu tout ce que je dois à Emmanuel Levinas, aujourd'hui mon plus ancien

surtout, écrire ne conduit pas à la 'vérité de l'être' [mais] à l'erreur de l'être – à l'être comme lieu de l'errance, à l'inhabitable.¹⁰

[For Heidegger already, art, understood in a non-aesthetic meaning, made the truth of being shine out, but it had this in common with other forms of existence. For Blanchot the vocation of art is unparalleled. But, above all, writing does not lead to the 'truth of being' [but] to the mistake of being – to being as a place of wandering, to the uninhabitable.]

Levinas clearly shows Blanchot's affinity with and divergence from Heidegger's understanding of art: both thinkers defy the traditional understanding of art as an object to be contemplated from a distance as well as the modern understanding of art as existing for its own sake. For both art is understood beyond any aesthetic meaning, since the artwork's mode of being puts forth and calls for another understanding of 'being'. However, art becomes unequalled for Blanchot, not as a site of disclosure of truth (including literary truth), but rather as a space, a spacing, of errancy ('err' here is meant in its double sense, both as wandering and as going wrong, being incorrect). As literature leads, to borrow Levinas's phrasing, '*à l'être comme lieu de l'errance*' [to being as a place of wandering],¹¹ Blanchot's spatial account of the artwork inverts the logic of manifestation that characterizes the Heideggerian movement of concealment and unconcealment, veiling and unveiling, and puts forth a resistance to visibility. In this sense, art for Blanchot is not inclined towards the pole of revelation and shining (being, truth, presence), as in Heidegger, but rather towards that of concealment and obscurity (disappearing, not being, absence). Nevertheless, as dissimulation adheres to a logic of movement, tension and strife, it does not correspond to – nor does it end up in – a new viewpoint from the other side, as in the Romantic exaltation of the nocturnal, in which the longing for the whole re-enters and the harmonious oneness of day and night is transfigured as 'the other night' (*l'autre nuit*).¹²

---

ami, le seul qui m'autorise d'un tutoiement' [I think it is well known how much I owe to Emmanuel Levinas, today my oldest friend, the only one I address using the familiar form of the second person singular] (Maurice Blanchot, 'Ce qu'il nous a appris' (1988) <http://ghansel.free.fr/blanchot.html> [accessed 22 February 2022]).

10   Levinas, *Sur Maurice Blanchot*, p. 19.

11   Levinas, *Sur Maurice Blanchot*, p. 19 (my emphasis).

12   The Romantic 'other night' is not merely the absence of daylight or the disappearance of things in darkness: it consists precisely in the apparition of the disappearance of things. Blanchot's distancing from the Romantic exaltation

Before paying attention to the resistance to visibility and to the importance of bewilderment rather than transparency, of obscurity rather than lucidity and sharpening, of dissonance and confusion rather than unison and fusion, this analysis will first linger on the questioning of an artwork, not in terms of 'what' but rather in terms of 'how' and 'that' – a displacement which Sontag encourages and which finds a radicalized formulation in *L'Espace littéraire*. In the chapter dedicated to Mallarmé, Blanchot endows art and literature with an ontological force and poses a vital question: 'Qu'arrive-t-il par le fait que nous avons la littérature? Qu'en est-il de l'être si l'on dit que "quelque chose comme les Lettres existe"?' [What is the result of the fact that we have literature? What would be at stake in the fact that 'something like art or literature exists'?].[13] The same question, a question which underlies and, in a way, stimulates the entire Blanchotian *œuvre*, is also found in a note which precedes *L'Entretien infini*, another of his crucial works, and is formulated as follows: 'Qu-est-ce qui est en jeu par ce fait que quelque chose comme l'art ou la littérature existerait?' [What is implied about being if one states that 'something like literature exists'?].[14] The crucial shift from 'what' to 'that', from *what* a being is to the fact *that* it is, has its precedent in Heidegger's famous essay *The Origin of the Work of Art*. In it, to summarize briefly, the artwork is conceptualized and rethought in terms of presentation (rather than representation) as an entity that, by not belonging to the familiar context of everyday objects, shows itself, positing itself (its own truth) and inviting the viewer to look upon it as something 'that is' (*es gibt*). Blanchot's thinking on the matter both builds on and diverges significantly from this Heideggerian

---

of the night occurs in his discussion of *Igitur*, in which he juxtaposes Mallarmé's account of death and suicide in *Igitur* to the Romantic attempt to find in death something more than – and beyond – death. In this regard, he writes: '[D]ans la mort, Novalis, comme la plupart des romantiques allemands, cherche un au-delà de la mort, un plus que la mort, le retour à l'état total transfiguré, comme dans la nuit, non pas la nuit, mais le tout pacifié du jour et de la nuit' [Novalis, like most of the German Romantics, seeks in death a further region beyond death, something more than death, a return to the transfigured whole – in that night, for example, which is not the night but the peaceful oneness of day and night] (Maurice Blanchot, 'L'Expérience d'*Igitur*', in Blanchot, *L'Espace littéraire*, pp. 135–50 (p. 140); Maurice Blanchot, 'The *Igitur* Experience', in Blanchot, *The Space of Literature*, pp. 108–19 (p. 111)).

13 Maurice Blanchot, 'L'Expérience de Mallarmé', in Blanchot, *L'Espace littéraire*, pp. 37–52 (p. 44); Maurice Blanchot, 'Mallarmé's Experience', in Blanchot, *The Space of Literature*, pp. 38–48 (p. 43).

14 Blanchot, 'Note', p. vi; Blanchot, 'Note', p. xi.

tribute to art. Following Heidegger, Blanchot's consideration of the 'that', the fact that art (or literature) is, goes in conjunction with the 'how', the particularity – as Heidegger would put it – 'its manner, its mode, its way of being'. At this point Blanchot distances himself from Heidegger and, echoing Mallarmé, asks 'whether' something like literature exists; and to Heidegger's affirmation that the artwork *is* (rather than is not) Blanchot adds that *it is* and *is not*:

> L'œuvre d'art se réduit à l'être. C'est là sa tâche, être, rendre présent 'ce mot même: *c'est*' … 'tout le mystère est là'. Mais en même temps, on ne peut pas dire que l'*œuvre* appartienne à l'être, qu'elle existe. Au contraire, ce qu'il faut dire c'est qu'elle n'existe jamais à la manière d'une chose ou d'un être en général. Ce qu'il faut dire, en réponse à notre question, c'est que la littérature n'existe pas.[15]
>
> [The work of art reduces itself to being. That is its task: to be, to make present 'those very words: *it is* … There lies all the mystery'. But at the same time it cannot be said that the work belongs to being, that it exists. On the contrary, what must be said is that it never exists in the manner of a thing or a being in general. What must be said, in answer to our question, is that literature does not exist.]

The above passage suggests how Blanchot's questioning about literature converges with, and can be approached through, a thinking about the imaginary, inasmuch as neither *properly* exists and yet both have a haunting presence. Imagination for Blanchot is not what the fantastic is for Todorov: it is not ascribed and confined to a particular genre but is the founding condition, the very essence, the real of literature. Moreover, in order to explore and designate the imaginary as the vital space of literature, a prior investigation into the key notion of the 'image' is required.

One should note that in the Blanchotian lexicon the terms art and literature are often used interchangeably, since for him they both belong to, and are defined as, the realm of images (in opposition to that of concepts or signs); a contention which is, more or less, acceptable regarding art but which seems odd with regard to literature. However, Blanchot insists on equating literature and literary language with the notion and the function of the 'image' and often uses the terms 'fiction', 'image' and 'imagination' (the latter

---

15 Blanchot, 'L'Expérience de Mallarmé', p. 44; Blanchot, 'Mallarmé's Experience', p. 43.

defined as the realm of images) as equivalent. In this respect, in the first section of *L'Espace littéraire* we read:

> [E]st-ce que, dans le poème, dans la littérature, le langage ne serait pas, par rapport au langage courant, ce qu'est l'image par rapport à la chose? [...] [E]st-ce que le langage lui-même ne devient pas, dans la littérature, tout entière image [...] image de langage [...] ou encore langage imaginaire, langage que personne ne parle, c'est à dire qui se parle à partir de sa propre absence, comme l'image apparaît sur l'absence de la chose?
>
> [[D]oesn't the language of the poem, of literature, compare to ordinary language as the image compares to the thing? [...] [I]n literature, doesn't language itself altogether become image? [...] an image of language [...], an imaginary language, one which no one speaks; a language, which issues from its own absence, the way the image emerges upon the absence of the thing?][16]

Then, right away, aware and disquieted that such a statement might be perceived as a conventional belief in art as mimetic, Blanchot adds:

> Ne sommes pas sur une voie où il nous faudrait revenir à des opinions, heureusement délaissées, analogues à celle qui voyait jadis dans l'art une imitation, une copie du réel? [...] D'après l'analyse commune, l'image est après l'objet. [...] Mais peut-être l'analyse commune se trompe-t-elle. Peut-être avant d'aller plus loin, faut-il se demander: mais qu'est-ce qu'est l'image?
>
> [Are we not on a path leading to suppositions happily abandoned, analogous to the one that defined art as imitation, a copy of the real? [...] According to the common analysis, the image comes after the object. [...] But perhaps the common analysis is mistaken. Perhaps before going further one ought to ask: but what is the image?][17]

There are two key points to investigate here, both of which are constructed around the notion of the 'image': the first concerns the alliance between literature and art, inasmuch as it is construed, for Blanchot, from their relation to the image; and the second the widespread belief in a divergence between reality and the image, along with the derivation of the latter from the former, a belief which Blanchot has the urge, albeit reluctantly, to defy. The comparison

---

16 Maurice Blanchot, 'La Solitude essentielle', in Blanchot, *L'Espace littéraire*, pp. 11–32 (pp. 31–32); Blanchot, 'The Essential Solitude', in Blanchot, *The Space of Literature*, pp. 19–34 (p. 34).

17 Blanchot, 'La Solitude essentielle', pp. 31–32; Blanchot, 'The Essential Solitude', p. 34.

between art and literature is, of course, quite ancient and common. Levinas, despite his personal disagreement with such a view, admits that art has always been, and still is, generally considered to be inextricably linked with expression, in the sense that an artist, whether a painter or a musician, tells, even of the ineffable, and that a poem or a painting speaks precisely where common language hesitates or gives up.[18] Against this context, Blanchot's contrivance lies in the fact that, as already mentioned, he frames the complicity between art and literature in their connection, not with expression but with the image. The question which therefore arises, and which this chapter investigates, is what new access is offered to art and literature if we displace our angle of attack from expression (and interpretation) to that of the image.

The Passion of the Image: The Becoming Image of the Thing

In the fragment cited above Blanchot brings to our attention, and seems to call into question, the prevalent philosophical tradition of the distinction between an original (reality) and a copy (the image or imagination), which comes after, in the double sense of being both posterior and inferior. However, even if we track the line of thought which strongly opposes the bad reputation the image has suffered from Plato onwards – be it the Kantian magnifying of imagination, as a synthetic power, presupposed in (and necessary to) experience and understanding, or the Husserlian stance, which appraises imagination as an effective resource for transcendence and hence the critique of the real – we realize that what has never been confronted and challenged is the firm separation between the real (what is) and its image. The following discussion argues that Blanchot's theory of the image (and the imaginary) casts the shadow of a doubt over the certainty of this solid separation of 'what is' over language, of a

---

18   Levinas claims that 'le poème ou le tableau parle' [a poem or a painting speaks] (Emmanuel Levinas, 'La Réalité et son ombre', in Emmanuel Levinas, *Les Imprévus de l'histoire* (Montpellier: Fata Morgana, 1994), pp. 123–48 (p. 123); Emmanuel Levinas, 'Reality and its Shadow', trans. by Alphonso Lingis, in *The Levinas Reader*, ed. by Sean Hand (Oxford: Blackwell, 1989), pp. 129–43 (p. 130)). The paradox of Levinas's essay 'La Réalité et son ombre' lies in the fact that although it contains some of the most astute comments on the ethical underpinnings of the image in its relation to 'being', it was initially written as an unrelenting attack on the visual arts and a privileging of criticism over art.

model over its image; or, to phrase the argument in a Blanchotian way, it will explore what it means 'to live an event as an image'.[19]

Of course, as might already be expected by now, the Blanchotian analysis of the 'image' does not avail itself of the common usage of the term. Inverting the premises, the image is not linked to seeing, sight, visibility and the virility of the gaze, but rather to the sensory, contact, touch and dispossession. In Blanchot's words:

> Mais qu'arrive-t-il quand ce qu'on voit, quoique à distance, semble vous toucher par un contact saisissant, quand la manière de voir est une sorte de touche, quand voir est un *contact* à distance? Quand ce qui est vu s'impose au regard, comme si le regard était saisi, touché, mis en contact avec l'apparence?
>
> [What happens when what you see, although at a distance, seems to touch you with a gripping contact, when the manner of seeing is a kind of touch, when seeing is contact at a distance? What happens when what is seen imposes itself upon the gaze, as if the gaze were seized, put in touch with appearance?][20]

The question is not rhetorical and the answer is provided a few lines further on: 'Ce qui nous est donné par un contact à distance est l'image, et la fascination est la passion de l'image' [What is given us by this contact at a distance is the image, and fascination is passion for the image].[21] The originality of Blanchot's view does not lie in the association of the image with tactility and the affective response on behalf of the viewer, but in its setting up of a double reversal: first, what is seen imposes itself, in an insistent presence, so it is not us who, voluntarily, see an image: it is, rather, the image that, despite us, seizes us. Second, and perhaps more importantly, distance (separation) unexpectedly becomes contact (a relation).

The formulation 'contact at a distance' is repeated twice and is given as the definition of the image. The distinguishing feature of distance here, or, more precisely, of distancing, is that it belongs to the heart of the thing itself. In 'Les Deux versions de l'imaginaire', a text

---

19 The phrasing 'vivre un événement en image' appears twice in the annexe 'Les Deux versions de l'imaginaire', in Blanchot, *L'Espace littéraire*, pp. 341–56 (pp. 352, 353); 'The Two Versions of the Imaginary', in Blanchot, *The Space of Literature*, pp. 254–63 (pp. 261, 262).

20 Blanchot, 'La Solitude essentielle', pp. 28–29; Blanchot, 'The Essential Solitude', p. 32.

21 Blanchot, 'La Solitude essentielle', pp. 28–29; Blanchot, 'The Essential Solitude', p. 32.

annexed to *L'Espace littéraire*, Blanchot describes the scene when we are face-to-face with things themselves, fixing our gaze upon a face (or a corner of the wall), and we let ourselves be taken by what we see, abandoning ourselves to its mercy. In the above scene, when the thing we stare at sinks (disappears) into its image, the following happens, says Blanchot: while the thing is grasped and offered to understanding, in its becoming image it is ungraspable and unreal: 'La chose était là, que nous saisissions dans le mouvement vivant d'une action comprehensive, – et, devenue image, instantanément la voilà devenue l'insaisissable, l'inactuelle, l'impassible' [The thing was there; we grasped it in the vital moment of comprehensive action – and, having become image, instantly it has become that which no one can grasp, the unreal, the impossible].[22]

The Blanchotian conception of the image as the dissolution, that is, the absence, the absenting of the thing, follows the Sartrean reasoning on this matter. In *L'Imaginaire*, Sartre famously gives the example of his friend Pierre, who is currently present in London and therefore, inasmuch as he appears to him as imaged, appears as absent.[23] Moreover, Sartre goes on to declare: 'Cette absence de principe, ce néant essentiel de l'objet imagé suffit à le différencier des objets de la perception' [This fundamental absence, this essential nothingness of the imaged object, suffices to differentiate it from the objects of perception].[24] For both Sartre and Blanchot imagination does not consist in the rearrangement, the reordering in an unused and inventive way, of images already given to perception; imagination rests upon, and is possible through, as Timothy Clark puts it, 'the ability to *detach* reality from itself'.[25] However, the distancing that constitutes the essence of imagination, its power of, in Clark's phrasing, 'sidestepping the world itself', is taken on quite divergently by Sartre and Blanchot.[26] Sartre opts for a phenomenological standpoint and, faithful to his political project, treats the image as the result of an act of consciousness and imagination as engaged in the task of freedom. For him, it is due to our imagination, our ability to detach and negate reality (the world as it is), that we can conceive of, and therefore

---

22 Blanchot, 'Les Deux versions de l'imaginaire', p. 343; Blanchot, 'The Two Versions of the Imaginary', p. 255.
23 Jean-Paul Sartre, *L'Imaginaire* (Paris: Gallimard, 2005 [1940]), p. 346; Jean-Paul Sartre, *The Imaginary* (London and New York: Routledge, 2004), p. 180.
24 Sartre, *L'Imaginaire*, p. 346; Sartre, *The Imaginary*, p. 180.
25 Clark, *Derrida, Heidegger, Blanchot*, p. 77.
26 Clark, *Derrida, Heidegger, Blanchot*, p. 77.

fight for, a world different from the one in which we actually live. As Sartre himself puts it, in terms that resonate with the Hegelian equation of determination with negation: 'Poser une image [...] c'est donc tenir le réel à distance, s'en affranchir, en un mot le nier' [To posit an image [...] is therefore to hold the real at a distance, to be freed from it, in a word, to deny it].[27] According to the Hegelian logic of negation followed by Sartre, something, to be what it is, needs to be determined conceptually, that is, negated and therefore also not be. Blanchot, on the other hand, lingers upon the ontology of the image and considers its inherent distance, its constitutive distancing, as an event with an ontological significance. The mode of being of the image is incompatible with consciousness, since the 'I' is stripped of its power to make sense, as well as with unconsciousness, since the image is nevertheless present and exerts a fascination upon us.

For Blanchot, an object, when it becomes image, turns into a non-object. In his definition, the image is 'cette chose comme éloignement, la présente dans son absence [...], apparaîssant en tant que disparue' [the thing as distance, present in its absence [...], appearing as disappeared].[28] Moreover, the relation between an image and its object is thought of in terms of 'resemblance' and 'doubleness'. At this point Blanchot makes an ontological claim about the image, showing how its existence affects the very being of the object: resemblance, the image, imagining, is possible because beings are bound with a certain non-being. In other words, to borrow Levinas's phrasing for the fundamental duality which constitutes a person or a thing (he also employs the key term *ressemblance*, situating resemblance within being): 'L'être n'est pas seulement lui-même, il s'échappe' [Being is not only itself, it escapes itself].[29] He further asserts: 'L'être est ce qui est [...] et, à la fois, il se ressemble, est sa propre image' [A being is that which is [...] and, at the same time, it resembles itself, is its own image].[30] Similarly, for Levinas reality is not only what is but at the same time *is* its double, its shadow, its image, as the very title of his essay 'La Réalité et son ombre' indicates: 'La réalité ne serait pas seulement ce qu'elle est, ce qu'elle se dévoile dans la verité, mais aussi

---

27   Sartre, *L'Imaginaire*, p. 352; Sartre, *The Imaginary*, p. 183.

28   Blanchot, 'Les Deux versions de l'imaginaire', p. 343; Blanchot, 'The Two Versions of the Imaginary', p. 256.

29   Levinas, 'La Réalité et son ombre', p. 133; Levinas, 'Reality and its Shadow', p. 135.

30   Levinas, 'La Réalité et son ombre', p. 134; Levinas, 'Reality and its Shadow', p. 135.

son double, son ombre, son image' [Reality would not be only what it is, what it is disclosed to be in truth, but would also be its double, its shadow, its image].³¹ To relate the (un)workings of the image to our discussion of the *il y a* in Chapter 2, through the image, reality (the things and the world, appearance and manifestation) begins to disintegrate and fade away, whereas the *il y a* indicates the reality of unreality. Furthermore, the *il y a* makes inoperative mainly the distinction between presence and absence, whereas the image – in Blanchot's rethinking of it – makes inoperative the distinctions of the sensible and the intelligible, the visible and the invisible as much as that of presence and absence.

The image, therefore, in its ontological dimension as put forth by Blanchot, offers a dis-incarnation of reality inasmuch as it alludes to the fact that something is and at the same time is not. This is why from a Blanchotian point of view the image is not bound up with freedom, as it is for Sartre, but is rather linked with the cadaver's strangeness, which occupies a fragile and indeterminate place, both here and behind, and whose unfamiliar presence fluctuates between being and not being. Additionally, the understanding of the Blanchotian image in terms of the cadaver's strangeness emerges not only as a re-inscription of resemblance against originality and authenticity but also as a radical critique of resemblance, to the extent that it consists of a resemblance which resembles nothing. The cadaver's presence radicalizes the logic of resemblance since it brings forth an excess of similarity: nothing but similarity and similarity to nothing (as the initial to which it resembles and directs is reduced to nothing).

The Passion of Writing: The Becoming Image of Language

If Blanchot's conception of the becoming image of the thing destabilizes the philosophical-metaphysical tradition (the privileging of 'the world' against its image), his definition of literature as the becoming image of language shakes the premises of aesthetics (the privileging of art and beauty) – be it the Kantian turn to the notion of beauty in his third *Critique*, the *Critique of Judgement* (in which Kant sets up the essential distinction between representation, in which 'what is' is reduced to an 'object' by and for the subject, and presentation, in which, crucially and conversely, the schematizing

---

31 Levinas, 'La Réalité et son ombre', p. 133; Levinas, 'Reality and its Shadow', p. 135.

powers of the subject are suspended);[32] or the Romantic postulate which posits imagination, in contrast to reason, as the supreme faculty of the mind (since it bestows upon human beings a creativity comparable to that of nature and God); or even the Heideggerian anti-aesthetic stance in its exaltation of art as a crucial site for the disclosure of truth (which moves away from the usual understanding of art in terms of representation – as a relation of equivalence and equation – towards a renewed understanding of it in terms of presentation – as an unveiling, a self-founding moment). Against this context, Blanchot sets up a heretical literary paradigm whose deviance is due to the notion and function of the image.

The Romantic tradition, in the aftermath of the Kantian crisis of presentation, praises the auto-sufficiency of the artwork as a unity complete in itself (inasmuch as it signifies nothing by itself), 'an expression for the sake of expression', as Novalis pronounces in his defence of literature as non-instrumental language.[33] In contrast to the inability of thought to become transparent and self-reflexive (the 'I think' brings about and comes with all my representations but it cannot re-present itself), art aspires to restore the unison between the subject of representation and the represented object. Andrew Bowie, in his account of the stakes of Romanticism, gives as an example of a self-reflexive painting *Las Meninas*, which unravels and, in an anticipatory way, resolves the subsequent Kantian, and post-Kantian, puzzle as crystallized in the formulation by Novalis: 'Can I look for a schema for myself, if I am that which schematizes?'.[34] As Bowie reminds us, Velásquez's *Las Meninas* both attests to the importance of the painter, without whom there would be no painting at all, and at the same time, by including him within the painting, inverts the state of affairs and renders him a result of reflection, an object as well, rather than merely the creating subject. In this sense, Bowie

---

32 Immanuel Kant, *Critique of Judgement*, intro and trans. by Werner S. Pluhar (Indianapolis, IN: Hackett, 1987). The *Kritik der Urteilskraft* was originally published in 1790: Immanuel Kant, *Kritik der Urteilskraft* (Berlin und Libau: Lagarde und Friedrich, 1790).

33 Novalis, *Logological Fragments II*, in Novalis, *Philosophical Writings*, ed. and trans. by Margaret Mahony Stoljar (Albany, NY: State University of New York Press, 1997), pp. 67–82 (p. 78).

34 Novalis, *Werke, Tagebücher und Briefe Friedrich von Hardenbergs*, 3 vols, II: *Das philosophisch-theoretische Werk*, ed. by Hans-Joachim Mähl (Munich; Vienna: Hanser, 1978), p. 162; Andrew Bowie, *Aesthetics and Subjectivity: From Kant to Nietzsche* (Manchester and New York: Manchester University Press, 1990, 2003), p. 90.

underlines, our direct access to (and the self-representation of) what generates the painting (Velásquez) is undermined, since the creator, as we see him painted, actually depends for his own depiction upon his reflection in a non-existent mirror. Indeed, as the viewer realizes, what the painter is looking at outside the painting is not himself in a mirror (in order to paint himself) but, as the mirror on the farthest wall of the painting indicates, he is looking at the supposedly empirical object he is painting, that is, the King and Queen of Spain. *Las Meninas* therefore stages an intricate interplay, interdependence and coexistence between its inner and outer space, presence and absence, the subject and the assumed object of the painting (Velásquez) and the King and Queen of Spain) and their respective reflections (in the painting itself and in the painted mirror). Nevertheless, in his analysis of *Las Meninas* in terms of a self-reflexive painting which chooses as its theme the undoing of the subject's self-representation, Bowie attests to the significance of the painter 'not least as the ironic creator of a baffling aesthetic object'.[35]

Against this context, which depends on and solidifies the notion and the endurance of the 'creator' and 'the aesthetic object', establishing between them – and an assumed 'reality' – a restless interdependence, as each term points constantly to another, in Blanchot's *L'Espace littéraire* the centre of attention is displaced around a triple dispersal. In this respect 'Le regard d'Orphée', which is portrayed as the hidden and attracting centre of the book, revolves around the dispersal of the subject (the writer, Orpheus), of the object (his artwork) and of the work's source (Eurydice). In the opening sentence of the section, we read: 'Quand Orphée descend vers Eurydice, l'art est la puissance par laquelle s'ouvre la nuit' [When Orpheus descends towards Eurydice, art is the power by which night opens].[36] Then, carried away by their encounter and oblivious to his task, namely to bring Eurydice back to the daylight, Orpheus looks at her, in her nocturnal darkness, while this look was forbidden. Therefore, writes Blanchot, 'trahit-il l'œuvre et Eurydice et la nuit' [he betrays the work and Eurydice and the night].[37] However, adds Blanchot in support of Orpheus: 'Si le monde juge Orphée, l'œuvre ne le juge pas. [...] Regarder Eurydice, sans souci du chant, dans l'impatience et l'imprudence du désir

---

35 Andrew Bowie, *Aesthetics and Subjectivity*, p. 91.

36 Maurice Blanchot, 'Le Regard d'Orphée', in Blanchot, *L'Espace littéraire*, pp. 225–32 (p. 225); Maurice Blanchot, 'Orpheus's Gaze', in Blanchot, *The Space of Literature*, pp. 171–76 (p. 171).

37 Blanchot, 'Le Regard d'Orphée', p. 226; Blanchot, 'Orpheus's Gaze', p. 172.

qui oublie la loi, c'est cela même, *l'inspiration'* [If the world judges Orpheus, the work does not. [...] To look at Eurydice, without regard for the song, in the impatience and imprudence of desire which forgets the law: *that is inspiration*].³⁸ In rendering inspiration the focal point and mythical Orpheus as the emblematic figure of the writer, Blanchot brings forth a literary paradigm in which writing tends not towards its end, towards its completion, towards the work as its result but, in an inverse movement, towards its starting point, its genesis, its source, its enabling (or rather disabling) condition. In Simon Critchley's astute remark, for Blanchot 'the goal of writing is not the work, the production of meaning and beauty. Writing is not the desire for the beautiful artwork; rather the writer writes out of a desire for the origin of the artwork'.³⁹

However, what is worth noting in Blanchot's account of the genesis of the artwork (and in its association with the fate of Orpheus) is that inspiration rather than an exaltation of creativity becomes that which ruins the work: the work consists of and emerges as the turning away and the silencing (rather than the expression) of inspiration and, conversely, inspiration is bound with worklessness (rather than with the work). In more explicit terms, the Blanchotian *quest* for the origin is a Levinasian-inspired attempt to break with ontology and thereby a *questioning* of the origin – a recasting of Heideggerian ontology in its aspiration for an original relation to Being, partly indebted to and echoing the relation between existence and existents as formulated by Levinas in *De l'existence à l'existant* (published in 1947). Leslie Hill has underlined how Blanchot's version of the genesis of the artwork parallels the Levinasian analysis of the emergence of the existent (the possibility of being in the world) from the impersonal anonymity of existence (the *il y a*).⁴⁰ The importance of conceiving the emergence of the artwork in such terms, that is, as the silencing and the intermittence of the work's source, lies in that emergence being recast as a suspension and origin recast as an interruption (and, therefore, not a beginning, a starting point, even less a ground or a foundation). The artwork, rather than constitutive, gifted with the power to establish or enact, is turned into an interruption and what proves primary (namely, the source of the artwork) is worklessness,

---

38   Blanchot, 'Le Regard d'Orphée', p. 228; Blanchot, 'Orpheus's Gaze', p. 173.
39   Critchley, *Very Little ... Almost Nothing*, p. 44.
40   Hill, *Blanchot: Extreme Contemporary*, pp. 115–16. Hill puts forward a reading of *L'Espace littéraire* as a recasting, via Levinas, of Heideggerian ontological difference.

darkness and anonymity, which both bring about the emergence of the work in the first place and, in their turn, suspend it. Therefore, Blanchot's recourse to the myth of Orpheus and his re-reading of it as the artwork's longing for its source do not simply expel origin to the realm of myth (thereby simply re-inscribing origin as mythic), nor are they an attempt to rewrite and create the myth of literature (making use of and speculating on the gaps of myths). On the contrary, designating the origin of the artwork as diffused and dispersed, Blanchot puts forth literature as that which dismantles the very logic of origin.

Pronouncing Orpheus's gaze at what resists being looked at as the very experience and fate of literature, Blachot deciphers Eurydice's instant disappearance as what can neither be grasped nor renounced in the attempt at poetic retrieval. Therefore, the poem and, more broadly, the artwork depend for their existence on something irretrievably lost which can neither be incorporated nor disclosed, but which lies within them as a ghostly presence, both doubling and separating them from themselves. In this respect, despite Blanchot's complicity with Levinas what Orpheus encounters in his descent is not, as Levinas would put it, the *visage* of Eurydice in its radical alterity, in its irreducible otherness; all that he bears witness to is her becoming image. The realm of literature, as the realm of the imaginary, is an exposure to the invisibility within the visible rather than the sheer transcendence of otherness, as in Levinasian ethics (or, to put it another way, the rethinking of the other in terms of ethical transcendence).

In order to elaborate on and illuminate the Blanchotian literary paradigm in its centrifugal search for the origin, it is necessary to cite Georges Didi-Hubermann and his laudatory reading of the film *Le Fils de Saoul* with the telling title *Sortir du noir*. Didi-Hubermann establishes a link between Saoul's desperate attempt in the Birkenau camp to salvage the body of a boy and Orpheus's descent towards Eurydice in Hades, the mythical space of death, as depicted by Blanchot. More precisely, Didi-Hubermann attributes to the maddening undertaking of Saul a literary structure:

> [C]ette folie avait une structure de conte: une structure d'objet mystérieux et, au fond, très littéraire. [...] Comme Orphée, Saul se confronte à l'espace de la mort. Comme Orphée, il fait s'ouvrir la nuit, en vouant toute sa vie à sortir du noir un seul être aimé. Comme Orphée, il échouera dans son geste pourtant miraculeux.[41]

---

41 Georges Didi-Hubermann, *Sortir du noir* (Paris: Minuit, 2015), pp. 40, 41.

> [[T]his madness had the structure of a tale: the structure of a mysterious object and a very literary one, in the end. [...] Like Orpheus, Saul confronts the space of death. Like Orpheus, he makes the night open up, devoting his whole life to bringing a loved one out of darkness. Like Orpheus, he will fail in his miraculous gesture.]

In the final lines of the text we read: 'Toute l'autorité de Saoul – et, partant, de cette histoire, de ce film – tient à ce qu'il crée de toutes pièces, à contre-courant du monde et de sa cruauté, une situation dans laquelle *un enfant existe*, fût-il déjà mort' [The whole authority of Saoul – and hence of this story, of this film – lies in that it creates from nothing, against the tide of the world and its cruelty, a situation in which *a child exists*, though already dead].[42] The authority of literature, the paradigm of literature, as espoused by Georges Didi-Hubermann and as put forth by Blanchot, lies in the fact that it occupies a tensional third space, lingering between being and not being, presence and absence, existence and non-existence. The Blanchotian experience of literature is close to the Derridean experience of the trace, which, against the authority of presence and the present (that is, against philosophy's preoccupation with the question of being – and the presupposition of presence and present that is bound with it), calls for a relation to something other than being, recasting the other as precisely what does not appear in terms of full presence.

This conception of the artwork in terms of an abiding duplicity is brought into even sharper focus in Blanchot's essay 'Le Chant des Sirènes. La rencontre de l'imaginaire'. This essay reverses the long-standing philosophical and aesthetic tradition according to which music is considered as accomplishing precisely what words always fail to realize: the absolute concordance between form and content, means and meaning. In the opening line of his essay Blanchot attempts to rethink and revitalize the relationship of music and language, as – in his retelling of the encounter between Ulysses and the Sirens – he notes that the Sirens derive their power of seduction from singing, not in a splendid but in a rather unsatisfactory way: 'Les Sirènes: il semble bien qu'elles chantaient, mais d'une manière qui ne satisfaisait pas, qui laissait seulement entendre dans quelle direction s'ouvraient les vraies sources et le vrai bonheur du chant' [The Sirens: it seems they did indeed sing, but in an unfulfilling way, that only gave a sign of where the real sources and the real happiness of the song

---

42   Didi-Hubermann, *Sortir du noir*, pp. 54–55.

opened].⁴³ In Blanchot's view Ulysses' encounter with the Sirens is what makes him become Homer and recount his tale about this extraordinary event. For Blanchot, it is the tale which is endowed with a world-disclosing power, as he puts it:

> Le récit n'est pas la relation de l'événement mais cet événement même, l'approche de cet événement, le lieu où celui-ci est appelé à se produire, événement encore à venir et par la puissance attirante duquel le récit peut espérer, lui aussi, se réaliser.
>
> [Narrative is not the relating of an event but this event itself, the approach to this event, the place where it is called on to unfold, an event still to come, by the magnetic power of which the narrative itself can hope to come true.]⁴⁴

In this way the Blanchotian notion of the *récit* appears as self-reflexive: it narrates itself and thereby brings into being both itself and that which it narrates (the event). The narration comes into being and, in so doing, it creates the event it narrates. Moreover, as the narration *is* (itself) the event, the event is yet to come and, as it comes, it brings narration into being. Nonetheless, in this depiction of narration, not as an account of the event distinct from it but as bound to the event, unlike contemporary theories of performance and enactment, the event and (its) narration never fully merge but elicit an asymptotic, an asymmetrical relationship. To put it another way, the fact that the narrated event is disentangled from the logic of representation does not amount to considering the narrative (in its capacity *as* an event, the event) in terms of enactment.

One cannot help but notice here that the narrated event, in Blanchot's analysis of the *récit*, is an encounter (first that of Ulysses with the Sirens and then that of Ahab with Moby Dick). Therefore, the encounter is both the theme of the *récit*, as the *récit* narrates an encounter, and the mode of being of the *récit*, as the *récit is* the encounter between itself and what it narrates. However, while the narrated encounter brings into being the *récit* and the encounter comes into being through its narration, these two encounters miss each other rather than coincide; rather than concurrent (existing in the same place at the same time) they are incompatible and discordant.

---

43 Maurice Blanchot, 'Le Chant des Sirènes. La Rencontre de l'imaginaire', in Blanchot, *Le Livre à venir*, pp. 9–18 (p. 9); Maurice Blanchot, 'The Song of the Sirens: Encountering the Imaginary', in Blanchot, *The Book to Come*, pp. 3–10 (p. 3).
44 Blanchot, 'Le Chant des Sirènes', p. 14; Blanchot, 'The Song of the Sirens', p. 6.

As Blanchot writes with regard to the unrealistic encounter of Ahab with Moby Dick in Melville's eponymous novel:

> Il est bien vrai que c'est seulement dans le livre de Melville qu'Ahab rencontre Moby Dick; il est bien vrai toutefois que cette rencontre permet seule à Melville d'écrire le livre, rencontre si imposante, si démesurante et si particulière qu'elle [...] paraît avoir lieu bien avant que le livre ne commence.
>
> [It is indeed true that it is only in Melville's book that Ahab encounters Moby Dick; but it is also true that this encounter alone allows Melville to write the book, such an overwhelming, immoderate, and unique encounter, that it [...] seems to take place well before the book begins.][45]

The *récit* is different to itself, inasmuch as the reality described by it and the reality of the *récit* itself (its reality as *récit*) never fully coincide. In other words, the entwinement of the event – which is here an encounter, the encounter of Ahab and Moby Dick – and the narration attests to a double origin: the encounter originates the narration (brings it into being) as much as the narration originates the encounter (makes it happen).[46]

In this sense, the mode of being of the *récit* (of literature), resembling itself but not fully identical to itself, is synonymous with the mode of being of beings, as sketched above. If, for reasons of methodological clarity, this chapter begins with 'being' (as not being, as double) to end up with literature (in its duplicity), for Blanchot it is through the latter that we are exposed to the former; in other words, it is the experience of literature which exposes us to the abiding duplicity of being. The theme of duplicity is explored in more detail in Part III, where the discussion focuses on doubling and masking. For now, it should be underlined that being, in its duplicity and doubleness as brought forth by the image, is equivocal, non-self-identical and thereby dispersed and dis-originated with regard to its unity or any possibility of totality. Thus, literature and art, defined as the realm

---

45   Blanchot, 'Le Chant des Sirènes', p. 15; Blanchot, 'The Song of the Sirens', pp. 7–8.

46   For Todorov the fantastic revolves around a hesitation regarding the *nature* of an uncanny event which is subsequently resolved as the event is acknowledged as reality or as imaginary (imaginary meaning here illusory), as it is decided whether the event 'is' or 'is not'. By contrast, the Blanchotian paradigm of inspiration focuses on the *origination* of the event, lingers over the undecidability of its origin and finally renders this undecidability unresolved, designating it precisely the space of literature.

of images, partake of an ontological density to the extent that they themselves are precisely an image without an original. In the work of art the so-called 'represented' object is always absent and the material elements which make the artwork – whether the strokes of the brush in a painting or the words in a novel – neither re-present nor disclose what they depict, but rather present it, pointing precisely towards its absence.

Drawing on Maurice Blanchot's key notions of the image, imagination, the event, the outside and distance, our discussion reconsiders – amongst other things – the definition of literature as a temporal art (which narrates events, contemplates time and memory) and, subsequently, its opposition to spatial arts such as painting and sculpture. Moreover, this analysis emphasizes the idea that literature's account of space (the space of literature) destabilizes the recurring dichotomies of here and nowhere, inside and outside, intimacy and distance, the visible and the invisible, what is and what is not, the real and the imaginary. In *L'Espace littéraire* Blanchot alludes to Rodin's *Balzac*, an artwork which exemplifies the alliance of literature – personified in the figure of Balzac – and art – condensed in Rodin's sculpture. As Blanchot writes, the *Balzac* cannot be gazed upon, in contrast to *The Kiss*, which allows itself to be gazed at: 'Le *Baiser* de Rodin se laisse regarder et même se plaît à l'être, le *Balzac* est sans regard, chose fermée et dormante, absorbée en elle-même jusqu'à disparaître' [The *Kiss* by Rodin lets itself be gazed at and even enjoys being thus regarded, but the *Balzac* goes without a look, it is a closed and sleeping thing, absorbed in itself to the point of disappearing].[47] Blanchot's tribute to art, via Rodin's tribute to literature, epitomizes what art and literature attain and offer us, what art and literature *are* for creators and writers, viewers and readers: presences not withheld but given in their withdrawal.

The space of literature – literature as space, the slot for which literature strives – can be resumed in terms of a change in focus, as a movement from 'what is' towards 'what is *not*' and thereby as a reconfiguration of existence in terms of invisibility and obscurity. The significance of *L'Espace littéraire* lies precisely, one can argue, in dissociating existence from presence and visibility and in considering spacing – making space for (the obscure and the invisible) – synonymous with the gesture – and the ethics – of writing. In *L'Espace*

---

47   Maurice Blanchot, 'Lire', in Blanchot, *L'Espace littéraire*, pp. 251–62 (p. 253); Maurice Blanchot, 'Reading', in Blanchot, *The Space of Literature*, pp. 191–97 (p. 192).

littéraire literature is designated a third space: neither that of death, as in Hegelian dialectics, nor that of eternal life, since Eurydice is not retrieved from the Underworld but is lost twice. Additionally, literature recasts the key measure of space, namely distance, since distance – and more particularly that of reality and the image – is no longer conceived in terms of *from/between* but in terms of *within*. In what follows, another reconfiguration of existence and another approach to the ethical will be examined, consisting in the dissociation of existence from teleology. In this respect, our spatial analysis of the Blanchotian image as the absenting of presence will be complemented by a temporal analysis of the Bataillean instant as the absenting of the present. To do so, we now turn to Bataille's *La Littérature et le mal*, in which time (rather than space) is the central preoccupation; here, 'what is' becomes disconnected from 'what it is *for*' and existence is reconfigured as gratuitous. In the disentanglement of the present from the hegemony of the future, existence (be it human or that of literature) comes forward freed from justification and redemption, yet bound to itself and to irredeemable loss.

5. The Instant: The Ethics of Literature

> Je dirais volontiers que ce dont je suis le plus fier, c'est d'avoir brouillé les cartes … c'est-à-dire d'avoir associé la façon de rire la plus turbulente et la plus choquante, la plus scandaleuse, avec l'esprit religieux le plus profond.[1]
>
> [I would happily state that what I am most proud of is that I have shuffled the cards … that is to say, that I have brought the most turbulent and shocking, the most scandalous laughter alongside the most profound religious spirit.]

In *Giving an Account of Oneself* Judith Butler argues that the inability of the subject to give a coherent and complete account of herself does not preclude ethical responsibility. As she puts it: 'Perhaps most importantly, we must recognise that ethics requires us to risk ourselves precisely at moments of unknowingness, […] when our willingness to become undone in relation to others constitutes our chance of becoming human'.[2] Pleading for the necessity of dispossession, the need to undress and undo the self-sufficient 'I', she goes on:

> To be undone by another is a primary necessity, an anguish, to be sure, but also a chance – to be addressed, claimed, bound to what is not me, but also to be moved, to be prompted to act, to address myself elsewhere, and so to vacate the self-sufficient 'I' as a kind of possession.[3]

---

1 'Georges Bataille' (Interview with Madeleine Chapsal, 10 February 1961), in Madeleine Chapsal, *Les Ecrivains en personne* (Paris: Julliard, 1973), pp. 21–33 (p. 29). The interview was previously published in Madeleine Chapsal, *Quinze écrivains. Entretiens* (Paris: Julliard, 1963), pp. 11–22.

2 Judith Butler, *Giving an Account of Oneself* (New York: Fordham University Press, 2005), p. 136.

3 Butler, *Giving an Account of Oneself*, p. 136.

Butler concludes by emphatically reasserting that a postulation of a divided, ungrounded and incoherent subject, of what she repeatedly calls 'an opaque subject', can serve and support a theory of ethics and responsibility: 'If we speak and try to give an account from this place, we will not be irresponsible, or, if we are, we will be forgiven'.[4]

Confronting the problem of (self-)identity, Butler's study rethinks the self as always already implicated with and interrupted by something outside itself, be it – from a Levinasian standpoint – the exorbitant call made by the Other, or – from a Foucauldian standpoint – our embeddedness within prior social structures. Similarly, giving an account of oneself, as her title promises, implicates and exposes the scene of address: the account necessitates and implies a structure of relationality, another to whom I give the account of myself. For Butler, it is due to its fundamental, essential, constitutive relationality that the self, rather than transparent, is opaque. Therefore, determined to work out a theory of ethics that is rooted in the reality of human existence, Butler unfolds her thesis as follows:

> [I]f it is precisely by virtue of its relations to others that it is opaque to itself, and if those relations to others are precisely the venue for its ethical responsibility, then it may well follow that it is precisely by virtue of the subject's opacity to itself that it sustains some of its most important ethical bonds.[5]

Butler's undertaking to recast the ethical subject resonates with the ethical experience as framed by Levinas. Simon Critchley observes that the Levinasian contribution to, and disruption of, ethics and, more precisely, Kantian ethics lie in the fact that the ethical is no longer linked to the autonomy of the subject: on the contrary, the ethical consists, precisely, of calling the subject's autonomy into question: 'The ethical subject in Levinas is constituted though a relation, an act of approval to the demand of the good to which it is fundamentally inadequate'.[6] For Levinas it is the radical alterity of the demand or, to use his terms, the face of the other which engenders the split within the self and gives rise to the subject as split. However, for Levinas, or rather in Critchley's reading of Levinas,

---

4 Butler, *Giving an Account of Oneself*, p. 136.

5 Judith Butler, 'Giving an Account of Oneself', *Diacritics*, 31:4 (2001), 22–40 (p. 22).

6 Simon Critchley, 'Demanding Approval: On the Ethics of Alain Badiou', *Radical Philosophy*, 100 (2000) <https://www.radicalphilosophy.com/article/demanding-approval> [accessed 14 April 2022].

there is a disposition towards alterity located, always already, at the heart of the self which enables its relation to the other as other. There is something at the heart of the subject which constitutes it but which remains opaque to the subject. Reading Levinas against Levinas or, rather, reversing the order preferred by Levinas and by Butler, Critchley posits the split subject (the otherness within) as the precondition for an ethical relation to the other and thereby ties ethics to a theory of the subject.

At the core of both Butler's and Critchley's thinking is the Levinasian critique of the Hegelian notion of a master subject. In *Subjects of Desire* Butler calls into question the totalizing and teleological aspects of Hegel's philosophy or, more precisely, of a certain reception of it. Following Kojève's reading, and thereby shifting her emphasis from ending, totality and conceptual domination towards break, interruption and loss, she aims to show how the Hegelian vision can be 'less totalizing than presumed' and the subject of mastery less whole and self-same than foreseen.[7] Similarly, and more emphatically, in *Le Temps et l'autre* Levinas stages a progressive journey in direct contrast to that of Hegelian phenomenology.[8] The Levinasian diagram of existence advances not towards totality and complete comprehension but towards alterity and the wholly other, rendering the subject's encounter with the irreducible mystery and otherness of the other person its culminating moment. As Richard Cohen remarks in his introduction, comparing and contrasting Levinas to Hegel: '[T]he end in Levinas is neither an end, a finality, nor a truth, a comprehension. Levinas' thought ends with what has no end: alterity, the infinite, the wholly other'.[9] Additionally, as Cohen demonstrates, it is not just the endings of Hegel and Levinas that are different, but also their yearnings: while Hegelian phenomenology is driven by a desire for the total truth, Levinasian phenomenology 'is driven by a desire for an exteriority which remains irreducible exterior'.[10]

Echoing the Levinasian craving for exteriority, Georges Bataille announces in *Sur Nietzsche*: 'Les êtres, les hommes, ne peuvent "communiquer" – *vivre* – que hors d'eux-mêmes' [Individuals or

---

7   Butler, *Subjects of Desire*, p. xx.
8   Emmanuel Levinas, *Le Temps et l'autre* (Montpellier: Fata Morgana, 1979).
9   Richard Cohen, 'Introduction', in Emmanuel Levinas, *Time and the Other*, trans. by Richard A. Cohen (Pittsburgh, PA: Duquesne University Press, 1987), pp. 1–27 (p. 2).
10 Cohen, 'Introduction', p. 2.

humans, can only 'communicate' – live – outside of themselves].[11] Bataille has thoroughly and persistently moulded the subject in terms of excess, in terms of an 'existential exaggeration', to use the words of Critchley. Bataille privileges moments of unknowingness, moments of 'anguish' and 'risk', when the 'self-sufficient I' is 'undone', to repeat the terminology of Judith Butler, since in precisely these moments the subject is given the chance to encounter itself. These links and comparisons do not aspire to suggest that Bataille can be considered a thinker concerned with ethical responsibility in the way that Levinas or Butler are. Besides, the (non-)relation to others is not a central concern in Bataille's thought and on many occasions he puts forward irresponsibility and carelessness over responsibility and care. Nevertheless, drawing on both Butler's and Critchley's remarks that a theory of ethics is interrelated with a theory of the subject, and on Critchley's view of the opaque, split subject as the precondition of the subject's capacity ethically to relate to the other, it is possible to make the minimum claim that Bataille's thought is relevant to ethics to the extent that it persistently unveils the subject as exposed to something other, outside itself, and that it takes good and evil as its theme(s).

La Littérature et le mal (published in 1957) is Bataille's collection of essays devoted to literature; as the title of the book testifies, it directly addresses the question of evil. Drawing on a series of writers in the modern literary tradition, Bataille demonstrates how evil becomes a privileged trope for ethical renewal against the rigidity of modern life.[12] Following – and at the same time going against – the literary tradition of Modernity, Bataille renders evil synonymous with an intense experience, something which is generally lacking in a world guided by the values of progress and rationality. However, unlike the Modernist tradition evil for Bataille does not confer or add another significance to life; it consists precisely of voiding, releasing and unbinding life from significance. As Critchley notes, Modernity is post-religious but not post-metaphysical, since it still fosters values, certainties and beliefs, what Nietzsche denominates and denunciates as 'the big words' (reason, equality, freedom, happiness, love)[13]

---

11 Georges Bataille, *Sur Nietzsche*, in *Œuvres complètes*, vi: *La Somme athéologique. Tome II* (1973), pp. 11–205 (p. 48); Georges Bataille, *On Nietzsche*, trans. by Bruce Boone, intro. by Sylvère Lotringer (New York: Paragon House, 2008), p. 25.

12 Damian Cattani has convincingly demonstrated the complex relationship between Modernity, evil and ethics in 'Modernity, Evil and Ethics: A Sartrean and Bataillean Reading of Baudelaire's "Le Jeu"', *Dix-Neuf*, 16 (2012), 260–70.

13 Critchley, *Very Little … Almost Nothing*, p. 11.

or what T. S. Eliot considers a *via negativa* towards the prospect of salvation. Commenting on Baudelaire's fascination with damnation, T. S. Eliot observes: '[D]amnation itself is an immediate form of salvation – of salvation from the ennui of modern life'.[14] Allying himself with Nietzsche, Bataille recasts evil as merely a moment of living which comes about due to the sheer abruptness of life. In this respect, Bataillean evil bears the resonance of and corresponds to the Nietzschean eternal return, namely 'existence as it is, without meaning or aim, yet recurring inevitably without any finale of nothingness'.[15] Nietzsche's understanding of being as becoming and of reality as a continual flow, as well as his corresponding recasting of temporality in terms of flux, fluctuation and tension rather than succession, inform and anticipate the Bataillean inversion of teleological thinking.

In *La Littérature et le mal* the Bataillean contrivance of evil addresses the Nietzschean challenge to reconfigure and endure 'existence as it is', that is, as inevitably recurring. By means of the trope of 'evil', the *telos* (the futurism and aim) of human existence is challenged and knocked down. Surya sketches the Bataillean reordering of morals as follows: '[L]e mal appartient au sommet, le bien au déclin' [[E]vil belongs to the summit, and good to the decline].[16] More importantly, in this new topography, where good and evil change places, good becomes evil and evil becomes good; or rather, to borrow the phrasing of Mikkel Borch-Jacobsen, evil becomes 'sovereignly good, because good for nothing'.[17] The moral of the summit, the hyper-moral, is designated by Bataille 'sovereign' inasmuch as it is 'not subjected, subordinated, subjugated to anything'.[18] In this respect, as Borch-Jacobsen observes, Bataille radicalizes Nietzschean superiority, height and nobility since he equates them with the filthiest baseness. Bataillean sovereignty is 'existence for itself', 'valid in itself', serving no purpose, nothing.[19]

Simon Critchley, criticizing the moral claims of liberal democracies as deficient to the extent that they are 'externally compulsory but not

---

14 T. S. Eliot, '*from* Baudelaire (1930)', in T. S. Eliot, *Selected Prose of T. S. Eliot*, ed. and intro. by Frank Kermode (New York: Harvest, 1975), pp. 231–37 (p. 236).

15 Friedrich Nietzsche, *The Will to Power*, ed. by Walter Kaufmann, trans. by Walter Kaufmann and R. J. Hollingdale (New York: Random House, 1967), p. 35.

16 Surya, *Georges Bataille*, p. 491; Surya, *Georges Bataille: An Intellectual Biography*, p. 425.

17 Borch-Jacobsen, 'The Laughter of Being', p. 153.

18 Borch-Jacobsen, 'The Laughter of Being', p. 153.

19 Borch-Jacobsen, 'The Laughter of Being', p. 153.

internally compelling', recalls Yeats's line in his poem 'The Second Coming', written in the aftermath of the First World War: 'The best lack all conviction, while the worst | Are full of passionate intensity'.[20] While for Critchley and his politics of resistance the aim is to fill the best with passionate intensity, according to Bataille's tragic outlook passionate intensity is recast as the best. In other words, Bataille's rearrangement of morality consists in a temporal rearrangement: it is the priority of the present over the future, the privileging of the intensity of the present over future planning, duration and survival. For Bataille, evil consists of the existential priority of the present, that is, the focalization of existence on itself and its refusal to be subordinated to a *telos*, a future goal, a principle. Again, the Nietzschean resonances of the Bataillean endeavour are sensed: breaking with the philosophical tradition from Plato to Kant and its quest for truth, Nietzsche's major concern is life and all that is life-enhancing. Additionally, breaking with the Aristotelian tradition of *eudaimonia* (and its recuperation by Bentham's utilitarianism), Nietzsche calls us to live not happy but tragic lives. Nonetheless, Bataille's insistence on evil differs from Nietzsche's sceptical attack on the concept and his advocacy to move *beyond* judgements of good and evil. Bataille asserts the necessity of evil for the same reasons as Nietzsche advocates its dismissal: while for the latter the concept of evil is life-denying, an invention of the powerless and weak due to their *ressentiment* towards the creative and vital forces of life, for the former evil is valued as an essential condition of life, precisely because it corresponds to the irreducible, sovereign part of ourselves that challenges the law of reason. As Bataille notes, '[L]e Mal [...] est aussi [...] d'une manière ambiguë, un fondement de l'être. L'être n'est pas voué au Mal, mais il doit, s'il peut, ne pas se laisser enfermer dans les limites de la raison' [[E]vil [...] is also, [...] in a somewhat ambiguous manner, a basis of existence. Though being is not doomed to evil, it must try to avoid becoming enclosed within the limitations of reason].[21] Elsewhere Bataille, quoting Jacques Brondel, affirms that '[i]l y a une volonté de rupture avec le monde, pour mieux étreindre la vie dans sa plénitude et découvrir dans la création artistique ce que la réalité refuse' [there is a desire to break with the world in order to embrace life in all its fullness and discover in artistic creativity that

---

20 Simon Critchley, *Infinitely Demanding: Ethics of Commitment, Politics of Resistance* (London: Verso, 2007), p. 39.
21 Bataille, *La Littérature et le mal*, p. 186; Bataille, *Literature and Evil*, p. 29.

which is refused by reality].²² It is in its defiance of reason and in the desire to break with the world as it is that evil becomes glorified for Bataille.

Evil and Literature

In *La Littérature et le mal* the seemingly paradoxical relation between evil and ethics is attested. In this regard, the irreducible, residual part within the subject that defies unity, coherence and understanding (the opaqueness to which both Critchley and Butler allude as the basis for ethical connection) is designated by Bataille as evil. In his commentary on *La Littérature et le mal*, Denis Hollier observes that evil corresponds to the moment when the wilful subject becomes helpless and vulnerable and thereby, instead of imposing its will, yields to something that is not its choice. This turning point, when the autonomy of the subject is compromised, is described by Hollier as follows:

> [W]hen, after having unconditionally desired the Good, the will arrives at the extreme point where it can no longer want [...] and nevertheless remains unsatisfied, [...] notices that there is a residue before which it remains helpless, a residue which has total power over it since the will becomes so vulnerable that it can only yield [...] [to what] in wanting, it did not want.²³

Bataille's vision of evil, as sketched above, can be compared, in its idiosyncrasy, with the Kantian account of the matter to the extent that both focus on the structure, the mode of the act as such. Bataille, like Kant, does not refer to the content of the act nor address its harmful consequences, yet, unlike Kant and the latter's equation of evil with a will that is not fully good, Bataillean evil is not considered in relation to the will but in relation to time, more precisely in relation to the moment in time when the will is suspended and silenced. In this sense, whereas Kantian evil consists in not acting out of principle, Bataillean evil lies in the displacement of action by passion.

Bataille appends evil to the field of literature, as the conjunction 'and' (*et*) in his title *La Littérature et le mal* makes evident. In so doing, he assigns to literature the deciphering of evil. Juxtaposing the moral

---

22 Jacques Brondel, *Emily Brontë. Expérience spirituelle et création poétique* (Paris: Presses Universitaires de France, 1995), p. 406.
23 Hollier, 'Dualist Materialism', p. 64.

virtuousness and the sheltered life of Emily Brontë to her exposure to the very depths of evil as attested in the writing of *Wuthering Heights*, he remarks: 'Mais sa pureté morale intacte, elle [Emily Brontë] eut de l'abîme du Mal une expérience profonde. [...] Ce fut la tâche de la littérature, de l'imagination, du rêve' [Yet, keeping her moral purity intact, she had a profound experience of evil [...], she fathomed the very depths of evil. This was the task of literature, imagination, dream].[24] Similarly, the double relationship of evil, on the one hand with literature, on the other hand with an ethical stance, is announced in the preface of Bataille's book:

> La littérature est l'essentiel, ou n'est rien. Le Mal – une forme aiguë du Mal – dont elle est l'expression, a pour nous, je le crois, une valeur souveraine. Mais cette conception ne commande pas l'absence de morale, elle exige une 'hypermorale'.
>
> [Literature is either the essential or nothing. I believe that evil – an acute form of evil – which it expresses, has a sovereign value for us. But this does not exclude morality: on the contrary, it demands a 'hypermorality'.][25]

Joseph Libertson underlines how the Bataillean terms communicate with, or become contaminated by, one another and that this act of interchange is an essential part of 'the process of their definition'.[26] It is precisely this complex relationship between these three key terms – literature, evil, and hypermorality – as well as the redefinition of each term due to its interplay with the others that this chapter seeks to explore. Initially, it should be noted that the 'hypermorality' put forth in *La Littérature et le mal* correlates with the distinction between morality and ethics and has qualities in common with the latter. According to the distinction drawn most notably by Foucault and Deleuze and bearing the mark of the Nietzschean transvaluation of values, morality posits a transcendental aspect and is meant as a set of rules against which a person's actions are evaluated, while ethics contain an element of immanence and correspond to a mode

---

24 Bataille, *La Littérature et le mal*, p. 173; Bataille, *Literature and Evil*, p. 15.

25 Georges Bataille, 'Avant-Propos', in Bataille, *La Littérature et le mal*, pp. 171–72 (p. 171); Georges Bataille, 'Preface', in Bataille, *Literature and Evil*, pp. ix–xi (p. ix).

26 Joseph Libertson, 'Proximity and the Word: Blanchot and Bataille', *Substance*, 14 (1976), 35–49 (p. 36).

of existence, a way of life.[27] For Bataille, as already mentioned, this way of life involves the primacy of the present. Additionally, given the implication of literature, one can go even further and suggest that hypermorality moves beyond the ethical and towards the aesthetic. As Todd May has argued with reference to Foucault, the ethical connotes that there is a right way, or several right ways, of living, while the aesthetic strives to bring into being a life, new and different, 'worthy of being lived'.[28] For May, the ethical slides towards the aesthetic when the question 'How ought we live?' is replaced by the question 'How might we live?'; and when life frees itself from principles and creates itself, becoming, as Foucault yearned for, itself a work of art.[29]

What is crucial and singular in the Bataillean re-examination of the question of evil is its framing in relation to modern literature. As Michel Surya notes, while the theme of evil – and (im)morality – is omnipresent in Bataille's texts, a systematic account of it was for a long time absent. As Surya observes with regard to the late writing of *La Littérature et le mal*: 'Ce qu'il ne lui est sans doute pas possible de dire en philosophe, il le dira en écrivain, en écrivain fasciné par d'autres écrivains' [What was no doubt impossible for him to say as a philosopher he would say as a writer, as a writer fascinated by other writers].[30] As a step towards highlighting and anticipating the complexity and subtlety of Bataille's thinking on the matter, it is helpful to bring in Simone Weil's *La Pesanteur et la grâce*, which was published in 1947, ten years before *La Littérature et le mal*. In the section titled 'Le Mal', more precisely in the fragment under the title 'Littérature et morale', Weil praises both imaginary evil (as opposed to real evil) and real good (as opposed to imaginary good): 'Le mal imaginaire est romantique, varié, le mal réel morne, monotone, désertique, ennuyeux. Le bien imaginaire est ennuyeux; le bien réel est toujours nouveau, merveilleux, enivrant' [Imaginary evil is romantic and

---

27 For the distinction and its relationship to the philosophy of the ancient world and more particularly to Stoicism, see John Sellars, 'An Ethics of the Event: Deleuze's Stoicism', *Angelaki*, 11 (2006), 157–71 (p. 166).

28 Todd May, 'Michel Foucault's Guide to Living', *Angelaki*, 11 (2006), 173–84 (pp. 176–77).

29 Foucault asks: 'But couldn't everyone's life become a work of art? Why should the lamp or the house be an art object, but not life?' (Michel Foucault, 'On the Genealogy of Ethics: An Overview of Work in Progress', in *The Foucault Reader*, ed. by Paul Rabinow (New York: Pantheon, 1974), pp. 340–72 (p. 350)).

30 Surya, *Georges Bataille*, p. 498; Surya, *Georges Bataille: An Intellectual Biography*, p. 431.

varied; real evil is gloomy, monotonous, barren, boring. Imaginary good is boring; real good is always new, marvellous, intoxicating].[31] Consequently, she evaluates literature (the field of the imaginary) as either boring when it picks good as its subject matter, or immoral when it makes the choice to contemplate evil: 'Donc la "littérature d'imagination" est ou ennuyeuse ou immorale (ou un mélange des deux). Elle n'échappe à cette alternative qu'en passant en quelque sorte, à force d'art du côté de la réalité – ce que le génie seul peut faire' [Therefore 'imaginative literature' is either boring or immoral (or a mixture of both). It only escapes from this alternative if in some way it passes over to the side of reality through the power of art – and only genius can do that].[32] As Weil seems to suggest, imaginary evil, that is, evil depicted in literature, rather than being immoral has the adeptness to pass over to the side of real good. Drawing on her insight, this chapter argues that Bataille's *Littérature et le mal* ventures precisely into this artful crossover of literary evil towards the side of good. In this sense, Bataille's position vis-à-vis evil proves to be more complex, tensional and ambiguous than it appears at first glance: rather than being an apologist for evil, he fluctuates between the fascination of evil and the dream of good, inclining towards darkness and nonetheless astonished by light. Indeed, pronouncing his admiration for *Wuthering Heights* he observes: 'La fin du très sombre récit d'Emily Brontë est la brusque apparition d'un rayon de tendre lumière' [The end of Emily Brontë's sombre tale is the sudden appearance of a faint ray of light].[33] Similarly, in a more confessional tone, commenting on his own disposition, he writes: 'N'étant pas plus moral qu'un autre, ayant même en cette matière toujours subi l'attrait du mal, j'ai dû comprendre néanmoins de bonne heure que l'attrait du bien me dominait' [Not being more moral than anyone else, having even in this matter always been under the attraction of evil, I must nevertheless have realized early on that it was the attraction of good that dominated me].[34] The following enquiry examines writing as a privileged occasion for the articulation of the topic of evil, reversing the order preferred by Bataille: evil will come first and literature

---

31   Simone Weil, *La Pesanteur et la grâce* (Paris: Plon, 1988 [1947]), p. 83; Simone Weil, *Gravity and Grace*, trans. by Emma Crawford and Mario von der Ruhr (London and New York: Routledge, 1952), p. 70.

32   Weil, *La Pesanteur et la grâce*, p. 83; Weil, *Gravity and Grace*, p. 70.

33   Bataille, *La Littérature et le mal*, p. 186; Bataille, *Literature and Evil*, p. 29.

34   Georges Bataille, 'Notes – La Souveraineté', in *Œuvres complètes*, VIII (1976), pp. 592–678 (p. 637).

second, i.e., evil and literature, rather than, as Bataille opted for, literature and evil. Inverting the terms in question, this section first explores the notion of evil as re-cast by Bataille and then examines what the domain of literature contributes (adds) to the problematic of evil. In other words, to what extent does evil require literature in order to think about itself? By way of an answer, it should be noted that *La Littérature et le mal* brings about a shift in emphasis with regard to Bataille's pre-war and post-war engagements which can be somewhat signalled in terms of a shift in emphasis from the real to the literary: while the Bataille of *Documents*, and to a certain extent the Bataille of *L'Expérience intérieure*, adopts the standpoint of the real (that is, materiality and experience) and revolts against aestheticism, idealization and the life of the spirit (namely, the Surrealists and Hegel), the Bataille of *La Littérature et le mal* adopts the standpoint of literature (that is, non-productive activity) and revolts against effective action (namely, Sartre).

Before exploring the Bataillean recasting of evil as put forth in *La Littérature et le mal*, this chapter will touch upon Bataille's fascination with evil in its common and broad signification as wrongdoing and suffering. 'Le mal est toujours pire' [Evil is always worse], notes Denis Hollier and he goes on by marking out *le pire* as an absolute comparative ('ce comparatif absolu') inasmuch as what is worse can always become (even) worse.[35] Evil challenges limits to the extent that the question of evil converges with the question of limits (discursive, subjective and ethical, limits of thought, of consciousness and of morality); thus it grows into a privileged trope for Bataille, who lived on the edge, who constantly pushed the boundaries of possibility and whose thinking – and life – were devoted to – and troubled by – the extreme. Crime and suffering, more specifically 'pure' crime and suffering, as Denis Hollier would add, are provocative in so far as they defy reason, in the double sense that they are without justification (motivation or purpose) and are beyond comprehension (threatening our ability to make sense).[36] However, one might object, if evil is considered synonymous with the unintelligible it runs the danger of being reduced to a useless concept. If the word 'evil' is

---

35   Denis Hollier, 'La Tragédie de Gilles de Rais', *L'Arc*, 32 (1967), 63–70 (p. 64).

36   Hollier, 'La Tragédie de Gilles de Rais', p. 64. On the case of Gilles de Rais, Hollier remarks: 'Sans la nudité de ses aveux étrangers à toute explication Gilles de Rais n'aurait pas été le "pur" criminel. En dernière instance, son crime, c'est de n'avoir aucune raison' [Without the nakedness of his confession, eluding all explanation, Gilles de Rais would not have been the 'pure' criminal. In the final analysis, his crime is to have no reason] (p. 64).

used to provide the missing explanation, when we lack a complete explanation, it might turn out to be, as Terry Eagleton remarks, 'a way of bringing arguments to an end' in a similar manner to the idea of taste.[37]

Bataille, of course, whose distaste for endings is widely known, does not appeal to the contrivance of evil in order to put an end to the debate but rather in order to re-open it. In post-war France, at the time when several of the essays that make up *La Littérature et le mal* were written, the depths of horror have entered history. Bataille is therefore urged to rethink some recurring themes in his writings (the desire for annihilation, expenditure, death), as well as respond to (and take responsibility for) the historical occurrence of radical evil. This response consists of an awakening to the possibility of evil. In his review of *Les jours de notre mort*, Rousset's novel on the universe of the concentration camps, Bataille renders humankind as a whole, himself and us, in charge of the question of evil by signalling:

> Nous ne pouvons pas être *humains* sans avoir aperçu en nous la possibilité de la souffrance, celle aussi de l'abjection. Mais nous ne sommes pas seulement les victimes possibles des bourreaux: les bourreaux sont nos semblables. Il nous faut encore nous interroger: n'y a-t-il rien dans notre nature qui rende tant d'horreur impossible? et nous devons bien nous répondre: en effet, rien. Mille obstacles en nous s'y opposent ... Ce n'est pas impossible néanmoins.

> [We cannot be *human* until we have perceived in ourselves the possibility for abjection in addition to the possibility of suffering. We are not only the possible victims of the executioners, the executioners are our fellow human beings. We must ask ourselves: is there anything in our nature that makes such horror impossible? And we should be correct in answering: no, nothing. A thousand obstacles in us stand against it ... Yet, it is not impossible.][38]

In this respect, Surya astutely notes that Bataille re-evaluates good as the *awakening* to evil, an awakening which (consisting of the consciousness of the *possibility* for abjection and suffering) is starkly

---

37 Terry Eagleton, *On Evil* (New Haven, CT; London: Yale University Press, 2010), p. 8.

38 Georges Bataille, 'Réflections sur le bourreau et le victime', in *Œuvres complètes*, XI: *Articles I. 1944–1949* (1988), pp. 262–67 (p. 266); Georges Bataille, 'Reflections on the Executioner and the Victim', trans. by Elizabeth Rottenberg, *Yale French Studies*, 79 (1991), 15–19 (p. 18)

distinct from the realization, the actual *doing* of evil.[39] Besides denoting that the very notion and existence of good implicate a contemplation of, an awakening to and a responsibility for evil, the significance of the above passage lies in the fact that Bataille, rather than establishing a link between the two forms of evil, suffering and abjection, adds the latter to the former; correspondingly, rather than placing sufferers and wrongdoers, victims and executioners face to face, he places them side by side. In so doing, he strives to put forward, against the prevailing dualism which determines two categories of evil, a broken dialectic.

The act of linking abjection and wrong on the one hand and suffering and misfortune on the other is old but persistent: it can be traced from Augustine's theological account of the Fall, in which affliction (natural evil) is logically connected to, and hence morally justified because of, man's Original Sin (moral evil) – a linkage which has nevertheless been shaken since the Lisbon earthquake (1755) – until the secular perspective within our current legal system, which associates crime with punishment. Indeed, in his commentary on Nietzsche's *On The Genealogy of Morals* Derrida wonders:

> D'où vient cette idée bizarre, bizarre, cette idée antique, archaïque (*uralte*), cette idée si profondément enracinée, peut-être indestructible, d'une équivalence possible entre le dommage et la douleur (*Schaden und Schmerz*). D'où vient cette étrange hypothèse ou présomption d'une équivalence de deux choses si incommensurables? Qu'est-ce qu'un tort et une souffrance peuvent avoir en commun?[40]

> [From where comes this bizarre, bizarre idea, this ancient, archaic (*uralte*) idea, so deeply rooted, perhaps indestructible, idea of a possible equivalence between injury and pain (*Schaden und Schmerz*)? From where comes this strange hypothesis or presumption of an equivalence between two such incommensurable things? What can a wrong and suffering have in common?]

In an attempt to cast light upon the penitentiary logic which permeates our legal system, Derrida, following Nietzsche, traces it back to the law of commerce and exchange.[41] As he remarks, commenting on the

---

39 Surya, *Georges Bataille*, p. 496; Surya, *Georges Bataille: An Intellectual Biography*, p. 430.

40 Jacques Derrida, *Séminaire. La peine de mort I (1999–2000)* (Paris: Galilée, 2012), p. 217.

41 Derrida, *Séminaire*, p. 217. In her review of the English translation of Derrida's book Judith Butler reminds us of Nietzsche's formulation 'festive cruelty', which

genesis and the genealogy of the legal system: '[L]'origine du sujet de droit et notamment du droit pénal, c'est le droit commercial, c'est la loi du commerce, de la dette, du marché, de l'échange entre les choses, des corps et des signes monétaires' [[T]he origin of the legal subject, and notably of penal law, is commercial law; it is the law of commerce, debt, the market, exchange between things, bodies and monetary signs].[42] To emphasize this, in her reading of both Derrida and Nietzsche Judith Butler insinuates the etymological coupling between counting (time and money) on the one side and accountability, being counted on (to count time and money) on the other. The alliance between criminality and punishment is based on the creditor-debtor relation, inasmuch as injury is considered a debt and punishment a repayment (literally, the price to be paid). Therefore, as Butler concludes, 'the field of suffering is pervasively economized, and the contract becomes the salient model for human exchange'.[43] The following discussion will show how Bataille disturbs the balance, the logic of equivalence and exchange which has reigned over the debate on evil, by inaugurating a logic of incommensurability, not only between the two forms of evil (suffering and wrongdoing) but also, and more crucially, between evil and good. This logic of the incommensurability of the broken dialectic sets in motion the repetitive temporality of the Nietzschean eternal recurrence against the linear temporality of the working dialectic (the Kojèvian/Hegelian master and slave dialectic).

Bataille approaches the question of the source of evil by taking human freedom as his point of departure. In the context of freedom Bataille inaugurates a new distinction concerning evil: an acute, asocial form of evil (upheld and celebrated in literature) and the social, political form of evil (that enters history). Thus in *La Littérature et le mal*, advancing two starkly different categories of evil, Bataille sets apart literary evil, that is, evil in its intimacy with modern literature (evil as a momentary expenditure, pure passion), from the historical and political occurrences of evil (evil as a relentless edifice of power, passion rendered servile in the service of power): '[L]e Mal envisagé sous le jour d'une attirance désintéressée vers la mort, diffère du mal dont le sens est l'intérêt égoïste' [[E]vil seen in the light of a

---

in his view is to be found in the domain of both law and morality (Judith Butler, 'On Cruelty', review of Jacques Derrida, *The Death Penalty*, vol. 1 (2013), trans. by Peggy Kamuf, *London Review of Books*, 36 (2014), 31–33 (p. 31)).

42 Derrida, *Séminaire*, p. 217.

43 Butler, 'On Cruelty', p. 1.

disinterested attraction towards death, differs from evil based on self-interest].[44] The better to understand Bataille's division, we might compare (or, more precisely, contrast) his modelling of an acute form of evil with Pasolini's film *Salò*, which draws precisely on, unveils and denounces the appropriation of passion by legal and political power. The film, which appeared in 1975 and whose complete title is *Salò, or the 120 days of Sodom*, transposes de Sade's eighteenth-century novel of enjoyment and pain, torment and humiliation into 1944 and the Italian town of Salò, which served as the capital of the Fascist Republic. The film focuses on the subjection of nine teenagers to 120 days of torture (physical, mental and sexual) at the hands of four corrupt Fascist libertines. Commenting on his adaptation of the novel, Pasolini remarks that in his film sex becomes 'an allegory of the commodification of bodies at the hands of power'.[45]

Evil and Time

In *La Littérature et le mal* Bataille breaks with and moves beyond the prevailing philosophical traditions on Good and Evil, namely both the Neo-Platonic logic, which considers evil as derivative, as a degraded form of Good, and the logic of opposites, which regards good and evil as antithetical and therefore as equivalent. Bataille's clash with Sartre brings into focus precisely these enduringly established philosophic postulates. Sartre, in his commentary on Baudelaire's *Les Fleurs du mal*, mistrusts evil and discredits it as self-defeating. In Sartre's view, quoted by Bataille, 'la création délibérée du Mal, c'est-à-dire la faute, est acceptance et reconnaissance du Bien; elle lui rend hommage et, en se baptisant elle-même mauvaise, elle avoue qu'elle est relative et dérivée, que sans le Bien, elle n'existerait pas' [the deliberate creation of evil – that is to say, wrong – is acceptance and recognition of good. It pays homage to it and, by calling itself wicked, it admits that it is relative and derivative – that it could not exist without good].[46] Against this oppositional logic, Bataille introduces a logic of asymmetry and essential otherness, since, as he writes in the section of *La Littérature et le mal* dedicated to Proust, 'si le Bien et le Mal sont complémentaires, il n'en résulte pas d'équivalence' [though good and

---

44 Bataille, *La Littérature et le mal*, p. 187; Bataille, *Literature and Evil*, p. 29.
45 Pier Paolo Pasolini, 'The Lost Interview' <https://mubi.com/notebook/posts/the-lost-pasolini-interview> [accessed 25 February 2022].
46 Jean-Paul Sartre, *Baudelaire* (Paris: Gallimard, 1946), p. 59.

evil are complementary, there is no equivalence].⁴⁷ Here it is helpful to recall Simone Weil's vision of a 'higher good', which accords and resonates with Bataille's demand for a 'hypermorality'. Weil's visualization of a higher good is entirely incompatible with evil as well as with what she calls 'degraded good', that is, a low form of good, the good of the penal code, order: 'Le bien comme contraire du mal lui est équivalent en un sens comme tous les contraires' [Good as the opposite of evil is, in a sense equivalent to it, as is the way with all opposites].⁴⁸ She goes on to provide a list of opposites which could have been similarly enumerated by Bataille (or by Foucault, in his critical review of Bataillean transgression), such as 'vol et respect bourgeois de la propriété, adultère et "honnête femme"; caisse d'épargne et gaspillage; mensonge et "sincérité"' [theft and the bourgeois respect for property, adultery and the 'respectable woman'; the savings-bank and waste; lying and 'sincerity'].⁴⁹

Against this oppositional and symmetrical logic, in each of the essays which make up *La Littérature et le mal* we find a variant on the main motif of evil as the predominance of the intensity of the instant, an intensity which challenges the path of reason, the calculations of interest and the will for survival and duration (all that which common morality designates Good). In the case of Emily Brontë, or rather in the character of Heathcliff, evil becomes synonymous with childhood, as crystallized in Heathcliff's frenzied attempt to regain his kingdom of childhood and concurrently his love for Catherine, which is bound – and irretrievably lost – with it. In this sense, evil, as personified by Heathcliff, is circumscribed as the infantile preference for the present moment, while Good assumes the form of consideration of the future, a concern which dominates the world of adults. Bataille's disagreement with Sartre unfolds around the key figure of Baudelaire, who, in both Sartre's and Bataille's view, refuses to assume responsibility for his freedom, denying the existing order while simultaneously sustaining and affirming it: 'Baudelaire [...], délibérément, refuse d'agir en homme accompli, c'est-à-dire en homme prosaïque. Sartre a raison: Baudelaire a choisi d'être en faute, comme un enfant' [Baudelaire deliberately refused to behave like a real man, that is to say, like a prosaic man. Sartre is right: Baudelaire chose to be wrong, like a child].⁵⁰ Two versions of freedom thus emerge: Sartre's

---

47   Bataille, *La Littérature et le mal*, p. 268; Bataille, *Literature and Evil*, p. 145.
48   Weil, *La Pesanteur et la grâce*, p. 84; Weil, *Gravity and Grace*, p. 70.
49   Weil, *La Pesanteur et la grâce*, p. 85; Weil, *Gravity and Grace*, p. 70.
50   Bataille, *La Littérature et le mal*, p. 192; Bataille, *Literature and Evil*, p. 39.

view of freedom as synonymous with human consciousness and, therefore, in terms of temporality, as future-oriented (to the degree that consciousness is necessarily future-oriented).[51] Bataille, on the other hand, considers freedom as correlated not with consciousness but with the fascination of evil and, in terms of temporality, as tied to an overwhelming, immersing and simultaneously receding present. Throughout *La Littérature et le mal* he insists on the reciprocal relation of evil and freedom, on the fact that evil and freedom are reciprocally constituted. Defining the freedom to go wrong and to disobey the Law as inherently human, he notes: 'La liberté n'est-elle pas le pouvoir qui manque à Dieu, ou qu'il n'a que verbalement, puisqu'il ne peut désobéir l'ordre qu'*il est*, dont il est garant?' [Is liberty not the power which God lacks, or which He only possesses verbally since He cannot disobey the order which *He is*, which He guarantees?].[52] Since God is dead and adulthood is assigned the task of acting as the guarantor of order, freedom for Bataille belongs to childhood. In his view, 'la liberté serait à la rigueur un pouvoir de l'enfant: elle ne serait plus pour l'adulte engagé dans l'ordonnance obligatoire de l'action qu'un rêve, un désir, une hantise' [strictly speaking liberty would be the power of a child. For the adult, bound by the obligatory regulations of action, it would be a mere dream, a desire, a spectre].[53]

While Sartre's liberating, dialectical view subscribes freedom (meant as empowerment) to the realm of the possible, the realizable and action, in Bataille's tragic view freedom (meant as powerlessness) is baptized 'sovereignty' and is bound to the realm of the impossible, the unrealizable, passion and failure. As Bataille notes, with reference to Genet: '[L]a souveraineté n'a pour elle que le royaume de l'échec' [[S]overeignty must inhabit the realm of failure].[54] As he concludes: 'Jamais nous ne pouvons *être* souverain' [Never can we *be* sovereign].[55] Against the Sartrean prospect of freedom, Bataille posits the attraction of freedom, freedom as an attraction. As Edward Greenwood points out, Bataillean sovereignty does not come to light as the happy end, the successful accomplishment of a progressing linear process, but bursts forth, repetitively, as an experience of

---

51 In *L'Être et le néant* human freedom consists in the ability of consciousness to transcend its material situation, in the ability of consciousness to deny and escape the present.
52 Bataille, *La Littérature et le mal*, p. 192; Bataille, *Literature and Evil*, p. 38.
53 Bataille, *La Littérature et le mal*, pp. 191–92; Bataille, *Literature and Evil*, p. 38.
54 Bataille, *La Littérature et le mal*, p. 306; Bataille, *Literature and Evil*, p. 194.
55 Bataille, *La Littérature et le mal*, p. 306; Bataille, *Literature and Evil*, p. 194.

failure. As Greenwood remarks, 'the story that Bataille tells about man's hunger for sovereignty has no happy ending. It is the tale of a repeated experience of failure'.[56] In this respect, the sovereign attitude is defined by Bataille as synonymous with '*l'attitude mineure*', 'une attitude d'enfant', 'un jeu gratuit' [a minor attitude, a child's attitude, a gratuitous game].[57]

Bataille's insistence on associating freedom with the plane of the present (an insistence that almost entraps freedom into the present), further coupled with the linkage between freedom, the present and childhood, echoes the doubt expressed by Ivan in the *Karamazovs* concerning the key figure of the child (the cost of a single tear, from a single child). Ivan's speech, cited and embraced by Simone Weil, goes as follows:

> 'Imagine [said Ivan] that you are creating a fabric of human destiny with the object of making men happy in the end, giving them peace and rest at last, but that it was essential and inevitable to torture to death only one tiny creature – that baby beating its breast with its fist, for instance – and to found that edifice on its unavenged tears, would you consent to be the architect on those conditions? [...].'
>
> 'No, I wouldn't consent,' said Alyosha softly.[58]

The figure of the child displays the ethical priority of the here and now; or rather, the reason the here and now are endowed with ethical underpinnings is manifest in the figure of the child. This means that the presence of the child, here and now, whether tearful, as in Ivan's speech, or savagely joyful, as Heathcliff in Bronte's novel, manifests what is miscalculated in the calculation of the future, what cannot and should not be overcome, annulled in its contingency, in and for the prospect of extraordinary marvels. In this sense, what Bataille says of Baudelaire is also true for himself; for Bataille as well 'la négation du bien [...] est d'une façon fondamentale la négation du primat du lendemain' [the denial of good was basically a denial of the primacy of the future], namely a denial of teleology.[59]

---

56 Edward Greenwood, 'Literature: Freedom or Evil? The Debate between Sartre and Bataille', *Sartre Studies International*, 4 (1998), 17–29 (p. 23).

57 Bataille, *La Littérature et le mal*, p. 191; Bataille, *Literature and Evil*, p. 38.

58 Fyodor Dostoevsky, *The Grand Inquisitor: With Related Chapters from The Brothers Karamazov*, ed. and intro. by Charles B. Guignon, trans. by Constance Garnett (Indianapolis, IN: Hackett, 1993), p. 16.

59 Bataille, *La Littérature et le mal*, p. 208; *Literature and Evil*, p. 58.

As a step towards understanding the correlation between freedom and evil and the temporality that goes along with it in Bataille's thinking, we might compare it with the reasoning of Paul Ricœur on the matter. For Ricœur, freedom is to take upon oneself the origin of evil (as literature does, according to Bataille, confessing its non-innocence, its guilt); evil, in its turn, is what reveals freedom, the terrible power to act against the Law.[60] As Ricœur underlines, to take upon oneself the origin of evil is to reject the ontology of evil, that is, the conception of evil as a 'being', and to recognize instead evil as a 'doing', as an act. Commenting on the temporality of the act of confession, which is an act of language that comes after the fact, the act of evil, Ricoeur notes that through it the three dimensions of time – past, present and future – are united, or, more precisely that the two dimensions of time – the future and the past – are tied together in the present:

> He who *will* bear the blame is the one who *now* takes the act upon himself and he who *has* acted [...]. The future of the sanction and the past of action committed are tied together in the present of confession.[61]

Ricœur further adds that the reason I hold myself in the present responsible for a past act is because 'I could, and should, have done otherwise' (in Kantian terms, I recognize my power of acting according to the representation of a law – which is a question of the will – despite the fact that I did not act according to the law). In this sense, freedom is set up by Ricœur as a tensional instance inasmuch as it resides in 'the power to act according to the representation of a law *and* not to meet the obligation'.[62]

Nonetheless, the unity of time which Ricœur comes upon and detects in the act of confession diverges from the unity of time which accompanies the Heideggerian call of conscience. In Heidegger's projective temporality, the call of conscience is a revelatory moment in which the human being, brought back to himself, that is, towards himself as a future projection, both seizes and projects

---

60 Paul Ricœur, 'Guilt, Ethics and Religion', in *Talk of God*, Royal Institute of Philosophy Lectures, 2 (London: MacMillan, 1969), pp. 100–17 (p. 107). The essay can also be found in Paul Ricœur, *The Conflict of Interpretations: Essays in Hernemeutics*, ed. by Don Ihde (Evanston, IL: Northwestern University Press, 1974), pp. 425–39.

61 Ricœur, 'Guilt, Ethics and Religion', p. 108.

62 Ricœur, 'Guilt, Ethics and Religion', p. 109.

himself towards its potential, towards its possibilities. Unlike this Heideggerian moment of vision, the Ricœurian act of confession is a moment that throws both the subject and thought into confusion.

The turning point in Ricœur's reasoning is when, attempting to exhaust the meaning of evil for ethics, he questions the foundation of evil and chooses to linger on the temporality of the evil act that comes before the act of confession. In so doing, he discloses within the evil action a discrepancy that takes the temporal configuration of a sliding. Pointing out evil as a first disposition of freedom which belongs and is bound to 'le fond démonique de la liberté humaine' [the demonic depth of human freedom], Ricœur argues that evil exists as a 'manner of being of freedom, which itself comes from freedom' and thereby proves as inscrutable as freedom itself.[63] In this sense, in the occurrence of evil action there is no origin in the sense of a temporal antecedent cause that can be retraced, but rather what Ricœur designates 'an instantaneous passage from innocence to sin'.[64] Following Kant, Ricœur acquiesces in what he calls 'the philosophical equivalent of the myth of the Fall', repeating the Kantian exclamation according to which, '[i]n the search for the rational origin of evil actions, every such action must be regarded as though the individual had fallen into it directly from a state of innocence'.[65] In other words, says Ricœur, it is '*as* Adam' (rather than '*in* Adam', because of Adam, the supposedly unique, anterior root of all expressions of evil) that we originate evil.[66]

What is compelling in Ricœur's reading of both the Adamic myth and its Kantian remodelling is his engagement with the point where they flounder, the point where the emergence of evil cannot be conceptualized as an act of the will and the loss of origin or foundation which this implies. The enigma – the initial difficulty – of the foundation of evil leads to the aporia – the terminal difficulty – of evil as already there. As Ricœur concludes, the paradox of ethics is interrelated with this inherent contraction of freedom (the non-power of power, the non-freedom of freedom): while evil is what I could not

---

63 Paul Ricœur, *Le Mal. Un défi à la philosophie et à la théologie* (Geneva: Labor et Fides, 2004), p. 44; Paul Ricœur, *Evil: A Challenge to Philosophy and Theology*, trans. by John Bowden (London: Continuum, 2007), p. 53; Ricœur, 'Guilt, Ethics and Religion', p. 111.

64 Ricœur, 'Guilt, Ethics and Religion', p. 111.

65 Immanuel Kant, *Religion within the Limits of Reason Alone*, trans. by T. M. Greene and H. H. Hudson (New York: Harper & Row, 1960), p. 36.

66 Ricœur, 'Guilt, Ethics and Religion', p. 111.

have done (while I am free not to do evil), evil is a prior captivity that compels me to do evil (in doing evil I discover the non-power of my freedom).

The glimpse of evil as a prior captivity and the instantaneous passage from good to sin which operate as the termination, the limit, in Ricœur's and Kant's argumentation constitute precisely the starting point and the core of Bataille's approach. Bataille persistently ties his thinking with what Foucault terms 'the opening' (*le décalage*) made by Kant in Western philosophy.[67] In *La Littérature et le mal* Bataille's deepening of the Kantian opening consists of the crack, the hiatus he inflicts upon the present. In his insistence on the priority of the present Bataille does not advocate the confinement of human existence within the present. Moreover, Bataille's thought constantly reflects the human need to escape, to find a way out. In this regard Bataille recites a passage from Baudelaire's *Journaux Intimes* which revolves around the centrality of time:

> À chaque minute […] nous sommes écrasés par l'idée de la sensation du temps. Et il n'y a que deux moyens pour échapper à ce cauchemar, – pour l'oublier: le plaisir ou le travail. Le plaisir nous use. Le travail nous fortifie. Choisissons.[68]

> [At every moment we are crushed by the idea and sensation of time. There are two ways of escaping from this nightmare, of forgetting it: pleasure and work. Pleasure exhausts us. Work strengthens us. Let us choose.]

A few lines further on Bataille elaborates on these two ways of escape, stating that, '[l]e travail répond au souci du lendemain, le plaisir à celui de l'instant présent. Le travail est utile et il satisfait, le plaisir, inutile, laisse un sentiment d'insatisfaction' [work corresponds to the care of tomorrow, pleasure to that of the present moment. Work is useful and satisfactory, pleasure useless, leaving a feeling of unsatisfaction].[69]

The response, the choice, of both Baudelaire and Bataille to the above dilemma is curious in three respects. First, the choice between pleasure and work, dissatisfaction and satisfaction, the present and

---

67 Foucault, 'Preface à la transgression', p. 756; Foucault, 'A Preface to Transgression', p. 30.

68 Charles Baudelaire, *Journaux Intimes* <https://www.bmlisieux.com/archives/coeuranu.htm> [accessed 14 April 2022].

69 Bataille, *La Littérature et le mal*, p. 203; Bataille, *Literature and Evil*, p. 52.

the future, in brief, evil and good, is not strictly speaking a matter of choice, an act of the will. Commenting on Baudelaire's refusal to act like a real man, that is, a prosaic man engaging in the world of action, Bataille notes:

> [Baudelaire] n'a pas de volonté, mais une attirance l'anime malgré lui. [...] Le Mal, que le poète fait moins qu'il en subit la fascination, est bien le Mal, puisque la volonté, qui ne peut vouloir que le Bien, n'y a pas le moindre part.

> [Baudelaire had no will power but an instinct animated him in spite of himself. [...] Evil, which the poet does not so much perpetrate as he experiences its fascination, is indeed evil since the will, which can only desire the good, has no part in it.][70]

Second, pleasure, unlike the conventional use of the term, is not pleasing, pleasant and gratifying. As Bataille clarifies, pleasure brings and is linked to dissatisfaction rather than satisfaction. In this respect the significance of the above passage lies neither in the opposition between work and pleasure and their association with usefulness and uselessness respectively, nor in the comprehension of work in terms of escape. The Romantic attack on the useful resides in the dissociation of leisure from work and in the reduction and impoverishment of life into a series of utilitarian ends to be reached and completed. Additionally, the Nietzschean condemnation of the work ethic lies in its serving of an escapist diversion that distracts from self-reflection and from pondering upon our human condition. Against this context, the interest of the above passage lies in the fact that it suggests and introduces another way to escape the sensation of time, to escape our present situation, apart from the structure of the project (that is, apart from both intentionality and projection).

The mode of escape for which Bataille looks and strives by introducing the ambiguous notion of an unsatisfying pleasure can be thought of in the framework provided by Levinas's work *De l'évasion* (1936–37). In this early work the question of being is raised, or rather the question of 'otherwise than being' is first tackled.[71] Levinas's contesting of the assumption that 'being is', namely, that being is at one with itself, displays a fundamental duality that is situated and stands at the heart of human existence. Of course, as Levinas acknowledges, the question of being was attacked long before him,

---

70   Bataille, *La Littérature et le mal*, p. 207; Bataille, *Literature and Evil*, p. 57.
71   The question finds its final articulation in Levinas's later work *Autrement qu'être ou Au-delà de l'essence* (1974).

as the opening line of the essay declares: 'La révolte de la philosophie traditionnelle contre l'idée de l'être procède du désaccord entre la liberté humaine et le fait brutal de l'être qui la heurte' [The revolt of traditional philosophy against the idea of being originates in the discord between human freedom and the brutal fact of being that assaults freedom].[72] The 'brutal fact of being' that restrains human freedom is both the being of the world, the fact that the external world is already there, and the being of existence, the givenness of human existence as such. Levinas's thinking both builds on and moves decisively beyond the attack of classical philosophy against the tautological assertion that 'being is'. As he writes, hinting at his distancing from classical debates: 'En combattant l'ontologisme, [...] [la philosophie occidentale] luttait pour un être meilleur, pour une harmonie entre nous et le monde ou pour le perfectionnement de notre être propre' [In combatting the tendency to ontologize [...] Western philosophy struggled for a better being, for a harmony between us and the world, or for the perfection of our own being].[73] The Levinasian critique of traditional philosophy consists in wrestling with the problem of being from the standpoint of, and towards the ideal of, sufficiency, fulfilment, contentment and peace. These struggles, as he puts it, 'ne brisent pas l'unité du moi qui [...] est promis à la paix avec soi-même, s'achève, se ferme et se repose sur lui-même' [do not break up the unity of the 'I', which [...] is given to peace with itself, completes itself, closes on and rests upon itself].[74] In more blatant terms, Levinas proclaims that the inadequacy of the human condition has always been understood in terms of limitation: 'L'insuffisance de la condition humaine n'a jamais été comprise autrement que comme une limitation de l'être, sans que la signification de "l'être fini" fût jamais envisagé' [The insufficiency of the human condition has never been understood otherwise than as a limitation of being, without our ever having envisaged the meaning of 'finite being'].[75]

In Levinas's overview of modern philosophy, both the eighteenth- and nineteenth-century Romantic revolt against reality (and its foreignness) and the twentieth-century philosophy of the vital urge and becoming (according to which the life force creates values

---

72   Emmanuel Levinas, *De l'évasion* (Montpellier: Fata Morgana, 1982 [1935]), p. 91; Emmanuel Levinas, *On Escape*, trans. by Bettina Bergo (Stanford, CA: Stanford University Press, 2003), p. 49.

73   Levinas, *De l'évasion*, p. 93; Levinas, *On Escape*, p. 51.

74   Levinas, *De l'évasion*, p. 91; Levinas, *On Escape*, p. 49.

75   Levinas, *De l'évasion*, p. 93; Levinas, *On Escape*, p. 51.

instead of being bound by pre-existing ones) aim at and are inscribed within the logic of full flowering (of a subject's proper reality) and fulfilment (of one's own destiny). Against the philosophical backdrop of revolt (opposing the world while assuring individual peace) and becoming (constantly creating and renewing 'being' and thereby ultimately serving and sustaining it, albeit in a less rigid form), Levinas introduces the notion of escape. Underlining the singularity of escape, he notes: 'L'évasion [...] met en question précisément cette prétendue paix avec soi [...]; c'est l'être même, le "soi-même", qu'elle fuit et nullement sa limitation' [Escape puts in question precisely this alleged peace-with-self [...]. It is being itself or the 'one-self' from which escape flees and in no way being's limitation].[76] Unlike becoming, which, in Levinas's view, denotes intentionality and directedness to the extent that it still implies 'going somewhere', escape consists of simply 'getting out': '[D]ans l'évasion nous n'aspirons qu'à sortir' [[W]ith escape we aspire only to get out].[77] It is precisely its capacity to get out of being that renders escape crucial for Levinas's thinking. Additionally, and perhaps more importantly, escape is put forward as intimately bound up with being to the extent that being is reconfigured in terms of an escape. Escape, in the Levinasian understanding of the term, is not about the fleeing of a limited being towards inexhaustible possibilities and infinity; neither is it about running away from the narrowness of a realized life towards the promise of unrealized possibilities: 'Dans l'évasion le moi se fuit non pas en tant qu'opposé à l'infini de ce qu'il n'est pas ou de ce qui ne deviendra pas, mais au fait même qu'il est ou qu'il devient' [In escape the I flees itself, not in opposition to the infinity of what it is not or of what it will not become, but rather due to the very fact that it is or that it becomes].[78] In an attempt to give a

---

76 Levinas, *De l'évasion*, p. 99; Levinas, *On Escape*, p. 55.

77 Levinas, *De l'évasion*, p. 97; Levinas, *On Escape*, p. 54.

78 Levinas, *De l'évasion*, p. 99; Levinas, *On Escape*, 55. Regarding the promise of unrealized possibilities, Levinas writes, 'l'évasion n'a donc que peu en commun avec ce besoin de "vies innombrables" qui est un motif analogue de la littérature moderne' [escaping therefore has little in common with that need for 'innumerable lives', which is an analogous motif in modern literature] (Levinas, *De l'évasion*, p. 98; Levinas, *On Escape*, p. 55). The literary motif of 'innumerable lives' brings to mind, alongside other famous examples, the unmarried sisters of 'The Supper at Elsinore', whom Karen Blixen characterizes, alongside their intimate friends – old maids like them or unhappily married women – as 'dames of the round table of possibilities'. In her attempt to introduce the reader to the sisters' idiosyncratic characters, Blixen (Isak Dinesen) notes: 'Perhaps to

content, from a phenomenological standpoint, to the notion of escape, Levinas describes the dual experience of need and pleasure. Arguing against the common understanding of need in terms of privation and lack which search for their appeasement and fulfilment in pleasure, Levinas challenges the metaphysical assumption which considers need synonymous with emptiness and the real synonymous with fullness: '[U]ne métaphysique où le besoin est d'avance caractérisé comme un vide dans un monde où le réel s'identifie avec le plein' [[A] metaphysics in which need is characterized in advance as an emptiness in a world where the real is identified with the full].[79] Contesting the common view of need and pleasure as states of privation and fullness respectively, Levinas reconfigures both as variants of an unending, dynamic process. More importantly, what need and pleasure unveil in their dynamism is the process of getting out of being (being itself, being oneself, being full and enriched). In the Levinasian view need tends towards escape rather than towards pleasure, satisfaction and appeasement; similarly, pleasure turns out to be disappointment and deceit rather than a re-establishment of, and a return to, a natural plenitude. In so doing, they compel us to rethink the question of being in terms of an escape, namely how being is split, how it tends towards, is interrelated to and finally *is* an

---

them the first condition for anything having real charm was this: that it must not really exist'. She goes on narrating how the unmarried sisters pitied and somehow scorned their happily married friends who had husbands, children and grandchildren; despite the fact that the sisters lived an uneventful life they felt that the path they had chosen was far more adventurous than that of their friends. Commenting upon and providing an explanation for their seemingly curious attitude, Dinesen writes: '[T]o them only possibilities had any interest; realities carried no weight. They had themselves had all possibilities in hand and had never given them away in order to make a definite choice and come down to a limited reality. They might still take part in elopements by rope-ladder, and in secret marriages, if it came to that' (Karen Blixen, 'The Supper at Elsinore', in *Seven Gothic Tales* (London: Penguin, 2002), pp. 189–235 (p. 211)). A first reading of the above passage might associate the sisters' choice of an unmarried life with the dream and the celebration of 'innumerable lives', a desire to keep open the multiplicity of unrealized possibilities that correspond to and appease the depths and the complexity of the self. However, the subtlety of the above passage invites another reading: the uneventful, non-gratifying lives of the sisters – whose intimate circle consists of *unhappily* married women, alongside old maids – 'bring into question', to return to Levinas's definition of escape, 'precisely this alleged peace-with-self'. To put it another way, what Blixen and Levinas suggest is that it is not the limits, the limitation, of being that urges us to escape, but the suffocating plenitude of being.

79   Levinas, *De l'évasion*, p. 103; Levinas, *On Escape*, p. 58.

escape. In Levinas's formulation, what need discloses is 'la pureté du fait d'être qui s'annonce déjà comme évasion' [the purity of the fact of being, which already looks like an escape];[80] 'le besoin exprime la présence de notre être et non pas sa déficience' [need expresses the presence of our being and not its deficiency].[81]

Whereas Levinas analyses need and pleasure as affective translations of finitude, Bataille, inversely, takes pleasure as his starting point and lingers on its temporal unfolding. This brings us to the third reason why Baudelaire's and Bataille's response to the burden of time is curious in so far as it consists in the pleasure of giving in the present. The Baudelairean and Batallean preference for the present leaks out as the temporality of the impossible, since the present opens up as non-present (as non-presence); the present unclothes not in and as a temporal immediacy but as it slips away. To put it another way, the present gives access to a temporality that is neither a moment of fullness/plenitude (as in Heidegger), nor a moment of emptiness (as in Beckett). It is neither the Heideggerian fulfilment of *kairos*, the right moment (as disclosed in the projective temporality of *Dasein*), nor the Beckettian affirmation of the lack of content of pure time (as realized in the attention to time as time, as too much time). What both Bataille and Baudelaire come across is the paradox of the instant whose paradox lies in the fact that we can access it only by fleeing from it while it withdraws as we try to seize it. Bataille terms it 'le paradoxe de l'instant – auquel nous n'accédons qu'en le fuyant, qui se dérobe si nous tentons de le saisir' [the paradox of the instant to which we can only accede by fleeing from it and which eludes us if we try to seize it].[82]

The key term of dissatisfaction, as it emanates from the temporality of the instant, brings into sharper focus the divergence between Sartre and Bataille. In Sartre's definition of poetry, unreservedly endorsed by Bataille, the poetic process consists in the fusion between subject and object, consciousness and the thing-in-itself, the man and the world, the perishable and the unchangeable. Subsequently, as poetic release fails to take the place of the objects once contemplated, the poet is condemned to permanent dissatisfaction. However, while Sartre considers dissatisfaction to be the moral deficiency of poetry and of Baudelaire, Bataille renders dissatisfaction the strength of poetry (and literature) and valorizes it as ethical. In his confrontation

---

80   Levinas, *De l'évasion*, p. 102; Levinas, *On Escape*, p. 57.
81   Levinas, *De l'évasion*, p. 107; Levinas, *On Escape*, p. 60.
82   Bataille, *La Littérature et le mal*, p. 208; Bataille, *Literature and Evil*, p. 58.

with Sartre, Bataille displaces the focal point of literature from the object, which is to be possessed, towards desire (the impossible), which is merely to be pursued: 'Sartre a beau dire de Baudelaire "son souhait le plus cher est d'*être* comme la pierre, la statue, dans le repos tranquille de l'immutabilité"' [It is all very well for Sartre to say of Baudelaire: his dearest wish was to be like the stone, the statue, in the repose of immutability].[83] As Bataille elucidates, the poet yearns to capture the fleeting instant and to extract an immutable icon of his beloved city, which was constantly changing due to Haussmannization.[84] However, through his poems and his attitude as a *flâneur* Baudelaire – essentially – ultimately participates in a life that is open, infinite, unsatisfiable: '[L]es images qu'il a laissés participent de la vie ouverte, infinie selon Sartre au sens baudelairien, c'est-à-dire insatisfaite' [[T]he images which he left participated in a life which was open, infinite in Baudelaire's sense of the word].[85] Bataille concludes: 'Ainsi, est-il décevant de dire de Baudelaire qu'il voulait l'impossible statue, [...] si l'on n'ajoute aussitôt que Baudelaire voulut moins la statue que l'impossible' [It is therefore misleading to maintain that Baudelaire wanted the impossible statue [...], unless we immediately add that he wanted the impossible far more than he wanted the statue].[86]

In praising the poetic image as synonymous with dissatisfaction and movement (as opposed to the tranquillity and immobility of the statue) and in shifting the poet's focus from the statue to the impossible, the above passage resonates in a way with the old condemnation of idols. As Jean-Luc Nancy reminds us, '[u]ne idole devient idole lorsque son adorateur est *satisfait* de l'adorer: n'importe quel Dieu ou diable peut ainsi devenir idole et peut-être tend toujours à le devenir' [[a]n idol is an idol when its worshipper is *satisfied* with worshipping it: any God or devil can become an idol

---

83   Bataille, *La Littérature et le mal*, p. 198; Bataille, *Literature and Evil*, p. 47.
84   Georges-Eugène Haussmann was appointed by Emperor Napoléon III radically to transform Paris. The reshaping, or 'Haussmannization' of Paris, as it came to be called, occurred between 1853 and 1870. Haussmann demolished entire neighbourhoods that were considered overcrowded and unhealthy, built new infrastructure and widened the winding medieval streets into broad, long, straight boulevards. The expansive avenues facilitated the control and suppression of political revolts, as they could better accommodate the free movement of the French army troops.
85   Bataille, *La Littérature et le mal*, p. 198; Bataille, *Literature and Evil*, p. 47.
86   Bataille, *La Littérature et le mal*, p. 198; Bataille, *Literature and Evil*, p. 47.

in this way and perhaps always has the tendency to do so].[87] In a daring gesture, Nancy equates immobility, or rather the satisfaction and appeasement which correspond to immobility, with evil: '[C]'est [...] dans une telle complétion – satisfaction, assouvissement, rassasiement, solution – que peut consister le mal: on s'y détourne de l'infini, on s'y complaît dans l'immobilité' [[E]vil can consist in such a completion – satisfaction, assuagement, contentedness, solution. Here one turns away from the infinite, one becomes complacent in immobility].[88] Nancy's idiosyncratic discerning and remodelling of evil as completion, satisfaction and stillness echo and align with Weil's equally unorthodox conception of good as 'always new, marvellous, intoxicating'. In this sense, the Baudelairean and poetic repugnance towards satisfaction, the impotence of poetic existence (in its quest for the impossible and its complicity with dissatisfaction) – condemned as evil by classic morality as advocated by Sartre, while endorsed as evil by Bataillean hypermorality – turns into a higher good, which is similarly unsatisfiable, infinite and – to return to Weil's definition – always 'new, marvellous, intoxicating'.[89]

The reconfiguration of good (through the trope of a concise form of evil) in terms of desire and impossibility offers an oblique response to the distressing question of theodicy, namely the justification of the existence of evil. In the final lines of her section dedicated to evil and entitled 'Le mal', Simon Weil raises the issue of the existence of evil in the world. Inverting the premises of theodicy, she does not wonder, 'How can there be evil in the world?'; instead, she asks, 'Comment n'y aurait-il pas du mal dans le monde?' [How could there be no evil in the world?].[90] By way of an answer she points towards desire, whose delirious purity *must* be, at any cost, shielded: 'Il faut que le monde soit étranger à nos désirs. S'il l'était sans contenir de mal, nos désirs alors seraient entièrement mauvais. Il ne le faut pas' [The world has to be foreign to our desires. If this were so without it containing evil, our desires would then be entirely bad. That must not happen].[91]

---

87 Jean-Luc Nancy, *L'Adoration (Deconstruction du christianisme, 2)* (Paris: Galilée, 2010), p. 98 (my emphasis); Jean-Luc Nancy, *Adoration: The Deconstruction of Christianity II*, trans. by John McKeane (New York: Fordham University Press, 2013), p. 66.

88 Nancy, *L'Adoration*, p. 98; Nancy, *Adoration*, p. 66.

89 Bataille terms it 'la crainte d'être satisfait' [the terror of being satisfied] (Bataille, *La Littérature et le mal*, p. 199; Bataille, *Literature and Evil*, p. 49).

90 Weil, *La Pesanteur et la grâce*, p. 82; Weil, *Gravity and Grace*, pp. 78–79.

91 Weil, *La Pesanteur et la grâce*, p. 82; Weil, *Gravity and Grace*, pp. 78–79.

Similarly, Bataille insists that the authors examined in *La Littérature et le mal* (authors of evil in the double sense of the world – writers and originators/makers) long for nothing but the good. In this regard, cross-fertilizing and moving beyond both Kantian idealism and the Nietzschean *amor fati*, the first opening a gap at the heart of being, between the world as it is and the world as it should be, and the second who suggested willing the world as it is (without wanting it to be different), Bataille's conception of evil, conjointly with Weil's, tends to suggest a third way, one in which we affirmatively desire the world as it is not.

The Time of Literature

La Littérature et le mal posits literature as an heir to religious sacrifice, assigned the task of expressing in the modern era the enduring human exigency of challenging and infringing the law. However, while religious rituals inaugurate transgression as an institutionalized violation of norms and taboos carried out collectively by the members of a community, literature gives voice to evil, that is, a denounced (rather than institutionalized) violation of norms, attempted in solitude (rather than shared within a community).[92] As Bataille puts it in *L'Érotisme*, 'le Mal n'est pas la transgression, c'est la transgression condamnée. Le Mal est exactement le péché' [evil is not transgression, it is transgression condemned. Evil is in fact sin].[93] Furthermore, in *La Littérature et le mal* Bataille insists on the solitary, asocial and unfoundational character of the literary endeavour, inasmuch as it privileges the instant (instantaneous loss) over the future (duration and survival):

> [U]n tel enseignement ne s'adresse pas, comme celui du christianisme – ou celui de la religion antique –, à une collectivité ordonnée dont il serait devenu le fondement. Il s'adresse à l'individu isolé et perdu, auquel il ne donne rien que dans l'instant: il est seulement *littérature*.

> [[I]ts doctrine, unlike that of Christianity or of ancient religions, is not aimed at the organized community of which it would be the

---

[92] For a more detailed account of the banishing of transgression from our modern societies due to the advent of Christianity and capitalism, see Libertson, 'Proximity and the Word', pp. 36–37.

[93] Georges Bataille, *L'Érotisme*, in *Œuvres complètes*, x (1987), pp. 11–270 (p. 140); Georges Bataille, *Eroticism*, trans. by Mary Dalwood (London: Penguin, 2010), p. 127.

foundation. It is aimed at the isolated and lost individual to whom it gives nothing except in this one instant: it is solely literature.]⁹⁴

As Surya has argued, in the aftermath of the war Bataille feels the urge to make a distinction between his liberty, the liberty of one (or some) and the liberty of all, the liberty of an organized society,⁹⁵ for, as Surya observes, '[c]e qui vaut pour un individu ne vaut pas pour tous, c'est-à-dire pour une société organisée dont l'enjeu est de durer' [[w]hat is true for the individual is not true for everyone, that is to say for an organized society, whose concern is to last].⁹⁶ In this regard, singular, Bataillean, morality (Bataille's challenge to morality, namely hypermorality) is set apart from collective, social morality: the latter is historical in so far as it belongs to history and time, while the former is ahistorical in so far as it belongs to the intensity of the instant.⁹⁷ Paying tribute to the hypermorality of the instant *in* and *as* literature, Bataille declares: 'La littérature ne peut pas assumer la tâche d'ordonner la nécessité collective' [Literature cannot assume the task of regulating collective necessity].⁹⁸

Literature has a strangely privileged place in relation to evil and its temporality. First, the act of writing as such can be, to some extent, considered synonymous with evil. Kafka and Baudelaire, to whom two of the essays of *La Littérature et le mal* are dedicated, consider themselves as being on the side of evil while writing, to the extent that writing is not really an occupation; it is not real work in the sense of a productive, commercial activity (in Bataille's definition, 'écrire, c'est faire le contraire de travailler' [writing is the opposite of working]).⁹⁹ Moreover, for Bataille the temporality of writing partakes of the instantaneous temporality of evil. In this respect, Bataille's dispute with Sartre and their divergent views on literature revolve precisely around the question of the temporality of literature. The preference for the present, a recurrent motif in *La Littérature et le mal*, separates,

---

94   Bataille, *La Littérature et le mal*, p. 182; Bataille, *Literature and Evil*, p. 25.

95   Surya, *Georges Bataille*, p. 499; Surya, *Georges Bataille: An Intellectual Biography*, p. 433.

96   Surya, *Georges Bataille*, p. 499; Surya, *Georges Bataille: An Intellectual Biography*, p. 433.

97   Surya, *Georges Bataille*, p. 499; Surya, *Georges Bataille: An Intellectual Biography*, p. 433.

98   Bataille, *La Littérature et le mal*, p. 182; Bataille, *Literature and Evil*, p. 25.

99   Pierre Dumayet, 'Georges Bataille à propos de son livre *La Littérature et le mal*', vidéo INA, 21 May 1958 <https://www.ina.fr/video/I00016133> [accessed 25 February 2022].

alongside childhood from adulthood, poetic existence (as condensed in the figure of Baudelaire) from the prosaic realm of action, the Sartrean conception of literature (equated to prose and, ultimately, philosophical ideas) from the Bataillean conception of it (paired with poetry, not as a *genre* but in the poetic capacity to disengage from the production of meaning).

In his well-known distinction between prose and poetry Sartre pleads for the transcendent signifying function of words in prose, namely the fact that they refer to something *beyond* themselves, as opposed to poetry's inward concern with the reality of language as such. While words in prose are associated with (pointing to and serving) the ideal of freedom, words in poetry are dissociated from any social or historical utility, as well as from the typical structure of language. Therefore, for Sartre, literature, to be worthy of its name, becomes identical to prose and is praised inasmuch as it offers a vision of a free future world. Going against Sartre, Bataille, as already mentioned above, asserts that 'the determination of the presence by the future', 'of what exists by what does not yet exist' – be it the signpost that points to the road, the bookmarker that shows the page of the book or the celebrated and handed-over-to-literature-by-Sartre *modus operandi* of philosophy, namely philosophical transcendence – corresponds to a subordinate vision of being. In Bataille's view, literature addresses (and should address) the sovereign part of existence: literature is not a medium that communicates idea(l)s, most notably that of freedom; rather, it is and conveys an unmediated experience in which – rather than the prospect of happiness – merely, instantly, the smile of life appears: '[L]e sourire auquel essentiellement la vie demeure égale y transparaît' [[T]he smile to which life essentially remains equal and shines through].[100]

Bataille renders literature a preferential site to address the intensity of the present moment, detached from those that follow for two reasons: first, unlike everyday life, it is not governed by the necessity to continue; second, unlike other forms of discontinuity and disruption, historical or philosophical, it is not governed by the necessity to conclude and to (re)create order. Indeed, in opposition to living – that is, living on, in opposition to life's essential and inescapable binding to continuance, the next day and thereby, inevitably, to some extent, the care of tomorrow – literature is made of inorganic stuff and is therefore intrinsically and enduringly free, as Bataille proclaims: 'Étant inorganique, elle est irresponsable. Rien ne

---

100   Bataille, *La Littérature et le mal*, p. 187; Bataille, *Literature and Evil*, p. 31.

repose sur elle. Elle peut tout dire' [Being inorganic, it is irresponsible. Nothing rests on it. It can say everything].[101] Then, pointing out literature's dissimilarity from other instances of revolutionary undertaking, both historical and intellectual, he highlights the idea that '[s]eule la littérature pouvait mettre à nu le jeu de la transgression de la loi – sans laquelle la loi n'aurait pas de fin – *indépendamment d'un ordre à créer*' [[o]nly literature could reveal the process of breaking the law – without which the law would have no end – *independently of the necessity to create order*].[102]

Regarding the last part of the sentence, which asserts literature's independence from the necessity to create order, the Bataillean reading of Kafka is insightful. Kafka's agonizing and desperate struggle, the continuing relevance and magnetism of the Kafkaesque, consist in sidestepping the frequent error of questioning, competing and, therefore, ultimately changing places with authority. As Bataille notes: 'L'attitude de Kafka devant l'autorité du père n'a de sens que l'autorité générale qui découle de l'*activité efficace*' [Kafka's attitude towards his father's authority symbolises hostility towards the general authority which stems from *effective activity*].[103] However, Kafka's distancing from effective activity, achievement and conclusion might be seen as standing for the distancing of literature not only from historical action but also from philosophical undertaking. The latter, depending on rational and systematic argumentation, is guided by the exigency to conclude; it thereby ends up by somehow re-establishing order. In other words, philosophical questioning, even when it encounters its limits, bears within it the assuredness and vigour of authority. The above considerations bring us back to the first part of the sentence, which attests to the transgressive element of literature. If we accept the distinctiveness of literature from other pursuits, we are still faced with the question of the way in which it reveals the process of breaking the law.

The interconnectedness of literature and the law is at the centre of Derrida's analysis 'Devant la loi', which bears and redoubles the title of Kafka's story 'Vor dem Gesetz' [Before the Law], a fable published both independently and as part of *Der Prozeß* [*The Trial*] (1925). For Derrida there are two distinct senses in which literature and the law are interlaced. The first sense involves the fact that the field of literature has its own laws. Literature is governed by laws (which

---

101   Bataille, *La Littérature et le mal*, p. 182; Bataille, *Literature and Evil*, p. 25.
102   Bataille, *La Littérature et le mal*, p. 182; Bataille, *Literature and Evil*, p. 25.
103   Bataille, *La Littérature et le mal*, p. 285; Bataille, *Literature and Evil*, p. 167.

determine what belongs to 'literature', classifying texts as 'literary' and 'non-literary') and concurrently (at least literature in the sense that interests Derrida) undermines and suspends its (own) laws. In an attempt to demonstrate the strange status of the laws of literature, Derrida draws on the ambiguous structure of the title of Kafka's story, 'Before the Law', inaugurating a line of separation between itself and the narrative body.[104] Though outside the narrative, it nevertheless belongs to fiction. Moreover, the same phrase is found again (a first or a second time? It is hard to tell) in the main body of the narrative, formulated as follows: 'Before the Law stands a doorkeeper'.[105] The expression 'Before the Law', as the title of the text, is before the text and external to its content, while it is also, as an incipit, inside the text as the initial internal element of the story's fictive content.[106] In its double status as both title and incipit the inaugural phrase of the fiction exposes the origin of the text as split, while the repetition of the phrase discloses the non-identicalness of two seemingly identical formulations.[107]

The second sense in which literature interlaces with the law involves the fact that the law is perpetually the subject of narratives. Kafka's story 'Before the Law' narrates precisely 'l'itineraire en vue du lieu et de l'origine de la loi' [the journey toward the place and the origin of law].[108] Nevertheless, the story and the law appear and unfold concurrently to the extent that, while the law gives rise to the story, it is the story which brings about the theme of the law. Moreover, as the narrative unfolds and investigates what makes the law stand as the law, namely the being-law of the law, the interlacing of law and literature proves less thematic than structural. For, as Derrida argues, being before the law and being before a literary text and, by the same token, the being of the law and the being of literature, turn out to be intimately alike. However, before addressing the structural similarity

---

104 Franz Kafka, 'Before the Law', trans. by Willa and Edwin Muir, in *The Compete Short Stories of Franz Kafka*, ed. by Nahum N. Glatzer (London: Vintage, 1999), pp. 3–4.

105 Kafka, 'Before the Law', p. 3.

106 Jacques Derrida, 'Devant la loi', in Jacques Derrida, *Philosophy and Literature*, ed. by A. Philipps Griffiths (Cambridge: Cambridge University Press, 1984), pp. 173–88 (p. 176); Jacques Derrida, 'Before the Law', in Jacques Derrida, *Acts of Literature*, ed. by Derek Attridge (London and New York: Routledge, 1992), pp. 181–220 (p. 189).

107 Derrida, 'Devant la loi', p. 181; Derrida, 'Before the Law', p. 200.

108 Derrida, 'Devant la loi', p. 179; Derrida, 'Before the Law', p. 192.

between literature and the law, let us first linger on the being of law, as explicated in Kafka's story and Derrida's analysis.

The parable raises one of the most significant issues concerning the law, namely the relationship between the singular and the universal. As the man from the country thinks when his entering is not allowed, the Law should be accessible, at all times, to everyone. However, as Derrida observes, while the Law is inaccessible, the gate is open. More crucially, entrance has never been denied; it has merely been delayed, deferred, enacting Derrida's favoured temporality, namely, deferral, *différance*: 'Tout est question de temps, et c'est le temps du récit' [It is all a question of time, and it is the time of the story].[109] In his commentary Derrida draws on how the oppositional positions of the man from the country and the doorkeeper further divide and redouble the inscription 'before the law', within the main body of the text this time. Despite the fact that both men are 'before the law', the one – in order to guard it effectively – turns his back to it, while the other – waiting to enter it – faces it.[110] Again, a unique expression and position – that of being before the law – is brought into view as divided, doubled, split. Moreover, in their oppositional positions before the law, no one sees, or is in presence of, the law. This is due to the fact that, as Derrida divulges, the law itself is also double: the law forbids itself. It only prohibits to the extent that it is prohibited. In its inaccessibility, as a prohibited place without access, it manifests itself by non-manifesting, withholding, itself. Its origin, its proper taking-place, is unlocated.[111] This originary division of the law, its self-prohibition, places humans in a contradictory position: humans are simultaneously given the freedom of self-determination (since the law does not prohibit) and self-prohibition from entering it (since the law is prohibited). As Derrida affirms, before the law the human being is concurrently a subject of law and an outlaw (since s/he remains outside it; s/he does not enter it; s/he is not in it): 'Elle [la loi] est l'interdit: cela ne signifie pas qu'elle interdit mais qu'elle est elle-même interdite, un lieu interdit. Elle s'interdit et se contredit en mettant l'homme dans sa propre contradiction' [[The law] is prohibition: this does not mean that it prohibits, but that it is itself prohibited, a prohibited place. It forbids itself and contradicts itself by placing the man in its own contradiction].[112]

---

109 Derrida, 'Devant la loi', p. 182; Derrida, 'Before the Law', p. 202.
110 Derrida, 'Devant la loi', p. 182; Derrida, 'Before the Law', p. 202.
111 Derrida, 'Devant la loi', p. 183; Derrida, 'Before the Law', p. 203.
112 Derrida, 'Devant la loi', p. 183; Derrida, 'Before the Law', p. 203.

In *Ethics of the Real* Alenka Zupančič observes that the fundamental paradox of ethics is that in order to set it up a certain conception of ethics, a certain notion of good and evil, already need to exist *prior* to it.[113] What Kant does, in an attempt to avoid the paradox (which nevertheless re-emerges at a following stage), is to set up the moral law as self-founded and self-identical; in this respect the good is defined as such *after* the moral law. By contrast, what Derrida and Kafka do is to expose the origin of the law (of what is before the law, both spatially and chronologically) as paradoxical. Alternatively, as Bataille put it earlier, in the respective gestures of Kafka and Derrida literature reveals 'the process of breaking the law' by exposing the law as fissured, self-prohibited, self-contradictory and double. This exposure is disclosed through the mode of being of the literary text, for, as Derrida argues, Kafka's story describes nothing but itself as a story, having no content beyond itself, and yet this does not mean that the text in its self-referentiality becomes transparent, but that our access to it (and its significance) is denied or, more precisely, deferred. In its readability (as we read it) and unreadability (as it leads nowhere), Kafka's parable, both tautological and allegorical (of the Law as well as of the drama of reading), presents itself and its subject matter, the Law, as self-contradictory and lacking in essence.

In this respect, literature, for Derrida as well as for Bataille, can be seen as primarily undoing the fictive elements of the laws which compose our reality (fictions of origin, unity, coherence). However, the temporal unfolding of this undoing is conceived divergently by Bataille and Derrida: while for the latter literary undoing (literature as undoing) enacts the temporality of deferral, for the former it bursts forth as an interruption. In his reading of 'Before the Law' Giorgio Agamben comments that all the interpreters of the story, including Derrida, focus on the element of openness, on the fact that 'the gate is open as usual'.[114] By contrast, Agamben directs his attention to the end of the story and to the doorkeeper's last words: 'I am now going to shut it'.[115] Focusing on the final closing of the door, Agamben does not consider the man from the country as defeated by the impossible

---

113 Alenka Zupančič, *Ethics of the Real: Kant and Lacan* (London; New York: Verso, 2000), p. 93.

114 Giorgio Agamben, 'The Messiah and the Sovereign: The Problem of Law in Walter Benjamin', in Giorgio Agamben, *Potentialities: Collected Essays in Philosophy*, ed. and trans. by Daniel Heller-Roazen (Stanford, CA: Stanford University Press, 1999), pp. 160–75 (p. 173).

115 Kafka, 'Before the Law', p. 4.

and enigmatic presence/absence of the Law, but rather as succeeding in interrupting the Law's being in force. Therefore, in Agamben's view the story is not about, as Derrida wants it, 'an event which arrives at not arriving, which manages not to happen', but about the opposite, about 'how something has really happened in seeming not to happen'.[116]

In the same way, for Bataille and his privileging of the intensity of the instant literature is not (about) something that does not take place, infinitely deferred, always to come; it is, rather, (about) how something happens in seeming not to happen. Nevertheless, this something that happens while seemingly not happening, namely, the closing which happens in and as literature, does not ultimately occur as the end (as it does in Kafka's story, being an allegory of the messianic event, both belonging and putting an end to historical time and its law): it occurs repetitively as the intensity of the instant. In *La Littérature et le mal* the trope of closing appears as the closing of the eyes, crystallized in René Char's saying: 'Si l'homme parfois ne fermait *souverainement* les yeux, il finirait par ne plus voir ce qui vaut la peine d'être regardé' [If human beings did not sometimes *sovereignly* close their eyes, they would end up no longer seeing what is worth being looked at].[117] In this respect, closing one's eyes is not simply an act of avoiding what is going on, but an act which enables us to see what is really worth seeing; and in Bataille's tragic vision what is worth seeing gives rise not to an image of happiness (in the end, as the end) but to the bursting violence of laughter or the fleeting appearance of a smile.

What is worth looking at and how it is to be looked at are also a major theme in the chapter on Blanchot. After going into detail about the way in which a literary work relates to and negotiates with what is and remains outside, what is exterior to both the advent of language and to the springing up of a world, we concluded that Orpheus's gaze and Eurydice's image crystallize what literature and art can (and cannot) attain, what they fulfil (and fall short of): a presence, presented in its withdrawal. However, one might raise the following objection: does this not amount to making a case for failure as the achievement, the accomplishment, the success of literature? If this is so, what makes it different from success? Conversely, if we consider

---

116 Agamben, 'The Messiah and the Sovereign', p. 174.

117 Char's aphorism appears as the incipit of Bataille's 'Méthode de méditation', p. 192 (René Char, *Feuillets d'Hypnos* (Paris: Gallimard, 2007 [1946]), aphorisme 59, p. 24).

the endeavour of literature in terms of pure failure, what difference does it make?

The chapter on Bataille emphasizes that the Bataillean moments in their absolute (unemployed) negativity are not constructive or productive and therefore are not to be considered moments *within* or moments *towards* (something better and greater). Nonetheless, the chapter guards against securing them as 'moments of being', moments in their own right – in particular because literature arises as one of these moments. Rather than substantiating and separating the Bataillean moments off as such, the chapter calls attention to their contact with and affecting of what comes before and after. Therefore, the leap of inspiration – in terms closer to Blanchot's lexicon – is not simply a moment of carelessness and transgression – in terms closer to the Bataillean lexicon – is not simply a momentary disruption. Our analysis of the Blanchotian literary paradigm of inspiration and the Bataillean entwinement of the literary with evil distances itself from a reading in terms of the plenitude of the void or the delirious purity of self-loss (that is, as instances when everything is lost but then everything resumes and continues). On the contrary, our emphasis on the key terms of the image (that is, the thing as distance) and the instant (that is, appearance as disappearance) shows how both thinkers install a void, a fissure, a rift within presence and the present due to which nothing changes but everything is transformed.

Writing is, therefore, rethought by both Bataille and Blanchot in terms of what would later be glossed in Nancy's major work from the 1970s, *Logodaedalus*, as syncopation. The term 'syncopation', which in music indicates a rhythmic deviation, a missed beat or a spin, and in medicine a fainting or a bump, is used in Nancy's tribute to Kant in the sense of discursive contingency (namely, as a demonstration that language is unavoidably embedded in the language of metaphysics). However, in music syncope is not the frailty of rhythm but, on the contrary, what gives the rhythm and the beat; in medicine as well what disrupts an organism's biological process (or a self's consciousness) is not a deficiency, but a pause, a black-out which discloses, for the first time in a self-evident way, that there is an organism. Similarly, Nancy's contrivance of the syncopation brings forth linguistic disruption not as the deficiency of the Kantian system but as the simultaneous presentation and withdrawal of secure foundation, whereby the attempt of thought to present and ground itself is not only withheld and held back (hindered) but held (determined).[118]

---

118 For a discussion of Nancy's *Logodaedalus* and the fateful implication of literature in the Kantian system, see Ian James, *An Introduction to the Philosophy*

The syncope put forth by Bataille and Blanchot does not designate merely discursive contingency (and therefore is not to be confined to the relation of literature with philosophy). It comes to designate, more broadly, a pause, a paralysis that is not merely a pause within a course, a disruptive moment after which things go on – resuming as if nothing had occurred or revitalized by what has occurred – but rather a pause which shows the joints and thereby affects both what comes before and what comes after while seemingly doing (changing) nothing.

In our analysis of *L'Espace littéraire* and *La Littérature et le mal* we have seen how both Blanchot and Bataille challenge the presence of metaphysics, that is, the conception of the presence as self-identical in relation to past and future instances of presence and how both writers bring forth an excessive non-self-identical presence which is always outside itself, unable to gain an identity by reference to a *telos* (in the case of Bataille), or an underlying substance (in the case of Blanchot), or any transcendent principle exterior to it (in both Bataille and Blanchot).

The attempt by literature to account for another reality – outside what is present, in its spatial and temporal dimension –, as explored above, is comparable to (both converging and fighting against) the psychoanalytical endeavour. Psychoanalysis, also drawing on another reality (the psychic reality), explores and challenges what counts as real. Moreover, as the psychic reality put forward by Freud is not the bracketing of the external reality in favour of the subject's internal reality but is, rather, situated indecisively at the crossroads of the imagined and the actual, and as the analytical method consists of an emphasis on 'speech' rather than subjectivity, psychoanalysis raises questions which are at heart of what is at stake in our discussion of the literary real. Designating the Freudian method as 'un champ nouveau, celui du dire' [a new field, that of saying], Laplanche and Pontalis emphatically note, 'non pas "c'est *vous* qui le dites", mais "c'est vous qui le *dites*"' [not 'it's *you* who says so', but 'it's you who *says* so'].[119] The analytical investigation of the real as well as the mutual implication of (psycho)analysis and literature in their corresponding attempts to approach the real are the theme of the next chapter.

---

of Jean-Luc Nancy: The Fragmentary Demand (Stanford, CA: Stanford University Press, 2006), pp. 44–47.

119 Jean Laplanche and J.-B. Pontalis, *Fantasme originaire. Fantasmes des origines. Origines du fantasme* (Paris: Hachette, 1985), p. 19.

6. The Speech of Analysis

> An unwritten law divides all texts in two categories, the ones that do the interpreting, and the ones that are there mostly to be interpreted.[1]

One of Freud's early essays, 'Creative Writers and Daydreaming', written in 1908, draws on the question of the origin of the artwork, as for Freud the latter attests to the fundamental human desire to transform the existing world of reality. Attempting to decipher the enigma of creativity, the father of psychoanalysis draws a parallel between the creator ('that strange being, the creative writer') and the child at play.[2] For Freud, every child who plays behaves like a writer; similarly and conversely, the writer does the same as a child who plays: they both create an imaginative world, sharply separating it from reality, and they take this world very seriously. In Freud's economic system of psychic stability, where there are only exchanges and substitutes and nothing is given up or lost, the growing child, instead of playing, fantasizes: '[The growing child] builds castles in the air and creates what are called day-dreams. I believe that most people conduct phantasies at times in their lives'.[3] For Freud, what differentiates a child's play from fantasizing is that the child, unlike the airy castles of adults, *links* the imagined objects with real objects in the world (for example, a chair that becomes a house). As for what differentiates creative activity from fantasizing, Freud points to 'ars poetica', of which a rather meagre definition is provided. According

---

1   René Girard, 'Narcissism: The Freudian Myth Demystified by Proust', in *Psychoanalysis, Creativity and Literature: A French-American Inquiry*, ed. by Alan Roland (New York: Columbia University Press, 1978), pp. 293–311 (p. 308).

2   Sigmund Freud, 'Creative Writers and Daydreaming', in Sigmund Freud, *Art and Literature*, trans. by James Strachey, ed. by Albert Dickson (London: Penguin, 1990), pp. 129–42 (p. 131).

3   Freud, 'Creative Writers and Daydreaming', p. 133.

to Freud, poetic art consists of softening the egoistic character of day-dreaming and in highlighting form: '[T]he writer softens the character of his egoistic day-dreams by altering it [i.e., the egoistic character] and disguising it and he bribes us by the purely formal – that is, aesthetic – yield of pleasure which he offers us in the presentation of his phantasies'.[4]

The essay's simplistic view of art as authorial wish-fulfilment has been widely criticized. Peter Brooks, restating the view of recent psychoanalytic criticism, notes that 'Freud speaks most pertinently to literary critics when he is not explicitly addressing art',[5] while Fredric Jameson suggests that the value of the essay lies not in the solution offered but in the formulation of the problem.[6] If, for Jameson, from the viewpoint of Marxist criticism Freud's formulation of the problem is interesting inasmuch as it unfolds a dialectic between private and public, pre-social and social, individual and collective (as he puts it, 'a dialectic between individual desire and fantasy and the collective nature of language and reception'),[7] here attention will be directed to the first point of the essay, which has been persistently overlooked and in which Freud illuminates the interrelatedness between literary activity and childhood, especially as Bataille and Blanchot seem to pick up the threads of the Freudian conjecture in their definitions of literature. In *La Littérature et le mal* literature is defined by Bataille as a return to, and of, childhood: 'La littérature, je l'ai, lentement, voulu montrer, c'est l'enfance enfin retrouvée' [I wanted to prove that literature is a return to childhood].[8] In *L'Espace littéraire* writing is linked by Blanchot to fascination: 'Écrire, c'est disposer le langage sous la fascination' [To write is to let fascination rule language]. In turn, fascination is traced back to childhood: 'Que notre enfance nous

---

4 Freud, 'Creative Writers and Daydreaming', p. 141.

5 Peter Brooks, *Psychoanalysis and Storytelling* (Oxford & Cambridge, MA: Blackwell, 1994), p. 27.

6 As Jameson writes in favour of the essay: '[F]ar from using the identification of literary productivity with private fantasy as a pretext for "reducing" the former to the latter, on the contrary [the essay] very specifically enumerates the theoretical difficulties such an identification must face' (Fredric Jameson, 'Imaginary and Symbolic in Lacan: Marxism, Psychoanalytic Criticism and the Problem of the Subject', in *Literature and Psychoanalysis: The Question of Reading: Otherwise*, ed. by Shoshana Felman (Baltimore, MD: Johns Hopkins University Press, 1982), pp. 338–95 (pp. 339–40)).

7 Jameson, 'Imaginary and Symbolic in Lacan', p. 342.

8 Bataille, 'Avant-Propos', in *La Littérature et le mal*, p. 172; Bataille, 'Preface', *Literature and Evil*, p. x.

fascine, cela arrive parce que l'enfance est le moment de la fascination' [If our childhood fascinates us, this happens because childhood is the moment of fascination].[9]

However, the Bataillean return to childhood, echoing to some extent the Freudian conception of the uncanny, rather than a homecoming turns out to be *unheimlich*; and Blanchotian fascination is a threatening and disarming moment rather than a moment of joy or pleasure. In this respect, Bataille's and Blanchot's conjoining of literature and childhood problematizes the idea of revival and recovery of an earlier condition that underlines the Freudian principle of constancy. Nonetheless, if we momentarily put aside the dimension of play that Freud associates with the child and, analogically, with the writer's imaginative activity, the child – the focal point of psychoanalysis in many ways – calls attention to, as Christopher Fynsk has argued, 'questions of general import concerning the human relation to language'.[10] Fynsk reminds us that the *in-fans*, as its etymology attests, is without language: it does not speak.[11] In this sense, the advent of the subject through language happens as a result of the death of the *infans* and also brings it forth. In other words, the death of the child marks and haunts the origin of our relation to language. Additionally, the Freudian primal scene, which triggers an enigma which the child cannot interpret, is close to Bataille's and Blanchot's conception of the literary experience in terms of a response to an alterity (rather than in terms of active interpretative mastery).

In *Freud, Proust and Lacan: Theory as Fiction* Malcolm Bowie opens his first chapter, dedicated to 'Freud's dreams of knowledge', with an epigraph by the Italian composer Giuseppe Verdi.[12] Verdi's epigram, 'Let us return to the past: that will be progress', offers a

---

9 Blanchot, 'La Solitude essentielle', pp. 31, 30; Blanchot, 'The Essential Solitude', p. 33. Showing how fascination unsettles passivity and activity by enacting a somehow active passivity, Blanchot notes how the fascinated child renders the mother fascinating: 'C'est parce que l'enfant est fasciné que la mère est fascinante' [[I]t is because the child is fascinated that the mother is fascinating] (Blanchot, 'La Solitude essentielle', p. 30; Blanchot, 'The Essential Solitude', p. 33).

10 Christopher Fynsk, 'Introduction', in *Infant Figures: The Death of the Infans and Other Scenes of Origin* (Stanford, CA: Stanford University Press, 2000), pp. 1–8 (p. 1).

11 The Latin term *in-fans* derives from the Latin *for, fari* and from the Greek *phemi* [I speak] and means the one who does not (yet) speak.

12 Malcolm Bowie, 'Freud's Dreams of Knowledge', in Malcom Bowie, *Freud, Proust, and Lacan: Theory as Fiction* (Cambridge: Cambridge University Press,

foretaste of the Freudian dream of knowledge.[13] Indeed, passion for the origin – a primary event, a primary scene – animates Freud and psychoanalysis. Moreover, the origin, the original persistently looked for, is understood in terms of anteriority and depth and is endowed with an exegetic power. Drawing on the theme of anteriority, which haunts and determines the Freudian enterprise, Bowie defines psychoanalysis, as well as archaeology, as 'the quest for, and the systematic study of, anterior states'.[14] Bowie, lingering over Freud's archaeological metaphors, goes on to add that this turning back, this stepping backwards towards the anterior, is due to the fact that for Freud 'that which came before, whether in a life of civilization or in the life of a mind' has a considerable influence on 'that which is'.[15] This anterior origin, the conception of origin as anterior and past, is also linked with layering and profundity. As Bowie remarks, the Freudian credo, inherited from the sciences of stratification, could be resumed as follows: 'that which is earlier is deeper', 'that which is deeper is closer to the origins'.[16] Finally, the depths are elevated to the guarantors of meaning, since 'it is only in the origin that scientific explanations can find their guarantee'.[17] Firmly believing not only in the indestructability of the past – be it a psychical or an archaeological object – but also, and perhaps more crucially, in the ability of the analytical and the archaeological endeavour to bring to light the buried and the inaccessible, Freud's dream of knowledge seems at first glance to be, as Malcolm Bowie suggests, synonymous with 'explanatory completeness'.[18] In this dialectic of burial and excavation, Bowie writes, 'the traumatic event "explains" the neurotic symptom just as the prior existence of Minoan-Mycenean civilization "explains" the glorious richness of Greek art'.[19]

1987), pp. 13–44. (p. 13). Verdi's saying is part of his correspondence with the librarian of the Conservatorio in Naples, Francesco Florimo.

13   Charles Osborne, *Letters of Giuseppe Verdi*, ed. and trans. by Charles Osborne (London: Victor Gollancz, 1971), p. 167.

14   Malcolm Bowie, 'Freud's Dreams of Knowledge', p. 18.

15   Malcolm Bowie, 'Freud's Dreams of Knowledge', p. 18.

16   Malcolm Bowie, 'Freud's Dreams of Knowledge', p. 23. More precisely, Bowie stages these two mottos as the teachings of the sciences of stratification (that is, archaeology, geology and palaeontology) handed on to psychoanalysis.

17   Malcolm Bowie, 'Freud's Dreams of Knowledge', p. 23. This is the third motto/teaching from the sciences of stratification handed on to psychoanalysis.

18   Malcolm Bowie, 'Freud's Dreams of Knowledge', p. 24.

19   Malcolm Bowie, 'Freud's Dreams of Knowledge', p. 24.

As becomes clear, the Freudian dream of knowledge, in its aspiration to decipher traces of the past, does not simply implicate the act of narration but intrinsically *is* a narrative. The talking cure, the method posited by Freud, consists of the moving from an incoherent, disordered, unintelligible narrative (an insufficient account of the event) towards a more coherent, connected, consistent narrative (a more adequate account of the past event).[20] Defining the talking cure in terms of a 'moving back' and a 'linking', Peter Brooks notes: '[M]oving back from present symptoms, and the incoherent narrative offered in explanation of them, to the traumatic events [...], then the linking of events in an uninterrupted causal series, provides a narrative that is itself curative'.[21]

Additionally, Peter Brooks shows how this motif of 'moving back', the quest for the origin, is thematized in the nineteenth-century novel. In his essay 'Freud's Masterplot' Brooks convincingly argues that the itinerary of the main character in *Great Expectations* – Dickens's novel standing in for the great nineteenth-century novel – seemingly opposes, but essentially falls into step with, Verdi's epigram, 'Let us return to the past; it will be a step forward', since all his steps forward are ultimately nothing but a return to his past (what Pip calls that old spell of his childhood). '[E]ach of Pip's choices in the novel', Brooks suggests, 'while consciously life-furthering, forward oriented, in fact leads back to the insoluble question of origins'.[22] 'Pip's story', Brooks goes on:

> while ostensibly the search for progress, ascension and metamorphosis, may after all be the narrative of an attempted homecoming: of an effort to reach the assertion of origin through ending, to find the same in the different, the time before in the time after.[23]

Brooks concludes that – despite the fact that the ending conflates with the origin, the different with the same, the time after with the time before – the novel finally offers more than their happy coincidence,

---

20 In this respect, the talking cure derives its power and persuasiveness in relation to its object, the narrated event, as well as from the internal relationship of the elements that constitute the narrative chain itself.

21 Brooks, *Psychoanalysis and Storytelling*, p. 49.

22 Peter Brooks, 'Freud's Masterplot: Questions of Narrative', in *Literature and Psychoanalysis*, ed. by Felman, pp. 280–300 (p. 298).

23 Brooks, 'Freud's Masterplot', p. 298. Here Brooks does not commit the common error of simply psychoanalyzing the literary character since what is at stake are the beginning and the ending of the text itself.

since 'recognition cannot abolish textuality' and the textual middle, in its oscillatory *in-betweenness*, is the truth of the narrative. Taking into account this remark, it could be suggested that literary and psychoanalytic truth (the space of literature and analysis) challenge and throw into confusion the very notions of origin and ending, rendering them problematic as such.[24] The value of the psychoanalytic model – and its convergence with literature – lies in its contribution to the determination (that is, the recasting) of the concept of truth. More crucially, the present analysis moves away from the prevailing view, which comprehends the truth of psychoanalysis – and its analogy with novelistic truth – in terms of plausibility, towards an understanding of psychoanalytic – and literary – truth in terms of impossibility. Against the consideration of truth in terms of coherence, continuity and persuasiveness (the redefinition of truth as what is plausible – in regard to the recounted event – and well-formed – in regard to the narrative chain itself), the Lacanian return to Freud brings forth a radical recasting of truth as heterogeneous, spasmodic and erratic which makes advances to the Real.

In Lacan's essay 'La Chose freudienne' truth becomes the narrator of a strange apologue, truth speaks (itself) and says the following:

> Je vagabonde dans ce que vous tenez pour être le moins vrai par essence: dans le rêve, dans le défi au sens de la pointe la plus gongorique et le nonsense du calembour le plus grotesque, dans le hasard, et non pas dans sa loi, mais dans sa contingence.
>
> [I wander about in what you regard as least true by its nature: in dreams, in the way the most far-fetched witticisms and the most grotesque nonsense of jokes defy meaning and in chance – not in its law, but rather in its contingency.] [25]

The most striking aspect of the passage is, of course, that Lacan stages the truth while it speaks, as that which speaks. However, before commenting on this quasi-performative element of truth

---

24 Brooks posits the obstinacy of the textual middle as a defiance of the linearity of recognition as follows: 'Yet recognition cannot abolish textuality, does not annul the middle which, in its oscillation between blindness and recognition, between origins and endings, is the truth of the narrative text' (Brooks, 'Freud's Masterplot', p. 296).

25 Jacques Lacan, 'La Chose freudienne ou Sens du retour à Freud en psychanalyse', in Jacques Lacan, *Écrits I* (Paris: Seuil, 1999 [1966]), pp. 398–433 (p. 407); Jacques Lacan, 'The Freudian Thing, or the Meaning of the Return to Freud in Psychoanalysis', in Jacques Lacan, *Écrits*, trans. by Bruce Fink (New York: Norton, 2006 [2002]), pp. 334–63 (p. 342).

attention will be directed to the distinct conception of truth which ensues from this essay. Against the common understanding of the term, truth converges on conceit, is found in dreams (rather than in reality), wanders (rather than being fixed) and defies, obstructs, suspends and interrupts (rather than makes, promotes, advances and furnishes us with) sense. Put briefly, an irregular conception of truth comes forth which does not evoke reality in terms of solidity and constancy. In other words, and in an attempt to gloss the above displacing in a Lacanian way, truth is not challenged in its relation with reality (the truth as revelation or adequation, presented or represented, uncovered or recovered, constructed or reconstructed), but in so far as it drifts towards the Real. However, before looking into Lacan's return to Freud, we first need to turn to Freud and consider his conception of desire, not as wish-fulfilment, but as what transcends – or rather decentres – being. Freud unties being from presence and permanence, the analytic process from interpretation (putting forward the primacy of interruption) and theory from firmness and rigidity.

As Bowie points out, for Freud the intellectual life of neurotics involves, first, a reversal and, second, a shift: in the reversal the thinking-process is not a sublimation of sexuality but becomes itself a source of (sexual) pleasure; in the shift pleasure is not linked to the content of thought but to the act of thinking itself: '[T]he intellectual feeling, so much desired, of having found a solution recedes more and more into the distance'.[26] The thought-process of neurotics (thinking in vain, in detachment from external material), Bowie argues, unfolds the ineliminable conditions of thought in general and Freud's theoretical constructions and writings in particular. The transformational process, the primary object of psychoanalytic inquiry (how an unconscious experience transforms itself), turns out to concern – and transform – primarily psychoanalytic inquiry. In this regard, as Bowie remarks, 'the psychoanalyst's constructions were similar in function with the delusions of his patients'.[27] Consequently, the Freudian dream of knowledge recedes from 'explanatory completeness' to find itself momentarily (un)realized in provisional, partial constructions that keep changing. Against the solidity of

26 Sigmund Freud, 'Notes upon a Case of Obsessional Neurosis', in *The Standard Edition of the Complete Psychological Works*, ed. by James Strachey, 24 vols (London: The Hogarth Press, 1953–74), x: *The Cases of 'Little Hans' and the Rat Man* (1955), pp. 155–318 (p. 245).

27 Malcolm Bowie, 'Freud's Dreams of Knowledge', p. 43.

theoretical constructions, Bowie and Freud put forward theory as fiction, thereby reconfiguring both the theoretical and the fictitious as that which does not last. Desire is not desire for the end (of solution), since, as Freud contends, 'the intellectual feeling, so much desired, of having found a solution recedes'. This chapter suggests that this receding is not to be understood as simply enacting a temporality of detour which will make the end even more gratifying, since theory as fiction, theory in its entwinement with fiction, shifts away from fulfilment and becomes concurrently articulated and unconsumed.[28]

Taking into consideration two key Freudian elements, namely dreams and children's play, and radicalizing their reading in terms of interruption (against continuity) and repetition (against mastery), this chapter dissociates the analytic process from interpretation and psychoanalytic theory from the scopic tradition and associates them with interruption and repetition respectively. In his study of dreams in 'Beyond the Pleasure Principle' (1920), an essay which marks a turning point since views and principles of earlier texts are revisited, Freud attests to the fact that dreams, in the case of traumatic neuroses, rather than enabling and facilitating one's sleep result in frightful awakenings. In this respect, as Critchley remarks, the primary function of dreams proves to be not the continuation of sleep, but its interruption: '[T]he original function of dreams is not the dreamwork (*die Traumarbeit*) that permits the sleeper to sleep on, it is rather the interruption of sleep, *die Trauma-Arbeit*, that is beyond the pleasure principle'.[29] Similarly, in the case of the famous *fort/da* game, the game of disappearance and return invented by Freud's grandson, among the many questions the child's repetitive gesture of loss and retrieval raises (questions of displacement – from the mother's disappearance to the toy's disappearance, transformation – of an unpleasant experience to a pleasurable one, entry into language – by means of the baby's exclamations 'Oh', 'Ah'), what interests us particularly here is whether repetition should be considered a movement from passivity to mastery (as the child's control of loss and, thereby, in Freudian terms, still bound to the primacy of the pleasure principle), or whether repetition needs to be reconsidered as primal (that is, in

---

28 Brooks opts for this temporality of detour, in which end and detour constantly nourish each other. For Brooks, 'desire is the wish for the end, for fulfilment but fulfilment delayed' (Brooks, 'Freud's Masterplot', p. 299).

29 Simon Critchley, 'The Original Traumatism: Levinas and Psychoanalysis', in Simon Critchley, *Ethics – Politics – Subjectivity: Essays on Derrida, Levinas, & Contemporary French Thought* (London and New York: Verso, 1999), pp. 181–97 (p. 193).

Freudian terms, beyond – and distinguishable from – the pleasure principle).[30] Drawing on and moving beyond the function of dreams and the significance of the *fort/da* game, this chapter shows the centrality of interruption and repetition in the analytic process and theory.

The Analytic Process: From Interpretation to Interruption

The Freudian revisiting of origins proves to be more complicated and less straightforward than initially anticipated. Freud's great discovery, the unconscious, persistently defies the characteristics of anteriority, depth and the etiologic as posited at the beginning of this chapter. First, in a similar manner to the Faulknerian past, which claims 'actually it's not even past', the Freudian unconscious is constantly and overwhelmingly present, in jokes, dreams and slips of the tongue. Second, as Freud makes clear in *The Interpretation of Dreams* (1899), unconscious desire should not be equated with the secret and what is hidden beneath the surface with the latent content (the dream-thought) behind the manifest form (the dream-text), since the unconscious is not (in the) latent but *between* the latent and the manifest. In this sense, Freud on the one hand directs our attention to dreams, rendering them meaningful rather than meaningless, worth being looked into rather than ignored; on the other hand, for Freud our attention should focus on the form of the dream rather than on its hidden meaning.[31] Finally, in his essay dedicated to Serge Leclaire, 'La psychanalyse comme anti-herméneutique' (1994), Jean Laplanche, invoking Freud in support and supporting Freud, insists on and

---

30   For these two readings of the *fort/da* game, see Brooks, 'Freud's Masterplot', pp. 286–87.

31   Freud writes: 'I used at one time to find it extraordinarily difficult to accustom readers to the distinction between the manifest content of dreams and the latent dream-thoughts. [...] The need to interpret (it) would be ignored. But now that analysts at least have become reconciled to replacing the manifest dream by the meaning revealed by its interpretation, many of them have become guilty of falling into another confusion which they cling to with an equal obstinacy. *They seek to find the essence of dreams in their latent content* and in so doing they overlook the distinction between the latent dream thoughts and the dream-work. At bottom, dreams are nothing but a particular form of thinking [...]. *It is the dream-work which creates that form, and it alone is the essence of dreaming*' (Sigmund Freud, *The Interpretation of Dreams*, ed. and trans. by James Strachey (London: Penguin, 1976), p. 650) (my emphasis).

fosters the anti-interpretative axis of the analytic method. Aware of the paradoxical attempt to dissociate the discipline which initiated us into the interpretation of dreams from the burden of interpretation, he writes: 'Comment la psychanalyse – ne serait-ce qu'avec son ouvrage fondamental intitulé L'*interprétation du rêve* – ne rencontrerait-elle pas tout naturellement le mouvement herméneutique [...] précisément comme théorie, méthode et pratique de l'interprétation?' [How can psychoanalysis – if only on the basis of its foundational work, *The Interpretation of Dreams* – not be directly connected to the hermeneutic movement [...], precisely in so far as it is a theory, method and practice of interpretation?].[32]

Hermeneutics is defined by Laplanche as a process of reading – 'd'un texte, d'une destinée, d'un *Dasein*' [of a text, a destiny, a *Dasein*] – which provides 'a translation code or a key' to the extent that it is based on 'a pre-comprehension or proto-comprehension'.[33] On the contrary, for Laplanche psychoanalysis and, more precisely, the analytic method are anti-hermeneutic, anti-exegetic (inasmuch as they offer no key or code but only individual and spontaneous associations) and anti-synthetic (in so far as personal associations defy and dissociate themselves from pre-established chains of meaning). Moreover, to return to the question of origins but from the angle of the origins of the method itself, psychoanalysis began as the study of neurosis, which emerges precisely as, and due to, a failure of synthesis. Laplanche posits the method as literally an ana-lysis, that is, a *lysis*, a loosening, a disintegration, a breaking down (from *lyein*: to unbind, to compromise integrity):

> La méthode est analytique au sens propre du terme, associative-dissociative, déliante. On la dirait 'déconstructive' – et le terme de *Rückbildung* est bien présent chez Freud – si le mot n'avait ensuite été accaparé et acclimaté dans une philosophie exogène.

---

32 Jean Laplanche, 'La psychanalyse comme anti-herméneutique', in Jean Laplanche, *Entre séduction et inspiration: l'homme* (Paris: Presses Universitaires de France, 1999), pp. 243–62 (p. 243); Jean Laplanche, 'Psychoanalysis as Anti-Hermeneutics', trans. by Luke Thurston, *Radical Philosophy*, 79 (1996), 7–12 (p. 7).

33 Laplanche puts it as follows: 'une lecture qui se fonde, évidemment, sur une précompréhension or protocompréhension préalable' [a reading based on a pre-comprehension or proto-comprehension] (Laplanche, 'La psychanalyse comme anti-herméneutique', p. 244; Laplanche, 'Psychoanalysis as Anti-Hermeneutics', p. 7).

[The method is ana-lytic in the true sense of the term, associative/dissociative, unbinding. One might call it 'deconstructive' – and the term *Rückbildung* is certainly there in Freud – if the word had not subsequently been monopolized, adapted by a philosophy elsewhere.]³⁴

The analytic process is not simply an interplay between filling in (the gaps) and opening up (calling for more and more interpretation); rather, it defies and subverts the interpretative act as such. As Ellie Ragland-Sullivan observes, the analytic method involves interruption rather than interpretation. The analyst intervenes not by filling in the gaps and reconstituting the thread of an incoherent narrative: the analyst punctuates the narrative by interrupting it: 'The technique relies less on interpretation, be it surface or deep, than on interruption. [...] The analyst interrupts to punctuate the discourse and to introduce a sense that eventually can be grasped by the analysand'.³⁵ Drawing on Laplanche's remark, and bringing in the psychoanalytic axiom 'analysis again and again', could it be, as Barbara Johnson suggests, that the speech of analysis, *la parole pleine*, against its connotation of fullness, approaches Derridean *writing*? In Johnson's words, '[i]s it not equally possible to regard what Lacan calls "full speech" as being *full* of what Derrida calls *writing*?'.³⁶

In his reading of Freud's essay 'Constructions in Analysis' Peter Brooks comments on how analytic reconstructions ultimately turn out to be constructions, as the dropping of the *re* in the title of the essay suggests. With regard to the Freudian talking cure, Brooks traces a shift of emphasis from the narrative chain itself ('the coherent, ordered, chronological story') towards the inseparability of the story (the events, the raw material, the Russian 'fabula', Genette's 'histoire') and narrating (telling, Genette's 'narration').³⁷ In this

---

34 Laplanche, 'La psychanalyse comme anti-herméneutique', p. 252; Laplanche, 'Psychoanalysis as Anti-Hermeneutics', p. 10.

35 Ellie Ragland-Sullivan, 'Lacan's Four Fundamental Concepts of Psychoanalysis', in Ellie Ragland-Sullivan, *Jacques Lacan and the Philosophy of Psychoanalysis* (Urbana, IL and Chicago, IL: University of Illinois Press), pp. 68–129 (p. 83).

36 Barbara Johnson, 'The Frame of Reference: Poe, Lacan, Derrida', in *Literature and Psychoanalysis*, ed. by Felman, pp. 457–505 (p. 473).

37 For Brooks, who insists on the place and the role of the reader, this shift is crucial as it brings about a redirection of focus as well as a temporal rearrangement: first, the act of narrating becomes significant inasmuch as the story (the narrative, Genette's 'récit') emerges due to, in and through narrating; second, the story (the material, Genette's 'histoire') turns out to come not before but after the narrative (the story as 'récit'). As Brooks writes: 'Though we tend to

respect, for Brooks as well as for Freud, narrative truth is redefined in terms of plausibility (and not of verifiability), since the aim is not the re-collection, the re-capturing or the re-construction of the events, but their 'figuring' in a construction. (The term 'figuring' is meant here as both a depiction and an assumption.) Brooks writes:

> Thus we learn that parts of the story of the past may not ever be recalled by the person whose story it is, or was, but may nonetheless be *figured* in a construction of them by the analyst-narratee – a construction which is unsubstantiated, unverifiable, yet carries conviction.[38]

Consequently, for Brooks narrative truth (be it analytic or literary):

> seems to be a matter of conviction, derived from the plausibility, and well-formedness of the narrative discourse, and also from […] its power to persuade us that things must have happened this way, since here lies the only explanatory narrative, the only one that will make sense of things.[39]

As a step towards approaching the Real, the most problematic (and elusive) term of Lacan's trilogy, this discussion now introduces the end of storytelling, as formulated most notably by Walter Benjamin's famous essay 'The Storyteller' (1936). Against Brooks's standpoint, which considers storytelling to be our ability to make sense, Benjamin brings in, abruptly, the end of storytelling, our inability to make a story. In so doing, Benjamin opposes the loss of the art of storytelling to the framework revolving around the loss of origin. Benjamin's main thesis is, as Shoshana Felman notes, that 'storytelling is lost to the twentieth century' since 'it has become impossible to tell a story'.[40] The reason for this loss is the dumbness caused by the First World War. The muteness of the body, as Felman puts it, due to the deafening noise of explosions, reduces narration to silence: 'Resonating to this dumbness of the body is the storyteller's dumbness'.[41] As she writes further, highlighting the dimension of the loss of narration: 'The First World War is the first war that can no

---

talk – as Freud does – of the "story" as primary, a moment's reflection allows us to see that it is in fact derivative of the "discourse", the product of the reader's interpretation of a normalized chronology from what the narrative discourse gives us' (Brooks, *Psychoanalysis and Storytelling*, p. 74 n. 8).

38 Brooks, *Psychoanalysis and Storytelling*, p. 59.
39 Brooks, *Psychoanalysis and Storytelling*, p. 59.
40 Shoshana Felman, 'Benjamin's Silence', *Critical Inquiry*, 25 (1999), 201–34 (p. 205).
41 Felman, 'Benjamin's Silence', p. 206.

longer be narrated. Its witnesses and its participants have lost their stories'.[42] In parallel, Felman, alluding to Benjamin's 'Theses on the Philosophy of History' (1940), elaborates what she terms 'his second theory of silence': here speechlessness arises due to World War II and affects not literature (and storytelling) but historical narration:

> [L]ike the storyteller who falls silent or returns mute from the First World War, the historian or the theorist of history facing the conflagration of the Second World War is equally reduced to speechlessness: no ready-made conceptual or discursive tool [...] turns out to be sufficient to explain the nature of this war.[43]

Psychoanalysis revolves around a comparable muteness and points to an analogous deficiency of conceptual and discursive tools. Indeed, what began as an aspiration to explanatory completeness and a model of symptomatic reading (moving from the surface towards the deeper, the hidden truth of the primary event) steadily brings forth an asymptotic relation, precisely due to the overwhelming power of the primary event which defies all attempts at mastery and understanding. Alluding to the paradoxical constitution of the analytic process and delineating it as a tensional space, Leclaire writes:

> D'une part, on dit que le travail analytique consiste à rendre conscient ce qui est inconscient; de l'autre part il est avéré que l'inconscient en tant que tel est irréductible, et qu'il échappe, de par sa nature, à toute saisie consciente.
>
> [On the one hand it is often said that analytical work consists in rendering conscious the unconscious; on the other, it is granted that the unconscious, as such, is irreducible, and that it eludes, by its very nature, any conscious grasp.][44]

Due to the nature of its object (the unconscious), the psychoanalytic endeavour (the representation of the unconscious) raises wider questions of representation and representability. The elusive and the irreducible enact a representational crisis which establishes and

---

42 Felman, 'Benjamin's Silence', p. 207.

43 Felman, 'Benjamin's Silence', p. 208.

44 Serge Leclaire, 'L'Inscription inconsciente: une autre mémoire', in Serge Leclaire, *Écrits pour la psychanalyse 1. Demeures de l'ailleurs. 1954–1993* (Paris: Seuil, 1996), pp. 177–86 (p. 180); Serge Leclaire, 'Unconscious Inscription: Another Memory', in *Psychoanalysis, Creativity, and Literature*, ed. by Alan Roland (New York: Columbia University Press, 1978), pp. 75–84 (p. 79).

increases the points of contact between art and analysis (bringing about 'the art of analysis'). Moreover, Leclaire underlines how this crisis of representation does not simply arise due to the nature – the distinguishing, or rather the disquieting, features – of the unconscious, but mainly due to its *presence*, since 'l'inconscient est, plus que tout autre chose au monde présent, là, "*hic et nunc*", dans tous les actes et paroles de notre vie la plus quotidienne' [the unconscious is, more than any other thing in the world, present, here, *hic et nunc*, in all the actions and utterances of our day-to-day lives].[45] The unconscious, whose presence is to be comprehended along the semantic axes of the spatial and the temporal, here and now, unmediated and immediate, misplaces and disrupts precisely 'that which is'.

To emphasize this Leclaire makes an effort to demystify, to strip off the aura of the (traumatic/unconscious) event. In this attempt he suggests and stages the following scenario: someone decides to confide some inspired, improvised thoughts to a recording machine; the next morning, (s)he realizes that the needle has been deceptive and that nothing has been recorded. Leclaire raises the following question: 'Que reste-t-il de votre géniale improvisation?' [What is left of your inspired improvisation?].[46] He offers the following answer – and some advice:

> À en juger par la violence de vos sentiments à cet instant précis, *infiniment plus* que si la machine vous renvoyait le reflet de votre voix. […] Un conseil, si vous en avez alors le courage, prenez cette fois du papier et un crayon et vous verrez que ce qui vous vient sous le coup de cette perte sera *bien meilleur* que ce que vous avez énoncé la veille au soir, comme si le nouveau texte, fort de cette perte, retrouvait les sources inconscientes de ce que l'on appelle la création. Et si ce n'est pas encore assez bon, vous n'avez qu'à perdre votre manuscrit dans le métro! Le tout est ne pas tenter de reproduire ce qui a été perdu, mais de prendre appui sur cette perte.
>
> [Judging by the violence of your feelings at that very moment, *infinitely more* than if the machine had yielded the reflection of your own voice. […] A bit of advice: if you have the courage to do so at the time, pick up paper and pencil, and you'll see that what comes to you, under the influence of this loss, will be *far better* than what you had dictated the night before. It is as if your new text, strengthened

---

45 Leclaire, 'L'Inscription inconsciente', p. 184; Leclaire, 'Unconscious Inscription', p. 83.

46 Leclaire, 'L'Inscription inconsciente', p. 181; Leclaire, 'Unconscious Inscription', p. 80.

by this loss, has discovered the unconscious sources of what we call creativity. And if this isn't enough, you need only to lose your manuscript in the subway. The main thing is not to try to reproduce what has been lost, but to make use of this loss.]⁴⁷

Such a framing of the problem of loss radically recasts the significance of origin. If, as Leclaire suggests, what is left is 'infinitely more' and what is written is 'far better', the significance of loss seems to give its place to the significance of repetition. In so doing, the psychoanalytic project seems to shift away from the preoccupation with the lost, absent, inaccessible origin and to gesture towards the problematization of the idea of unity. The remnant – being more – and the (re)written – being better (and better) – contribute to the determination of the concept of double and doubling, suggesting, as Barbara Johnson does, that 'one equals two' (1=2). In her discussion of doubleness and doubles Johnson asks: 'What is the relation between a divided unity and a duality? Are the two *two's* synonymous? […] If the doubles are forever redividing or multiplying, does the number "2" really apply? If 1=2, how can 2=1+1?'.⁴⁸

As Lacan suggests in his essay 'Fonction et champ de la parole et du langage', the most fundamental and unsettling double is that of reality as it emerges in and as speech. For Lacan, we (and our thinking) are embedded in language:

> L'ambiguïté de la révélation hystérique du passé ne tient pas tant à la vacillation de son contenu entre l'imaginaire et le réel, car il se situe dans l'un et dans l'autre. Ce n'est pas non plus qu'elle soit mensongère. C'est qu'elle nous présente la naissance de la vérité dans la parole, et que par là nous nous heurtons à la réalité de ce qui n'est ni vrai, ni faux.
>
> [The reason for the ambiguity of hysterical revelation of the past is not so much the vacillation of its content between the imaginary and reality, for it is situated in both. Nor is it the fact that it is made up of lies. It is that it presents us with the birth of truth in speech, and thereby brings us up against the reality of what is neither true or false.]⁴⁹

---

47   Leclaire, 'L'Inscription inconsciente', p. 181; Leclaire, 'Unconscious Inscription', p. 80 (my emphasis).

48   Johnson, 'The Frame of Reference', p. 472.

49   Jacques Lacan, 'Fonction et champ de la parole et du langage', in Lacan, *Écrits I*, pp. 235–321 (p. 254); Jacques Lacan, 'The Function and Field of Speech in Psychoanalysis', in Lacan, *Écrits*, pp. 197–268 (p. 212).

The passage, first, displays what Bowie terms 'Lacan's ambitious philosophy of the human', in which everything counts and is embraced as true (lies, the Imaginary and the Real).[50] Second, it underlines how words have made us and continue to do so. In Bowie's remark, 'it is the peculiar privilege of man the language-user to remain oblivious, while making things with words, of the extent to which words have made, and continue to make, him'.[51] Third, and perhaps more crucially, read together with the above-mentioned essay 'La Chose freudienne' the passage elucidates the significance of the fact that truth speaks. Speech bears and gives birth to truth – to a truth, neither true or false, as there is no signified (no truth) in a pure, separable form. In his later essay 'La Science et la vérité' (1965) Lacan sheds further light on the fact that truth does not speak *about* but merely speaks[52] when he writes: '[I]l n'y a pas de métalangage [...], nul langage ne saurait dire le vrai sur le vrai, puisque la vérité se fonde de ce qu'elle parle et qu'elle n'a pas d'autre moyen pour ce faire' [[T]here is no such thing as a metalanguage [...], no language being able to say the truth about truth, since truth is grounded in the fact that truth speaks, and that it has no other means by which to become grounded].[53] In a similar way, theory, as suggested by Lacan, does not write about but mainly writes and (re)writes. In its entwinement with language, theory approaches the act of writing.

Psychoanalytic Theory: From Seeing to Writing

In the essay 'La psychanalyse comme anti-herméneutique' and in his effort to dissociate psychoanalysis from exegetic reduction, Jean Laplanche raises the following question: 'Une théorie, pour quoi faire? Pour maîtriser une énigme, proposée par le monde des adultes, à l'enfant' [What is a theory for? To master an enigma, which the adult world offers to the child].[54] In this definition of theory as a

---

50 Malcolm Bowie, *Lacan* (London: Fontana, 1991), p. 111.

51 Malcolm Bowie, *Lacan*, p. 109. In this respect, the relationship between language and the unconscious is twofold: the unconscious exerts pressure upon language, but equally language creates the unconscious.

52 He claims: 'Moi, la verité, je parle' [I, truth, speak] (Jacques Lacan, 'La Science et la verité', in Jacques Lacan, *Écrits II* (Paris: Seuil, 1999 [1966]), pp. 335–58 (p. 347); Jacques Lacan, 'Science and Truth', in Lacan, *Écrits*, pp. 726–45 (p. 736)).

53 Lacan, 'La Science et la verité', p. 348; Lacan, 'Science and Truth', p. 737.

54 Laplanche, 'La psychanalyse comme anti-herméneutique', p. 250; Laplanche, 'Psychoanalysis as Anti-Hermeneutics', p. 7.

mastery of enigmas, the question which subsequently arises is how we are to give an account of and specify a theory which revolves precisely around an enigma, that of childhood, and posits the child as its central figure, the child who we, adults, once were. In other words, how could the figure of the child contribute to theory – or rather, how does the child upset the adult world of theory? Additionally, how can the enigmatic be approached other than from a position of mastery or, as Laplanche warns us, its exoneration as 'mysterious', 'hard to get at' or 'inexplicable'?[55]

Theory is not only linked with the mastery of enigmas, as Laplanche argues, but also with sight and seeing; or rather, theory becomes associated with mastery in so far as it is associated with seeing. In *Lacan, le maître absolu* [*Lacan: The Absolute Master*] Mikkel Borch-Jacobsen designates the history of Western philosophy 'L'histoire de l'œil' [The Story of the Eye] and inscribes Lacan – or, more specifically, Lacan's mirror stage – within that scopic tradition.[56] Quoting Heidegger, Borch-Jacobsen underlines the etymological coupling between theory and seeing: 'The Greeks conceived knowledge as a kind of seeing and viewing, a state of affairs suggested by the expression "theoretical", an expression that is still common today. In it, the words *thea*, "view", and *horan*, "seeing" [...], speak'.[57] Additionally, Borch-Jacobsen points out that knowledge has been thought of in terms of vision and seeing, since being has been thought of in terms of presence and permanence. Indeed, as Heidegger writes: 'Because Being means presence and permanence, "seeing" is especially apt to serve as an explanation for the grasping of what is present and what is permanent'.[58] With particular reference to the Platonic Idea, Heidegger shows how *idea* acquires a double sense, that of Being and that of vision: 'According to Plato's doctrine, Being is idea, visuality, presence as outward appearance'.[59] He continues: 'As visual, Being is presence, but at the same time is what man brings before the eyes'.[60]

---

55 Laplanche, 'La psychanalyse comme anti-herméneutique', p. 257; Laplanche, 'Psychoanalysis as Anti-Hermeneutics', p. 11.

56 Mikkel Borch-Jacobsen, *Lacan, le maître absolu* (Paris: Flammarion, 2015 [1990]), pp. 72–77; Mikkel Borch-Jacobsen, *Lacan: The Absolute Master*, trans. by Douglas Brick (Stanford, CA: Stanford University Press, 1991), pp. 53–57.

57 Martin Heidegger, *Nietzsche*, ed. by David Farrell Krell, 4 vols (New York: Harper & Row, 1979–87), IV: *Nihilism* (1982), p. 167.

58 Heidegger, *Nietzsche*, IV: *Nihilism*, p. 167.

59 Heidegger, *Nietzsche*, IV: *Nihilism*, p. 173.

60 Heidegger, *Nietzsche*, IV: *Nihilism*, p. 173.

Consequently, following Heidegger's critique of the Cartesian *cogito* and the modern metaphysics of subjectivity, Borch-Jacobsen concludes that in the equation of Being to what is brought before the eyes 'begins the progressive transformation of the idea into perception and representation'.[61] As Borch-Jacobsen notes, in the Heideggerian critique of the Cartesian *cogito* 'I think' means 'I represent myself' and ultimately 'I see myself'. In this respect, Heidegger insists that 'every "I represent [I pose before myself] something" simultaneously represents a "myself" [poses me before myself]'.[62]

Borch-Jacobsen claims that Lacan, despite his aspiration to break from 'any philosophy directly issuing from the cogito', prolongs and completes this specular line of thought. This is due to the fact that in the Lacanian mirror stage, when the formation of the ego takes place, the ego comes forth outside itself, represented and posited in front of itself.[63] For Borch-Jacobsen, '[t]he Lacanian ego is the ego as it theorises itself, never as it feels itself or experiences itself'.[64] Nevertheless, while Lacan inscribes himself into this specular tradition he also reverses it. First, the mirror stage itself, and the Imaginary Order which arises from it, problematize the very notion of representation, underlining the idea that every representation is essentially a mis-representation. Second, Lacan introduces and insists on the primacy of the letter and the Symbolic Order, in which representation is further problematized since it corresponds to absence (the subject is represented insofar as it is excluded).

In the mirror stage the child is caught up in its mirror reflection. The child recognizes itself in its specular image, but this recognition already consists of a mis-recognition since the child who – in reality – feels itself fragmented sees itself – in its image, its *imago* – whole.[65] The Imaginary Order and the formation of the ego which arise along with the mirror stage consist of identification (the infant identifies with, and assumes, its specular image) and alienation (the self does not coincide with its image, yet the image becomes confused with

---

61 Borch-Jacobsen, *Lacan: The Absolute Master*, p. 54.

62 Heidegger, *Nietzsche*, IV: *Nihilism*, p. 106.

63 Borch-Jacobsen, *Lacan: The Absolute Master*, p. 56.

64 Borch-Jacobsen, *Lacan: The Absolute Master*, p. 57.

65 The Latin term *imago*, introduced in psychoanalytical theory by Jung, is used by Lacan to underline, apart from the visual component of the image, its subjective and emotional dimension, that is, the feelings associated with it. The term *imago* is widely used in Lacan's writings until 1950, whereas afterwards it is replaced by the term 'image'.

the self). As becomes clear, alienation for Lacan does not mean that the subject is alienated from itself, but rather that the subject *is* alienated from its very beginning. In this sense, Sean Homer defines alienation as the fact that 'the infant's realization (in both senses of the term: forming a distinct concept in the mind and becoming real) lies in an-other place'.[66] According to Lacan:

> [L]e stade du miroir est un drame dont la poussée interne se précipite de l'insuffisance à l'anticipation – et qui pour le sujet, pris au leurre de l'identification spatiale, machine les fantasmes qui se succèdent d'une image morcelée du corps à une forme que nous appellerons orthopédique de sa totalité – et à l'armure enfin assumée d'une identité aliénante, qui va marquer de sa structure rigide tout son développement mental.
>
> [[T]he mirror stage is a drama whose internal pressure pushes precipitously from insufficiency to anticipation – and for the subject caught up in the lure of spatial identification, turns out fantasies that proceed from a fragmented image of the body to what I will call an orthopedic form of its totality – and to the finally donned armor of an alienating identity that will mark his entire mental development with its rigid structure.][67]

The term 'stage' should, first, be understood temporally. However, and against its usual connotation, it should not be thought of as a precise period, a step or a phase in a process of development but rather as a dialectic of projection and anticipation. Additionally, the term should be understood spatially, in the sense that the formation of the ego – the image of mastery and wholeness – takes place outside the self as well as theatrically, in terms of a platform on which the subject's drama of non-coincidence takes place. Indeed, in the formation of the ego an irreducible and unbridgeable gap is introduced between the subject and the ego, its image, which will re-occur in the subject's relations with the external world (people and things). As we read in 'Le Stade du miroir':

> le point important est que cette forme [that is, the subject in the mirror stage, the *je-idéal*] situe l'instance du moi, dès avant sa détermination sociale, dans une ligne de fiction, à jamais irréductible pour le seul individu, – ou plutôt qui ne rejoindra qu'asymptotiquement le devenir

---

66 Sean Homer, *Jacques Lacan* (London and New York: Routledge, 2005), p. 26.

67 Jacques Lacan, 'Le Stade du miroir comme formateur de la fonction du Je', in Lacan, *Écrits I*, pp. 92–99 (p. 96); Jacques Lacan, 'The Mirror Stage as Formative of the *I* Function', in Lacan, *Écrits*, pp. 75–81 (p. 78).

du sujet, quel que soit le succès des synthèses dialectiques par quoi il doit résoudre en tant que *je* sa discordance avec sa propre réalité.

[the important point is that this form situates the agency known as the ego, prior to its social determination, in a fictional direction that will forever remain irreducible for any single individual or, rather, that will only asymptotically approach the subject's becoming, no matter how successful the dialectical syntheses by which he must resolve, as *I*, his discordance with his own reality.]⁶⁸

Consequently, the Imaginary is delimited by Lacan as visual (to the extent that it is the realm of images), fictive (inasmuch as it is illusory) and haunting (in so far as it has real effects on the subject's life). Additionally, it becomes synonymous with immobility, similarity and identification, since the subject constantly attempts to appropriate and invalidate (his/her) otherness in order to remain, in Malcolm Bowie's phrasing, 'what one is'.⁶⁹ As Bowie notes, 'the Imaginary is the scene of a desperate delusional attempt to be and remain "what one is" by gathering to oneself ever more instances of sameness, resemblance and self-replication'.⁷⁰

In contrast to the Imaginary, the Lacanian Symbolic order is the realm of language, difference and movement. While the Imaginary rests on a dual logic (a dual relation between the self and its specular image), the Symbolic involves a divisional logic (a relationship of exclusion between the subject and the signifier). The Symbolic brings forth representation in terms of absence, to the extent that the subject is represented in language by a stand-in: a personal pronoun ('I'), a name, or a denomination ('daughter of'). The subject is represented in, as well as excluded by, language, or rather it becomes represented inasmuch as it becomes excluded. In this respect, the Symbolic corresponds to the coming-into-being of the subject as well as of the unconscious, as that reality of the subject which is excluded in and due to the process of naming and representation. The unconscious is both bound together with and repressed by language, as Lacan's emblematic phrase 'the unconscious is the discourse of the Other' attests. As Bowie puts it: '[[T]he symbolic] is the realm of language,

---

68   Lacan, 'Le Stade du miroir', pp. 93–94; Lacan, 'The Mirror Stage', p. 76. Commenting on the passage, Jameson notes that it is not simply the mirror-image that is fictive (alienating), but that fiction, meant as fantasy and narration, plays a central role in the subsequent efforts of the subject to re-appropriate his/her alienated image (Jameson, 'Imaginary and Symbolic in Lacan', p. 353).

69   Malcolm Bowie, *Lacan*, p. 92.

70   Malcolm Bowie, *Lacan*, p. 92.

the unconscious and an otherness that remains other'.[71] He adds: 'It is a res publica that does not allow any of its members to be himself, keep himself to himself or recreate in his own image the things that lie beyond him'.[72]

The primacy and significance of the Symbolic as opposed to the Imaginary are put forward in Lacan's reading of Poe's 'The Purloined Letter' (1844). In 'Le séminaire sur la "Lettre volée"', Lacan reads Poe's story as an allegory of the signifier.[73] In Lacan's reading, Poe's story is about the centrality of the Letter, since the subjects occupy their positions in relation to it (in Lacanian terms, Poe's story is about the symbolic as constitutive of subjectivity). In parallel, the story, for Lacan, discredits the act of seeing (upon which lies the imaginary) since, as the story shows, the best way to protect the letter from inquisitive eyes is to leave it in the open. In this respect, dramatizing an excess of visibility, the story undermines the assumption that what is not seen is hidden and subverts fantasies of hiddenness and unveiling. In Lacan's illustrious formulation, the story revolves around *la politique de l'autruiche* and thereby brings together the ostrich (*autruche*), which by sticking its head in the ground sees (imagines) that it is not seen whereas (in reality) it is seen not seeing; the others (*autrui*), which constitute the intersubjective order of the Symbolic (the big Other); and Austria (*Autriche*), the birthplace of psychoanalysis.[74]

Lacan's interest in 'The Purloined Letter' lies in the fact that it displays and coincides with the stakes of psychoanalysis; or, rather, Lacan's reading of the story elucidates the points of contact between

---

71 Malcolm Bowie, *Lacan*, p. 92.

72 Malcolm Bowie, *Lacan*, p. 93. This otherness that remains other refers to the foreignness of language, since for Lacan language is an alienating structure that speaks us, rather than we – as an aesthetic of expression wants it – speak it. In parallel, it refers to the otherness of the desires of others, through which we learn to desire (to articulate our desire). In this sense, the conception (and emergence) of the unconscious as the 'discourse of the Other' conflates with the definition (and emergence) of desire as 'the desire of the Other', a definition which in the late Lacan points to the impossibility of desire (in so far as it is always a desire for something else). In the early Lacan (under the influence of Kojève), the phrase 'the desire is the desire of the Other' refers mainly to the desire of recognition (humans desire to be desired by others).

73 Jacques Lacan, 'Le Séminaire sur *La Lettre volée*', in Lacan, *Écrits I*, pp. 11–61; Jacques Lacan, 'Seminar on "The Purloined Letter"', in Lacan, *Écrits*, pp. 6–50.

74 Lacan, 'Le Séminaire sur *La Lettre volée*', pp. 15–16, 31; Lacan, 'Seminar on "The Purloined Letter"', pp. 10, 22.

Poe's literary text and psychoanalytic theory as put forward by Lacan. First, in Lacan's reading Dupin's strategy demonstrates how the sender receives from the receiver his proper message in reverse form; this phrase correlates with Lacan's definition of the unconscious as the discourse of the Other, in which the subject receives in the inverted form his own forgotten message. Second, Poe's configuration of 'The Purloined Letter' – as a literary text which calls into question the notions of 'self' and 'analysis' in so far as, in Barbara Johnson's words, it 'both analyses itself and shows that it actually has neither a self nor any neutral metalanguage with which to do the analysing'[75] – corresponds to the Lacanian demarcation of psychoanalysis not as a meta-language (a discourse of mastery) that speaks *on* or *about*, but as a language that enters *into* whatever it speaks of (as, for Lacan, it is the world of words that creates the world of things rather than the inverse). In this respect, Poe's text – acting for literature – and Lacan's texts – speaking for psychoanalytic theory – do not simply create a dialogue of equals, showing how literature and psychoanalysis are mutually implicated, but throw into confusion a fundamental law according to which, as Girard puts it, all texts are divided into two categories: 'the ones that do the interpreting, and the ones that are there mostly to be interpreted'.[76]

In its progression Poe's story unsettles the (Oedipal) desire to see, to know, to uncover, since the content of the letter is never revealed. As the story moves on, the letter itself moves, circulates and changes hands; constantly displaced, the letter goes missing from its place again and again. Finally, Poe's text involves a crucial shift: the mystery is solved and the letter is found, as the focus shifts away from the act of looking towards the act of repeating, as Johnson convincingly argues: 'Dupin finds the letter "in" the symbolic order *not* because he knows where to look, but because he knows *what to repeat*'.[77] Dupin's act crystallizes and parallels not only the psychoanalytic process but

---

75 Johnson, 'The Frame of Reference: Poe, Lacan, Derrida', p. 457.

76 Girard, 'Narcissism', p. 308. Girard unsettles this law in his own way, showing how Proust's *À la recherche du temps perdu* offers a critique and a more complete vision of narcissism than Freud's essay on narcissism.

77 Johnson, 'The Frame of Reference', p. 498. Freud coined the term 'primal scene' (*Urszene*) to argue that an experience which is incomprehensible for a child is often organized into scenarios which subsequently have an effect on its psychosexual development and adult life. The term 'primal scene' refers to a sexual act, usually between the parents, which the child observes, or deduces and (mis)conceives from certain clues. As the scene is not understood by the child, it is often constructed, fantasized about and interpreted as a scene of violence.

also psychoanalytic theory in its shift from seeing to writing, a shift enacted by Lacan's numerous writings, several of which are collected and entitled *Écrits*. Commenting on and arguing against one of the most common reproaches to psychoanalysis (iterated by Derrida, in his critique of Lacan's reading of 'The Purloined Letter'), namely that psychoanalysis always finds itself in whatever it studies, Johnson promotes this denunciation to one of the most acute definitions of psychoanalysis. For Johnson, psychoanalysis, as the first occurrence of what has been repeating itself, revolving around an event that never took place as such, problematizes the terms 'event' and (its) 'repetition': 'psychoanalysis is not itself the interpretation of repetition; it *is* the repetition [of a trauma of interpretation]'; 'it has content insofar as it repeats the dis-content of what never took place'.[78] This discontent, the displeasure without content, is, for Johnson, an 'interpretative infelicity'. The (traumatic) event (the Real, in Lacanian terms) is and consists of a traumatic interpretation, an inability to understand which never properly took place. As a result, psychoanalysis proves to be, as Johnson writes, 'itself the primal scene it is seeking: it is the first occurrence of what has been repeating itself [in the patient without ever having occurred]'.[79]

The Lacanian enterprise could be sketched as a passage from the Imaginary to the Symbolic, from the *ego* (and illusions of wholeness) to the *je* (as split and divided), from theory (as an act of seeing) to writing (as an act of repetition). The entry of and to the Symbolic is, as Johnson points out, the entrance of difference, otherness and temporality into identity.[80] The entrance of difference, otherness and temporality recasts the notion of repetition (as the repetition of sameness) and renders it synonymous with the impossibility of equation (as in Poe's story, where the message is received in reverse form). Alternatively, as Johnson puts it in numerical terms, the Symbolic is 'the impossibility not of the number 2 but of the number 1 [...]; something which subverts not the symmetry of the imaginary couple but the possibility of the independent unity of any term whatsoever'.[81] In the Lacanian topology, what further disjoins the possibility of unity as well as of the Imaginary and the Symbolic as an opposing and interdependent pair is the third Lacanian locus, the Real. The Real, as what precedes and exceeds phenomenalization,

---

78 Johnson, 'The Frame of Reference', p. 499.
79 Johnson, 'The Frame of Reference', p. 499.
80 Johnson, 'The Frame of Reference', p. 499.
81 Johnson, 'The Frame of Reference', p. 469.

language and subjectification, is a resistance to symbolization. However, in its defiance of integration and symbolization, in its approximation of the impossible and the ineffable, it exerts pressure on the Symbolic, setting it in motion.

As becomes evident, Lacan's return to Freud rewrites both the analytic process and psychoanalytic theory as primarily a relation to language. In his privileging and use of, his alliance and recourse to, the Symbolic as the order of movement, deferral, difference and irreducible otherness, Lacan shifts away from Freud's (hermeneutic) inclination towards meaning – and the questioning of the relation between signifier and signified – and directs his attention to the (structural) relation between signifiers, along with the (unstructural) unstoppability of the signifying chain. Freud remoulds theory to the extent that he yields at last to doubt, authorizing it to permeate the solidity and certainty of knowledge, as he writes to his friend Marie Bonaparte: 'I always envy the physicists and mathematicians who can stand on firm ground. I hover, so to speak, in the air'.[82] On the contrary, Lacan's reward, despite – or precisely due to – his laborious refusal to stop, pause and be satisfied, is, as Bowie remarks, to become a writer and hence momentarily to savour the relief of truth in its most absolute incarnation as promised by Hegel:

> When the theorist has completed his long apprenticeship and travelled far along the *via negativa* that psychoanalysis recommends to all those who would presume to construct theories, he is eligible for his reward. In Lacan's case the reward is to become a writer, and in his writing to discover not the foothills of Truth but its delirious summits.[83]

Without deluding himself with Hegel's cognitive satisfactions, truth is glimpsed – and reconfigured – by Lacan as a rupture, in and as the delight of speech. In Bowie's words, '"[t]ruth" of the kind that Hegel had foretold, breaks in upon him, momentarily relieves him of the need to say "always anOther thing", and breathes upon his writing an unmistakable air of bliss'.[84]

The momentary crystallizations of Lacanian truth can be discerned in his definitions, or rather his problematization, of 'existence'. From the viewpoint of the Symbolic, existence becomes synonymous with

---

82 Ernest Jones, *Sigmund Freud: Life and Work*, 3 vols (London: The Hogarth Press, 1953–57), II: *Years of Maturity: 1901–1919* (1955), p. 466.
83 Malcolm Bowie, *Lacan*, p. 120.
84 Malcolm Bowie, *Lacan*, p. 121.

absence, since 'nothing exists insofar as it does not exist'. From the viewpoint of the Real, existence becomes synonymous with the impossible, since 'only that which is impossible to symbolise exists'.[85] The above depictions come into contact with the remoulding of existence in terms of impossibility, as suggested by the Blanchotian and the Bataillean experience of literature. Nonetheless, drawing on Shoshana Felman's remark that literature, in its connection to psychoanalysis, destabilizes the assigned places (in so far as the literary critic, in his/her relation to the text, is both the analyst, since s/he analyses the text, and the analysand, to the extent that the text is supposed to possess some hidden knowledge and assumes the function of the 'subject supposed to know' that is embodied by the analyst),[86] Blanchot's contribution to Lacan's theory is a re-evaluation of the 'Imaginary' and the 'image'. Both Blanchot and Lacan depart from the philosophical conception of imagination as an ability (a faculty) and render it synonymous with the world and realm of images. However, for Lacan the image and the Imaginary are understood in terms of a disabling fixity which 'imprisons the subject in a series of static fixations', while for Blanchot, as we saw in the previous section, the image becomes synonymous with movement and withdrawal.[87] Additionally, while for Lacan the Imaginary is defensive and protective (protecting us from the Real), the Blanchotian Imaginary might be considered an opening towards the Real as designated by Lacan. Indeed, whereas the Lacanian image leads back to and reassures the 'I' (the 'eye', the ego), the Blanchotian image opens to the not-I, to the indivisibility and anonymity of the Lacanian Real. To put it a different way, for Lacan the image entails and sustains a dual relationship between the self and its specular image, while Blanchot advances the image as a tensional doubleness between the subject and its disappearance. In this respect, the Imaginary, for Lacan, is synonymous with fantasy, inasmuch as it

---

85   This definition of existence in relation to the Real is given by Dylan Evans, 'Existence (existence)', in Dylan Evans, *An Introductory Dictionary of Lacanian Psychoanalysis* (London and New York: Routledge, 1996), p. 58.

86   The phrase 'subject supposed to know' or the 'supposed subject of knowledge' (*sujet supposé savoir*) is used by Lacan in his definition of transference as the attribution of knowledge to a subject. During the analytic process, transference occurs when the analyst is perceived by the analysand as the possessor of some kind of knowledge. The phrase 'subject supposed to know' designates a function that the analyst embodies during the treatment and not the analyst as such.

87   Dylan Evans 'Imaginary (imaginaire)', in Evans, *An Introductory Dictionary of Lacanian Psychoanalysis*, pp. 82–84 (p. 83).

functions as a setting, a staging, a *mise en scène* and a fulfilment of the subject's desire for unity and wholeness (that is, for what the subject is not); the Blanchotian Imaginary is an exposure to the dispersal of the subject as it sinks to the anonymity of the language of literature.

Additionally, Lacan's analysis of Holbein's *The Ambassadors* suggests to some extent how the impossible – and one's relation to it – is configured differently in the literary and the analytic endeavour. The painting as well as Lacan's reading of it, while revolving around and insisting on the obliqueness of a register, nevertheless calls for another point of view, albeit ec-centric; the literary undertaking, on the contrary, scatters and withholds the possibility of any point of view whatsoever. In Lacan's reading of *The Ambassadors* the painting exemplifies how the subject's existence is sustained by a fundamental relation of obliquity and suspension with the subject's annihilation, as the latter is symbolized in the skull. The annihilating subject which grasps and understands the world, as portrayed in the assertive pose of the two majestic figures, is undercut by a residue of knowledge that is impossible for the conscious subject (or, in Sartrean terms, the subject of consciousness). Lacan's analysis focuses on the fact that, due to this strange distorted object which appears in the foreground, the viewer, who equally enjoys the certainty of being a subject in control of his/her looking, in the attempt to decipher this strange object, which turns out to be a skull, finds himself being watched. Therefore, the viewer's eye is caught by the skull, which somehow looks back at the viewer. For Lacan, I who look (who looks at the painting) find myself under a gaze, I am looked upon: 'Nous verrons alors se dessiner [...] le regard comme tel, dans sa fonction pulsatile, éclatante et étalée [...]; ce tableau n'est rien d'autre que ce que tout tableau est, un piège à regard' [We shall then see emerging on the basis of vision [...] the gaze as such, in its pulsatile, dazzling and spread out function, as it is in this picture].[88]

While most Lacanian critics emphasize the incompatibility between the two scopic regimes glossed by Lacan as the eye (*l'œil*) and the gaze (*le regard*), the painting nevertheless invites the viewer to position and situate himself properly in order to face (look

---

88 Jacques Lacan, 'L'Anamorphose', in Jacques Lacan, *Les Quatre concepts fondamentaux de la psychanalyse. Texte établi par Jacques-Alain Miller* (Paris: Seuil, 1973 [1964]), pp. 92–104 (p. 102); Jacques Lacan, 'Anamorphosis', in Jacques Lacan, *The Four Fundamental Concepts of Psycho-Analysis*, ed. by Jacques-Alain Miller, trans. by Alan Sheridan (London; New York: Karnac, 1977), pp. 79–90 (p. 89).

towards and accept) this oblique register of death (the fact that s/he is looked upon): '[N]ous retournant, nous voyons ce que signifie l'objet flottant magique. Il nous reflète notre propre néant, dans la figure de la tête de mort' [[T]urning around, we see what the magical floating object signifies. It reflects our own nothingness, in the figure of the death's head].[89] Similarly, psychoanalysis, in its claim that the subject might – and must – position itself properly towards and reconcile with the obscurity of its desire (which is somehow death-bound), calls for an analogous confrontation. Though Lacan revolts against the bourgeois dream of happily settling within reality and puts forth a relation of ongoing confrontation (*contra mundum*) – and hence should constantly be defended against the appropriation of him by ego-psychology (in the latter's emphasis on the normalization and social rehabilitation of the subject) – in psychoanalysis, to put it bluntly, there is a goal and there is a way (albeit strenuous). The goal and the way consist of a double realization, which is summed up by Critchley as the realization of the unrealizable of our desire and of the fact that we are, fundamentally, beings of lack, lacking *in* being: 'In Lacanian terms, sublimation is the realization of one's desire, where one realises that one's desire will not be realized, where one realises the lack of being that one is'.[90]

As the stakes of psychoanalysis and its *raison d'être* are crystallized in terms of an itinerary from the *Es* to the *Ich*, the psychoanalytic subject, in its subjection to the symbolic order, is put forward – that is, both constituted and celebrated – as split (rather than whole and unitary).[91] Against the analytic route from the *Es* towards the

---

89 Jacques Lacan, 'La Ligne et la lumière', in Lacan, *Les Quatre concepts fondamentaux de la psychanalyse*, pp. 105–19 (p. 107); Jacques Lacan, 'The Line and Light', in Lacan, *The Four Fundamental Concepts of Psycho-Analysis*, pp. 91–104 (p. 92).

90 Simon Critchley, '*Das Ding*: Lacan and Levinas', in Critchley, *Ethics – Politics – Subjectivity*, pp. 198–216 (p. 202).

91 On how Lacan reinterprets the famous Freudian proclamation 'Wo Es war, soll Ich werden', see Ellie Ragland-Sullivan, 'What is "I"? Lacan's Theory of the Human Subject', in Ragland-Sullivan, *Jacques Lacan and the Philosophy of Psychoanalysis*, pp. 1–67 (p. 12). Ragland-Sullivan underlines the fact that in Lacan's return to Freud the announcement does not mean that the conscious subject (the *Ich*) replaces the unconscious subject (the *Es*) but rather that it emerges from it: 'Freud's formula means that it is one's duty to emerge from a place of unconscious being to recognize the truth, that one's being derives from having been an object of unconscious and alien principles' (Ragland-Sullivan, 'What is "I"?', p. 12).

Ich, the last chapter will focus on the itinerary of literature in terms of a movement from the *je* to the *il* for Blanchot and as a series of disguises for Bataille. In so doing, and in putting forth the tropes of the 'neuter' with reference to Blanchot and the 'mask' with reference to Bataille, the chapter attempts to advance a more radical dispersal and defiance of subjectivity, reality and relationality.

Part III
(Re)turns

7. Blanchot: Turning and Reveiling[1]

Toute recherche est une crise. Ce qui est cherché n'est rien que le tour de la recherche qui donne lieu à la crise: le tour critique.

[All research is crisis. What is sought is nothing other than the turn of seeking, of research, that occasions the crisis: the critical turn.][2]

Throughout his work Maurice Blanchot never tires of restating – never tires of repeating – that to write is 'to pass from the first to the third person'.[3] This definition of writing as the downfall of subjectivity is first found in his collection *La Part du feu* (1949) with particular reference to Kafka. In his seminal essay 'Kafka et La littérature' Blanchot considers the passage from the 'I' to the 'he', namely from the personal to the impersonal, as the defining characteristic of the literary: 'Kafka [a] éprouvé la fécondité de la littérature (pour lui-même, pour sa vie et en vue de vivre) du jour où il a senti que la littérature était ce passage du *Ich* au *Er*, du Je au Il' [Kafka grasped the fecundity of literature (for himself, for his life, and to go on living) from the moment that he felt literature was the passage from *Ich* to *Er*, from I to he].[4] Blanchot goes on to bring in the theme of Kafka's state and *expression* of unhappiness and adds to literature's dimension of

---

1   In *L'Entretien infini* the term 'reveiling' appears in Blanchot's definition of the image as the veil which reveals by reveiling: '[L]'image est [...] le voile qui révèle en revoilant' [[T]he image is [...] the veil that reveals by reveiling] (Maurice Blanchot, 'Parler, ce n'est pas voir', in Blanchot, *L'Entretien infini*, pp. 35–45 (p. 42); Maurice Blanchot, 'Speaking is Not Seeing', in Blanchot, *The Infinite Conversation*, pp. 25–32 (p. 30)).
2   Blanchot, 'Parler, ce n'est pas voir', p. 45; Blanchot, 'Speaking is Not Seeing', p. 32.
3   Blanchot, 'La Solitude essentielle', p. 31 ('[Écrire] c'est passer du Je au Il'); Blanchot, 'The Essential Solitude', p. 33.
4   Blanchot, 'Kafka et la littérature', p. 29; Blanchot, 'Kafka and Literature', p. 21.

impossibility (alluded to in the previous chapters) its signalling of the transition from the 'I' to the 'he':

> Il ne me suffit pas donc d'écrire: *Je* suis malheureux. [...] Ce n'est qu'à partir du moment où j'arrive à cette substitution étrange: *Il* est malheureux, que le langage commence à se constituer en langage malheureux pour moi, à esquisser et à projeter lentement le monde du malheur tel qu'il se réalise en lui.
>
> [So it is not enough for me to write 'I am unhappy'. [...] It is only from the moment I arrive at this strange substitution, 'He is unhappy', that language begins to be formed into a language that is unhappy for me, to sketch out and slowly project the world of unhappiness as it occurs in him.][5]

There are two remarks to be made at this point concerning the occurrence of the 'he'. The first is that the overthrowing of the 'I' is described in the respective terms of a 'passage' and a 'substitution'. The second is that the occurrence of the 'he' in place of the 'I' brings together another language and another world (a language that is unhappy and a world of unhappiness). In other words, writing puts a triple pressure on received notions of subjectivity, language and, ultimately, reality. Against the conception of writing in terms of the stream of consciousness which renders possible immediate presence (though, in reality, this immediacy is artificial inasmuch as it is *mediated* through writing), the Blanchotian conception of writing presents itself as – and imposes – the suspension of presence. As will be shown in the discussion that follows, for Blanchot writing brings forth a logic of doubleness which disperses the possibility of ontology – the opening of a horizon – as well as the logic of dialectics – the promise of closure due to the equation of negativity with work.

The definition of writing in terms of a passage to the third person is given again in Blanchot's major work of the 1950s, namely *L'Espace littéraire,* and is explicitly interrelated with anonymity and repetition: '[Écrire] c'est passer du Je au Il, de sorte que ce qui m'arrive n'arrive à personne, est anonyme par le fait que cela me concerne, se répète dans un éparpillement infini' [[To write] is to pass from the first to the third person, so that what happens to me happens to no one, is anonymous insofar as it concerns me, repeats itself in an infinite dispersal].[6] To put it another way, the passage from the 'I'

---

5 Blanchot, 'Kafka et la littérature', p. 29; Blanchot, 'Kafka and Literature', p. 21.
6 Blanchot, 'La Solitude essentielle', p. 31; Blanchot, 'The Essential Solitude', p. 33.

to the 'he' is not simply a replacement (simply a substitution) but a more profound transformation, to the extent that the 'he' is actually a no-one, bringing on a language that no-one speaks, addressed to no-one, which reveals no-thing. Additionally, as is emphasized in *L'Espace littéraire*, this passage does not obey a logic of continuity but of discontinuity. In this regard, it is described in terms of a break, destruction and withdrawal. For Blanchot, to write is to untie the bond between words and the world, between words and myself, between myself and you (I and you):

> Écrire c'est briser le lien qui unit la parole à moi-même, briser le rapport qui, me faisant parler vers 'toi', me donne parole dans l'entente que cette parole reçoit de toi [...]. Écrire, c'est en outre, retirer le langage du cours du monde.
>
> [To write is to break the bond that unites the word with myself. It is to destroy the relation which, determining that I speak toward 'you', gives me room to speak within the understanding which my word receives from you [...]. To write is, moreover, to withdraw language from the world.][7]

The definition of writing in terms of a passage recurs in the essay 'La Voix narrative' in *L'Entretien infini*, Blanchot's major work from the late 1960s. Having sufficiently secured the definition of writing in terms of the impersonal *il*, while providing a laconic definition of the *il* as 'l'événement inéclairé de ce qui a lieu quand on raconte' [the unlighted event that occurs when one tells a story], Blanchot declares that 'il reste à savoir ce qui est en jeu, quand écrire répond à l'exigence de ce "il" incaractérisable' [what remains to be discovered is what is at stake when writing responds to the demands of this uncharacterizable 'he'].[8]

The recurring definition of writing in terms of a passage that runs through Blanchot's works from the 1940s to the 1970s seems to invite Roger Laporte's insightful remark that Blanchot, like all great writers, always says – spends his life trying to say – 'qu'une chose' [one and the same thing]. However, Laporte warns us against any deceitful impression that this one and same thing can be approached by a specific text – even less, that it can be adequately articulated by

---

7 Blanchot, 'La Solitude essentielle', pp. 20–21; Blanchot, 'The Essential Solitude', p. 26.

8 Maurice Blanchot, 'La Voix narrative *(le "il", le neutre)*', in Blanchot, *L'Entretien infini*, pp. 556–67 (p. 558); Maurice Blanchot, 'The Narrative Voice *(the "he", the neutral)*', in Blanchot, *The Infinite Conversation*, pp. 379–87 (p. 380).

a specific term. Briefly, Laporte suggests that this one thing Blanchot keeps telling us permeates the entire Blanchotian *œuvre* without it being localized or crystallized somewhere – be it a text or a notion:

> Comme tout grand écrivain, Blanchot ne nous dit qu'une chose, ou plutôt il passe sa vie à tenter de la dire, mais le lecteur a parfois l'illusion que tel texte est celui où ce qui cherche à se dire est dit au plus près.[9]
>
> [As all great writers, Blanchot tells us only one thing, or rather he spends his life trying to say it. But the reader sometimes has the illusion that this text is the one in which what is trying to be said is said as acutely as possible.]

Challenging Laporte's remark or, rather, further developing and augmenting it, Leslie Hill singles out Blanchot from other major thinkers such as Levinas or Heidegger precisely because Blanchot's thinking cannot be assembled 'in one central intuition, thought or concept'.[10] This is due to the fact that Blanchot, as Hill underlines, 'never has only one idea, but always two' and 'these two are never reducible to attributes of the one'.[11] Thus, Hill suggests that Blanchot's constantly recurring main consideration is a 'commitment to doubleness', that is, 'to that which is more than One, or otherwise than One'.[12] This resolute and recurrent commitment is, for Hill, formulated in *L'Entretien infini* as the 'twofold task of "naming the possible, responding to the impossible"'.[13] Drawing on both Hill and Laporte, the following discussion will show that the Blanchotian key term of the neuter – which appears throughout *L'Entretien infini* – is the one, recurrent idea which permeates all Blanchot's works, precisely to the extent that it names and responds to an irreducible doubleness.

Blanchot's definition of writing in terms of a 'passage' and the definition of the latter in term of breaking the bond with the world are analogous (similar in some ways, starkly different in others) to the bracketing posed by the phenomenological *epoché*. Both notions have in common a gesture of suspension; yet they differ radically

---

9   Roger Laporte, 'Le Oui, Le Non, le Neutre', *Critique*, 229 (1966), 579–90 (p. 582).

10 Leslie Hill, 'After Blanchot', in *After Blanchot*, ed. by Hill, Nelson and Vardoulakis, pp. 1–12 (p. 1).

11 Hill, 'After Blanchot', p. 1.

12 Hill, 'After Blanchot', p. 2.

13 Hill, 'After Blanchot', p. 2.

with regard to what is suspended and the outcome of suspension. The Husserlian *epoché* is and calls for a suspension of reference to the empirical world according to the 'natural attitude'.[14] The existence of the external world and of its objects – if any – is bracketed and emphasis is given on the subject, or more precisely on the existence of the world as experienced (that is, both perceived and intended) by the subject. This emphasis on subjective experience results in equating being with appearing and in rendering the bodily self the anchor and the producer of meaning. The free subject, freed from the external world, becomes the site (and the guarantor) of the continuous *flow* of lived experience. The phenomenological first-person point of view and the flowing of experience within the self is precisely what is interrupted by the Blanchotian contrivance of the 'passage', a passage which consists of moving away from the 'I' and the world towards impersonality and worldlessness. Blanchot's account of the neuter in terms of 'passage' and 'substitution' suggests, in contrast to Husserl, a third-person point of view (rather than a first) and indicates the suspension of the world, worldly identity and linguistic meaning (rather than a suspension of the natural attitude). Additionally, contrary to Levinas (but mainly the Levinas of *Totalité et infini* (1961)), this third-person point of view is not that of the other (*autrui*) but that of no-one.[15] To put it another way, the double logic of the neuter succeeds in *not* relocating transcendental subjectivity to a conception of the other in terms of transcendence.

14 The 'natural attitude' is a key term in phenomenology and is juxtaposed onto the phenomenological perspective of the world. The natural attitude (which characterizes both our everyday way of being in the world and ordinary science) naively takes the world and its objects as granted, simply real, (f)actually 'being there' in themselves, starkly separated, independent of and prior to our perception. By contrast, the phenomenological approach focuses on the structures which make possible the perception of the world and its objects by us, that is, the structures that precede or accompany the world and its objects, allowing them to constitute themselves *in* and *for* our consciousness and allowing us to identify them.

15 The Blanchotian suspension within – and challenging of – the transcendental character of subjectivity can be compared to the Levinasian concept of 'substitution', which is both a key term and the name of one of the core chapters in Levinas's major work *Autrement qu'être ou Au-delà de l'essence* (1974). Substitution, as developed by Levinas, is a radicalization of Husserlian *epoché* in so far as it refers to a first experience of alterity, an 'alterity within', and attempts to think of intersubjectivity in non-dialectical terms and, more crucially, relationality in terms of immanence.

The logic of the double, in terms of an initial division, is already displayed in the key term of the previous chapter on Blanchot, namely, the image. There it is shown how the becoming image of a thing – requiring its absenting – suspends the understanding of being in terms of presence and calls for a different understanding, one in which things both are and are not. The image attests to the fact that absence is not derivative of, but actually partakes in, presence, as the very possibility of figuration. As Blanchot notes, coming back to the notion of the image in *L'Entretien infini*: 'L'image est image en cette duplicité, non pas le double de l'objet, mais le dédoublement initial qui permet ensuite à la chose d'être figurée' [The image is image by means of this duplicity, being not the object's double but the initial division that permits the thing to be figured].[16] Contesting the understanding of being in terms of presence, manifestation and unveiling, the image points to and brings forth the world of the imaginary, where the prevalent terms are absence, withdrawal and obscurity. Nonetheless, the demand to which *L'Espace littéraire* responds, through the contrivance of the image, is the unworking of presence, visibility and the hiatus between contact and distance, while the demand to which *L'Entretien infini* responds, through the contrivance of the neuter, is that of otherness. Therefore, it is in this late work that the logic of the double, as the suspension of the one, acquires its full force. In this sense, while *L'Entretien infini* continues some of the Blanchotian preoccupations articulated throughout the 1940s and the 1950s, it also marks a turning point since the question of otherness acquires an urgency and a centrality it did not have in Blanchot's previous works.

Alongside the prominence of the neuter, one needs to point to a shift from 'literature' to 'writing' in the lexicon of *L'Entetien infini*, as the terms *littéraire*, *literature* and *œuvre*, which figure in the early essays of the 1940s and, of course, in *L'Espace littéraire* in the 1950s, are dropped in favour of the terms *écrire* and *écriture*. Additionally, while the earlier works can be distinctly situated within the theoretical field as critical essays, Blanchot's later works of the 1970s and 1980s, with their fragmentary writing, waver indecisively between theory of literature and literature. Nevertheless, as far as Blanchot's conception of literature is concerned, this shift is more reflective of the Derridean (post-)Structuralist paradigm of *écriture* than a substantial change in his own thinking. Blanchot's main shift from literature to writing

---

16 Blanchot, 'Parler, ce n'est pas voir', p. 42; Blanchot, 'Speaking is Not Seeing', p. 30.

(that is, in Bident's phrasing, from a conception of literature in terms of revelation towards a conception of writing in terms of contestation) can be traced back to the 1940s.[17]

It is also in the 1940s that Blanchot's preference for Kafka over Thomas Mann is revealed – a preference which can be seen as indicative of Blanchot's rejection of an understanding of culture from a conservative standpoint. While the early Blanchot of the 1930s, the Blanchot of *L'Insurgé* still attached to and motivated by the cultural and political conservatism with which he was raised, reviews one of the volumes of Mann's tetralogy *Joseph und seine Brüder* [*Joseph and His Brothers*] (1933–43), from the 1940s onwards it is Kafka who becomes the major and recurring reference in all Blanchot's major works.[18] As already mentioned, it is with reference to Kafka that Blanchot's definition of the literary in terms of a passage to the impersonal is formulated and developed (from the essay 'Kafka et la littérature' in *La Part du feu* to the essay 'La Voix narrative' in *L'Entretien infini*).

In the case of Thomas Mann's novels there is an aspiration to literary greatness, due not only to Mann's personal aspiration to become a great man, write great books and be a dominant intellectual figure in German culture but also, more crucially, to the striving of his novels, especially of *Joseph und seine Brüder* (which is reviewed by the young Blanchot), to provide a myth for modern times. *Joseph und seine Brüder*, in providing a *Bildungsroman* centred on the biblical figure of Joseph (Genesis 37–50), rewrites and re-enacts Joseph's story employing psychological insight into the protagonist's journey from his fall into slavery up to his rise to the position of regent appointed by the Pharaoh of Egypt. It thereby exemplifies and attests to a belief in the human capacity to adapt, move on, come to terms with and thrive in the flux of the modern world, but also in the ability of literature to provide a response to the crisis of modern times, when the founding political and moral principles of the western world have been shaken, social and economic changes have occurred and

---

17 Bident locates this shift to the 1940s onwards and notices Bataille's role in it (that is, the conversation between Bataille and Blanchot out of which Bataille's *L'Expérience intérieure* emerged) when he writes: 'What first of all needed to happen was little short of a veritable Copernican Revolution: the move from a classical conception of literature as revelation to a modern conception of writing as contestation; this was what was at stake in the debate with Bataille' (Bident, 'Movements of the Neuter', p. 26).

18 Maurice Blanchot, 'Notes de lecture sur *Joseph et ses frères* de Mann', *L'Insurgé*, 14, 14 avril 1937, p. 5.

individual lives have been dizzyingly affected. Kafka's novels, on the contrary, inhabited by characters unable to find their way (in the world or even out of it), offer a view of literature which, far from providing a response to the modern deadlock, is enfolded in it and emerges wounded.

Thus, the turning point of *L'Entretien infini* does not refer to the question of literature but rather to the question of otherness to the extent that the other – though a central concern which informs all Blanchot's post-war writings – is displayed more prominently in it. While literature in *L'Espace littéraire* is suspended between being and non-being, in *L'Entretien infini* it is constituted in and by its detour as always other to itself, thereby undoing every attempt to confine existence in terms of identity, sameness, unity and origin.[19]

The Logic of the Double: To Find is to Turn

In his essay dedicated to Blanchot and entitled 'La Pensée du dehors', Foucault traces the difference between two simple but crucial assertions: 'I lie' and 'I speak' (with the latter amounting to 'I write'). For Foucault, while the first makes Greek truth shudder, the second puts modern fiction on trial.[20] He notes in the opening lines of the essay: 'La vérité grecque a tremblé, jadis, en cette seule affirmation: "je mens". "Je parle" met à l'épreuve toute la fiction moderne' [In ancient times, this simple assertion was enough to shake the foundations of the Greek truth 'I lie'. 'I speak', on the other hand, puts the whole of modern fiction to the test].[21] The intention

---

19 On the contrary, in Kevin Hart's theological reading of Blanchot there is a crucial turning point in *L'Entretien infini* as it shifts from the lexicon of the imaginary that dominates *L'Espace littéraire* to a lexicon of transgression and thereby implicates a different kind of 'beyond'. For Hart, while *L'Espace littéraire*, in its emphasis on the imaginary, points towards (and is interested in) what is beyond reality, possibility and negativity, *L'Entretien infini*, calling attention to contestation and transgression, points towards what is beyond history (the history of meaning), that is, for Hart, 'the infinite God, a deity beyond all dialectic' (Kevin Hart, 'The Counter-Spiritual Life', in *The Power of Contestation*, ed. by Kevin Hart and Geoffrey H. Hartman (Baltimore, MD and London: Johns Hopkins University Press, 2004), pp. 156–77 (p. 177)).

20 Greek truth here stands for the quest for truth in ancient Greek philosophy.

21 Michel Foucault, 'La Pensée du dehors', *Critique*, 229 (1966), 523–46 (p. 523); Michel Foucault, 'Maurice Blanchot: The Thought from Outside', in Michel Foucault and Maurice Blanchot, *Foucault. Blanchot*, trans. by Jeffrey Mehlman and Brian Massumi (New York: Zone, 1990), pp. 7–58 (p. 9).

here is not to read the divergence between these two statements as a recurrence of the old dispute between literature and philosophy, a dispute as old as ancient philosophy itself inasmuch as it already appears in the Platonic Dialogues.[22] Framing the question of both representation (crystallized in the axioms of philosophy 'I lie', 'I think') and presentation (crystallized in the statement of literature 'I write') in terms of duplicity, Foucault shows how writing puts forth a different kind of duplicity, a duplicity which moves beyond the dual logic, the binary logic of 'I think' and 'I lie', bringing forth the logic of the double.

The essential duality of the paradox 'I lie', says Foucault, concerns the non-coincidence, the split, between the announcement and its content/object (I say – the truth – that I lie). This essential duality derives from the fact that the subject *who* speaks is the same as the subject *about* which it speaks. Contrary to 'I lie', which is self-defeating, 'I speak' is self-assertive. In its exact coincidence, in its self-reference, the statement 'I speak' (and I say that I speak) is undeniably true. However, continues Foucault, while as a formal proposition 'I speak' raises no problems, its *meaning* raises a variety of questions in so far as it has no other object, no other content than itself (which is precisely what secured its truth). Providing the meaning – the definition, consequences and significance[23] – of 'I speak' ('I speak' crystallizing modern literature), Foucault writes: 'Bref, il n'est plus discours et communication d'un sens, mais étalement du langage en son être brut, pure extériorité déployée' [In short, it is no longer discourse and the communication of meaning, but a spreading forth of language in its raw state, an unfolding of pure exteriority]:[24]

> Le 'sujet' de la littérature (ce qui parle en elle et ce dont elle parle), ce ne serait pas tellement le langage en sa positivité, que le vide où il trouve son espace quand il s'énonce dans la nudité du 'je parle'.

---

22 The Platonic Dialogues were written between 399 BC and Plato's death in 347 BC.

23 The question of meaning could be formulated as follows: what is meant by these two words 'I speak'; what do I mean when I speak; what is the meaning of speaking when the sovereignty of speech lies in the deficiency of an object (other than itself)?

24 Foucault, 'La pensée du dehors', p. 524; Foucault, 'Maurice Blanchot: The Thought from Outside', p. 11.

[The 'subject' of literature (what speaks in it and what it speaks about) is less language in its positivity than the void language takes as its space when it articulates itself in the nakedness of 'I speak'.][25]

The raw state of language, its void and nakedness mentioned by Foucault, designate the dissociation of speech (of 'the speech of writing', to use a Blanchotian term) from content as well as from communicative exchange.

In this sense, for Foucault the case of writing, the statement 'I write', in its self-reference, can no longer be understood in terms of an 'essential duality', as is the case with telling the truth (or lying about the truth), but in terms of a 'redoublement' (a doubling back).[26] This doubling back, far from resulting in the solidification of language, brings about its dispersal, since language, in its self-reference, approaching itself, gets away from itself (that is, its conception as meaningful discourse). To put it another way – and to bring in the term 'the outside' which appears in Foucault's title – in its interiorization language passes towards the outside (that is, outside the discourse of representation). Having no object, language becomes intransitive. 'I speak', as opposed to 'I lie' (which is always a lying about, always in need of an object), involves a displacement from an object to a movement. This movement can be thought of in terms of a turn, a detour, a folding: the assertion 'I speak', having no object, folds back upon itself (to find itself naked and void); turning towards itself, it turns away (from the traditional conception of discourse).

In Foucault's essay the dispersal of language is coupled with the dispersal of the speaking subject. The initial opposition of 'I lie', 'I speak' is brought together with the opposition of 'I think', 'I speak'. For Foucault, unlike the self-evidence of 'I think', the self-coincidence of 'I speak' proves perilous. While the thought of thought leads to the deepest interiority and brings the certainty of the 'I' and its existence, the speech of speech (the being of language), in its passage to the outside, brings the effacement of the 'I'. Hence, concludes Foucault: 'Sans doute est-ce que pour cette raison que la réflexion occidentale a si longtemps hésité à penser l'être du langage: comme si elle avait pressenti le danger que ferait courir à l'évidence du "Je suis" l'expérience nue du langage' [No doubt this is why Western thought took so long to think the being of language: as if it had a

---

25 Foucault, 'La pensée du dehors', p. 525; Foucault, 'Maurice Blanchot: The Thought from Outside', p. 12.

26 Foucault, 'La pensée du dehors', p. 524; Foucault, 'Maurice Blanchot: The Thought from Outside', p. 11.

premonition of the danger that the naked experience of language poses for the self-evidence of 'I am'].[27] It is in this nakedness that lies the aporetic logic of writing for Blanchot or, more precisely, the experience of aporia which deposes the subject and being from their conception as univocal or from the order of the 'possible'.

In this sense, the Blanchotian exclamation 'I write', as endorsed by Foucault, distances itself both from the Heideggerian self-representation of the artwork (in its celebration of a beginning, an opening, an origin) and the Hegelian end of history/end of the story (in its celebration of the ending, completion, termination). Writing does not found or find itself, it merely turns upon itself (to find itself missing). In this sense, the logic of the double as set forth in writing is that of an internal doubling. However, internal, against what the term traditionally defines, does not mean interior, it means not external, that is, essential. Similarly, doubling (*redoublement* in Foucault's terminology) is not to be understood as a secondary distortion (of an initial identity) but as an inherent part of the act of writing as it turns back upon itself (to find the deficiency that constitutes it).

In one of the opening sessions of *L'Entretien Infini* ('Parler, ce n'est pas voir') Blanchot makes the link between finding and turning. As he notes, the initial meaning of finding has nothing to do with a goal, a result and a stopping (stopping since a result has been found). Rather than a stop, a halt, to find involves movement. Rather than a goal, a result, it involves searching. To find, *trouver* in French (from the Greek *trepein*: to turn), is to take a turn and to make something turn. The initial definition of trope (from the Latin *tropus* and the Greek *tropos*) is a turn – and hence a way, a manner or a style, according to Blanchot: 'Trouver, c'est tourner, faire le tour, aller retour. Trouver un chant, c'est tourner le mouvement mélodique, le faire tourner' [To find is to turn, to take a turn, to go around. To come up with a song is to turn a melodic movement, to make it turn].[28]

In the same section, Blanchot raises the demand for a speech in which things exist in their 'non-truth', which, as he goes on to add, would mean that things are neither unveiled nor veiled, neither visible nor invisible, neither showing themselves nor hiding (in other words, not showing is not equated with hiding): '[I]l y a une parole où les choses ne se cachent pas, ne se montrant pas. Ni

---

27 Foucault, 'La pensée du dehors', p. 525; Foucault, 'Maurice Blanchot: The Thought from Outside', p. 13 (modified).

28 Blanchot, 'Parler, ce n'est pas voir', p. 35; Blanchot, 'Speaking is Not Seeing', p. 25.

voilées ni dévoilées: c'est là leur non-verité' [[T]here is a speech in which things, not showing themselves, do not hide. Neither veiled nor unveiled: this is their non-truth].[29] The (anti-)phenomenological resonance of Blanchot's endeavour contests not only the Heideggerian conception of death as one's ownmost possibility,[30] but also Merleau-Ponty's equation of the manifest world as being on the 'carte de ce que je peux' [plane of possibility].[31] For Blanchot the speech of writing breaks (and should break) from the optical metaphor (lexicon) that has permeated phenomenological thought and the history of the novel. The privileged viewpoint of the novel lies in the notion that speech presents itself not simply as another way of seeing, but as a superior and transcendent way of seeing (which has the possibility of surpassing the limits of the common experience of seeing). According to Blanchot: 'Le romancier soulève les toits et livre son personnage au regard pénétrant' [The novelist lifts up the rooftops and gives his characters over to a penetrating gaze].[32] Speech, therefore, becomes 'une vue affranchie des limitations de vue. Non pas une manière de dire, mais une manière transcendante de voir' [sight freed from the limitations of sight. Not a way of saying, but a transcendent way of seeing].[33] Against the configuration of literary speech in terms of the possible (in terms of a privileged viewpoint, absolute vision, namely, ultimate possibility), Blanchot puts forward a reconfiguration of speech in terms of the impossible. Indeed, Blanchot gives rise to a narrative voice (in both his *récits* and his essays) that does not enjoy the

---

29 Blanchot, 'Parler, ce n'est pas voir', p. 40; Blanchot, 'Speaking is Not Seeing', p. 29.

30 Heidegger uses the term *ownmost* (*eigenst*) to characterize death and to show that it belongs to an individual individually and fundamentally: I, on my own, will die my death. For Heidegger, death is non-relational, as it is an experience that cannot be shared with others.

31 Maurice Merleau-Ponty, *L'Œil et l'esprit*, in Maurice Merleau-Ponty, *Œuvres*, édition établie et préfacée par Claude Lefort (Paris: Gallimard, 2010 [1964]), pp. 1591–1628 (p. 1594). The whole phrase reads as follows: 'Tout ce que je vois par principe est à ma portée du moins à la portée de mon regard, relevé sur la carte du "je peux"' [Everything I see in principle is within my reach, or at least within the reach of my gaze, within the plane of possibility]. On the dominance of the visual in our tradition and Maurice Blanchot's place in challenging this, see Ian James, 'Lucidity and Tact', in *Lucidity: Essays in Honour of Alison Finch*, ed. by Ian James and Emma Wilson (Oxford: Legenda, 2016), pp. 9–19.

32 Blanchot, 'Parler, ce n'est pas voir', p. 40; Blanchot, 'Speaking is Not Seeing', p. 29.

33 Blanchot, 'Parler, ce n'est pas voir', p. 40; Blanchot, 'Speaking is Not Seeing', p. 29.

privileged viewpoint of the omnipresent narrator, the viewpoint of absolute and resolute possibility that renders possible the impossible (lifting the roof and seeing everything from all sides). Instead of longing for access to (and rendering possible) an impossible point of view, Blanchot's theory of narration, as it emerges in his *récit* *L'Instant de ma mort*, insists on the significance of turning (going around against unveiling) and folding (against unfolding). In what follows, this is juxtaposed with Benjamin's monumental essay on narration, 'The Storyteller'.

In his melancholic essay 'The Storyteller', Benjamin, who celebrated the dismantling of the aura of the artwork in the age of mechanical reproduction, pays tribute to and extols the virtues of the aura of storytelling. While providing several definitions and identifying the distinguishing features of the extinct art of storytelling, Benjamin repeatedly designates death as the source and the birthplace of stories: '[D]eath is the sanction of everything that the storyteller can tell. He has borrowed his authority from death'.[34] For Benjamin, stories are rooted in death and death bestows authority on storytelling, not because the question of death is their central theme, but because real life, which is the material of stories, is grasped and becomes graspable at the moment of death: 'It is […] characteristic that not only a man's knowledge or wisdom, but above all his entire life – and this is the stuff that stories are made of – first assumes transmissible form at the moment of his death'.[35]

In the above-cited fragment, Benjamin makes three distinct but interrelated claims about stories, death and life: the first is that narrative and, more crucially, narratability, the governing law of the narrative, are not thematically but constitutively bound to the moment of death. The second is that the end (the human end, actual death) allows the beginning (the beginning of narration) since the ending confers meaning (the meaning of life). The third is that the meaning of life conferred by death is understood in terms of unity and entirety: what the end offers, and what is grasped due to the end, is the unity of an entire life, life in its entirety. In this regard, Benjamin appropriates and amends – slightly but crucially – the

---

34 Walter Benjamin, 'The Storyteller: Reflections on the Works of Nikolai Leskov', in Walter Benjamin, *Illuminations*, trans. by Harry Zorn (London: Pimlico, 1999), pp. 83–107 (p. 93). The essay was first published in 1936: Walter Benjamin, 'Der Erzähler. Betrachtungen zum Werk Nikolai Lesskows', *Orient und Occident*, 3 (1936), 16–33.

35 Benjamin, 'The Storyteller', p. 93.

phrase 'a man who dies at the age of thirty-five is, at every point of his life, a man who dies at the age of thirty-five'.[36] Setting right the sentence and placing the man's life and death in the past, Benjamin brings forth the end as determinant. Therefore, in his rephrasing, the man's life, fastened in the past, is seen in retrospect and the sentence becomes: a man who *died* at the age of thirty-five is, at every point of his life, *remembered* as a man who dies at thirty-five.

In comparison with Benjamin's philosophical chronicle of narration, accompanied by his emphasis on the existential stakes of the narrative in its interrelatedness with death, the radical reversal in Maurice Blanchot's very short narrative *L'Instant de ma mort* (1994) is that it emerges from and revolves around a death that does not take place. Blanchot's last book – in Lacoue-Labarthe's expression, 'his testamentary book and legacy' ('[son] livre testamentaire') – recounts a death that does not occur.[37] In this sense, death is not the constitutive element, the enabling condition of the story, but (in)directly its main theme – indirectly, since death is depicted by the story as essentially evasive. In opposition to Benjamin's thesis that life is the stuff of stories, Blanchot seems to make the claim that death is the stuff of his story and of writing. Moreover, the evasiveness of death (against its positing as an ending point) renders life ungraspable as well as evasive. To phrase it in Benjamin's terms, but to reverse his statement, since death is not posited as an ending point, life, in its turn, cannot assume transmissible form.

A reasoning similar to Benjamin's is adopted by Sartre in his attempt to trace the difference between living and narrating. Contemplating the mode of being of the sentence, 'Je me promenais, j'étais sorti du village sans m'en apercevoir, je pensais à mes ennuis d'argent' [I was out walking, I had left the village without realizing it, I was thinking about my money troubles], Sartre, or more precisely Antoine Roquentin, the troubled protagonist of Sartre's *La Nausée*, points out the significance of the end.[38] The end of the novel functions as the guarantor of meaning of the phrase – or rather of the situation described in the phrase: 'Mais la fin est là, qui transforme tout' [But the end is there, transforming everything].[39] Indeed, the end transforms

---

36 Benjamin, 'The Storyteller', p. 99.

37 Lacoue-Labarthe, 'La Contestation de la mort', p. 58; Lacoue-Labarthe, 'The Contestation of Death', p. 143.

38 Jean-Paul Sartre, *La Nausée* (Paris: Folio, 2019 [1938]), p. 65; Jean-Paul Sartre, *Nausea*, trans. by Lloyd Alexander (New York: New Directions, 2007 [1964]), p. 40.

39 Sartre, *La Nausée*, p. 65; Sartre, *Nausea*, p. 40.

the banality and triviality of the situation into a story that is worthy of our attention. While the man is a hundred miles from adventure, in the story he is the hero of the story: 'Pour nous, le type est déjà le héros de l'histoire' [For us, the man is already the hero of the story].[40] Commenting on the above passages and on the 'sense of an ending' as determinant, Peter Brooks underlines the idea that while in real life moments like those recounted in *La Nausée* (walking absorbed in one's thoughts and troubles) happen – and are lived – in a haphazard and disorderly way, since the future (which will illuminate and reveal their significance) has not yet arrived, in the narrative these seemingly unimportant moments are already caught up by the end of the story, 'enchained toward a construction of significance', and are thereby lived and read 'as annunciations and promises of final coherence'.[41] In a similar manner to that of storytelling, the unity of life is grasped and offered by the novel, since a novel's beginning and composition entail – as a constitutive requirement – the end of the novel (figurative death).

In this regard, Sartre accedes to a long philosophical tradition according to which the endless, the unending, is synonymous with meaninglessness. For Sartre, the specificity (and privilege) of narrating lie in their ability to stand in the end, adopt the viewpoint of the end and hence start backwards, whereas life falls prey to and disintegrates under the 'not yet', since the end is not yet there. Against this tradition, Blanchot renders this endless 'not yet' the space of literature. Against the Sartrean view that narrative, *unlike* life, starts from the end, while life hovers in the 'not yet' (as the end is not yet there), for Blanchot writing, *like* life and like death, inhabits the 'not yet', in its double connotation of the interminable and the undecidable. In his commentary on *L'Instant de ma mort* Lacoue-Labarthe provides a definition of writing and suggests that writing

---

40 Sartre, *La Nausée*, p. 65; Sartre, *Nausea*, p. 40.

41 Brooks, 'Freud's Masterplot', p. 283. As we read in *La Nausée*: 'Et nous avons le sentiment que le héros a vécu tous les détails de cette nuit comme des annonciations, comme des promesses, ou même qu'il vivait seulement ceux qui étaient promesses, aveugle et sourd pour tout ce qui n'annonçait pas l'aventure. Nous oublions que l'avenir n'était pas encore là; le type se promenait dans une nuit sans presages' [And we feel that the hero has lived all the details of this night as annunciations, promises, or even that he lived only the those that were promises, blind and deaf to all that did not herald adventure. We forget that the future was not yet there; the man was walking in a night without forethought] (Sartre, *La Nausée*, pp. 65–66; Sartre, *Nausea*, p. 40).

is not about life, or a way of living; it is rather about death, a way of dying. In his words:

> La 'leçon' de *L'Instant de ma mort*, son legs testamentaire si l'on veut, est d'affirmer qu'écrire [...] ce n'est pas raconter [...] comment l'on vit ou comment vivent les autres, ce qui revient au même. Mais c'est dire comment l'on est mort.
>
> [The 'lesson' of *L'Instant de ma mort*, its testamentary legacy if you will, is to affirm that to write [...] is not to recount [...] how one lives, or how others live, which is one and the same thing. But it is to say how one has died.][42]

In an attempt to sketch out what the recounting of one's death might entail and necessitate, Lacoue-Labarthe notes that it consists of a double shifting. The 'I am' shifts to an 'I am no longer', 'I never have been'. This first shift is accompanied by a second, more crucial one: the transition from a position of amazement and admiration to a sensation of puzzlement, defeat and ravage. Briefly, I am no longer 'surprised or enraptured' by the fact that I am; I am rather 'devastated and overwhelmed' by the fact that I am no longer (I never have been).[43]

Blanchot's *L'Instant de ma mort* – mainly written in the third person but largely autobiographical, as the title, the concluding lines and some elements within and outwith the text indicate – has as its theme the inexperienced experience of death, an experience of death as impossible and interminable.[44] It draws on a young man, possibly Blanchot himself, brought before a firing squad during World War II and then suddenly released from his near death. As we read in the opening lines of the narrative: 'Je me souviens d'un jeune homme – un homme encore jeune – empêché de mourir par la mort même' [I recall a young man – a man who was still young – prevented from dying by death itself].[45] The incident is again described, or rather called into question, a few lines later in the following formulation: 'La rencontre de la mort et de la mort?' [The encounter of death with death?]. Therefore, in Blanchot's narrative, the incident of death

---

42   Lacoue-Labarthe, 'La Contestation de la mort', p. 58; Lacoue-Labarthe, 'The Contestation of Death', p. 143.

43   Lacoue-Labarthe, 'La Contestation de la mort', p. 58; Lacoue-Labarthe, 'The Contestation of Death', p. 143.

44   Maurice Blanchot, *L'Instant de ma mort* (Paris: Gallimard, 2002). The book was initially published in 1994 by Fata Morgana.

45   Blanchot, *L'Instant de ma mort*, p. 9.

becomes an incident of life, the end proves unending and death is not constitutive of subjectivity but belongs to anonymity (as attested to by the surrounding omnipresence of catastrophe and the execution of three young boys whose names are not given). To phrase the above in Blanchotian terms, death (*la mort*, the possibility of death) is replaced, or rather doubled, by 'dying' (*mourir*, the impossibility of death). Death's double, the impossibility of death, sends us back to the infinity of existence. In this sense Blanchot's narrative gives rise to a notion of return which challenges the usual understanding of it.

For Benjamin the importance of the novel and the uniqueness of the storyteller lie in their ability to return, reach back and unfold an entire (a complete) life and thereby disclose its meaning. This disclosure, unlike the coldness and unconcern that characterize knowledge and information, is endowed with warmth, consumption and flame. Additionally, the existential underpinnings of reading and storytelling are emphasized, as Benjamin writes, from the viewpoint of the novel and the reader:

> The novel is significant [...] not because it presents someone's else's fate to us, perhaps didactically, but because this stranger's fate by virtue of the flame which consumes it yields us the warmth which we never draw from our own fate. What draws the reader to the novel is the hope of warming his shivering life with a death he reads about.[46]

Additionally, from the viewpoint of the storyteller, praising his distinctiveness and accounting for his unique aura, Benjamin writes: 'The storyteller: he is the man who could let the wick of his life be consumed completely by the gentle flame of his story. This is the basis of the incomparable aura about the storyteller'.[47]

The storyteller's life is not simply transformed into his story but is dissolved and consequently completely absorbed by it. Unlike the novel, which follows a linear logic (in so far as the end is posited as the ending point), storytelling seems to comply with a circular logic (in so far as it involves a return which brings – and should be understood as – a completion of a circle). Storytelling joins the part-whole relation characteristic of the hermeneutic circle: the spirit of the whole is discovered and obtained through the individual and, conversely, the individual is grasped through the whole. To put it another way, the individual and the whole, life and stories, can only be understood in reference to one another.

---

46 Benjamin, 'The Storyteller', p. 100.
47 Benjamin, 'The Storyteller', p. 107.

In Benjamin's account, through the recourse to the novel and storytelling, the Heideggerian conception of being as a confrontation with finitude ('being-towards-death') is both repeated and essentially renounced. At first glance Benjamin's essay seems to accord with Heidegger's view that the meaning of life is revealed in and through death, since death renders a lifetime complete (be it the lifespan of a person, or that of a story). However, Benjamin's 'Storyteller' diverges crucially from Heidegger in two ways. First, with regard to the reader, Benjamin points out that this fundamental relation to death is experienced not through a focus on one's own death, as one's ultimate and ownmost possibility, but, conversely, through the death of others. As he indicates, this is precisely what draws us to reading: the promise of warmth of our shivering lives through a death we read about (in other words, reading offers an affectionate response to our finitude). Contrary to Heidegger's assertion that death is non-relational, since no one else can die in our place, for Benjamin it is through exposure to the death of others – an exposure occurring precisely through reading – that death is experienced (be it the figurative end of the novel or the actual death of a character in a novel). Second, with regard to the storyteller, Benjamin's underscoring of the centrality of death is different to Heidegger's, since the storyteller's relation to death is understood not in terms of a free, decisive projection but in terms of a consumptive retrospection. Unlike the Heideggerian projective call of *being-towards* and his conception of being as 'being-towards-death', Benjamin's storyteller enacts – through narrative – a retrospective relation that consists in a *reaching back*.

Against this framework, Blanchot's narrative suggests a relation to the end (death) that is neither projective nor retrospective, neither anticipatory nor consumptive/redemptive; it brings forth a relation to the end that is double, thereby untying both dialectics and finitude. As the end is doubled by (its) non-ending, a double relation to the end is established. The end, the ending point, becomes a turn, a turning point. As the end becomes a turn, it does not bring or allow an unfolding (the unfolding of a complete life offered to understanding), but a folding (the folding of an incomplete life falling back on itself, as self-referring and self-deferring). Therefore, the turn is not only to be thought of in terms of a return and a detour, as turning towards and away, but also in terms of an original torsion, an initial division, a fundamental doubleness. Furthermore, a different relation between life and writing is brought forth: life is no longer the stuff, the material of stories; stories are not about a lifetime (or a shorter period within it) brought to an end (the end accrediting precisely the beginning of narration). Stories, like life, are unending; stories and life cease to exist in reference to each other – in a logic of absolute continuity – and are instead equated to each other. To put it another way, their relation is no longer one of transformation but of equation; yet this equation should not be understood in terms of a stabilizing equality and a balancing symmetry, but in terms of ceaseless – infinite – movement and dissymmetry.

The relation between writing and life might be thought of in terms of the famous Borgesian equation of the book with the world and, additionally and conversely, of the world with a book. In the essay 'L'Infini littéraire: L'Aleph', part of the collection *Le Livre à venir* (1959), Blanchot, suspecting Borges of having come upon the infinity – that is, the truth – of literature, notes that what is destabilizing in this 'innocent tautology' (of the book and the world) is the lack of a (stable) point of reference. The world and the book incessantly, dizzyingly, send to each other their reflected (and deflected) images, without either world having priority over the other, without either world acting as a (stable) point of reference for the other. It is precisely this infinite, interminable *errance* that is designated by Blanchot, via Borges, as the truth of literature (the truth as reconfigured by literature): 'La vérité de la littérature serait dans l'erreur de l'infini' [The truth of literature might be in the error of the infinite].[48]

Blanchot elucidates that the distinguishing feature of the infinite, or rather what transforms the finite into the infinite, is that there is no exit and no stop. With regard to the impossibility of exit, he notes: '[D]u fini qui est pourtant fermé on peut toujours espérer sortir [...]; [...] tout lieu absolument sans issue devient infini' [[F]rom the finite, which is still closed, one can always hope to escape [...] – [...] any place absolutely without exit becomes infinite].[49] With regard to the impossibility of stopping he notes: 'L'erreur, le fait d'être en chemin sans pouvoir s'arrêter jamais, changent le fini en infini' [The error, the fact of being on the go without ever being able to stop, changes the finite into infinity].[50] The re-conception of truth as wandering is further developed and practised in *L'Entretien infini*, in which the truth wanders and passes from speaker to speaker without

---

48   Maurice Blanchot, 'L'Infini littéraire: L'Aleph', in Blanchot, *Le Livre à venir*, pp. 130–34 (p. 130); Maurice Blanchot, 'Literary Infinity: The Aleph', in Blanchot, *The Book to Come*, pp. 93–96 (p. 93).
49   Blanchot, 'L'Infini littéraire', p. 131; Blanchot, 'Literary Infinity', p. 94.
50   Blanchot, 'L'Infini littéraire', p. 131; Blanchot, 'Literary Infinity', p. 93.

ever being retained or appropriated. In *L'Entretien infini* the truth as wandering becomes synonymous with the truth as always other.

In the Borgesian universe, the liquidation of a stable point of reference is coupled with the liquidation of the idea of origin. In this respect, Blanchot alludes to the fictional twentieth-century French writer Pierre Menard, who, reproducing and repeating phrase by phrase an identical section from Cervantes' *Don Quixote* (1605/1615), creates a perfect double to the original text.[51] What is disquieting in this identical production or, as Blanchot puts it, 'dans cette identité qui n'en est pas une' [in this identity that is not one], is that it throws into confusion the very idea of identity (in its equation to the one).[52] In other words, 'là où il y a un double parfait, l'original est effacé et même l'origine' [where there is a perfect double the original is erased, and even the origin].[53] In his own tribute to *Don Quixote* in *L'Entretien infini* (whose unparalleled originality as a created work lies in the fact that it deliberately offers itself as an imitation), Blanchot brings in the theme of the double in terms of an initial doubling and an original torsion, as he alludes to 'un redoublement plus initial, celui qui précède et met en cause l'unité supposée de la "literature" et de la "vie"' [a more initial doubling that precedes and puts into question the supposed unity of 'literature' and 'life'].[54] This unity of literature and life here called into question should be considered both in terms of coherence (as the harmonious relationship/correspondence *between* literature and life) and in terms of oneness, the state of being one (the unity *of* literature, the unity *of* life). This unity is thrown into confusion by Cervantes' *Don Quixote* as well as by Cervantes himself.

The madness and extravagance of Don Quixote, whose life has been permeated by literature (by what he has read), is, says Blanchot,

---

51 In Borges' short story 'Pierre Menard, Author of the *Quixote*', the narrator, who knew the fictitious French poet Pierre Menard, informs the reader about Menard's admirable undertaking: to produce himself, without copying, a number of pages which would be verbally identical to those by Cervantes. At the end, the narrator quotes and juxtaposes three lines as written by Cervantes in his *Don Quixote* and, directly after, the exact same lines as rewritten, word for word, in the *Don Quixote* of Pierre Menard. See Jorge Luis Borges, 'Pierre Menard, Author of the *Quixote*', in Jorge Luis Borges, *Collected Fictions*, trans. by Andrew Hurley (London: Penguin Books, 1999), pp. 88–95 (pp. 91, 94).

52 Blanchot, 'L'Infini littéraire', p. 133; Blanchot, 'Literary Infinity', p. 95.

53 Blanchot, 'L'Infini littéraire', p. 133; Blanchot, 'Literary Infinity', p. 95.

54 Maurice Blanchot, 'Le Pont de bois *(la répétition, le neutre)*', in Blanchot, *L'Entretien infini*, pp. 568–82 (p. 570); Maurice Blanchot, 'The Wooden Bridge *(repetition, the neutral)*', in Blanchot, *The Infinite Conversation*, pp. 388–96 (p. 389).

to abandon his library, to become a character of action and to live adventurously, as one does in books. Therefore, writes Blanchot, 'ce qu'il fait est toujours déjà une réflexion, de même qu'il ne peut être lui-même qu'un double, tandis que le texte où se racontent ses exploits n'est pas un livre, mais une référence à d'autres livres' [his feats are always already a reflection, just as he himself cannot but be a double, while the text in which his exploits are recounted is not a book but a reference to other books].[55] For Blanchot the madness of Don Quixote – the 'not reasonable', but 'nonetheless logical', madness of everyone who reads – is his trust in recounting and his belief that the truth of books might hold for life. To Don Quixote's logical madness, Blanchot introduces the asymmetrical (even greater) and dissimilar (illogical) madness of Cervantes. Cervantes is the reverse case of Don Quixote inasmuch as, unlike his character, who decides to abandon his library and goes out in an attempt to put the life of books into practice, Cervantes puts all his efforts into a book, doing nothing but writing without living. As Blanchot writes: '[C]'est dans un livre encore qu'il s'évertue, ne quittant pas sa librairie et ne faisant rien, vivant, s'agitant, mourant, qu'écrire sans vivre, sans se mouvoir ni mourir' [[I]t is still into a book that he puts all his efforts, not leaving his library and doing nothing while he lives, acts and dies other than writing – without living, and without either moving or dying].[56] What interests Blanchot in the strange case of Don Quixote (and the even stranger case of Cervantes) is that a relation (between life and literature) is put forth that defies unity. Life is not transformed, turned into a story, and stories, as the disenchanted Don Quixote realizes, do not reflect the reality of life. Nonetheless, this does not mean that literature and life are cut off from each other: on the contrary, their relation is one of mutual implication and entanglement, which can be thought of in terms of an original torsion.

The Logic of the Neuter: Neither/Nor

In *L'Entretien infini*, in the footnote to the section entitled 'La Question la plus profonde', Blanchot designates as the most profound question the questioning of the 'One'.[57] Accommodating Levinas's criticism of all Western philosophies as philosophies of the Same, he criticizes and

---

55 Blanchot, 'Le Pont de bois', p. 569; Blanchot, 'The Wooden Bridge', p. 389.
56 Blanchot, 'Le Pont de bois', p. 569; Blanchot, 'The Wooden Bridge', p. 389.
57 Maurice Blanchot, 'La Question la plus profonde', in Blanchot, *L'Entretien infini*, pp. 12–34 (pp. 32–34 n. 1); Maurice Blanchot, 'The Most Profound Question',

equates, despite their differences, Hegelian dialectics, Heideggerian ontology and the critique of ontology to the extent that all three are based on and conclude with the postulate of the One:

> L'Un, le Même restent les premiers, les derniers mots. Pourquoi cette référence à l'Un comme référence ultime et unique? En ce sens, la dialectique, l'ontologie et la critique de l'ontologie ont le même postulat: toutes trois se remettent à l'Un.
>
> [The One, the Same, remain the first and the last words. Why this reference to the One as the ultimate and unique reference? In this sense, the dialectic, ontology, and the critique of ontology have the same postulate: all three deliver themselves over to the One.][58]

Blanchot goes on to enumerate the different ways in which the above systems of thought reinforce the idea of the One, incorporating otherness under the promise of the whole or the Absolute or on the premise of gathering, light and unity, 'soit que l'Un s'accomplisse comme tout, soit qu'il entende l'être comme rassemblement, lumière et unité de l'être, soit que par-delà et au-dessus de l'être, il s'affirme comme l'Absolu' [be it that the One accomplishes itself as everything, be it that it understands being as gathering, light, and unity of being, or be it that, above and beyond being, it affirms itself as the Absolute].[59] Therefore, concludes Blanchot, 'ne faudrait-il pas dire: "la question la plus profonde" est la question qui échappe à la référence de l'Un? C'est l'autre question, question de l'Autre, mais aussi question toujours autre' [must we not say: 'the most profound question' is the question that escapes reference to the One? It is the other question, the question of the Other, but also a question that is always other].[60]

There are three remarks to be made here: first, the insistent questioning of the One marks Blanchot's difference from Heidegger, especially the late Heidegger, who insists on the intimacy, the association and the interchangeability between being and oneness

---

in Blanchot, *The Infinite Conversation*, pp. 11–24 (pp. 439–40 n. 3). In the English translation the notes to 'The Most Profound Question' are on pages 439–40.

58 Blanchot, 'La Question la plus profonde', pp. 32–34 n. 1; Blanchot, 'The Most Profound Question', pp. 439–40 n. 3.

59 Blanchot, 'La Question la plus profonde', pp. 32–34 n. 1; Blanchot, 'The Most Profound Question', pp. 439–40 n. 3.

60 Blanchot, 'La Question la plus profonde', pp. 32–34 n. 1; Blanchot, 'The Most Profound Question', pp. 439–40 n. 3.

(ὄν, ἔν).⁶¹ Second, the questioning of the One overlaps with, but is not the same as, the question of the Other; it goes together but does not coincide with it. In so doing, it also marks, as we shall see, Blanchot's divergence from Levinas. Third, as always in Blanchot, this question is, and is posed as, the question of writing. In this sense the question of 'the other' is a demand which is not only set forth in the first sections of *L'Entretien infini* but also, and more crucially, is responded to throughout the numerous pages of this immense work.

In the introductory note of *L'Entretien infini* Blanchot, alluding to the exigency of writing, repeats his earlier definition of writing as it appeared mainly in the 1940s, namely, in terms of a contestatory force. Additionally, he provides a definition of writing as an anonymous and dispersed way of being in relation. Among the many things which writing challenges, Blanchot includes the Truth and the One (to which we could add the conception of the Truth as one and the idea of the One as the Truth). The passage reads as follows:

> [L'] écriture qui [...] dégage des possibilités tout autres, une façon anonyme, distraite, différée et dispersée d'être en rapport par laquelle tout est mise en cause, et d'abord l'Idée de Dieu, du Moi, du Sujet, puis de la Vérité et de l'Un, puis l'idée du Livre et de l'Œuvre [...] écriture qu'on pourrait dire hors discours, hors langage.
>
> [[W]riting [...] brings forth possibilities that are entirely other: an anonymous, distracted, deferred and dispersed way of being in relation, by which everything is called into question – and first of all the ideal of God, of the Self, of the Subject, then of the Truth and the One, then finally the idea of the Book and the Work – [...] a writing that could be said to be outside discourse, outside language.]⁶²

As Blanchot suggests, the contestatory force of writing ends up contesting not only the notion of the One (through the notion of the other) but also the way of being in relation, since the very notion of the other demands an-other way of being in relation. In this respect, the key notion of the neuter, namely Blanchot's way of thinking about and addressing alterity, is advanced not only with reference to the subject and reality (as the dispersal of subjectivity and worldhood) but also in terms of another language (neutral speech) and another

---

61 For the late Heidegger: 'Oneness makes up beingness. And oneness here means: unifying, originary gathering unto sameness of what presences' (Martin Heidegger, *Contributions to Philosophy (From Enowning)*, trans. by Parvis Emad and Kenneth Maly (Bloomington, IN: Indiana University Press, 1999), p. 138).

62 Blanchot, 'Note', p. vii; Blanchot, 'Note', p. xii.

way of relation (the neutral relation as a relation of a third kind, one which goes beyond both dialectical progression and mystical fusion). Additionally, the neuter is the Blanchotian response to, as well as a reworking of, the Levinasian *autrui* (where alterity is restricted to the unconceptualizable radical alterity of the other person).

Although *L'Entretien infini* begins by evoking the term 'autrui', the dropping of it in favour of the neuter characterizes Blanchot's singular approach to the question of otherness and marks his divergence from Levinas (in so far as it neutralizes the relation of transcendence). For Blanchot our subjection to the other, as Levinas demands, is still tied up in a logic of subordination and dominance. In the Levinasian demand of ethics as the first philosophy, the other (the second of traditional philosophy) comes first, while in Blanchot's elaboration of the other in terms of the neuter the other is what alters (what makes other) the one. Blanchot distances himself from the absolute priority of the other person (*autrui*) in place of (instead of) oneself, as he remarks: '– [L]a souveraineté est en l'Autre qui est le seul Absolu. – Et l'autre, dans ce cas, n'est encore qu'un substitut de l'Un' [– [S]overeignty is in the Other who is the sole absolute. – And the other, in this case, is still no more than a substitute for the One].[63] To put it another way, a critique of the Levinasian *autrui* from a Blanchotian standpoint is that the priority of the other against subjectivity still remains within the framework of dialectics to the extent that it still rests on reconciliation – albeit the reconciliation (our reconciliation) with the absolute primacy of the other against the self (ourselves) – and, as transcendental subjectivity, is relocated to a conception of the other in terms of transcendence. Put somewhat schematically, as in Levinas's thought, alterity is overemphasized, the other is what transcends relation, whereas Blanchot's aim is to find an-other way of relating. This other relation, which is the relation to the other, is radicalized in

---

63 Blanchot, 'Le Rapport du troisième genre', p. 95; Blanchot, 'The Relation of the Third Kind', p. 66. Similarly, in *L'Écriture du désastre* (1980) Blanchot expresses his reluctance to accept the absolute priority of the other and asks: '[S]i moi sans moi je suis à l'épreuve (sans l'éprouver) de la passivité la plus passive lorsque autrui m'écrase jusqu'à l'aliénation radicale, est-ce à autrui que j'ai encore affaire, n'est-ce pas plutôt au "je" du maître, à l'absolu de la puissance égoïste, au dominateur qui prédomine et qui manie la force jusqu'à la persécution inquisitoriale?' [[I]f I, deprived of myself, am put to the test (without experiencing it) of the most passive passivity, as the other crushes me to the point of radical alienation, is it really the other to whom I relate – or is it rather the 'I' of the master, the absolute of egoistic power, the dominator who prevails and who wields force to the point of inquisitorial persecution?] (Maurice Blanchot, *L'Écriture du désastre* (Paris: Gallimard, 1980), pp. 37–38).

L'Entretien infini as a double relation (doubly asymmetrical), as '[un] rapport neutre, rapport sans rapport' [the neutral relation, a relation without relation].[64]

The logic of doubleness is at first set up in *L'Espace littéraire* under the contrivance of a 'double death' and, consequently, of a 'double relation to death'. The theme, or rather 'the strange project', of the double death ('l'étrange projet ou la double mort' [the strange project, or double death]) is defined as 'non pas la certitude de la mort accomplie, mais "l'éternel tourment de mourir"' [not the certainty of death achieved, but 'the eternal torments of dying'].[65] In a lengthier passage a more analytical description of the notion of the double death is provided and a double relation to death is instituted as both possible and impossible:

> [I]l y a comme une double mort, dont l'une circule dans les mots de possibilité, de liberté, qui a comme extrême horizon la liberté de mourir et le pouvoir de se risquer mortellement – et dont l'autre est l'insaisissable, ce que je ne puis saisir, qui n'est liée à *moi* par aucune relation d'aucune sorte, qui ne vient jamais, vers laquelle je ne me dirige pas.
>
> [[D]eath is somehow doubled: there is one death which circulates in the language of possibility, of liberty, which has for its furthest horizon the freedom to die and the capacity to take mortal risks; and there is its double, which is ungraspable. It is what I cannot grasp, what is not linked to *me* by any relation of any sort. It is that which never comes and toward which I do not direct myself.] [66]

The redoubling of death, as death turns into the impossibility of dying, can be seen in the fate of Kafka's characters, whose story and torment lie precisely in their inability to die. The space of death they inhabit is sketched not in terms of the end as definite but in terms of the endless time of dying. In Blanchot's words, 'c'est dans l'espace de la mort que les héros de Kafka accomplissent leurs démarches, c'est au temps indéfini du "mourir" qu'ils

---

64 Blanchot, 'Le Rapport du troisième genre', p. 104; Blanchot, 'The Relation of the Third Kind', p. 73. For two re-readings and critical approaches to Levinas through Blanchotian lenses, see Critchley, *Very Little ... Almost Nothing*, pp. 94–97; and Clark, *Derrida, Heidegger, Blanchot*, pp. 102–05, 107.

65 Maurice Blanchot, 'L'Œuvre et l'espace de la mort', in Blanchot, *L'Espace littéraire*, pp. 103–210 (pp. 129, 150); Maurice Blanchot, 'The Work and Death's Space', in Blanchot, *The Space of Literature*, pp. 85–160 (pp. 103, 119).

66 Blanchot, 'L'Œuvre et l'espace de la mort', pp. 129–30; Blanchot, 'The Work and Death's Space', p. 104.

appartiennent' [Kafka's heroes carry out their actions in death's space, they belong to the indefinite time of 'dying'].[67] One thinks here of the dead Hunter Gracchus, who finds out that his death does not after all consist of a peaceful end (a final termination of and deliverance from existence), but of carrying on, wandering eternally over the seas;[68] or of the peculiar destiny of Gregor Samsa, who causes great distress to his family not when he finally dies (which is a relief to the family), but when he refuses to do so and turns into an insect. In his earlier essay 'La Lecture de Kafka' (1949), Blanchot describes Gregor Samsa's state as 'l'état même de l'être qui ne peut pas quitter l'existence' [the state of the being who cannot depart from existence]; and his existence as his condemnation 'à retomber toujours dans l'existence' [to falling continually back into existence].[69] By the same token Blanchot finds the end of the story – '[l'] appel à la volupté sur lequel le récit s'achève' [the call to the sensual on which the story ends] – to be the climax of horror in so far as it certifies that 'il n'y a pas eu de fin, l'existence continue' [there is no end, life goes on].[70] *Die Verwandlung* [*The Metamorphosis*] (1915) ends with Gregor's sister awakening to life and, despite the hardships of her family and the paleness of her face, turning into a pretty girl who, as her parents think, might be in need of a husband. According to Blanchot's commentary on the ending, 'il n'y a rien de plus effrayant dans tout ce conte. C'est la malédiction même et c'est aussi le renouveau, c'est l'espérance, car la jeune fille veut vivre, et vivre c'est déjà échapper à l'inévitable' [there is nothing more frightening in the entire story. It is the curse and it is revival, hope, for the girl wants to live, when to live is just to escape the inevitable].[71] In a similar way, the early Levinas of *De l'existence à l'existant* (1947) desperately exclaims, repeating Baudelaire's lament which anticipates the claustrophobic Beckettian universe: '[D]emain, hélas!, il faudra vivre encore'

---

67 Blanchot, 'L'Œuvre et l'espace de la mort', p. 112; Blanchot, 'The Work and Death's Space', p. 92.

68 'Der Jäger Gracchus' [The Hunter Gracchus] is a short story by Franz Kafka (written in 1917, published posthumously in 1931).

69 Maurice Blanchot, 'La Lecture de Kafka', in Blanchot, *La Part du feu*, pp. 9–19 (p. 17); Maurice Blanchot, 'Reading Kafka', in Blanchot, *The Work of Fire*, pp. 1–11 (p. 9).

70 Blanchot, 'La Lecture de Kafka', p. 18; Blanchot, 'Reading Kafka', p. 10.

71 Blanchot, 'La Lecture de Kafka', p. 18; Blanchot, 'Reading Kafka', p. 10.

[[T]omorrow, alas, she will still have to live].⁷² Critchley puts it as follows: 'But what if tomorrow does not bring death but only the infinity of today, the irremissibility of an existence one is unable to leave?'.⁷³

The displacement brought about by the term 'dying' can be thought of with reference to another limit, that of the limited forces which limit life, as the theme of weariness that invades the beginning of *L'Entretien infini* reminds us. In the case of weariness, the limit, rather than compromising the integrity of life, becomes an integral part of life: in other words, the limit is displaced from the outside towards the inside, it is not a limit on life but a limit within life. In the phrasing of *L'Entretien infini*, in the preliminary dialogue which follows the introductory note and precedes the main text, the main dialogue, we read: '± *Pourquoi donne-t-il le nom de fatigue à ce qui est sa vie même?*' [± Why does he give the name weariness to what is his very life?].⁷⁴ Moreover, as Blanchot argues in his essay 'La Lecture de Kafka', the complexity and subtlety of Kafka's universe (the experience not only of Kafka's characters but also of Kafka himself) lie in its depiction of existence not only as dreadful and interminable (dreadful to the extent that it is interminable), but also as primarily indeterminate: '[N]ous ne savons pas si nous en sommes exclus (et c'est pourquoi nous y cherchons vainement des prises solides) ou à jamais enfermés (et nous nous tournons désespérément vers le dehors)' [[W]e do not know if we are excluded from it (which is why we search vainly in it for something solid to hold onto) or whether we are forever imprisoned in it (and so we turn desperately toward the outside)].⁷⁵

---

72   Levinas, *De l'existence à l'existant*, p. 102; Charles Baudelaire, 'Le Masque', in *Les Fleurs du mal*; Charles Baudelaire, 'The Mask', trans. by William Aggeler, in *The Flowers of Evil* < https://fleursdumal.org/poem/201> [accessed 17 April 2022].

73   Critchley, *Very Little ... Almost Nothing*, p. 70.

74   Maurice Blanchot, 'Sans titre', in Blanchot, *L'Entretien infini*, pp. ix–xxvi (p. xx); Marice Blanchot, 'Untitled', in Blanchot, *The Infinite Conversation*, pp. xiii–xxiii (p. xix). The displacement of the limit is borne by the place and the staging of this preliminary dialogue. Bearing the double sign (±), written in italics, it presents itself as a liminal text: since it has no title and it does not appear in the table of contents, it is not strictly speaking part of the book. Rather, it questions its being part of the book, since it is both in and outside it, both belonging and not belonging, both a component and not a component. Additionally, despite its status as an interval between the introductory note and the main text, it nevertheless is, and acts like, an introductory act: it opens the scene, initiates us to and sets the tone for the main conversation that follows, bearing its echo.

75   Blanchot, 'La Lecture de Kafka', p. 17; Blanchot, 'Reading Kafka', p. 9.

The double relation which is first established in *L'Espace littéraire* with reference to death reoccurs in *L'Entretien infini* with reference to life. Indeed, in *L'Entretien infini* the relation to the impossible depends primarily on existence. As we read in Blanchot's homage to Bataille and to the Bataillean key term of the impossible (one of the last words he made public, as Blanchot informs us):

> Il faut entendre que la possibilité n'est pas la seule dimension de notre existence et qu'il nous est peut-être donné de 'vivre' chaque événement de nous-même dans un double rapport, une fois comme ce que nous comprenons, saisissons, supportons et maîtrisons [...] en le rapportant à quelque bien, quelque valeur [...], une autre fois comme ce qui se dérobe à tout emploi et échappe à toute fin [...]. oui, comme si l'impossibilité [...] nous attendait derrière tout ce que nous vivons, pensons et disons.
>
> [It must be understood that possibility is not the sole dimension of our existence, and that it is perhaps given to us to 'live' each of the events that is ours by way of a double relation. We live it one time as something we comprehend, grasp, bear and master [...] by relating it to some good or to some value [...]; we live it another time as something that escapes all employ and all end [...]. Yes, as though impossibility [...] were waiting for us behind all that we live, think and say.][76]

Alongside this double relation, in *L'Entretien infini* the third term of the neuter is brought about, which problematizes precisely the idea of Unity (the idea of the One). Christophe Bident, providing a brief definition of the neuter as 'neither the one nor the other, neither clear nor obscure', as well as its etymological origin from the Latin *ne-uter* (not either), neither this nor that, characterizes the term as one of Blanchot's crucial creative conceptual achievements. Alluding to Deleuze's remark that the creation of true concepts is what makes a philosopher, Bident suggests that the contrivance of the neuter would suffice to render Blanchot a philosopher. He nevertheless adds that the neuter is not a concept either:

> For if the neuter is irreducible to the clear or the obscure, it is in the first instance because it is also irreducible to itself: broadly undefined, it does not present itself as a concept which is clear, or that clarifies, or that serves as a source of clarification [...].[77]

---

76 Blanchot, 'L'Expérience-limite', pp. 307–08; Blanchot, 'The Limit-Experience', p. 207.
77 Bident, 'The Movements of the Neuter', p. 13.

However, if the peculiar status of the neuter as a concept might bring into question Blanchot's adhesion to philosophy, the neuter is indisputably what draws him to literature.

Critics have argued that the neuter is not a term invented by Blanchot (although Blanchot proves incomparably inventive concerning its use and function, its workings and its unworkings). It is preferable to allude briefly to the theme of the neutral *within* the Blanchotian *œuvre*, since well before *L'Entretien infini* the theme of neutrality appeared in the early essays of the 1940s under the name of the *il y a* (the key term that figured in Part I), a device which designated precisely the neutrality of being. The *il y a*, a term shared by Blanchot and Levinas, is a contestation of both the destructive force of Hegelian negativity and the Heideggerian positing of Being. Against Hegelian negation, the *il y a*, the simple fact that 'there is', always already affirmed (the presence of absence as extreme affirmation, the extreme affirmation of the presence of absence) designates, contra Hegel, the impossibility of negation. Additionally, the *il y a* recasts being as the neutrality of being. Against the Heideggerian ontological difference (the relation between Being and beings and the event of Being against beings), the *il y a* (in Paul Davies's terms 'the Levinasian contribution to ontology that ruins ontology') corresponds to the undifferentiated unity of being and remoulds existence in terms of worldlessness, anonymity and neutrality.[78]

The neuter, on the contrary, has nothing to do with being or non-being; it responds to the question of the other. In so doing, while the *il y a* serves to designate the impossibility of negation, the neuter designates the impossibility of the one. While the *il y a* points to the unity of being, the neuter contests precisely the idea of unity and brings forth the multiple and the fragmentary. While grammatically the *il y a* [there is] has an affirmative character, the neuter (neither this nor that) has an indeterminate character. More crucially, whereas the *il y a* corresponds to the otherness of language, the preconceptual materiality (and singularity) of things before the cataclysmic event (the calamity) of their naming, the neuter is plural speech, the speech of writing (as anonymous and neutral) which challenges the discourse of unity and identity. While, with the contrivance of the *il y a*, Blanchot and Levinas join forces to problematize the Heideggerian question of being (to suspend and pass beyond the

---

78 Paul Davies, 'A linear narrative? Blanchot with Heidegger in the Work of Levinas', in *Philosophers' Poets*, ed. by David Wood (London: Routledge, 1990), pp. 37–69 (p. 42).

alternative between being and non-being), with the contrivance of the neuter Blanchot both addresses and problematizes the question of Levinasian otherness. The neuter therefore marks both Blanchot's proximity to and his distancing from Levinas. It is in this sense that Timothy Clark provides a further definition of the neuter as 'neither Heidegger nor Levinas'.[79] For Clark, Blanchot's reconfiguration of language in terms of the neuter, which is the voice of no one, diverges both from Heideggerian *Dichtung* (and the conception of language as the saying – and the poetic gathering – of Being) and from Levinasian otherness (and the conception of language as a form of transcendence). Put differently, Blanchot does not impose another language, that of the neuter, against dialectical language (negativity) or against the language of ontology (being) but reconfigures the relation between the two languages in non-dialectical terms, since – rather than being opposed – they are bound together; and the neuter – rather than being privileged – merely undermines, shadows, interrupts and disperses both Hegelian negativity and Heideggerian being.

The elusive character of the neuter can be signalled in its convergence with the everyday, that is, the unobservability of the everyday. In this respect, another difference between the neuter and the *il y a* emerges: the *il y a* corresponds more to a biblical, post-apocalyptic scene, while the neuter converges more with everyday life, whose constitutive trait it is to be unperceived. The *il y a*, inasmuch as it attests to the presence of absence, is (and invites us – impossibly – to experience) what exists (always has and will exist) without us, while the everyday is relational, as it is what we (always) see again. The everyday, as that which never happens for the first time but always again, more evidently brings forth repetition, whereas the *il y a* attests to what is without beginning or end. In this respect, the *il y a* (already there and still there) challenges creation and destruction, whereas the everyday, as that which always already happens and to which we always already have access, more evidently challenges the beginning, the possibility of access and the idea of creation.

By directing our attention to the neuter as one of the prominent terms of *L'Entretien infini*, we have seen how, against all the semantic connotations of the neutral as of no particular kind or characteristics and of neutrality as an impartial, disengaged position, as not taking sides in a dispute, the Blanchotian neuter breaks through as a distinct term which contests what no philosophical system – despite their

---

79   Clark, *Derrida, Heidegger, Blanchot*, p. 107.

disagreements – has contested, namely, the order of the One as well as the conception of relation in terms of opposition, incompatibility or hierarchy. Thus, despite the common association of the neutral with the dispassionate, the neutral is precisely what empassions Blanchot about – nearly captivates him in – the space of literature. Picking up and singling out the neuter as the most characteristic term of *L'Entretien infini*, we have seen how it is bound up with the less noticeably displayed but nevertheless pervasive logic of the 'double', which appears throughout all parts of *L'Entretien infini* and, more largely, throughout Blanchot's entire *œuvre*. Indeed, all the prevalent terms in *L'Entretien infini*, namely fragmentation, multiplicity and repetition, can be delineated under the constellation of the neuter – a term whose defining particularity is its adherence to (and its enactment of) a double logic against wholeness, duality and unity and of a double relation against the dialectics of progression, recognition and reconciliation or the hierarchy of the ontic-ontological difference. In this respect, the neuter advances a relation of radical horizontality (rather than a hierarchical relation), a shifting and disjunctive movement (rather than a progressive movement). In the end, one might say that the neuter eventually has a neutralizing function: in its association with the double, it tones down the Levinasian predominance (and burden) of otherness and in its affinity with the everyday it counteracts the Bataillean preference for (and fostering of) the limit(less) in terms of the extreme.

8. Bataille: Returning and Masking

La vie humaine ne peut suivre sans trembler – sans tricher – le mouvement qui l'entraîne à la mort. Je l'ai représentée trichant – louvoyant – dans les voies dont j'ai parlé.

[Human life cannot follow without trembling – without cheating – the movement that leads it to death. I have depicted it cheating – navigating – in the ways I have spoken of.][1]

Il y a donc le 1 et le 2, le simple et le double. Le double vient *après* le simple, il le multiplie *par suite*. […] [J]amais la discernabilité absolue entre l'imité et l'imitant, ni l'anteriorité de celui-là sur celui-ci, n'auront été déplacées par un système métaphysique.

[There is thus the 1 and the 2, the single and the double. The double comes *after* the simple; it multiplies it as a *follow-up*. […] But never have the absolute distinguishabilty between imitated and imitator, and the anteriority of the first over the second been displaced by any metaphysical system.][2]

Among the various readings of *Histoire de l'œil* two of the most insightful commentaries are those of Patrick ffrench and Michel Leiris. The first insists on its visual dimension and underlines the broader project of dislocation which it sets out, while the second focuses on its temporal dimension and reads the story as a vacuum in time. Despite their dissimilarities – the former provides a more structural close reading (zooming in, magnifying the chopping of the eye and raising broader questions of visuality and form), while the latter offers a more thematic reading (construing the cut as a cut in time and linking this vacuum with holidays and childhood) – both

---

1   Georges Bataille, *L'Érotisme*, p. 158; Georges Bataille, *Eroticism*, p. 146.
2   Jacques Derrida, 'La Double séance', in Jacques Derrida, *La Dissémination* (Paris: Seuil, 1993 [1972]), pp. 215–347 (p. 235–36); Jacques Derrida, 'The First Session', in Derrida, *Acts of Literature*, pp. 127–80 (p. 140).

show how Bataille, in his first novel, distances himself from any idea of origin, because what truly counts are subversion (of vision) and disruption (of time). In his seminal study dedicated to the novel, *The Cut: Reading Bataille's Histoire de l'œil*, ffrench advances a reading of it as a story of the de-sublimation of the visual, as a narrative which traces the eye's displacement downwards to the sexual parts. As he puts it: 'The "Story of the Eye" is the story of an imaginary regression of the eye along a chain of displacements from its sublimated position within the corpus of the human'.[3] One can compare this regressive journey of the eye with the Deleuzian contrivance of 'bodies without organs', that is, without organization, as the eye, in Bataille's novel, is not relinquished but displaced, liberated, diffused. In Deleuzian terms, the eye is no longer part of an organism: as it escapes from the organization of the organism, it becomes transitory, sticks in the material reality of bodies and re-emerges through the sexual organs of Simone. However, this displacement, as ffrench insists throughout his book, is not to be confused with a replacement, since the latter would amount to an attempt to foreground the body, physicality or sexuality as an origin or a primary site.[4] Instead, the story has recourse to all means in order to make us see and realize the complete absence of firm ground, fixity and stability – which is why urination also comes in, as a process of liquification that attacks and dismantles solidity, inflicting a vision of the world as flux. Sharing, and quoting, Krauss's view as expressed in her *Optical Unconscious*, ffrench claims that the task of de-sublimation is, in principle, to unform, 'to knock meaning off its pedestal, to bring it down in the world, to deliver it a low blow'.[5] To put it another way, the process of de-sublimation of the privileged organ of cognition and perception does not aspire to replace one ideal with another.

Michel Leiris, on the other hand, in his short article entitled 'Le Temps de Lord Auch', while not ignoring the fact that in the novel the recurrent and major attack and assault are against the eye as the most eminent and loftiest organ, reads 'ce festival du dérèglement et de l'insulte aux idoles' [this festival of misbehaviour and insult to idols], as he calls *Histoire de l'œil*, as bound to childhood and holidays.

---

3   ffrench, *The Cut*, p. 32.

4   A similar remark can be made with regard to Bataille's dark eroticism in general: it does not aspire to posit sexuality as predominant nor to appoint death as an all-encompassing force.

5   Rosalind E. Krauss, *The Optical Unconscious* (Cambridge, MA: The MIT Press, 1993), p. 157.

Noting that in this frenzied festival only one character is an adult, he puts forward a reading of the novel as a story of irreducible (unrestrained) childishness and endless holidays:

> Par quelque flamme qu'ils soient rongés et à quelque noirceur qu'atteignent finalement leurs actes, le fait c'est que les héros [...] demeurent empreints d'une irréductible gaminerie, à travers des tribulations qui sont impossibles à situer ailleurs que dans une période des grandes vacances.[6]
>
> [By whatever flame they are consumed and whatever darkness their acts finally reach, the fact is that the heroes [...] remain imbued with an irreducible childishness, through tribulations that are impossible to situate elsewhere than in a period of the long holidays.]

Drawing on Leiris's remark and pushing it further, one can argue that the definition of literature as a return to childhood ('la littérature, c'est l'enfance retrouvée'), as it appears twenty years later in *La Littérature et le mal*, is anticipated and set (staged) in Bataille's first book (which can be read as a reverse coming-of-age story).[7] However, as both childhood and holidays depart from their conventional meaning, the Bataillean return resembles more a break, a rupture, a fissure. In both Bataille's book and Leiris's commentary, childhood and holidays designate a vacant, unoccupied period, a breach in time rather than a definable period within time (opposed, and thereby complementary, to adulthood and work). Indeed, childhood is not considered to be the beginning of a lifetime, an initial phase located back in the past, but rather a leap out of time, a time of absolute, and hence terrifying, leisure.[8] Similarly, holidays are literally meant as time off and acquire the sense of a vacancy, a vacuum, a radical break in time. In this sense, the returns launched in *Histoire de l'œil* (the return of the eye within the body and the return to childhood) are rather to be considered reversals, overturnings (of the primacy of sight, of the order of the world).

---

6 Michel Leiris, 'Du temps de Lord Auch', *L'Arc*, 32 (1967), 6–15 (p. 15).

7 Bataille, 'Avant-Propos', in Bataille, *La Littérature et le mal*, p. 172; Bataille, 'Preface', in Bataille, *Literature and Evil*, p. x.

8 Leiris also renders childhood synonymous with amusement, adding right away that, against the tamed version of entertainment in modern culture (in which entertainment is complementary to work, a break in order to return to work re-energized and to work more efficiently), for Bataille amusement is outrageous and terrifying. In Bataille's definition, 'l'amusement est le besoin le plus criant, et bien entendu, le plus terrifiant de la nature humaine' [amusement is the most blatant and, of course, the most terrifying need of human nature] (Leiris, 'Du temps de Lord Auch', p. 15).

The longing for return, which first appears in *Histoire de l'œil*, is a recurrent motif in Bataille's thought. The Bataillean return echoes the Nietzschean device of eternal recurrence in its attempt to disengage life (and thought) from being future-directed. In (anti-)Hegelian and (anti-)Heideggerian terms, the motif of return eschews both the aspiration to represent the totality of the world as well as the attempt to disclose an original moment. The erotic and the deathly, Eros and (as) Thanatos, two of the most predominant and pervading themes in the Bataillean universe, cannot be considered apart from a yearning for return inasmuch as they designate a movement from discontinuity (the separateness of individual beings) towards continuity (a state, or rather an ec-static mode, in which individuals escape the confinements of their limits and merge into the limitlessness from which they have emerged). Nonetheless, this return is to be conceived neither in terms of retrieval (of a prior, initial, antecedent origin which is recovered), nor in terms of revelation (of a newly found origin which is to be laid as a foundation), but rather in terms of overturning (that is, as a problematization of the very idea of origin).

In our previous chapters on Bataille we have already looked into a series of overturnings which, despite their thematic divergence, testify to the insistent recurrence of the gesture of reversal as a way of problematizing the logic of origin and foundation. Adopting the viewpoint of economy, Chapter 1 demonstrates how discharge is asserted as constitutive of life and hence expenditure and loss are considered primary, while production and acquisition are considered secondary operations. Adopting the viewpoint of ethics, Chapter 5 focuses on the primacy of the present and the valorization of the intensity of the instant against the future and that which lasts. In this way it is shown how Bataille brings forth pleasure (designated the surrender to the present and hence termed a sovereign moment when existence obeys nothing outside itself) against work (designated as the care for – and hence the subordination of existence to – the future). This last chapter (adopting the viewpoint of art and history or, more precisely, pre-historic art), by making particular reference to Bataille's text *Lascaux ou la naissance de l'art* (1955), in which the celebrated Greek miracle is overthrown and displaced by the miracle of Lascaux, brings in a third reversal, one which concerns the birth of art and humanity.[9] As Bataille puts it: 'À

---

9 The Greek miracle, or the Athenian miracle, is the blooming of democracy, philosophy, tragedy, comedy, architecture, sculpture and mathematics in the fifth century BC in Athens. The outburst of creative spirit occurred in parallel with the rise of ancient Athens as a Mediterranean power.

Lascaux, ce qui, dans la profondeur de la terre, nous égare et nous transfigure est la vision du plus lointain' [In Lascaux, in the depths of the earth, what leads us astray and transfigures us is the vision of the most distant past].[10] He asserts: '[C]e n'est pas tellement du miracle grec que nous devrions parler désormais mais du miracle de Lascaux' [[I]t is not so much about the Greek miracle that we should talk from now on but rather about the miracle of Lascaux].[11] Going further back (into the depths of time) and further down (into the depths of a cave), decentring the luminosity and radiance of the Greek miracle with the chthonic site of Lascaux, Bataille's text on Lascaux emphasizes how humanity is concurrently affirmed and disguised *in* (not behind) animal masks. In so doing, it suggests disguise and masking as constitutive and sheds light on what Bataille is trying to do in writing. This chapter also looks into how the Bataillean recurring movement of returning and overturning is bound to an unappeased demand for truth and how truth is requalified in terms of a radical withdrawal, masking and doubling.

It may at first sound paradoxical to suggest that Bataille's thought, a thought that renewed the intellectual scene by privileging experience against understanding, positing the unknowable and the excessive against the knowable and measurable, imposing base materiality as a considerable matter for thought – briefly, a thought the distinctive mark of which is the preference for exposure and an aversion to mastery – is driven by a commitment to a question as old and worn out, as used and misused and as closely associated with the tradition of metaphysics as that of truth. In this regard, as one might expect, the Bataillean truth, sharing the Nietzschean inheritance of dispiritedness, is neither liberating nor empowering: it is, merely and primarily, truthful (faithful) to existence as it is – or, to use more of a Bataillean term, to existence in its nakedness (against the artifice of social conventions and intellectual constructions). In this way, one can contend that the truth which concerns Bataille is the truth of the body.

As the truth of the body is rendered the central axis, in *L'Érotisme*, Bataille declares: 'L'action décisive est la mise à nu' [The decisive action is laying bare].[12] Bataille has also announced that the act of denuding is registered on his thought: 'Je pense comme une fille

---

10   Georges Bataille, *Lascaux ou la naissance de l'art*, in *Œuvres complètes*, ix (1979), 7–101 (p. 12).

11   Bataille, 'Préface', in Bataille, *Lascaux*, pp. 9–10 (p. 9).

12   Bataille, *L'Érotisme*, p. 23. The translation in the English edition has been modified ('stripping naked in the decisive action' (Bataille, *Eroticism*, p. 17)).

enlève sa robe' [I think in the way a girl takes off her dress].[13] Drawing on these preliminary remarks, the following discussion shows how denuding proves decisive to the extent that, dispersing all fantasies of revelation (and secrecy), it does not consist in the majestic power of the revelatory but in the minimal act of laying bare. Additionally, and conversely, the analysis demonstrates how the act of denuding can be conceived in terms of acting rather than action and how masking becomes inflected with laying bare. In this way, the mask will be introduced as a useful term in order to approach how truth, as put forward by Bataille, consists of an irreducible doubleness, since it is distanced from its conception both in terms of correctness and correspondence (truth as a correct vision) and in terms of drawing the veil and bringing into the open (truth as bringing to light). In other words, for Bataille there is neither representation nor presentation, since he does not aim for the unmediated transmission of truth (the fiction of truth) but rather points to the inevitable entanglement of truth with the fictitious (the truth of fiction).

Truth precedes – as a prefatory statement – several of Bataille's fictional texts. In a way that echoes Cézanne's famous promise to the younger artist Emile Bernard, 'I owe you the truth in painting and I will tell it to you', the prefaces of many of Bataille's texts announce a similar commitment.[14] In both cases the announcement has a double meaning: first, inasmuch as it is directed towards the interlocutor – the reader, in the case of Bataille; the young fellow craftsman, in the case of Cézanne – it makes a pact with, and a promise to, the addressee; second, inasmuch as it is articulated with regard to art, it formulates and fosters the principle of alliance between truth and art – the art of painting, for Cézanne; the art of writing, for Bataille. Nonetheless, if one takes a closer look at Cézanne's saying ('I owe you the truth in painting and I will tell it to you'), one realizes that its meaning is rather dubious and slippery, which is precisely what urges Derrida to comment on it extensively. What is this 'truth in painting'? Is it to be told or to be painted? To put it another way, is it the truth *about* painting (on the subject of painting, what truly counts as painting) or is it the truth as it emerges *through* painting (as the subject of painting, truth as depicted by painting)? Finally, should the promise be fulfilled – or, in so far as it is a promise, should its force and spell

---

13   Georges Bataille, 'Méthode de méditation', in Œuvres complètes, v: *La Somme athéologique. Tome I*, pp. 191–227 (p. 200).

14   The phrase 'Je vous dois la vérité en peinture, et je vous la dirai' appears in a letter from Paul Cézanne to his friend Émile Bernard dated 23 October 1905.

depend on its unfulfillment? If this is the case, one's duty might as well be to secure and guard the non-fulfilling of the promise (in a similar but inverse logic to that of the secret, whose existence and very condition of secrecy are enabled and sustained by disclosure – if not of its content, at least of its existence). As Derrida sums up the above: '*Cézanne a-t-il* promis, vraiment *promis, promis de* dire, *de dire* la verité, *de dire* en peinture *la verité* en peinture? Et *moi*?' [*Did Cézanne* promise, really *promise, promise* to tell, *to tell* the truth, *to tell* in painting *the truth* in painting? And what about *me*?].[15]

Drawing on Derrida's aporia, one feels the urge to ask: and Bataille? How does he position himself and his writings with regard to truth? Does he share Derrida's questioning and mistrustful attitude or does he take sides with Cézanne's decisive commitment to truth? On the one hand, it seems incomprehensible that the same Bataille who tirelessly denounced all the facets of metaphysical solace, who famously proclaimed 'Je vis d'expérience, et non pas d'explication logique' [I live by experience and not by logical explanation], who celebrated, against duration and coherence, the elusive and the convulsive – in its visual, temporal and bodily manifestations, in blinding illuminations, in the intensity of the instant and erotic spasms – that this same Bataille does not simply use a term as scholarly as that of 'truth' but posits the will to truth as the precept of his writings. On the other hand, as Surya argues, Bataille is not a homogenous man: 'Il n'y a pas *un* Georges Bataille tout entier révélé, livre après livre, homegène d'un bout à l'autre de son œuvre et de son existence' [There is not *one* Georges Bataille but *several*].[16] However, while taking this remark into account, this study does not suggest that there is a Bataille who denounces truth and another one who takes it upon himself; rather, despite – or precisely *in* – the heterogeneity of Bataille's thought an enduring and persistent engagement to the search for truth can be detected.

The Logic of the Double: Acting (What it is *Like*)

In the preface of *Le Bleu du ciel*, his novel written in 1937, Bataille sketches out in a quite straightforward way the truth in literature in its

---

15   Jacques Derrida, *La Vérité en peinture* (Paris: Flammarion, 2010 [1978]), p. 14.

16   Surya, *Georges Bataille*, p. 111; Surya, *Georges Bataille*, p. 88. A more complete, exact translation would be: 'There is not *one* Georges Bataille wholly revealed, book after book, thoroughly homogenous from one end of his work and his existence to the other'.

double sense, as dissected above by Derrida with reference to painting and Cézanne. Indeed, we are told both what kind of truth counts *for* literature and what truly counts *as* literature: the interference of life is given as the criterion for truth, whereas the implication of constraint, the imperative to write, is given as the criterion of true literature. In the opening lines of the preface Bataille announces that narratives reveal – and should reveal – 'la vérité multiple de la vie' [the multiple truth of life]. The whole phrase reads as follows: 'Un peu plus, un peu moins tout homme est suspendu aux récits, aux romans qui lui relèvent la vérité multiple de la vie' [A little more or a little less, every man depends on stories, on novels that reveal to him the multiple truth of life].[17] Here, the multiplicity of life is meant as its vibrancy and not as the coexistence of multiple, various forms of life; or, to phrase the above in Deleuzian terms, Bataille here refers to zones of intensity that constitute (and destitute) life and not to the multiplicity of living forms, as the latter is simply another variant of the 'one'. Furthermore, as becomes clear further on, the truth of life for Bataille, far from being multiple, is rather unequivocal. The definition of literary truth in its second sense, that of true literature, is provided a few lines further on, formulated as follows: 'Comment nous attarder à des livres auxquels, sensiblement, l'auteur n'a pas été contraint?' [How can we dwell on books to which, essentially, the author was not compelled?].[18] Despite its interrogative form, the formulation is not to be taken as a question, even less as a hesitant suggestion; it is, rather, to be taken as a statement in its strictest sense. The fact – or rather the principle – according to which one does not freely choose to write but is forced to write is given in a quasi-aphoristic, almost dogmatic tone, as Bataille's general – or, more precisely, his personal – truth about books. In this regard Bataille offers clarification: 'J'ai voulu formuler ce principe. Je renonce à le justifier' [I wanted to formulate this principle. I renounce its justification].[19] What he provides us with is just a series of books which have moved him as a reader.[20] Despite

---

17 Georges Bataille, 'Avant-Propos', in Bataille, *Bleu du Ciel*, in *Œuvres complètes*, III: *Œuvres littéraires*, pp. 381–82 (p. 381).
18 Bataille, 'Avant-Propos', in *Le Bleu du ciel*, p. 381.
19 Bataille, 'Avant-Propos', in *Le Bleu du ciel*, p. 381.
20 Whereas truth in its joining forces with life recurrently appears in many of Bataille's prefaces, the definition of true literature appears only in the preface of *Le Bleu du ciel*. The coercive element, the Batalliean measure of true literature, while given as the distinctive characteristic of a writer, also involves the reader: what initially compels the author to the book (to write it) subsequently drives the reader to the book (to read it).

Bataille's refusal to provide explanations for picking out the element of compulsion, his choice is justifiable by his widespread preference for experiences in which agency is suspended, namely, experiences which, however willed or striven for, ultimately and essentially befall us, occur despite us (like fate), are given, rather than acquired (like grace), take hold of us and possess us (like religious or erotic ecstasy).

In the preface to *L'Impossible* the depiction of truth is again designated the steadfast aim of the Bataillean project: 'Comme les récits fictifs des romans, les textes qui suivent [...] se présentent avec l'intention de peindre la vérité' [Like the fictional narratives of novels, the texts that follow [...] are presented with the intention of sketching the truth].[21] Additionally, desire and death are designated the appropriate means for the attainment of truth to the extent that they suspend consciousness and throw identity into confusion: 'L'outrance du désir et de la mort permet seule d'atteindre la vérité' [The excess of desire and death is the only way to reach the truth].[22] In (anti-)Hegelian and (anti-)Sartrean terms, desire and death show how we are not only subjects *of* desire but primarily subjected *to* desire, inasmuch as, far from fostering or imposing subjectivity, they ex-pose us, despite ourselves, to something other than ourselves. In the extremity of death and desire, subjects (or, in terms closer to the Bataillean lexicon, *les êtres vivants*) do not impose their will but become possessed and disarmed. In this respect death is not to be understood in substantive terms, that is, in terms of decease or disappearance, but in terms of a process, an operation (which defies both immediacy and mediation). Rather than actual death, this should be understood as an act of dying. Furthermore, the act which interests Bataille is neither (from an internal viewpoint) an act of consciousness – in which what is negated appears as an object of consciousness – nor (from an external viewpoint) a worldly action – in which the given is negated and a world which was not is created. In the preface to *Madame Edwarda* the undertaking is described in the following terms: 'L'être nous est donné dans un dépassement *intolerable* de l'être' [The act whereby being – existence – is bestowed upon us is an *unbearable* surpassing of being].[23] Whereas for Hegel to exist is to act (negate the world as it is and transform it into something that was not) and

---

21 Georges Bataille, 'Préface', in Bataille, *L'Impossible*, in *Œuvres complètes*, III: *Œuvres littéraires*, pp. 101–02 (p. 101).

22 Bataille, 'Préface', in *L'Impossible*, p. 101.

23 Bataille, 'Préface', in Bataille, *Madame Edwarda*, pp. 11–14 (p. 11); Bataille, 'Preface', in Bataille, *Madame Edwarda*, pp. 123–29 (p. 126).

for Heidegger, contra Hegel, possibility is valorized against actuality and action (to be is to let the world and beings be), Bataille, contra Heidegger, valorizes impossibility against possibility: truly to be, for Bataille, is to be outside of being. Human existence consists not in a privileged access to the world (as Heidegger's largely criticized anthropocentric vision asserts), but in escaping from the world.

The element of impossibility and outsideness, glossed again as the unbearable, returns decisively a few lines further on in the preface of *Madame Edwarda*. Here, truth is resolutely termed unbearable – unbearable to see, unbearable to know – and sight and vision, knowledge and thought are implicated only to be dismissed:

> Que signifie la vérité [...] si nous ne voyons ce qui excède la possibilité de voir, ce qui est intolérable de voir, comme, dans l'extase il est intolérable de jouir? si nous ne pensons ce qui excède la possibilité de penser ...?
>
> [What does truth signify if we do not see that which exceeds sight's possibilities, that which it is unbearable to see as, in ecstasy, it is unbearable to know pleasure? what if we do not think that which exceeds thought's possibilities? ...][24]

As becomes evident, the Bataillean truth drifts towards the Lacanian Real, which is precisely that against which reality – in all the constructions that make it up – protects us. However, if we accept the unbearable as the definition of truth (in its verging upon the Real), the problem which follows is that of its access: how can the unbearable be borne (be it from the viewpoint of subjectivity, by a human body, or from the viewpoint of art and literature, by a visual or a written form)? If we accept the extremity of desire and death as the means of the attainment of truth, as Bataille suggests, how are they to be endured? In other words, the desire of the separate individual to escape the confinements of individuality, however strong, cannot be considered apart from the struggle against the terror of losing oneself, as Bataille writes in *L'Érotisme*: 'Mais sortant des limites, ou mourant, nous nous efforçons d'échapper à l'effroi que la mort donne, et que la vision d'une continuité par-delà ces limites peut elle-même donner' [But as we break through the barriers, as we die, we strive to escape the terror of death and the terror that belongs

---

24 Bataille, 'Préface', in Bataille, *Madame Edwarda*, p. 12; Bataille, 'Preface', in Bataille, *Madame Edwarda*, p. 126.

even to the continuity beyond those boundaries].²⁵ In this regard, as ffrench suggests, fear, anxiety and terror are not in front of (and due to) nothingness but in front of (and due to) metamorphosis, incessant movement, pure fluidity.²⁶

As the human condition is rethought in terms of a fundamental, unsurpassable contradiction and the unitary subject becomes a torn subject – torn between the desire to be lost in continuity and the will to survive (go on living a discontinuous life) – the following question arises: as Kristeva would frame the problem, from the viewpoint of subjectivity, knowledge and eroticism, how can the encounter between the subject and *jouissance* (which throws the subject outside itself) take place? In Deleuzian terms, and from the viewpoint of presentation, how can excessive presence be presented and how can invisible forces be rendered visible? In his book dedicated to Francis Bacon, Deleuze also raises the question of how sound could be painted and, conversely, how colours could be made audible. Thus, the questioning of visibility/ invisibility does not revolve around the limits of vision, neither is it an attack merely on vision; rather, it touches on, in broader terms, the forms of creation if we exclude representation – and, in even broader terms, on the forms of relation if we exclude mediation.

The section from *Madame Edwarda* quoted above, alongside the reformulation of truth in terms of the unbearable and the excessive and the analogy between truth and the ecstatic, calls for the imperative to see it, to think of it, to know it. Truth, in its unbearableness, becomes a demand upon literature. As Surya says: 'Insoutenable est cette vérité; [...] Insoutenable doit être la littérature' [This truth is unbearable; [...] Unbearable is what literature must be].²⁷ In his book on Bacon Deleuze makes a similar claim about painting. Repeating Paul Klee's aphorism which crystallizes the task of painting as 'non pas rendre le visible, mais rendre visible' [not to render the visible, but to make visible], Deleuze underscores the idea that the task of painting is to render visible the invisible ('invisible forces', in terms

---

25 Bataille, *L'Érotisme*, pp. 139–40; Bataille, *Eroticism*, p. 140. A more precise translation would be: 'But by crossing the limits, or by dying, we strive to escape the dread that death gives and that the vision of continuity beyond those limits can itself give'.

26 ffrench, *The Cut*, p. 54. As ffrench writes, terror is a terror of the *informe*, that is, 'pure movement, pure flux without stasis'. The Bataillean key term *informe* is examined later.

27 Surya, *Georges Bataille*, p. 488; Surya, *Georges Bataille: An Intellectual Biography*, p. 422.

closer to the Deleuzian lexicon).²⁸ Applied in the case of Bataille, that is, the case of language and literature, the task is to approach silence, make silence speak. In the essay 'Molloy's Silence', Bataille provides one more definition of literature which highlights its alliance with silence as well as with recoil: '[I]l se peut même que la littérature ait déjà profondément le même sens que le silence, mais elle recule devant le dernier pas que le silence serait' [[I]t may even be that literature already has profoundly the same meaning as silence, but it recoils before the ultimate step that silence would be].²⁹ Beckett's greatness, as Bataille notes, lies in the fact that he rendered, exposed – and exposed us to – reality in its pure, that is, its poorest, state, the 'state of a wreck'; or, as Adorno expresses it (with reference to *Endgame*), Beckett takes 'the theological "unto dust shalt thou return" literally', since 'the Old Testament saying "You shall become dust again" is translated here into "dirt"'.³⁰ As signalled in the title of Bataille's essay, this reality of dirt and dust, fundamental and minimal, dreadful and repelling as it is, strikes one dumb; it cannot be spoken of or named. In truth, it is and renders one silent: '[C]e que nous nommons que par impuissance vagabond, misérable, [...] en vérité est innommable (mais innommable est encore un mot qui nous embrouille)' [[W]hat we call by impotence vagabond, miserable, [...] in truth is unnamable (but unnamable is still a word that confuses us)].³¹

Since reality in its pure state is – in truth – unnamable, the Bataillean truth, like death, is not understood in terms of 'what' but in terms of an operation: as the endless process of laying bare, without depending on something transcending this life or this world as an answer or a remedy. In terms closer to Hegel, the desire for interrogation is more fundamental than the desire to know and the desire to be undone is more fundamental than the desire for recognition (which is why Bataille puts forward the erotic struggle against the Hegelian master-and-slave struggle until death). While there is, arguably, an element of transcendence in Bataille's thought, for Bataille transcendence takes place in this world: it is not to be encountered once we exit

---

28 Gilles Deleuze, *Francis Bacon. Logique de la sensation* (Paris: Seuil, 2002 [1981]), p. 58.

29 Georges Bataille, 'Le Silence de Molloy', in *Œuvres complètes*, xii: *Articles II. 1950–1961* (1988), pp. 85–94 (p. 88).

30 Theodor W. Adorno, 'Notes on Beckett', trans. by Dirk Van Hulle and Shane Weller, *Journal of Beckett Studies*, 19 (2010), 157–78 (p. 171).

31 Bataille, 'Le Silence de Molloy', p. 86.

this life but while we live. Though unseizable, it is not higher, superior, outside existence, but both within and beyond this life and world. For Surya, therein lies Bataille's distance from Dostoevsky, since the infinity of remorse and of confession which permeates the Dostoevskian universe ultimately corresponds not to an endless laying bare but to religiosity.[32] Dostoevsky's remorse and shame remain idealistic and sentimental, inasmuch as they demonize and move away from 'l'hideuse matérialité de ce monde' [the hideous materiality of this world].[33] On the contrary, notes Surya, Bataille's profound affinity with Beckett lies in the fact that they do not flee materiality, hideous as it is, but respond to the endless laying bare by endlessly laying bare.[34] In this respect, as the materiality of the real expropriates truth, the function and the texture of the narrative plot changes. Narration, far from being a reliable ally in the search of truth, worthy of our trust, proves to be unworthy and risible, riddled with and ridiculed due to the outbursts of the real.[35]

Beckett and Bataille, the latter turning to the materiality of bodies, the former turning to the materiality of objects, join forces to attack the two basic postulates of Existentialism, namely meaning and inwardness. Commenting on Beckett's clinging to objects, Critchley, following Adorno, notes how the Beckettian turn to objects – to 'their

32 Surya, *Georges Bataille*, p. 487; Surya, *Georges Bataille: An Intellectual Biography*, p. 421.

33 Surya, *Georges Bataille*, p. 487; Surya, *Georges Bataille: An Intellectual Biography*, p. 421.

34 Surya, *Georges Bataille*, p. 488; Surya, *Georges Bataille: An Intellectual Biography*, p. 422. Additionally, alongside their different approaches to confession, Bataille's and Dostoevsky's conceptions of evil also differ on the grounds of religiosity. Apart from a thematic divergence, since Bataillean evil is not only or necessarily wrongdoing but, bound to the Bataillean notion of sovereignty, refers – both more broadly and in the strictest sense – to a specific temporality of existence (in which the priority of future survival gives way to the intensity of the present), a second divergence consists in the fact that, in the case of Dostoevsky, unlimited affection for criminal figures is animated by religiosity and, more precisely, redemption. As Freud remarks in his article 'Dostoevsky and Parricide', the case of *The Brothers Karamazov* demonstrates that guilt does not only concern the one who actually commits the crime: the one who longs for the crime before it happens and the one who happily accepts it once it has happened are equally guilty. In this sense, Freud adds, 'a criminal is to [Dostoevsky] almost a redeemer', inasmuch as 'he has taken on himself the guilt which must else have been borne by others' (Sigmund Freud, 'Dostoevsky and Parricide', in Freud, *Art and Literature*, ed. by Albert Dickson, pp. 435–60 (p. 443)).

35 ffrench analyses how the narrative structure of the story of the eye is interrupted and undermined by the obscene (ffrench, *The Cut*, pp. 86–89).

extraordinary ordinariness', as he puts it – diverges radically from Existentialism in a double sense: first, the meaninglessness of existence (in a Godless, absurd, world) is not translated into a meaning, as that would turn it into – and equate it with – idealism (meaninglessness would then become another universal, another idea).[36] Second, the world's meaninglessness is no longer seen from the point of view of individuality and hence as subjectivity's claim to freedom.[37] Adhering to the main critique against existential philosophy, Critchley notes that Existentialism has not just left intact the conception of the subject, but that it ends up solidifying and setting free individuality in terms of autonomy and emancipatory freedom. Reacting against the Sartrean 'desire for being' which renders the subject (and its choices) the guarantor of (the) meaning (of meaninglessness), Beckett empties, impoverishes, the subject, reducing it to nothingness, whereas Bataille reconfigures subjectivity in terms of a torn subject, torn by a desire to be (to maintain itself) and a desire not to be (to exceed the bounds which secure it but also doom it to confinement). Consequently, while the Beckettian universe is occupied by desolate, dispirited beings, alone amidst various leftovers, worthless among scraps, the aesthetic vision which emanates from Bataille's torn subject involves an attack on form as closed and clearly defined and an emphasis on slippage rather than equivalence. Focusing on the movement of differentiation, Bataille resists the conception of meaning in terms of either fixity or transfer, as meaning occurs neither through formation (the positing of form as the ascription of meaning) nor through the use of metaphor (the conception of meaning in terms of transference, exchange, resemblance).

The *informe*, as many critics have argued, is a key notion that crystallizes the Bataillean battle to unform, to undo the closedness of forms, the positing of meaning and the fixity of interpretation. The *informe* is not to be thought of in terms of presence or absence, as it designates neither the absence of form nor the substantiation of nothingness, but rather highlights rhythm and movement, slippage and metamorphosis. Thus it has been defined by Rosalind Krauss as the 'threat carried by metamorphic rhythm', which nevertheless is the rhythmic condition of form,[38] and as 'the movement of slippage, difference, differentiation' by Patrick ffrench.[39] The operational

---

36 Critchley, *Very Little ... Almost Nothing*, pp. 173–75.
37 Critchley, *Very Little ... Almost Nothing*, pp. 173–75.
38 Krauss, *The Optical Unconscious*, p. 137.
39 ffrench, *The Cut*, p. 20.

character of the *informe* as it undoes the logic of oppositions has been highlighted by critics. As ffrench writes with reference to materiality and idealism, '[The *informe*] does not define a base materiality in opposition to the domain of ideas […] but the operation of materiality upon the ideal'.[40] Additionally, as the *informe* is an *operation upon* – rather an *opposition to* – form, the internal enabling – rather than the absence – of form, it puts forward, in ffrench's words, 'the movement of becoming present as always conditioned by an operation of re-presentation and difference'.[41] In its capacity as the generator of form, the *informe*, apart from the oppositional logic of presence/absence and material/ideal, also defies the logic of cause and effect: form emerges as the residue of the *informe* and the *informe* (which is precisely what is lost when form comes into view) comes, in its turn, to be the (invisible) residue of form.

In his own definition of the *informe* Bataille, faithful to the practical disposition which characterizes the whole *Documents* venture, announces that our focus should be directed towards what words do (rather than what they mean), towards their task (rather than their meaning). In this regard the *informe* is (its task is) 'un terme servant à déclasser' [a term that serves to bring things down in the world].[42] Bataille continues by giving a more detailed account:

> Il faudrait en effet, pour que les hommes académiques soient contents, que l'univers prenne forme. La philosophie entière n'a pas d'autre but: il s'agit de donner une redingote à ce qui est […]. Par contre, affirmer que l'univers ne ressemble à rien et n'est qu'*informe* revient à dire que l'univers est quelque chose comme une araignée ou un crachat.
>
> [In fact, for academic men to be happy, the universe would have to take shape. All of philosophy has no other goal: it is a matter of giving a frock coat to what is […]. On the other hand, affirming that the universe resembles nothing and is only *formless* amounts to saying that the universe is something like a spider or a spit.][43]

Commenting on the passage, ffrench guards the operational character of the *informe* against its substantiation – not even as an *araignée* or

---

40 ffrench, *The Cut*, p. 22.
41 ffrench, *The Cut*, p. 20.
42 Georges Bataille, 'Informe', in *Œuvres complètes*, I: *Premiers écrits. 1922–1940*, p. 217; Georges Bataille, 'Formless', in Bataille, *Visions of Excess*, p. 31.
43 Bataille, 'Informe', p. 217; Bataille, 'Formless', p. 31.

a *crachat*, as Bataille willingly seems to suggest. Following Krauss, and in contrast to Kristeva, ffrench insists that the *informe* should be considered in terms of an operation rather than in terms of a referent, a thing, an attribute or an object, and thereby strongly opposes the reification of the process through the fetishization of certain states as abject (such as the material or the maternal).

In 'L'Anus solaire' (1927) the theory of the universe as *informe* is paired with a view of the world (a worldview) as parodic, that is, in flux. As the world is parodic, fluid, the relation of the objects which constitute it lies in the constant movement of circulation. The logic of circulation, unlike the circular logic that relies on the completion of the circle, is one of endless flow. As Bataille declares: 'Il est clair que le monde est purement parodique, c'est à dire que quelque chose qu'on regarde est la parodie d'une autre, ou encore la même chose sous une forme décevante' [It is clear that the world is purely parodic, in other words that each thing seen is the parody of another, or is the same thing in a deceptive form].[44] He adds, asserting the lack of any principle and providing a list of things as parodies of other things:

> Tout le monde a conscience que la vie est parodique et qu'il manque une interprétation. Ainsi le plomb est la parodie de l'or. L'air est la parodie de l'eau. Le cerveau est la parodie de l'équateur. Le coït est la parodie du crime.
>
> [Everyone is aware that life is parodic and that it lacks representation. Thus lead is the parody of gold. Air is the parody of water. The brain is the parody of the equator. Coitus is the parody of crime.][45]

To say that the world is parodic is to endorse the Heraclitean doctrine of flux, in its comparison of existing things to the flow of a river, against the Platonic theory of forms and ideas. Additionally, to say that the world is parodic is to subsume language with the worldly movement of circulation and to make it proceed via copulation. In the omnipresence of a constant state of flux, the copula 'is' becomes, as ffrench observes, 'the mark not of an equivalence but of slippage'.[46] Copulative joining, in both its grammatical and corporeal sense, is a

---

44 Georges Bataille, 'L'Anus solaire', in *Œuvres complètes*, I: *Premiers écrits. 1922–1940*, pp. 79–86 (p. 81); Georges Bataille, 'The Solar Anus', in Bataille, *Visions of Excess*, ed. by Stoekl, pp. 5–9 (p. 5).
45 Bataille, 'L'Anus solaire', p. 81; Bataille, 'The Solar Anus', p. 5.
46 ffrench, *The Cut*, pp. 21, 27.

movement out of and back into limits.⁴⁷ The copula (the connecting verb) acts as the link, the tie that connects and allows the possibility of relation (the circulation of words, the formulation of sentences); copulation (the coming together of bodies, sexual intercourse) connects and links through leakage, setting up contact in terms of the leakage of the self rather than in terms of a connection with the other. In this respect, in *L'Érotisme* Bataille makes a remark that is close to Susan Sontag's observation that 'making love resembles having an epileptic fit'.⁴⁸ Underscoring how the erotic act brings no real union but consists, rather, in a shared state of crisis, he writes:

> [A]u moment de la conjonction […] il n'y a pas à proprement parler d'union, deux individus sous l'empire de la violence […] partagent un état de crise où l'un comme l'autre est hors de soi. Les deux êtres sont en même temps ouverts à la continuité.
>
> [[A]t the moment of conjunction […] there is no real union; two individuals in the grip of violence […] share a state of crisis in which both are outside themselves. Both creatures are simultaneously open to continuity.]⁴⁹

The conception of the erotic act in terms of both solitude and overwhelming diffusion echoes the Bataillean conception of dramatization, which is similarly described both as solitary and as profoundly communicative. As Bataille has already asserted in *L'Expérience intérieure*:

> Si nous ne savions dramatiser, nous ne pourrions sortir de nous-même. Nous vivrions isolés et tassés. Mais une sorte de rupture – dans l'angoisse – nous laisse à la limite des larmes: alors nous nous perdons, nous oublions nous-mêmes et communiquons avec un au-delà insaisissable.
>
> If we didn't know how to dramatize, we wouldn't be able to leave ourselves. We would live isolated and turned in on ourselves. But a sort of rupture – in anguish – leaves us at the limit of tears: in such a case we lose ourselves, we forget ourselves and communicate with an elusive beyond.]⁵⁰

---

47 In this respect, ffrench, in highly structural terms, notes that sexual relation involves two axes: the vertical axis (erection) towards the sun and the horizontal axis (copulation) between objects (ffrench, *The Cut*, p. 56).
48 Sontag, 'The Pornographic Imagination', p. 57.
49 Bataille, *L'Érotisme*, pp. 103–04; Bataille, *Eroticism*, p. 103.
50 Bataille, *L'Expérience intérieure*, p. 23; Bataille, *The Inner Experience*, p. 11.

Dramatization has a double meaning: the term 'dramatic' designates both a play and a turbulent event. 'To dramatize' means both to present a performance and to present in a dramatic way, to exaggerate; it means both to act and to overact. Bataille uses the term in both ways: dramatization is meant as insistence and intensification, since continuous effort and repetition are required in order to have a glimpse of instantaneous rupture.[51] However, on the occasion of *Madame Edwarda* the second meaning of dramatization is put forward, that of acting, staging, performing, as God is brought on stage, appearing (masked or laid bare?) as a public whore. Edwarda shows how the experience of ecstasy, be it mystic or sexual, though comparable, is preferable to the act of dying, since in death '[l'être] en même temps qu'il nous est donné, il nous est retiré' [being is taken away from us at the same time it is given].[52] Therefore, death is – and must be – sought 'dans le *sentiment* de la mort' [in the feeling of dying], in moments when 'il nous semble que nous mourons' [it seems to us that we are dying].[53] All that we can receive (and to which we can aspire) is merely an impression, a sensation, or, one could add more emphatically, a pretence, an *as if*. In this respect the Bataillean act is also an acting, an undertaking but also a performance, a venture but also a pretence, yet this pretence is not to be dismissed as false or presented as truth. This glimpse of death is fictive but the fictive here is not juxtaposed with the real or with truth but rather points to the inescapability of the fictitious in one's relation to death.[54]

Alongside the *informe*, the importance of which has rightly been highlighted by scholarship inasmuch as it registers the movement of openness and continuity of the Bataillean venture, the mask merits attention as another model that accounts for the tension and doubleness of Bataille's narratives, as well as for their apparent theatrical character. The mask, neither self-present nor simply absent, shows boldly how Bataille undermines representation

---

51 In *L'Expérience intérieure* the experience of rupture occurs, as we are told, through the successive and insistent projection (both through evocation and imagination) of images of rupture.

52 Bataille, 'Préface', in Bataille, *Madame Edwarda*, p. 11; Bataille, 'Preface', in Bataille, *Madame Edwarda*, p. 126.

53 Bataille, 'Préface', in Bataille, *Madame Edwarda*, p. 11; Bataille, 'Preface', in Bataille, *Madame Edwarda*, p. 126.

54 In his analysis of Bataille's text 'Hegel, la mort et le sacrifice' Leslie Hill underlines the element of the 'fictitious', pointing out how spectatorship ultimately offers a paradox of proximity and distance, tragedy and comedy (Hill, *Bataille, Klosswoski, Blanchot*, pp. 67–69).

in its traditional sense without completely abandoning it. Like the *informe*, the mask does not simply oppose form; yet while the *informe* emphasizes movement, since it both generates and undoes form, the mask designates more emphatically the centrality of re-presentation in Bataille's writing. Additionally, alongside Nancy's logic of exscription, developed in Chapter 1, the mask – defying both presence and absence – offers another way of approaching the residual logic of Bataille's writing and its embedding in the real. Nancy, in his description of how exscription works, notes that 'le cri de Bataille n'est pas masqué ni étouffé: il se fait entendre *comme le cri qu'on n'entend pas*' [Bataille's cry is not masked or muffled: it is heard as the cry that is not heard].[55] In this respect the cry, in its intensity, is not represented, inscribed, tamed, stifled or muted in the text; yet neither is it outside, beyond the text, unrepresentable: the cry is in the text, presented in it (heard), yet presented as exscribed, not fully contained (not heard). The mask, however, can also be thought of not in terms of a trope that masks and covers but in terms of the Derridean conception of 'mimesis without imitation'. In this sense, the mask ruins imitation and destabilizes resemblance without discarding them altogether. There is masking (mimesis), not because there is something to see (to imitate), but because there is nothing to see (and nothing to mask). To bring into play the term Bataille uses in his definition of the *informe*, alluding to the attempt by philosophy to dress up the world, instead of a *redingote* Bataille offers a mask. With reference to Bataille's text on Lascaux, what follows will show in what way masking proves more fitting than clothing.

The Logic of Masking/Showing

Tension, one can unreservedly argue, is the distinctive mark of and the driving force in Bataille's thought and life. However, since tension is not simply asserted as something then to be overcome but, rather, becomes a matter of attainment and maintenance, Bataille's thought is characterized by a series of tensional couplings in which each term neither opposes nor excludes but rather agitates the other – both inflaming and disturbing it. As Bataille strives to break free from the actual and the possible only to bind himself to the impossible, these couplings include, most notably, life and death – or, in other words, experience and communication. More importantly, these couplings both ask for and emanate from a daring gaze at the world (and life)

---

55 Nancy, 'L'excrit', p. 62; Nancy, 'Exscription', p. 64.

as it is, as well as a fondness for artistic practice.⁵⁶ The Bataillean desire to embrace the real – both in its totality and in its bareness – is accompanied by a profound affection for art. Commenting on the central place which art occupies in Bataille's work, Surya notes that '[l]'art […] [a induit] Bataille […] à penser la même chose [ce qu'il a sans cesse pensé] au moyen de nouveaux éléments' [art […] made him […] think about the same things through new elements].⁵⁷ Additionally and conversely, Bataille's texts on art, apart from intensifying and developing some of the key themes of his thought, provide us with, as ffrench observes, a useful model of how his own literary texts work.⁵⁸

Bataille's affection for art, on the same plane as his devotion to life, can be traced back to his famous letter to Kojève. The question of *négativité sans emploi* that is raised in the letter is linked not only to his existence (to the open wound that is his life – eluding thereby the closedness of the Hegelian system), but also to artworks:

> Je la [la négativité sans emploi] suis dans les formes qu'elle engendre non tout d'abord en moi-même, mais en d'autres. Le plus souvent, la négativité impuissante se fait œuvre d'art: cette métamorphose dont les conséquences sont réelles d'habitude répond mal à la situation laissée par l'achèvement de l'histoire (ou par la pensée de son achèvement) […] [;] quand éluder n'est plus possible (quand arrive l'heure de la vérité).⁵⁹

> [I follow it [unemployed negativity] in the forms it generates not just in myself but rather in others. In most of the cases, unemployed negativity becomes a work of art: this metamorphosis, whose consequences are usually real, responds badly to the situation left by the end of history (or by the thought of its end) […] [;] when eluding is no longer possible (when the time of truth comes).]

To respond to the question of how art breaks through at the moment of truth, Bataille does not take the standpoint of the end of history but

---

56   As Jean Bruno comments, 'ses écrits ultérieurs manifestent une avidité de connaître la totalité du réel et une rare finesse dans l'appréciation des formes les plus diverses de l'art' [his later writings show an urge to know the totality of reality and a rare subtlety in the consideration of the most diverse forms of art] (Jean Bruno, 'Techniques d'illumination chez Georges Bataille', *Critique*, 195/196 (1963), 706–21 (pp. 717–18)).

57   Surya, *Georges Bataille*, p. 537; Surya, *Georges Bataille: An Intellectual Biography*, p. 465.

58   ffrench, *The Cut*, p. 111.

59   Bataille, 'Lettre à X', p. 370.

turns to another decisive moment. 'En prenant [le] chemin à rebours' [Following the same path in reverse], as Kristeva aptly phrases the Bataillean convergence and divergence from Hegel, Bataille directs his attention to the birth of humanity, which is bound to the parietal art of Lascaux.[60] As we read in his text *Lascaux ou la naissance de l'art*: 'Le nom de Lascaux est le symbole des âges qui connurent le passage de la bête humaine à l'être délié que nous sommes' [The name of Lascaux is the symbol of the times that witnessed the passage from the human beast to the delicate being that we are].[61]

For Bataille, contrary to Hegel, the birth of humanity coincides with – and is carried through – the birth of art inasmuch as the passage from animality to humanity is not effectuated through and due to work but is, rather, due to figuration. Additionally, while the logic of work is that of negation, figuration puts forward a logic of return. Indeed, the abundance of animal figures in the Lascaux cave bear the mark of a return – not a return *to* but a return *of* animality, at the very moment at which humanity is attained and by the very gesture by which humanity is enacted. Nonetheless, the importance of Lascaux for Bataille and, consequently, of Bataille's text on Lascaux for us, is that what returns (as the repressed) is not only animality but also, and perhaps more crucially, fiction, pretence and masking.[62]

In the paintings which decorate the Lascaux cave human faces are masked with animal heads and human figures are absent, ruled out by innumerable animal figures. In the section 'La représentation de l'homme', under the title 'L'homme paré du prestige de la bête', commenting on what he glosses as the 'miracle of Lascaux' and demonstrating in what sense Lascaux introduces a paradox into the heart of figuration, Bataille writes that 'ce qui nous fige en un long étonnement est l'effacement de l'homme devant l'animal – et de l'homme justement devenant humain – est le plus grand que nous puissions imaginer' [what leaves us astonished and thunderstruck is that the effacement of man before the animal – and, more precisely,

---

60 Kristeva, 'Bataille, l'expérience, et la pratique', p. 269; Kristeva, 'Bataille, Experience and Practice', p. 239. Kristeva underlines the fact that Bataille and Hegel share the same preoccupations, most notably the desire to embrace the totality of the real, but their methods radically differ.

61 Bataille, *Lascaux*, p. 22.

62 On the importance of reading Lascaux as a problematization of cultural origins (as opposed to proposing Lascaux as the alternative or the authentic origin of both art and humanity) in the historic and cultural context of post-war France, see Douglas Smith, 'Beyond the Cave: Lascaux and the Prehistoric in Post-War French Culture', *French Studies*, 58 (2004), 219–32.

of man becoming human – is the greatest that we can imagine].[63] In his comments on the abundance of animal figures and the absence of human figures, we read:

> Dans la mesure où il [l'homme de l'Age du renne] s'est lui-même représenté, le plus souvent, il dissimulait ses traits sous le masque de l'animal. [...] S'il avouait la forme humaine, il la cachait dans le même instant; il se donnait à ce moment la tête de l'animal. Comme s'il avait honte de son visage et que, voulant se désigner, il a dû en même temps se donner le masque d'un autre.[64]

> [To the extent that he [the man of the Reindeer Age] represented himself, most of the time he concealed his features under the mask of an animal. [...] Whenever he admitted his human form, at the same time he concealed it; he gave himself an animal's head. As if he was ashamed of his face and, wanting to depict himself, he had to give himself the mask of another.]

In the above passages Bataille employs both effacement and masking with regard to representation. However, this analysis will, somewhat in contrast to Bataille, pose the logic of masking as more central, in so far as it considers the mask a key term which accounts for both effacement and masking.

Bataille's text on Lascaux, in its emphasis on the representation of animals (which either disguises or erases the representation of humans), does not aim to foreground animality as the (re)discovered origin of humanity; rather, it aspires to show how the animal figures of the Lascaux cave bring about a tensional logic which opposes representation whilst not discarding it altogether. More broadly, one can argue on the one hand that Bataille's writings cannot be labelled non-representative since everything in Bataille is represented and representative. Bataille's fictions are made up of all his favoured themes: eyes and blindness, bodies and sexuality, death and dying, priests and whores, breaking and escaping the law, Paris and Spain; even God is represented in the character of Edwarda. On the other hand, however, Bataille's writings do not represent anything in the sense that they offer nothing to see, understand or untangle. Edwarda does not *stand for* but bluntly introduces herself as God. Additionally, rather than offering access to the divine she blocks vision; whilst willing to offer herself, her most intimate parts and her divine tatters, all that she offers is the thickness of her nudity. Edwarda, as the

---

63   Bataille, *Lascaux*, p. 63.
64   Bataille, *Lascaux*, p. 63.

narrator informs us, is still, thick, impenetrable like a rock; there is nothing behind (her).

At this point, it should be stressed that Bataille's commentary on the miracle of Lascaux is, above all, Bataille's personal vision of the miracle. The history of the Lascaux cave is construed as Bataille's personal narrative not only in the sense that Bataille lingers over unintelligible traces, gathers dispersed figures and turns them into a coherent story – somehow imposing order on the disorderly figures, endowing them with an abundance of meaning and thereby rendering Lascaux the birthplace of art and humanity – but also in the sense that Bataille populates the earthly site of Lascaux with all the pairs that inhabit his own universe, namely the sacred and the profane, human life and animality, conscious and instinctual life, history and nature. The Bataillean text on Lascaux is not a veracious account of prehistoric art or humanity, but accounts for Bataille's conceptions of the human, art and representation and sets up what is the focal point in our inquiry into the literary real, namely the intimate connection between art and humanity. As Bataille notes, 'cette manière de voir me conduisait à montrer à quel point l'œuvre de l'art était intimement liée à la formation de l'humanité' [this way of seeing led me to show to what extent the work of art was intimately connected to the formation of humanity].[65]

In the Bataillean quest for the origin, and as Lascaux is construed as a tale of origin (of both humanity and art), origin is not understood in terms of a starting point, a place where something begins, but is recast in terms of a passage and a becoming. Additionally, this passage is not evolutionary but hybrid; therefore, it is to be understood as a movement *within* rather than a progression *from-to* (from animality to humanity).[66] Furthermore, the passage is not meant in spiritual terms and therefore effectuates a celebration of animal and not of spiritual life. In this respect Lascaux invites a reconfiguration of the relation between the human and the animal which does not consist in the destruction, transformation and transcendence of animality in favour – and in the name – of humanity but shows how humans are inescapably fascinated by and divided between humanity and animality. Bataille's re-conception of humanity, via Lascaux, as not clearly distinguished from, or distinctly opposed to, animality,

---

65 Bataille, 'Préface', in *Lascaux*, p. 9.

66 For two detailed accounts of the significance of Lascaux in our reconfiguration of the human, see Jean-Michel Rey, 'Le Signe aveugle', *L'Arc*, 44 (1967), 54–63; and René de Sollier, 'L'Homme de Lascaux', *L'Arc*, 32 (1971), 58–62.

approaches Agamben's suggestion that humans should be thought of anew as both the site and the result of divisions and caesurae; and, by the same token, the relationship between humanity and animality should be recast in terms of an irreducible betweenness, incongruity and separation rather than settlement, articulation and conjunction.[67] This relation can be also described in the Deleuzian terms of 'pure becoming', 'pure difference' or 'pure variation' (in brief, 'pure movement' – as opposed to the reality of things in terms of the actual and the identifiable). However, the most interesting tension here is not that of the tensional relationship between animality and humanity but how figuration comes to play a crucial role in this relationship.

The gesture of figuration, first, attests that the passage is not accomplished once and once only. As the innumerable superimposed animal figures show, the passage relies on the repetition of gesture. Additionally, the blurred and indistinct animal figures, which cover – and are drawn on – fragments, marks and lines, the shades and shadows of other previous figures, show that it is the gesture, momentary appearance and the moment of appearance which truly count rather than the image, the enduring object, the result.[68] One can understand why the figures – in their superimposition – coming into view as a celebration of confusion and the momentary, defying any logic of coherent whole and endurance, grasp Bataille's attention. Labelling the cave 'une scène théâtrale' [a theatrical scene], Bataille renders it a moveable feast, claiming that 'une constellation de la vie animale, divergente, y est mouvante autour de nous' [a constellation of divergent animal life is moving around us].[69]

The theatrical scene and the troupe of animal life – shifting and unstable as it comes forth – evoke the Deleuzian theatre of repetition, with its emphasis on movement and directness and its consideration of masking as constitutive. Deleuze sketches an order of movement, change, difference and directness which, operating through sensation and affect, runs counter to the order of representation, conceptualization and mediation. For Deleuze, emotions, bodies and contexts can neither 'be' nor be 'represented', belonging neither to

---

67 Giorgio Agamben, *The Open: Man and Animal*, trans. by Kevin Attell (Stanford, CA: Stanford University Press, 2004), p. 16.

68 The execution of the paintings is part of a hunting ritual, as hunting, despite its productive nature, is primarily a game rather than simply a job. The figures become part of a rite of evocation in which what is vital is the moment of appearance and not the thing, the durable object.

69 Bataille, *Lascaux*, p. 51.

the order of 'being' nor to that of 'representation'. Thus, he erects a universe of prior dynamic communication – composed of language, gestures, masks and phantoms – that come before words, bodies, faces and characters:

> Dans le théâtre de la répétition, on éprouve des forces pures, des tracés dynamiques qui agissent sur l'esprit sans intermédiaire, et qui l'unissent directement à la nature et à l'histoire, un langage qui parle avant les mots, des gestes qui s'élaborent avant les corps organisés, des masques avant des visages, des spectres et des fantômes avant les personnages – tout l'appareil de la répétition comme 'puissance terrible'.
>
> [In the theatre of repetition, we experience pure forces, dynamic lines in space which act without intermediary upon the spirit, and link it directly with nature and history, with a language which speaks before words, with gestures which develop before organized bodies, with masks before faces, with spectres and fantoms before characters – the whole apparatus of repetition as a 'terrible power'.][70]

The Deleuzian theatre of repetition defies the logic of manifestation (the theatre of representation) in that it puts forward masking as constitutive. In this regard and contrary to manifestation, repetition does not enact a movement of (un)concealment and unveiling, but one of disguise and constitution. Correspondingly, in the paintings of Lascaux the birth of the human – the passage from animality to humanity – brings forth the rebirth of the animal in figuration. While humans deny their animal nature and gain their humanity by painting, their rejected animality returns as the favoured leitmotif of their paintings. As Bataille writes:

> Ce qu'avec une force juvénile annoncent ces figures inhumaines n'est pas seulement que ceux qui les ont peintes ont achevé de devenir des hommes en les peignant, mais qu'ils l'ont fait en donnant de l'animalité, non d'eux-mêmes, cette image suggérant ce que l'humanité a de fascinant.[71]
>
> [What these inhuman figures announce in all their youthful force is not only that those who painted them became human by painting them, but that they became so by bestowing upon animality, not upon themselves, an image that suggests what is fascinating about humanity.]

---

70 Gilles Deleuze, *Différence et répétition* (Paris: Presses Universitaires de France, 2019 [1968]), p. 19; Gilles Deleuze, *Difference and Repetition*, trans. by Paul Patton (New York: Columbia University Press: 1994), p. 10.
71 Bataille, *Lascaux*, p. 62.

The act of figuration involves disguise (inasmuch as an abundance of animal figures masks the newly constituted humanity) as well as detour (inasmuch as humans turn away from the presently gained humanity). Figuration shows and – concurrently – hides the formation of the human; in parallel, it involves the denial and – simultaneously – the return of animality (as the repeated figure of painting). In this respect the denial of animality, contrary to Hegel, does not obey a logic of dialectical suppression but a spectral logic, since negation is not seen in terms of conservation (or more precisely in terms of transformation, conservation and finally transcendence) but in terms of return.

Additionally, as Bataille glosses figuration in terms of a 'sacred moment' there are three remarks to be made. First, because the temporality of figuration is that of the moment, Bataille includes figuration among his various privileged moments – instantaneous ruptures, disruptive instants – such as laughter, erotic or religious ecstasy. Figuration is conceived as momentary (rather than as lasting), since, as already mentioned, it is thought of in terms of appearance (rather than in terms of an object). Second, because figuration is not evidently, that is, lastingly, useful, it underlines the idea that the difference between the sacred and the profane is above all a temporal difference. The multiplicity of figures, rendered redundant after their appearance, point to the difference between the structured time of work and a time that does not conform to the logic of utility and duration. Third, as figuration is linked to the sacred it goes against both the logic of immediacy (usually associated with the sacred) and the logic of mediation (usually associated with figuration). The moment of figuration suggests another way of relation (and of representation) which corresponds to the moment of transgression. Against Hegelian self-consciousness and negative (creative) action, Bataille privileges transgression as the crucial anthropogenic moment when the negated returns as desirable and is rendered as such in figuration. Alternatively, as Suzanne Guerlac notes in more Freudian terms, Bataille posits the unconscious negativity of interdiction and transgression against the Hegelian negativity of consciousness and action.[72]

Against the dialectical logic that advances and proceeds through a binary structure of opposition and synthesis, Bataille insists on the double operation of negation and return and adds – to the creation of

---

72 Suzanne Guerlac, '"Recognition" by a Woman!: A Reading of Bataille's *L'Érotisme*', *Yale French Studies*, 78 (1990), 90–105 (p. 95).

man and the world of work, culture and history through the negation of the given, the natural world – a second negation – the negation of the world of work – which gives rise to the sacred and which 'truly' constitutes humanity. Reviewing Bataille's monograph on Lascaux, Blanchot insists on the importance of this twofold negation in so far as it disperses the birth of the human and the origin of humanity, rendering it unlocatable, recasting the origin as what is 'originellement différée' [originally deferred].[73]

Drawing on Blanchot's remark, it should be highlighted that the crucial element of this second negation is that it does not consist of a further step; rather, a double logic – of negation and return – is entangled in the binary logic of opposition. To put it briefly, to the progressive logic of the beginning and the end of history Bataille opposes a tensional logic according to which the entry into history is concurrently a leap out of history, since the time of the sacred (the time of figuration) is both within and outside (pre)history. We read in *L'Érotisme* about the paradoxical temporality of the two realms which constitute the human world:

> La societé humaine n'est pas seulement le monde du travail. Simultanément – ou successivement – le monde profane et le monde sacré la composent, qui en sont les deux formes complémentaires. Le monde profane est celui des interdits. Le monde sacré s'ouvre à des transgressions limitées.
>
> [Human society is not only the world of work. Simultaneously – or successively – it is made up of the profane and the sacred, its two complementary forms. The profane world is the world of taboos. The sacred world depends on limited acts of transgressions.][74]

Dissecting the paradoxical temporal relation between the sacred and the profane, ffrench shows how, on the one hand, the sacred is radically opposed to the profane whilst, on the other hand, since there is a passage from the profane to the sacred the two realms are linked through sacrifice (which is to be understood here etymologically, as the act of making sacred rather than as an act of slaughtering).[75] The relationship between the sacred and the profane needs to be successive because if the sacred comes too early, the two realms will not be able

---

73 Maurice Blanchot, 'Naissance de l'art', in Maurice Blanchot, *L'Amitié* (Paris: Gallimard, 1971), pp. 9–20 (p. 19).
74 Bataille, *L'Érotisme*, p. 70; Bataille, *Eroticism*, pp. 67–68.
75 ffrench, *After Bataille*, p. 64.

to communicate and two closed totalities will be formed. As ffrench warns, '[i]mmediacy prior to mediation, animalistic immediacy, is a totality which does not allow for any mediation, any relation'.[76] However, if the sacred in its immediacy comes afterwards, it will have no power to disrupt the process and the possibility of relation will again be closed off. It must, therefore, come both simultaneously and successively.

In this respect, in *L'Érotisme* we read about two dispositions that make up humans:

> Les hommes sont en un même temps soumis à deux mouvements: de terreur, qui rejette, et d'attrait qui commande le respect fasciné. L'interdit et la transgression répondent à ces deux mouvements contradictoires: l'interdit rejette, mais la fascination introduit la transgression. L'interdit, le tabou ne s'opposent au divin qu'en un sens, mais le divin est l'aspect fascinant de l'interdit: c'est l'interdit transfiguré.
>
> [Human beings] are swayed by two simultaneous emotions: they are driven away by terror and drawn by an awed fascination. Taboo and transgression reflect these two contradictory urges. The taboo would forbid the transgression but the fascination compels it. Taboos and the divine are opposed to each other in one sense only, for the sacred aspect of the taboo is what draws [humans] towards it and transfigures the original interdiction.][77]

Commenting on the passage, Suzanne Guerlac argues that there is a double relationship between interdiction and transgression, or rather that the relationship between interdiction and transgression follows two different logics: a logic of opposition, to some extent, as well as a logic of recoil and return.[78] In the first case, interdiction is opposed to transgression and, accordingly, the profane to the sacred, whilst in the second case interdiction and transgression are both considered as moments belonging to the sacred. Additionally, as Guerlac notes, in the first case there is wilful action (agency), whilst in the second case there is yielding (affectivity).[79] In this way, in the first case interdiction of the violence of nature is actively imposed and results in the division

---

76 ffrench, *After Bataille*, p. 64. ffrench makes the above remarks mainly with reference to the constitution of the subject and the possibility of experience, that is, exposure.
77 Bataille, *L'Érotisme*, p. 71; Bataille, *Eroticism*, p. 68.
78 Guerlac, '"Recognition" by a Woman!', pp. 97–98.
79 Guerlac, '"Recognition" by a Woman!', pp. 95–96.

between the sacred and the profane: interdiction renders violence sacred and enables the emergence of the realm of reason; transgression is, subsequently, the regulated introduction of violence (of the sacred) into the profane, which reinvigorates the system and keeps it going. By contrast, in the second case there is no active but a responsive attitude to the violence of nature. We are not acting upon nature: we are, rather, acted upon. In this case interdiction is bound to horror, while transgression is bound to fascination. Here, the sacred is not opposed and hence complementary to the profane: it is constituted by two contradictory moments – fear and rejection (resulting in interdiction); attraction and fascination (resulting in transgression) – and it jeopardizes the system, putting it at risk.

To phrase the above in more explicitly Hegelian terms, at issue is the question of the moment and whether it is subordinated to a process, a result, a gain, a project; or whether it constitutes a cut, a pure loss, an interruption from within. Derrida, in his essay dedicated to Bataille, considers him to be a Hegelian without reserve, one who turns mastery into sovereignty, sacrifice for something into sacrifice for nothing, resolution and absolute knowledge into interruption and laughter.[80] As Derrida emphasizes, while both Hegel and Bataille share a crucial moment – the exposure to absolute negativity – Hegel construes it in retrospect, whereas Bataille, looking back at it, guards it like a night watchman.[81] While Hegel retrospectively gives a response, Bataille returns to this prior moment and gives no response. Thus the Hegelian and Battaillean undertakings, in their divergence, demonstrate how turning one's back is not the same as turning away and how fleeing is not the same as stepping back, retreating in fright and returning.[82]

The better to understand Bataille's response to nature and, more specifically, the issue of recoil before nature, it is necessary to introduce, alongside Hegelian negativity, the Kantian sublime. The sublime, in opposition to the beautiful, which involves a judgement of taste and an experience of harmony and serenity, is an experience of the power and the intimidating greatness of nature. Additionally, this experience throws subjectivity and appearance into confusion since the sublime

---

80 Derrida, 'De l'économie restreinte'.

81 Derrida, 'De l'économie restreinte'.

82 ffrench notes that natural life, for Hegel, is sacrificed in favour of something else (essential spiritual life, reason, meaning and truth, human reality and the birth of the subject), while Bataille assents to life as it is, that is, as exposure (ffrench, *After Bataille*, pp. 78–79).

marks a failure of representation in a double sense. As Thomas Huhn points out in his commentary on the sublime, subjectivity fails not only to present the sublime *to* itself but, due to the power of the sublime, it also fails to present (sense) *itself*.[83] However, as subjectivity for Kant is constituted (elevated above nature) through and due to its subjection to awe (the awe of nature), the power of the subject is never really suspended in the case of the Kantian sublime.

Indeed, the encounter of the subject with the sublime is marked by a double peculiarity: the sublime constitutes, solidifies and elevates the subject since, first, it is the subject which attributes to nature an overwhelming power, presenting nature as fearful; and, second, since the sublime has the paradoxical status of being what Kant terms 'a power without dominance'.[84] Regarding the paradoxical status of the sublime, Kant insists that the dynamically sublime (as opposed to the mathematical sublime) consists of our contemplation of nature as a power that 'has no dominance over us': 'When in an aesthetic judgement we consider nature as a power that has no dominance over us, then it is dynamically sublime'.[85] In other words, we consider nature fearful without, in fact, being afraid of it. Underlining the two-faced disposition of fear with reference to the sublime, Kant notes: '[W]e can however consider an object fearful, without being afraid of it'.[86] The power of nature therefore forces us to experience, alongside our physical powerlessness, our independence and superiority – or, in more Kantian terms, the power of nature sets up our capacity to judge ourselves independent and superior (over the power of nature). Therefore, the experience (the judgement) of the sublime finally reveals ourselves and gives rise to a feeling of superiority due to our power to reason. Huhn, terming the judgement of the sublime 'a record of our having overreached ourselves', stresses that it is primarily a founding moment of subjectivity: '[W]hen we realize that we have been overwhelmed', he

---

83 Additionally, here one should bear in mind that in the aesthetic judgement what is under consideration is not nature itself, as such, but a presentation of nature, as Huhn writes: 'When I judge nature to be sublime [...], I am judging not nature but the manner in which I have presented nature to myself. I am judging a representation of nature' (Thomas Huhn, 'The Kantian Sublime and The Nostalgia for Violence', *The Journal of Aesthetics and Art Criticism*, 53 (1995), 269–75 (p. 270)).

84 Immanuel Kant, *Critique of Judgement*, intro. and trans. by Werner S. Pluhar (Indianapolis, IN: Hackett, 1987), p. 119, §28.

85 Kant, *Critique of Judgement*, p. 119, §28.

86 Kant, *Critique of Judgement*, p. 119, §28.

writes, 'what we also thereby realize is ourselves'.[87] Put differently, '[w]e realize and found the self in that moment when we judge that which is beyond the self'.[88] In this regard the sublime also involves pleasure, apart from (or more precisely after) fear and pain, since, as Huhn observes, in our *consideration* of nature as fearful we distance ourselves both (externally) from nature and (internally) from our fear of nature (and the pain it causes us).[89]

The Kantian sublime is essentially and ultimately bound to the demand of positing subjectivity and the moral law – briefly, freedom – against nature; it is not simply part of, but goes to the centre of, the constitution of the self. As Huhn points out, the powerlessness of the subject is caught up within the economy of the self to the extent that it supports (both justifying and grounding) an exchange, the exchange of a powerful self.[90] In similar terms, Roger Scruton, framing our disposition towards the sublime within the logic of the self, argues that in the very awe of nature we sense 'our own ability as free beings to measure up against it'.[91]

However, we need to insist on the temporality of our judgement, as it leads to the first peculiarity of the sublime, as mentioned above. When faced with nature, first, we are overwhelmed, afraid of nature; then we realize that we have been overwhelmed and we distance ourselves from our fear. However, the tour de force of Kant's argumentation lies in the fact that there is still another moment which precedes our overwhelming, a moment which initiates the process and leads the way. Taking into account this prior moment, the temporality becomes the following: first of all, it is we who present nature as fearful; subsequently, we are, at first, afraid of it and then we *consider* it fearful, overcoming thereby – and distancing ourselves from – our previous horror-struck reaction. As Huhn writes with

---

87   Huhn, 'The Kantian Sublime', p. 272.

88   Huhn, 'The Kantian Sublime', p. 272.

89   These considerations make it evident that aesthetic pleasure lies not in the content of judgement but in the judgement itself, in the act of judging as such. Huhn makes the helpful distinction between external and internal distancing, showing how our external distancing from nature (while fear is immersive, the very *consideration* of nature as fearful requires a distance between ourselves and the object of our fear) is further internalized (after fearing and being overwhelmed by nature, we overcome our fear; hence, we consider nature as fearful but we are not afraid of it) (Huhn, 'The Kantian Sublime', pp. 271–72).

90   Huhn, 'The Kantian Sublime', p. 273.

91   Roger Scruton, *Beauty: A Very Short Introduction* (Oxford: Oxford University Press, 2011), p. 63.

reference to this prior moment: 'The paradox of the sublime is that *we* accord nature an overwhelming power'. He continues: 'Nature is empowered when we *present* it as an object of fear'.[92] Nonetheless, in this set up subjectivity is not fully installed, which is why, instead of occurring once only, the process is repeated, as Huhn writes, with particular emphasis on the artfulness and the trickery involved:

> The sublime is the realization of our dominance, our power over the supposed power of nature. But in order to feel this power of ours, in order to realize our dominance, we must insist upon nature being a fearful power – and in repeatedly staging its redoubtable character we repeatedly stage our dominance. (One suspects we would tire of so much rehearsal.)[93]

Against this context, and while Bataille's thought adheres to both the Kantian overwhelming and the Hegelian exposure, in the Bataillean experience there is no passing through, as in Hegel, nor a rendering of it as a moment of being, as in Kant. Thus, the Bataillean analysis of the animal figures of Lascaux sidesteps the two major risks of representation, namely, the Hegelian aspiration of complete representation and the Kantian positing of a controllable – for the mind – beyond. Through the key term of the mask, Bataille, in contrast to Hegel, neither renders identical the symbol and the symbolized nor, in contrast to Kant, contents himself with designating the impossibility that surrounds possibility (of representation, subjectivity); he insists instead on the impossible representation of this beyond, reconfiguring it in terms of masking. As masking consists of showing and hiding – in the same gesture – it operates both within and outwith the representational system. The animal masks of Lascaux, as a coalescence of non-coincidence, can be thought of as a suspense of suspension – inasmuch as they display (hang) the interruption (of animality) and interrupt (put on hold) the display (of humanity).

The mask, corresponding to a liminal state in which one is oneself and (an)other, differs from the veil that hides. In contrast to the veil and the dialectic of concealment and unveiling it enacts, wearers of masks are neither fully themselves (their self that is masked) nor fully their mask, but suspended between the two – reminding us that 'person' is etymologically derived from *persona*, which originally means theatrical mask (as *personae* are masks worn by actors on stage).

---

92 Huhn, 'The Kantian Sublime', p. 271.
93 Huhn, 'The Kantian Sublime', p. 272.

Re-con-figuring

The animal figures left by the first humans give rise to the Bataillean redrawing of the Adamic myth, as humans clothe themselves in animal grace:

> Les traces, qu'après des millénaires nombreux ces hommes nous ont laissé de leur humanité, se bornent à de représentations d'animaux. [...] Ces hommes de Lascaux rendirent sensible le fait qu'en étant des hommes, ils nous ressemblaient, mais ils l'ont fait en nous laissant l'image de l'animalité qu'ils quittaient. Comme s'ils avaient dû parer un prestige naissant de la grâce animale qu'ils avaient perdue.[94]

> [The traces of their humanity left to us by these men numerous millennia later are limited to representations of animals. [...] These people of Lascaux made it clear that in being human, they resembled us, but they did so by leaving us the image of the animality they were leaving behind. As if they had had to adorn an emerging prestige with the animal grace that they had just lost.]

In his commentary on the Adamic myth, Agamben points not only to the paradoxical conception of human nature that lies at the heart of it, but also to the crucial role played by nudity and clothing in its foundation and sustenance.[95] According to the myth, Adam, created in grace, enjoys an originally graceful nature and is unashamedly naked. After the Fall, after his disobeying of God's command (through sin), grace is lost, corrupted nature appears and nudity needs to be concealed. However, as Agamben observes, in the beginning there is no nudity, since nudity is already cloaked (clothed) in grace. Thus, in Agamben's de-composition and re-composition of the myth, there is no prior nudity but the clothing of grace; correspondingly, afterwards, there is no nudity – which needs to be covered – but denudation – from the clothing of grace.

In a reversal which registers the Bataillean primacy of transgression in the theological lexicon of sin, Agamben puts forward sin as original and nature as derivative: 'With the removal of grace an original nature comes to light that is no longer original, because only sin is original, and so this nature has become merely a derivation of this sin'.[96] In other words, the supposedly 'pure' human nature, which is actually

---

94 Bataille, *Lascaux*, p. 62.
95 Giorgio Agamben, *Nudities*, trans. by David Kishik and Stefan Pedatella (Stanford, CA: Stanford University Press, 2011), pp. 70–71.
96 Agamben, *Nudities*, pp. 70.

considered impure and corrupted since it is not created in grace, does not exist as such. Agamben underlines that there is no nature in the absence of sinning and no nudity outside or before denudation. In his words, '[n]ature is now defined by the non-nature (grace) that it has lost, just as nudity is defined by the non-nudity (clothing) that has been stripped from it'.[97]

Put differently, what *supposedly* comes before *actually* comes after. However, this does not simply mean that what is considered preceding is subsequently construed as preceding but that it emerges – for the first time – as preceding consequently. What is presupposed as prior, emerges as such afterwards. Thus, there is no truth, no secret behind, as the secret and the truth are to be found not behind the act of tearing apart but *in* the very act of tearing apart. As Agamben remarks, in truth there is only the act of laying bare, the act of denuding. There is no prior nudity, no pre-existing nudity (apart from the act of denuding): 'In truth, there is only baring, only the infinite gesticulations that remove clothing and grace from the body'.[98]

Considering fashion as the 'profane heir of the theology of clothing', Agamben comments on how Helmut Newton's diptych *Sie Kommen [Dressed and Naked]* both inscribes and reverses the theology of clothing.[99] The diptych, originally published as a two-page spread in French *Vogue* in 1981, shows four super-women (top-models) on the march. On the left page they appear naked with the exception of high heels, while on the right page they wear high fashion suits. Moving away from John Berger's opposition between being naked (wearing no costume in order to be looked at by a male gaze) and being nude (wearing no costume and being yourself), between nakedness (as a representation of nudity) and nudity (as a process of relief and banality in which mystery is dissolved), Newton directs his attention to the opposition between nudity and clothing, showing how the two images, despite their apparent difference, amount to the same. Conforming to the conventions of the fashion industry, the women in both photos have the same stiff postures, glacial looks and expressions of indifference on their faces. While a more Berger-inspired commentary would linger on the objectification of women in both images (as objects of the male gaze), Agamben focuses on how their confident *appearance* unmakes the myth of the Fall, showing that

---

97 Agamben, *Nudities*, pp. 71.
98 Agamben, *Nudities*, pp. 78–79.
99 Agamben, *Nudities*, p. 80.

denudation unveils nothing. In Newton's diptych nothing is revealed, nothing but fashion's endless promise of delivering and designing fashionable clothes. As Agamben suggests, there is nothing left to be unveiled by denudation: '[N]udity has not taken place'.[100] Moreover, as he adds: 'The models *wear their nudity* in exactly the same way that [...] they wear their attire'.[101]

Nonetheless, our discussion on nudity as analysed by Agamben does not suggest that denudation is rendered redundant; on the contrary, it underlines that its use and significance consist in showing that there is nothing to denude, nothing hidden to reveal and nothing on the other side to hope for. In this respect Bataille's two key movements of accessing (and showing us) the truth – namely, laying bare and masking, denuding and duplicating – amount to showing the disguise. Bataillean nudity consists of pure appearance, pure visibility and presence – and is, as a result, horrific. The mystery of nudity, like the mystery of beauty, consists after all in the lack of mystery: standing for nothing else, it signifies nothing but itself; and yet, despite – or precisely due to – its straightforwardness, it takes hold of us. In other words, sheer presence does not equal transparency but the impenetrable. In this regard, Bataille's comment about Manet's *Olympia* (her 'exactitude provocante' [provocative literalness] against the artifice of naturalism and her majesty, her pure charm and straightforward humanity) allows us to understand how the nudity of his own text (and of Edwarda) work:

> [S]a nudité (s'accordant il est vrai à celle du corps) est le silence qui s'en dégage comme celui d'un navire échoué, d'un navire vide: ce qu'elle est, est l'horreur sacrée de sa présence – d'une présence dont la simplicité est celle de l'absence [...]. C'est la précision d'un charme à l'état pur, celui de l'existence ayant souverainement, silencieusement tranché le lien qui la rattachait aux mensonges que l'éloquence avait créés.
>
> [[H]er real nudity (not merely that of her body) is the silence that emanates from her, like that of a sunken ship. All we have is the sacred horror of her presence – presence whose sheer simplicity is tantamount to absence [...]. We feel a charm refined to its purest – a pure state of being, sovereignly, silently cut off from the old lies set up in the name of eloquence.][102]

---

100 Agamben, *Nudities*, p. 80.

101 Agamben, *Nudities*, p. 80 (my emphasis).

102 Georges Bataille, *Manet*, in *Œuvres complètes*, IX, 103–69 (p. 142); Georges Bataille, *Manet: Biographical and Critical Study*, trans. by Austryn Wainhouse

Nudity and masking do not conform to a relation of opposition, but bring forth a double relation, since the wearer of the mask is both himself and another, or rather neither himself nor another. In Hegelian terms, the mask, rather than the fictive death of the dialectically suppressed, advances a fiction of death (as it is a display of endurance without future – with no end or ending). The mask is not a mask *of* something but pure masking, masking as such. In psychoanalytic terms, the mask points to and brings back fiction as the return of the repressed. Because the operation of masking is the literary operation, the latter consists not in the presentation of presentation but in the display of fiction as fiction. Fiction, etymologically deriving from *fingere*, that is, to form and shape, but also to pretend and feign, shows how formation partakes of pretence.

The mask can be approached through the Derridean contrivance of mimesis without imitation. Commenting on Mallarmé's 'Mimique' (1897), Derrida argues that in Mallarmé's text the mimic (Paul Marguerite) does not imitate his act (Pierrot Assassin de sa Femme).[103] There is no imitation, says Derrida, because there is nothing to imitate, nothing prior to the act of the mime, no anterior referent, no thematic content, no event to be imitated. In this sense, the face of the mimic – in its whiteness – parallels the blank page in writing.[104] Nevertheless, and this is the core of Derrida's argument, this does not mean that there is no mimicry, as the mime gives us mimesis as such.[105] The mimic's gestures *are*, in their very emergence, imitative. Therefore, the mimic's act neither points to (imitates) the real nor 'is' (inaugurates) the real in its own right. One can say that the gestures of the mime parallel the Bataillean gesture of writing, since literature, for Bataille, neither 'resembles' the real nor 'is' real.

Advocating the differential structure of literature, Bataille and Blanchot write 'true', 'real' texts, since the double is not suppressed

---

and James Emmons (New York: Skira, 1955), p. 67. Elsewhere, we read: 'C'est la majesté retrouvée dans la suppression de ses atours. C'est la majesté de n'importe qui, et déjà de n'importe quoi ... – qui appartient, sans plus de cause, à ce qui *est*, et que révèle la force de la peinture' [Thus was majesty retrieved by the suppression of its outward blandishments – a majesty for everyone and no one, for everything and nothing, belonging simply to what *is* by reason of its *being*, and brought home by the power of painting] (Bataille, *Manet*, p. 147; Bataille, *Manet: Biographical and Critical Study*, p. 75).

103 Derrida, 'La double séance', p. 239; Derrida, 'The First Session', p. 144.

104 Derrida, 'La double séance', p. 240; Derrida, 'The First Session', p. 144.

105 Derrida, 'La double séance', pp. 254–57; Derrida, 'The First Session', pp. 156–57.

or rendered dialectical: in the case of Blanchot, writing doubles back, folds back on itself, questions itself and finds no answer (thereby undoing the dialectics of question and answer). Bataille puts forward writing as a relation of disguise, but a disguise which reveals itself as such (thereby undoing the opposition between disguise and authenticity). Blanchot brings into representation, into the represented space of literature, the material limitations and the spatial properties of writing (its fundamental deficiency, its being always other to itself), whereas for Bataille in literature nothing is represented but representation itself, staging and performance. While for Blanchot what recurringly returns is the anonymous murmur of wor(l)dly existence, for Bataille what recurrently returns is the inescapabilty of disguise.

Conclusion

Toutefois, le travail et la recherche littéraires – gardons ce qualitatif – contribuent à ébranler les principes et les vérités abrités par la littérature.

[However, literary work and research – let's keep this qualitative – contribute to undermine the principles and truths sheltered by literature.]¹

Tout problème en un certain sens en est un d'*emploi du temps*. Il implique la question préalable: – Qu'ai-je à faire (que dois-je faire ou qu'est-il est de mon intérêt de faire ou qu'ai-je envie de faire) ici (en ce monde où j'ai ma nature humaine et personnelle) et maintenant? Écrivant, je voulais toucher le fond des problèmes. Et m'étant donné cette occupation, *je me suis endormi*.²

[Every problem is in a way a problem *related to time*. It involves the prior question: What do I have to do (what should I do, what is it in my interest to do or what do I want to do) here (in this world where I have my human and personal nature) and now? Writing, I wanted to reach the depths of these problems. And having given myself this occupation, *I fell asleep*.]

The contrivance of the 'literary real', bringing together the literary and the real, attempts to make inoperative the hiatus between the conceptual and the sensuous, the conscious and the immediate, form and matter and, ultimately, fiction and truth. The component of the 'real' designates a resistance and an irreducibility to fictionality and

---

1 Blanchot, 'Note', in *L'Entretien infini*, p. vi; Blanchot, 'Note', in *The Infinite Conversation*, p. xi.
2 Bataille, *Méthode de méditation*, p. 201.

textuality and therefore all discursivity and conceptual determination as such, while the 'literary' attests to an insistence on the question of literature as such. Literature, as has been shown throughout this discussion, becomes a way of addressing – and relating to – that which escapes the order of representation, presence, consciousness and knowledge. The literary, although it partakes of language, runs against the discursive and notional logic (the logic according to which concepts are adequate accounts of the world); in so doing, it also goes against the world bound to and produced by such a logic (the day world of utility and reason).

In this regard, literature, especially in Blanchot's conception of it, can be paralleled to the Husserlian *epoché*, with the crucial difference that the suspension of the natural attitude now becomes a suspension of worldliness. As literature comes to stand for our relation to some kind of otherness (which manifests itself in the variants of the unknown, the obscure, the distant and the unfamiliar), it allows a rethinking of worldly relationality as always already preceded and passing through a radical relation of non-relation which makes relationality possible as such. Thus, literature enables us not only to think anew worldly relationality without recourse to substance, presence and fusion (briefly, all sorts of metaphysical groundedness) but also brings about an ethical affirmation of a relation (without relation). Indeed, each of Blanchot's redefinitions of literature – in terms of the *il y a*, the image, the neuter – calls for, accordingly, a reconfiguration of our relation to existence in terms of extreme affirmation (rather than negation), dissimulation (rather than unveiling), strangeness and intimacy (rather than sameness or radical otherness). In parallel, the terms adopted in order to designate Bataille's model of literature, namely exscription, simulacrum, withdrawal and the mask, either by way of reintroducing some sort of referentiality or by insisting on both the crisis and the inescapability of representation and figuration, go against a relation of adequation, coincidence, equivalence and, above all, identification (be it between the literary text and its subject matter).

The relation between the literary and the real moves towards neither the glorification of literature and, more broadly, art (adopting the elite standpoint of a closed-off aestheticism), nor the fetishization of the real as irrecuperable, inaccessible and ineffable (adopting the quietist standpoint of a world-renouncing passivity). As neither term has priority over the other, art is neither at the third remove, as in Plato, nor at the forefront, as in Romanticism, unrivalled and delighting in its capacity for auto-production and self-realization (of both the subject and the artwork). The literary demand, throughout this discussion, both rivals and complements the demands of the real and vice versa: the question of the existence of literature brings into question worldly existence in the case of Blanchot, whereas the conception of the real in terms of excess exerts pressure on literature and more broadly on forms of representation in the case of Bataille. As both Bataille and Blanchot are concerned with and foster the unplanned and the unexpected, the surprising and the unanticipated, the intersection between literature and the real is thought over as an encounter, to designate the element of chance and wonder which goes along with it. Additionally, the encounter is considered critical, inasmuch as it enacts a crisis – a crisis of representation and of subjectivity.

The re-evaluation of the real in terms of flux and becoming, while following the Nietzschean overcoming of being in terms of substance, essence and presence, does not yield to a comforting rejoicing in undecidability or a firm belief in the continuous plasticity of the world – ready, thereby, to offer itself to be appropriated and shaped by a determined subject. On the contrary, and as shown throughout this study, the real is approached in terms of resistance and withdrawal. The real is first thought along the lines of materiality: in its material capacity, it requires us to address things in their distinctive existence (in their preconceptual singularity), rethink ourselves as vulnerable subjects (rather than as disembodied agents) and approach others in their opacity (rather than as transparent objects of our consciousness). Alongside its dimension of materiality, the real also has the Lacanian connotation of that which defies conceptual specification and resists symbolization; or, to use an optical metaphor which brings its dimension of the unbearable closer to Bataille's favoured figure of the sun, the real is thought of as what cannot be looked at directly – or, more precisely, as that which might be looked at only fleetingly (rather than for a long time).

The engagement of both thinkers with the question of the real is entangled with the question of origin – as a prior moment, a primal and more fundamental state is entailed in their respective approaches to the real. Blanchot's tenacious search for the moment that precedes literature leads to the *il y a*, a state prior to ontology and being-in-the-world and more final than dialectics and worldly action. Similarly, one finds in Bataille an enduring longing for a primal state of excessive continuity that escapes the separateness of discontinuous beings and the confinements of individuality. Nonetheless, as has been argued throughout this discussion, the origin, in both Bataille and Blanchot, is finally offered as a fleeting point of contact rather than as something to hold on to. The logic of encounter displaces the logic of origin, with the former coming to designate precisely that which overturns the notion of origin – be it in its spatial account, as a ground; in its temporal dimension, as a beginning; or in its aesthetic and canonical dimension, as an original. Additionally, the term 'encounter' is not used in its traditional sense, as that of two separate, distinct, well-defined entities, but as that which undoes the logic of autonomy, enacting a double logic which precisely prevents oneself from being properly oneself. Against the dialectic of opposites, in the logic of the double terms are together (rather than opposed) and result in constant (unresolvable) tension (rather than in resolution), as in their entanglement they undermine and interrupt (rather than balance) each other.

All Blanchot's spatial accounts of literature – as inescapably divided between two slopes (Chapter 2), as a tensional space between being and non-being (Chapter 4) and as synonymous with the indeterminate zone of the neuter (Chapter 7) – sketch the mode of existence of literature in terms of a fundamental duplicity which, in its turn, undoes every attempt to confine existence in terms of unity, identity, sameness and origin. In parallel, the terms that are used in order to address and approach Bataille's model of literature display an irresolvable tension (an irreducible doubleness) that undoes the economy of sameness as well as that of exchange: the terms of exscription and simulacrum (Chapter 1) overturn the antithesis between inside and outside, original and copy respectively; the notions of the instant and withdrawal (Chapter 5) undermine both presence and absence; while the mask, concurrently showing and hiding a face (Chapter 8), suspends the opposition between visibility and invisibility, veiling and unveiling. The lexicon of initial division and originary torsion in Blanchot precludes any horizon of Being, while the terminology of masks and simulacra in Bataille outsteps every aspiration of an authentic existence.

Throughout this study, by way of the key notion of the encounter a model of communication has been put forward which defies unity (be it dialectical progression or mystical fusion) and redefines connection as always bound to separation. The logic of encounter is that of a double relation which undoes the order of hierarchy and opposition as well as fantasies of fusion and self-productivity (be it by the self or of the artwork). Blanchot's consideration of Orpheus as the emblematic figure of the writer renders turning towards and turning away the prevailing movement and shows how contact is always bound up with distance. Similarly, the Bataillean conceptualization of communication as synonymous with subjectivity recasts both in terms of linkage and leakage, (over)flowing and rupture.

Confronting Bataille and Blanchot not only with the demand of the real, a current demand in new French thought, but also with older concerns, such as that of truth, representation and subjectivity, demonstrates that the ongoing legacy of Bataille and Blanchot is that notions of subjectivity, truth and representation are not completely abolished or invalidated but rather, and perhaps more crucially, thrown into confusion and problematized. In this respect, both thinkers keep reminding us that subverting such precepts is not a finished task but an endless process of which we need to be a part, as readers and commentators who run into and critically engage not only with their texts but also with the texts of others which, whether coming before or after them, both accompany and haunt them – and us.

Bibliography

Works by Georges Bataille

'L'Anus solaire', in *Œuvres complètes*, 12 vols (Paris: Gallimard, 1970–88), I: *Premiers écrits. 1922–1940* (1970), pp. 79–86

'Avant-Propos', in *Bleu du Ciel*, in *Œuvres complètes*, 12 vols (Paris: Gallimard, 1970–88), III: *Œuvres littéraires* (1974), pp. 381–82

'Avant-Propos', in *La Littérature et le mal*, in *Œuvres complètes*, 12 vols (Paris: Gallimard, 1970–88), IX (1979), pp. 171–72

'Le Bas matérialisme et la gnose', in *Œuvres complètes*, 12 vols (Paris: Gallimard, 1970–88), I: *Premiers écrits. 1922–1940* (1970), pp. 220–26

Le Bleu du ciel, in *Œuvres complètes*, 12 vols (Paris: Gallimard, 1970–88), III: *Œuvres littéraires* (1974), pp. 377–487

Le Coupable, in *Œuvres complètes*, 12 vols (Paris: Gallimard, 1970–88), V: *La Somme athéologique. Tome I* (1973), pp. 235–92

L'Érotisme, in *Œuvres complètes*, 12 vols (Paris: Gallimard, 1970–88), X (1987), pp. 11–270

L'Expérience intérieure, in *Œuvres complètes*, 12 vols (Paris: Gallimard, 1970–88), V: *La Somme athéologique. Tome I* (1973), pp. 7–189

'Le Gros orteil', in *Œuvres complètes*, 12 vols (Paris: Gallimard, 1970–88), I: *Premiers écrits. 1922–1940* (1970), pp. 200–04

Histoire de l'œil, in *Œuvres complètes*, 12 vols (Paris: Gallimard, 1970–88), I: *Premiers écrits. 1922–1940* (1970), pp. 9–77

L'Impossible, in *Œuvres complètes*, 12 vols (Paris: Gallimard, 1970–88), III: *Œuvres littéraires* (1974), pp. 97–223

'Informe', in *Œuvres complètes*, 12 vols (Paris: Gallimard, 1970–88), I: *Premiers écrits. 1922–1940*, p. 217

Lascaux ou la naissance de l'art, in *Œuvres complètes*, 12 vols (Paris: Gallimard, 1970–88), IX (1979), 7–101

'Lettre à X', in *Œuvres complètes*, 12 vols (Paris: Gallimard, 1970–88), v: *La Somme athéologique. Tome I* (1973), pp. 361–71

La Littérature et le mal, in *Œuvres complètes*, 12 vols (Paris: Gallimard, 1970–88), ix (1979), 171–315

Madame Edwarda, in *Œuvres complètes*, 12 vols (Paris: Gallimard, 1970–88), iii: *Œuvres littéraires* (1974), pp. 7–31

Manet, in *Œuvres complètes*, 12 vols (Paris: Gallimard, 1970–88), ix (1979), 103–69

'Méthode de méditation', in *Œuvres complètes*, 12 vols (Paris: Gallimard, 1970–88), v: *La Somme athéologique. Tome I* (1973), pp. 191–227

Sur Nietzsche, in *Œuvres complètes*, 12 vols (Paris: Gallimard, 1970–88), vi: *La Somme athéologique. Tome II* (1973), pp. 11–205

'Notes – La Souveraineté', in *Œuvres complètes*, 12 vols (Paris: Gallimard, 1970–88), viii (1976), 592–678

'La Notion de dépense', in *Œuvres complètes*, 12 vols (Paris: Gallimard, 1970–88), i: *Premiers écrits. 1922–1940* (1970), pp. 302–20

Œuvres Complètes, 12 vols (Paris: Gallimard, 1970–88)

'Post-scriptum. 1953', in *Œuvres complètes*, 12 vols (Paris: Gallimard, 1970–88), v: *La Somme athéologique. Tome I* (1973), pp. 229–34

'Préface', in *L'Impossible*, in *Œuvres complètes*, 12 vols (Paris: Gallimard, 1970–88), iii: *Œuvres littéraires* (1974), pp. 101–02

'Préface', in *Lascaux ou la naissance de l'art*, in *Œuvres complètes*, 12 vols (Paris: Gallimard, 1970–88), ix (1979), 9–10

'Préface', in *Madame Edwarda*, *Œuvres complètes*, 12 vols (Paris: Gallimard, 1970–88), iii: *Œuvres littéraires* (1974), pp. 11–14

'Réflections sur le bourreau et le victime', in *Œuvres complètes*, 12 vols (Paris: Gallimard, 1970–88), xi: *Articles I. 1944–1949* (1988), pp. 262–67

'Le Silence de Molloy', in *Œuvres complètes*, 12 vols (Paris: Gallimard, 1970–88), xii: *Articles II. 1950–1961* (1988), pp. 85–94

'La Valeur d'usage de D. A. F de Sade', in *Œuvres complètes*, 12 vols (Paris: Gallimard, 1970–88), ii *Écrits* xii: *Articles II. posthumes. 1922–1940* (1970), pp. 54–69

Works by Maurice Blanchot

'Artaud', in *Le Livre à venir* (Paris: Gallimard, 1959), pp. 50–58

'Ce qu'il nous a appris' (1988) <http://ghansel.free.fr/blanchot.html> [accessed 22 February 2022]

'Le Chant des Sirènes. La Rencontre de l'imaginaire', in *Le Livre à venir* (Paris: Gallimard, 1959), pp. 9–18

'Comment la littérature est-elle possible?', in *Faux pas* (Paris: Gallimard, 1971 [1943]), pp. 92–101

'Les Deux versions de l'imaginaire', in *L'Espace littéraire* (Paris: Gallimard, 1955), pp. 341–56
L'Écriture du désastre (Paris: Gallimard, 1980)
'Une édition des *Fleurs du mal*', in *Faux pas* (Paris: Gallimard, 1971 [1943]), pp. 180–88
L'Entretien infini (Paris: Gallimard, 1969)
L'Espace littéraire (Paris: Gallimard, 1955)
'L'Expérience d'*Igitur*', in *L'Espace littéraire* (Paris: Gallimard, 1955), pp. 135–50
'L'Expérience intérieure', in *Faux pas* (Paris: Gallimard, 1971 [1943]), pp. 47–52
'L'Expérience-limite', in *L'Entretien infini* (Paris: Gallimard, 1969), pp. 300–42
'L'Expérience de Mallarmé', in *L'Espace littéraire* (Paris: Gallimard, 1955), pp. 37–52
Faux pas (Paris: Gallimard, 1971 [1943])
'L'Infini littéraire: L'Aleph', in *Le Livre à venir* (Paris: Gallimard, 1959), pp. 130–34
L'Instant de ma mort (Paris: Gallimard, 2002 [1994])
'Kafka et la littérature', in *La Part du feu* (Paris: Gallimard, 1949), pp. 20–34
'La Lecture de Kafka', in *La Part du feu* (Paris: Gallimard, 1949), pp. 9–19
'Lire', in *L'Espace littéraire* (Paris: Gallimard, 1955), pp. 251–62
'La Littérature et le droit à la mort', in *La Part du feu* (Paris: Gallimard, 1949), pp. 291–331
Le Livre à venir (Paris: Gallimard, 1959)
'Naissance de l'art', in *L'Amitié* (Paris: Gallimard, 1971), pp. 9–20
'Note', in *L'Entretien infini* (Paris: Gallimard, 1969), pp. 6–8
'Notes de lecture sur *Joseph et ses frères* de Mann', *L'Insurgé*, 14 (14 avril 1937), 5
'L'Œuvre et l'espace de la mort', in *L'Espace littéraire* (Paris: Gallimard, 1955), pp. 103–210
'Parler, ce n'est pas voir', in *L'Entretien infini* (Paris: Gallimard, 1969), pp. 35–45
'La Parole quotidienne', in *L'Entretien infini* (Paris: Gallimard, 1969), pp. 355–66
La Part du feu (Paris: Gallimard, 1949)
Le Pas au-delà (Paris: Gallimard, 1973)
'Le Pont de bois (*la répétition, le neutre*)', in *L'Entretien infini* (Paris: Gallimard, 1969), pp. 568–82
'La Question la plus profonde', in *L'Entretien infini* (Paris: Gallimard, 1969), pp. 12–34

'Le Rapport du troisième genre (homme sans horizon)', in *L'Entretien infini* (Paris: Gallimard, 1969), pp. 94–105

'Le Regard d'Orphée', in *L'Espace littéraire* (Paris: Gallimard, 1955), pp. 225–32

'Les Romans de Sartre', in *La Part du feu* (Paris: Gallimard, 1949), pp. 188–203

'Sans titre', in *L'Entretien infini* (Paris: Gallimard, 1969), pp. ix–xxvi

'La Solitude essentielle', in *L'Espace littéraire* (Paris: Gallimard, 1955), pp. 11–32

'La Voix narrative (*le "il"*, *le neutre*)', in *L'Entretien infini* (Paris: Gallimard, 1969), pp. 556–67

Selected Translations of Works by Georges Bataille

'Base Materialism and Gnosticism', in *Visions of Excess: Selected Writings, 1927–1939*, ed. by Allan Stoekl, trans. by Allan Stoekl with Carl R. Lovitt and Donald M. Leslie, Jr. (Minneapolis, MN: University of Minnesota Press, 1985), pp. 45–52

'The Big Toe', in *Visions of Excess: Selected Writings, 1927–1939*, ed. by Allan Stoekl, trans. by Allan Stoekl with Carl R. Lovitt and Donald M. Leslie, Jr. (Minneapolis, MN: University of Minnesota Press, 1985), pp. 20–23

Eroticism, trans. by Mary Dalwood (London: Penguin, 2010)

'Formless', in *Visions of Excess: Selected Writings, 1927–1939*, ed. by Allan Stoekl, trans. by Allan Stoekl with Carl R. Lovitt and Donald M. Leslie, Jr. (Minneapolis, MN: University of Minnesota Press, 1985), p. 31

The Inner Experience, trans. by Leslie Anne-Boldt (Albany, NY: State University of New York Press, 1988)

Literature and Evil, trans. by Alastair Hamilton (London; New York: Marion Boyars, 1973)

'Madame Edwarda', in *My Mother, Madame Edwarda, The Dead Man*, trans. by Austryn Wainhouse (London: Penguin, 2012), pp. 121–44

Manet: Biographical and Critical Study, trans. by Austryn Wainhouse and James Emmons (New York: Skira, 1955)

On Nietzsche, trans. by Bruce Boone, intro. by Sylvère Lotringer (New York: Paragon House, 2008)

'The Notion of Expenditure', in *Visions of Excess: Selected Writings, 1927–1939*, ed. by Allan Stoekl, trans. by Allan Stoekl with Carl R. Lovitt and Donald M. Leslie, Jr. (Minneapolis, MN: University of Minnesota Press, 1985), pp. 116–29

'Post-Scriptum 1953', in *Inner Experience*, trans. by Stuart Kendall (New York: State University of New York Press, 2014), pp. 203–07

'Preface', in *Literature and Evil*, trans. by Alastair Hamilton (London: Marion Boyars, 1973), pp. ix–xi

'Preface', in 'Madame Edwarda', in *My Mother, Madame Edwarda, The Dead Man*, trans. by Austryn Wainhouse (London: Penguin, 2012), pp. 123–29

'Reflections on the Executioner and the Victim', trans. by Elizabeth Rottenberg, *Yale French Studies*, 79 (1991), 15–19

'The Solar Anus', in *Visions of Excess: Selected Writings, 1927–1939*, ed. by Allan Stoekl, trans. by Allan Stoekl with Carl R. Lovitt and Donald M. Leslie, Jr. (Minneapolis, MN: University of Minnesota Press, 1985), pp. 5–9

'The Use Value of D. A. F. de Sade', in *Visions of Excess. Selected Writings, 1927–1939*, ed. by Allan Stoekl, trans. by Allan Stoekl with Carl R. Lovitt and Donald M. Leslie, Jr. (Minneapolis, MN: University of Minnesota Press, 1985), pp. 91–104

Visions of Excess: Selected Writings, 1927–1939, ed. by Allan Stoekl, trans. by Allan Stoekl with Carl R. Lovitt and Donald M. Leslie, Jr. (Minneapolis, MN: University of Minnesota Press, 1985)

Selected Translations of Works by Maurice Blanchot

'Artaud', in *The Book to Come*, trans. by Charlotte Mandell (Stanford, CA: Stanford University Press, 2003), pp. 34–40

The Book to Come, trans. by Charlotte Mandell (Stanford, CA: Stanford University Press, 2003)

'The Essential Solitude', in *The Space of Literature*, intro. and trans. by Ann Smock (Lincoln, NE; London: University of Nebraska Press, 1982), pp. 19–34

'Everyday Speech', in *The Infinite Conversation*, trans. by Susan Hanson (Minneapolis, MN and London: University of Minnesota Press, 1993), pp. 238–45

'The *Igitur* Experience', in *The Space of Literature*, intro. and trans. by Ann Smock (Lincoln, NE; London: University of Nebraska Press, 1982), pp. 108–19

The Infinite Conversation, trans. by Susan Hanson (Minneapolis, MN and London: University of Minnesota Press, 1993)

'Kafka and Literature', in *The Work of Fire*, trans. by Charlotte Mandell (Stanford, CA: Stanford University Press, 1995), pp. 12–26

'The Language of Fiction', in *The Work of Fire*, trans. by Charlotte Mandell (Stanford, CA: Stanford University Press, 1995), pp. 74–84

'The Limit-Experience', in *The Infinite Conversation*, trans. by Susan Hanson (Minneapolis, MN: University of Minnesota Press, 1993), pp. 202–29

'Literary Infinity: The Aleph', in *The Book to Come*, trans. by Charlotte Mandell (Stanford, CA: Stanford University Press, 2003), pp. 93–96

'Literature and the Right to Death', in *The Work of Fire*, trans. by Charlotte Mandell (Stanford, CA: Stanford University Press, 1995), pp. 300–44

'Mallarmé's Experience', in *The Space of Literature*, intro. and trans. by Ann Smock (Lincoln, NE; London: University of Nebraska Press, 1982), pp. 38–48

'The Most Profound Question', in *The Infinite Conversation*, trans. by Susan Hanson (Minneapolis, MN and London: University of Minnesota Press, 1993), pp. 11–24

'The Narrative Voice (the "he", the neutral)', in *The Infinite Conversation*, trans. by Susan Hanson (Minneapolis, MN and London: University of Minnesota Press, 1993), pp. 379–87

'Note', in *The Infinite Conversation*, trans. by Susan Hanson (Minneapolis, MN and London: University of Minnesota Press, 1993), pp. 11–12

'The Novels of Sartre', in *The Work of Fire*, trans. by Charlotte Mandell (Stanford, CA: Stanford University Press, 1995), pp. 188–203

'Orpheus's Gaze', in *The Space of Literature*, intro. and trans. by Ann Smock (Lincoln, NE; London: University of Nebraska Press, 1982), pp. 171–76

'Reading', in *The Space of Literature*, intro. and trans. by Ann Smock (Lincoln, NE; London: University of Nebraska Press, 1982), pp. 191–97

'Reading Kafka', in *The Work of Fire*, trans. by Charlotte Mandell (Stanford, CA: Stanford University Press, 1995), pp. 1–11

'The Relation of the Third Kind', in *The Infinite Conversation*, trans. by Susan Hanson (Minneapolis, MN and London: University of Minnesota Press, 1993), pp. 66–74

'The Song of the Sirens: Encountering the Imaginary', in *The Book to Come*, trans. by Charlotte Mandell (Stanford, CA: Stanford University Press, 2003), pp. 3–10

The Space of Literature, intro. and trans. by Ann Smock (Lincoln, NE; London: University of Nebraska Press, 1982)

'Speaking is Not Seeing', in *The Infinite Conversation*, trans. by Susan Hanson (Minneapolis, MN and London: University of Minnesota Press, 1993), pp. 25–32

'The Two Versions of the Imaginary', in *The Space of Literature*, intro. and trans. by Ann Smock (Lincoln, NE; London: University of Nebraska Press, 1982), pp. 254–63

'Untitled', in *The Infinite Conversation*, trans. by Susan Hanson (Minneapolis, MN and London: University of Minnesota Press, 1993), pp. xiii–xxiii

'The Wooden Bridge (*repetition, the neutral*)', in *The Infinite Conversation*, trans. by Susan Hanson (Minneapolis, MN and London: University of Minnesota Press, 1993), pp. 388–96

'The Work and Death's Space', in *The Space of Literature*, intro. and trans. by Ann Smock (Lincoln, NE; London: University of Nebraska Press, 1982), pp. 85–160

The Work of Fire, trans. by Charlotte Mandell (Stanford, CA: Stanford University Press, 1995)

Other Primary Sources

Baudelaire, Charles, *Journaux Intimes* <https://www.bmlisieux.com/archives/coeuranu.htm> [accessed 14 April 2022]

— Le Masque', in *Les Fleurs du mal* <https://fleursdumal.org/poem/201> [accessed 17 April 2022]

— 'The Mask', trans. by William Aggeler, in *The Flowers of Evil* <https://fleursdumal.org/poem/201> [accessed 17 April 2022]

Blixen, Karen, 'The Supper at Elsinore', in Karen Blixen, *Seven Gothic Tales* (London: Penguin, 2002), pp. 189–235

Borges, Jorge Luis, 'Pierre Menard, Author of the *Quixote*', in Jorge Luis Borges, *Collected Fictions*, trans. by Andrew Hurley (London: Penguin Books, 1999), pp. 88–95

Dostoevsky, Fyodor, *The Grand Inquisitor: With Related Chapters from The Brothers Karamazov*, ed. and intro. by Charles B. Guignon, trans. by Constance Garnett (Indianapolis, IN: Hackett, 1993)

Eliot, T. S., '*from* Baudelaire (1930)', in T. S. Eliot, *Selected Prose of T. S Eliot*, ed. and intro. by Frank Kermode (New York: Harvest, 1975), pp. 231–37

Freud, Sigmund, 'Creative Writers and Daydreaming', in Sigmund Freud, *Art and Literature*, ed. by Albert Dickson, trans. by James Strachey (London: Penguin, 1990), pp. 129–42

— 'Dostoevsky and Parricide', in Sigmund Freud, *Art and Literature*, ed. by Albert Dickson, trans. by James Strachey (London: Penguin, 1990), pp. 435–60

— *The Interpretation of Dreams*, ed. and trans. by James Strachey (London: Penguin, 1976)

— 'Notes upon a Case of Obsessional Neurosis', in *The Standard Edition of the Complete Psychological Works*, ed. by James Strachey, 24 vols (London: The Hogarth Press, 1953–74), x: *The Cases of 'Little Hans' and the Rat Man* (1955), pp. 155–318

Heidegger, Martin, *Contributions to Philosophy (From Enowning)*, trans. by Parvis Emad and Kenneth Maly (Bloomington, IN: Indiana University Press, 1999)

— *Nietzsche*, ed. by David Farrell Krell, 4 vols (New York: Harper & Row, 1979–87), IV: *Nihilism* (1982)

— 'The Origin of the Work of Art', in Martin Heidegger, *Poetry, Language, Thought*, trans. by Albert Hofstadter (New York: Harper & Row, 1971), pp. 15–88

Kafka, Franz, 'Before the Law', trans. by Willa and Edwin Muir, in *The Compete Short Stories of Franz Kafka*, ed. by Nahum N. Glatzer (London: Vintage, 1999), pp. 3–4

Kant, Emmanuel, *Critique of Judgement*, intro. and trans. by Werner S. Pluhar (Indianapolis, IN: Hackett, 1987)

— *Religion within the Limits of Reason Alone*, trans. by T. M. Greene and H. H. Hudson (New York: Harper & Row, 1960)

Nietzsche, Friedrich, *Twilight of the Idols*, in *The Portable Nietzsche*, ed. and trans. by Walter Kaufmann (London; New York: Penguin, 1982 [1954]), pp. 463–564

— *The Will to Power*, ed. by Walter Kaufmann, trans. by Walter Kaufmann and R. J. Hollingdale (New York: Random House, 1967)

Novalis, *Werke, Tagebücher und Briefe Friedrich von Hardenbergs*, 3 vols, II: *Das philosophisch-theoretische Werk*, ed. by Hans-Joachim Mähl (Munich; Vienna: Hanser, 1978)

— *Logological Fragments II*, in Novalis, *Philosophical Writings*, ed. and trans. by Margaret Mahony Stoljar (Albany, NY: State University of New York Press, 1997), pp. 67–82

Sartre, Jean-Paul, *Baudelaire* (Paris: Gallimard, 1946)

— *L'Imaginaire* (Paris: Gallimard, 2005 [1940])

— *The Imaginary* (London and New York: Routledge, 2004)

— *La Nausée* (Paris: Folio, 2019 [1938])

— *Nausea*, trans. by Lloyd Alexander (New York: New Directions, 2007 [1964])

— *Qu'est-ce que la littérature?* (Paris: Gallimard, 1948)

Verdi, Giuseppe, *Letters of Giuseppe Verdi*, ed. and trans. by Charles Osborne (London: Victor Gollancz, 1971)

Secondary Literature

Adorno, Theodor W., 'Notes on Beckett', trans. by Dirk Van Hulle and Shane Weller, *Journal of Beckett Studies*, 19 (2010), 157–78

Agamben, Giorgio, 'The Messiah and the Sovereign: The Problem of Law in Walter Benjamin', in Giorgio Agamben, *Potentialities: Collected Essays in Philosophy*, ed. and trans. by Daniel Heller-Roazen (Stanford, CA: Stanford University Press, 1999), pp. 160–75

— *The Open: Man and Animal*, trans. by Kevin Attell (Stanford, CA: Stanford University Press, 2004)

— *Nudities*, trans. by David Kishik and Stefan Pedatella (Stanford, CA: Stanford University Press, 2011)

Artaud, Antonin, *Le Théâtre et son double* (Paris: Gallimard, 1964)

Baugh, Bruce, *French Hegel* (London: Routledge, 2003)

Benjamin, Walter, 'Der Erzähler. Betrachtungen zum Werk Nikolai Lesskows', *Orient und Occident*, 3 (1936), 16–33

— 'The Storyteller: Reflections on the Works of Nikolai Leskov', in Walter Benjamin, *Illuminations*, trans. by Harry Zorn (London: Pimlico, 1999), pp. 83–107

— 'On the Mimetic Faculty', in Walter Benjamin, *Reflections: Essays, Aphorisms, Autobiographical Writings*, ed. by Peter Demetz (New York: Schocken, 1986), pp. 333–36

Bident, Christophe, *Maurice Blanchot. Partenaire Invisible. Essai Biographique* (Seyssel: Champ Vallon, 1998)

— 'The Movements of the Neuter', trans. by Michael FitzGerald and Leslie Hill, in *After Blanchot: Literature, Criticism, Philosophy*, ed. by Leslie Hill, Brian Nelson and Dimitris Vardoulakis (Newark, DE: University of Delaware Press, 2006), pp. 13–34

Borch-Jacobsen, Mikkel, 'The Laughter of Being', in *Bataille: A Critical reader*, ed. by Fred Botting and Scott Wilson (Oxford: Blackwell, 1998), pp. 146–66

— *Lacan, le maître absolu* (Paris: Flammarion, 2015 [1990])

— *Lacan: The Absolute Master*, trans. by Douglas Brick (Stanford, CA: Stanford University Press, 1991)

Bowie, Andrew, *Aesthetics and Subjectivity: From Kant to Nietzsche* (Manchester: Manchester University Press, 2003 [1990])

Bowie, Malcolm, *Freud, Proust, and Lacan: Theory as Fiction* (Cambridge: Cambridge University Press, 1987)

— *Lacan* (London: Fontana, 1991)

Brondel, Jacques, *Emily Brontë. Expérience spirituelle et création poétique* (Paris: Presses Universitaires de France, 1995)

Brooks, Peter, 'Freud's Masterplot: Questions of Narrative', in *Literature and Psychoanalysis: The Question of Reading: Otherwise*, ed. by Shoshana Felman (Baltimore, MD and London: Johns Hopkins University Press, 1982), pp. 280–300

— *Psychoanalysis and Storytelling* (Oxford & Cambridge, MA: Blackwell, 1994)

Bruno, Jean, 'Techniques d'illumination chez Georges Bataille', *Critique* 195/196 (1963), 706–21

Bruns, Gerard L., 'Anarchic Temporality: Writing, Friendship, and the Ontology of the Work of Art in Maurice Blanchot's Poetics', in *The Power of Contestation: Perspectives on Maurice Blanchot*, ed. by Kevin Kart and Geoffrey H. Hartman (Baltimore, MD and London: Johns Hopkins University Press, 2004), pp. 121–40

Butler, Judith, *Subjects of Desire: Hegelian Reflections in Twentieth Century France* (New York: Columbia University Press, 1987)

— 'Giving an Account of Oneself', *Diacritics*, 31:4 (2001), 22–40

— *Giving an Account of Oneself* (New York: Fordham University Press, 2005)

— 'On Cruelty', review of Jacques Derrida, *The Death Penalty, Vol. I* (2013), trans. by Peggy Kamuf, *London Review of Books*, 36 (2014), 31–33

Cattani, Damian, 'Modernity, Evil and Ethics: A Sartrean and Battaillean Reading of Baudelaire's "Le Jeu"', *Dix-Neuf*, 16 (2012), 260–70

Chapsal, Madeleine, 'Georges Bataille', in Madeleine Chapsal, *Les écrivains en personne* (Paris: Juillard, 1973), pp. 21–33; first published in Madeleine Chapsal, *Quinze écrivains. Entretiens* (Paris: René Julliard, 1963), pp. 11–22

Char, René, *Feuillets d'Hypnos* (Paris: Gallimard, 2007 [1946])

Clark, Timothy, 'Blanchot and the Literary', in Timothy Clark, *Derrida, Heidegger, Blanchot: Sources of Derrida's Notion and Practice of Literature* (Cambridge: Cambridge University Press, 1992), pp. 64–107

Cohen, Richard A., 'Introduction', in Emmanuel Levinas, *Time and the Other*, trans. by Richard A. Cohen (Pittsburgh, PA: Duquesne University Press, 1987), pp. 1–27

Critchley, Simon, '*Das Ding*: Lacan and Levinas', in Simon Critchley, *Ethics – Politics – Subjectivity* (London; New York: Verso, 1999), pp. 198–216

— *Ethics – Politics – Subjectivity: Essays on Derrida, Levinas & Contemporary French Thought* (London; New York: Verso, 1999)

- 'The Original Traumatism: Levinas and Psychoanalysis', in Simon Critchley, *Ethics – Politics – Subjectivity: Essays on Derrida, Levinas, & Contemporary French Thought* (London: Verso, 1999), pp. 181–97
- 'Demanding Approval. On the Ethics of Alain Badiou', *Radical Philosophy*, 100 (2000) <https://www.radicalphilosophy.com/article/demanding-approval> [accessed 14 April 2022]
- 'Preface to the Second Edition: As my father I have already died', in Simon Critchley, *Very Little ... Almost Nothing*, 2nd edn (London: Routledge, 2004 [1997]), pp. xv–xxviii
- *Very Little ... Almost Nothing*, 2nd edn (London: Routledge, 2004 [1997])
- *Infinitely Demanding: Ethics of Commitment, Politics of Resistance* (London: Verso, 2007)

Crowley, Martin, 'Bataille's Tacky Touch', *MLN*, 119 (2004), 766–80

Deleuze, Gilles, 'Simulacre et philosophie antique', in Gilles Deleuze, *Logique du sens* (Paris: Minuit, 1969), pp. 292–324
- 'La Littérature et la vie', in Gilles Deleuze, *Critique et clinique* (Paris: Minuit, 1993), pp. 11–17
- 'Literature and Life', trans. by Daniel W. Smith and Michael A. Greco, *Critical Inquiry*, 23 (1997), 225–30
- *Francis Bacon. Logique de la sensation* (Paris: Seuil, 2002 [1981])
- *Différence et répétition* (Paris: Presses Universitaires de France, 2019 [1968])
- *Difference and Repetition*, trans. by Paul Patton (New York: Columbia University Press: 1994)

Derrida, Jacques, 'De l'économie restreinte à l'économie générale. Un hégélianisme sans réserve', *L'Arc*, 32 (1967), 24–45
- 'Devant la loi', in *Philosophy and Literature*, ed. by A. Philipps Griffiths (Cambridge: Cambridge University Press, 1984), pp. 173–88
- 'Before the Law', in Jacques Derrida, *Acts of Literature*, ed. by Derek Attridge (London and New York: Routledge, 1992), pp. 181–220
- 'La double séance', in Jacques Derrida, *La Dissémination* (Paris: Seuil, 1993 [1972]), pp. 215–347
- 'The First Session', in Jacques Derrida, *Acts of Literature*, ed. by Derek Attridge (London and New York: Routledge, 1992), pp. 127–80
- 'From Restricted to General Economy: A Hegelianism without Reserve', in *Bataille: A Critical Reader*, ed. by Fred Botting and Scott Wilson (Oxford: Blackwell, 1998), pp. 102–38
- *La Vérité en peinture* (Paris: Flammarion, 2010 [1978])
- *Séminaire. La peine de mort I (1999–2000)* (Paris: Galilée, 2012)

Didi-Hubermann, Georges, *Sortir du noir* (Paris: Minuit, 2015)

Dumayet, Pierre, 'Georges Bataille à propos de son livre *La Littérature et le mal*', vidéo INA, 21 May 1958 <https://www.ina.fr/video/I00016133> [accessed 25 February 2022]

Eagleton, Terry, *On Evil* (New Haven, CT; London: Yale University Press, 2010)

Evans, Dylan, *An Introductory Dictionary of Lacanian Psychoanalysis* (London and New York: Routledge, 1996)

Felman, Shoshana, 'Benjamin's Silence', *Critical Inquiry*, 25 (1999), 201–34

Foucault, Michel, 'Préface à la transgression', *Critique*, 195/196 (1963), 751–69

— 'A Preface to Transgression', in *Bataille: A Critical Reader*, ed. by Fred Botting and Scott Wilson (Oxford: Blackwell, 1998), pp. 24–40

— 'La Pensée du dehors', *Critique*, 229 (1966), 523–46

— 'Sur les façons d'écrire l'histoire' (entretien avec R. Bellour*)*, *Les Lettres françaises*, 1187 (1967), 6–9

— 'On the Genealogy of Ethics: An Overview of Work in Progress', in *The Foucault Reader*, ed. by Paul Rabinow (New York: Pantheon, 1974), pp. 340–72

— 'Maurice Blanchot: The Thought from Outside', in Michel Foucault and Maurice Blanchot, *Foucault. Blanchot*, trans. by Jeffrey Mehlman and Brian Massumi (New York: Zone, 1990), pp. 7–58

ffrench, Patrick, *The Cut: Reading Bataille's* Histoire de l'œil (Oxford: Oxford University Press, 1999)

— 'Georges Bataille', in *Encyclopedia of Modern French Thought*, ed. by Christopher John Murray (New York and London: Routledge, 2004), pp. 55–59

— *After Bataille: Sacrifice, Exposure, Community* (Oxford: Legenda, 2007)

Fynsk, Christopher, *Language and Relation ... that there is language* (Stanford, CA: Stanford University Press, 1996)

— 'Introduction', in Christopher Fynsk, *Infant Figures: The Death of the Infans and Other Scenes of Origin* (Stanford, CA: Stanford University Press, 2000), pp. 1–8

Girard, René, 'Narcissism: Demystified by Proust', in *Psychoanalysis, Creativity and Literature: A French-American Inquiry*, ed. by Alan Roland (New York: Columbia University Press, 1978), pp. 292–311

Greenwood, Edward, 'Literature: Freedom or Evil? The Debate between Sartre and Bataille', *Sartre Studies International*, 4 (1998), 17–29

Guerlac, Suzanne, '"Recognition" by a Woman!: A Reading of Bataille's *L'Érotisme*', *Yale French Studies*, 78 (1990), 90–105

Hart, Kevin, 'The Counter-Spiritual Life', in *The Power of Contestation: Perspectives on Maurice Blanchot*, ed. by Kevin Hart and Geoffrey H. Hartman (Baltimore, MD and London: Johns Hopkins University Press, 2004), pp. 156–77

Hill, Leslie, *Blanchot: Extreme Contemporary* (London: Routledge, 1997)

— *Bataille, Klossowski, Blanchot: Writing at the Limit* (Oxford: Oxford University Press, 2001)

— 'After Blanchot', in *After Blanchot: Literature, Criticism, Philosophy*, ed. by Leslie Hill, Brian Nelson and Dimitris Vardoulakis (Newark, DE: University of Delaware Press, 2005), pp. 1–12

Hollier, Denis, 'La Tragédie de Gilles de Rais', *L'Arc*, 32 (1967), 63–70

— 'De l'équivoque entre littérature et politique', in Denis Hollier, *Les Dépossédés (Bataille, Caillois, Leiris, Malraux, Sartre)* (Paris: Minuit, 1993), pp. 109–30

— 'La Littérature doit-elle être possible?', in Denis Hollier, *Les Dépossédés (Bataille, Caillois, Leiris, Malraux, Sartre)* (Paris: Minuit, 1993), pp. 7–22

— *La Prise de la Concorde, suivi de Les Dimanches de la Vie. Essais sur Georges Bataille* (Paris: Gallimard, 1993)

— 'La Prise de la Concorde', in Denis Hollier, *La Prise de la Concorde, suivi de Les Dimanches de la Vie. Essais sur Georges Bataille* (Paris: Gallimard, 1993), pp. 11–298

— 'La Valeur d'usage de l'impossible', in Denis Hollier, *Les Dépossédés (Bataille, Caillois, Leiris, Malraux, Sartre)* (Paris: Minuit, 1993), pp. 153–78

— 'The Dualist Materialism of Georges Bataille', in *Bataille: A Critical Reader*, ed. by Fred Botting and Scott Wilson (Oxford: Blackwell, 1998), pp. 59–73

Homer, Sean, *Jacques Lacan* (London and New York: Routledge, 2005)

Huhn, Thomas, 'The Kantian Sublime and The Nostalgia for Violence', *The Journal of Aesthetics and Art Criticism*, 53 (1995), 269–75

James, Ian, *Pierre Klossowski: The Persistence of a Name* (Oxford: Legenda, 2001)

— *An Introduction to the Philosophy of Jean-Luc Nancy: The Fragmentary Demand* (Stanford, CA: Stanford University Press, 2006)

— 'From Recuperation to Simulacrum', in *The Beast at Heaven's Gate: Georges Bataille and the Art of Transgression*, ed. by Andrew Hussey (Amsterdam: Rodopi, 2006), pp. 91–100

— 'Lucidity and Tact', in *Lucidity: Essays in Honour of Alison Finch*, ed. by Ian James and Emma Wilson (Oxford: Legenda, 2016), pp. 9–19

Jameson, Fredric, 'Imaginary and Symbolic in Lacan: Marxism, Psychoanalytic Criticism and the Problem of the Subject', in *Literature and Psychoanalysis: The Question of Reading: Otherwise*, ed. by Shoshana Felman (Baltimore, MD and London: Johns Hopkins University Press, 1982), pp. 338–95

Johnson, Barbara, 'The Frame of Reference: Poe, Lacan, Derrida', in *Literature and Psychoanalysis: The Question of Reading: Otherwise*, ed. by Shoshana Felman (Baltimore, MD and London: Johns Hopkins University Press, 1982), pp. 457–505

Jones, Ernest, *Sigmund Freud: Life and Work*, 3 vols (London: The Hogarth Press, 1953–57), II: *Years of Maturity: 1901–1919* (1955)

Kaufman, Eleanor, *The Delirium of Praise: Bataille, Blanchot, Deleuze, Foucault, Klossowski* (Baltimore, MD: Johns Hopkins University Press, 2002)

Klossowski, Pierre, 'Le simulacre dans la communication de Georges Bataille', *Critique* 195/196 (1963), 742–51

— 'Of the Simulacrum in Georges Bataille's Communication', in *On Bataille: Critical Essays*, ed. by Leslie Anne Boldt-Irons (Albany, NY: State University of New York Press, 1995), pp. 147–56

Kojève, Alexandre, *Introduction à la lecture de Hegel*, ed. by Raymond Queneau (Paris: Gallimard, 1947)

Krauss, Rosalind E., *The Optical Unconscious* (Cambridge, MA: The MIT Press, 1993)

Kristeva, Julia, 'Bataille, l'expérience, et la pratique', in *Bataille*, ed. by Philippe Sollers (Paris: Union Générale d'Éditions, 1973), pp. 267–301

— 'Bataille, Experience and Practice', in *On Bataille: Critical Essays*, ed. by Leslie Anne Boldt-Irons (Albany, NY: State University of New York Press, 1995), pp. 237–64

Lacan, Jacques, 'L'Anamorphose', in Jacques Lacan, *Les Quatre concepts fondamentaux de la psychanalyse*, ed. by Jacques-Alain Miller (Paris: Seuil, 1973 [1964]), pp. 92–104

— 'Anamorphosis', in Jacques Lacan, *The Four Fundamental Concepts of Psycho-Analysis*, ed. by Jacques-Alain Miller, trans. by Alan Sheridan (London; New York: Karnac, 1977), pp. 79–90

— 'La Ligne et la lumière', in *Les Quatre concepts fondamentaux de la psychanalyse*, ed. by Jacques-Alain Miller (Paris: Seuil, 1973 [1964]), pp. 105–19

— 'The Line and Light', in *The Four Fundamental Concepts of Psycho-Analysis*, trans. by Alan Sheridan, ed. by Jacques-Alain Miller (London; New York: Karnac, 1977), pp. 91–104

— 'La Chose freudienne ou Sens du retour à Freud en psychanalyse', in Jacques Lacan, *Écrits I* (Paris: Seuil, 1999 [1966]), pp. 398–433

— 'The Freudian Thing, or the Meaning of the Return to Freud in Psychoanalysis', in Jacques Lacan, *Écrits*, trans. by Bruce Fink (New York; London: Norton, 2006 [2002]), pp. 334–63
— 'Fonction et champ de la parole et du langage', in Jacques Lacan, *Écrits I* (Paris: Seuil, 1999 [1966]), pp. 235–321
— 'The Function and Field of Speech and Language in Psychoanalysis', in Jacques Lacan, *Écrits*, trans. by Bruce Fink (New York; London: Norton, 2002 [1966]), pp. 197–268
— 'La Science et la verité', in Jacques Lacan, *Écrits II* (Paris: Seuil, 1999 [1966]), pp. 335–58
— 'Science and Truth', in Jacques Lacan, *Écrits*, trans. by Bruce Fink (New York; London: Norton, 2002 [1966]), pp. 726–45
— Le Séminaire sur *La Lettre volée*', in Jacques Lacan, *Écrits I* (Paris: Seuil, 1999 [1966]), pp. 11–61
— 'Seminar on "The Purloined Letter"', in Jacques Lacan, *Écrits*, trans. by Bruce Fink (New York; London: Norton, 2002 [1966]), pp. 6–50
— 'Le Stade du miroir comme formateur de la fonction du Je', in Jacques Lacan, *Écrits I* (Paris: Seuil, 1999 [1966]), pp. 92–99
— 'The Mirror Stage as Formative of the *I* Function as Revealed in Psychoanalytic Experience', in Jacques Lacan, *Écrits*, trans. by Bruce Fink (New York; London: Norton, 2002 [1966]), pp. 75–81
— 'Subversion du sujet et dialectique du désir dans l'inconscient freudien', in Jacques Lacan, *Écrits II* (Paris: Seuil, 1999 [1966]), pp. 273–308
— 'The Subversion of the Subject and the Dialectic of Desire in the Freudian Unconscious', in Jacques Lacan, *Écrits*, trans. by Bruce Fink (New York; London: Norton, 2002 [1966]), pp. 671–702
Lacoue-Labarthe, Philippe, 'La Contestation de la mort', *Le Nouveau Magazine Littéraire*, 424 (2003), 58–60
— 'The Contestation of Death', in *The Power of Contestation: Perspectives on Maurice Blanchot*, ed. by Kevin Hart and Geoffrey H. Hartmann (Baltimore and London: Johns Hopkins University Press, 2004), pp. 141–55
Laplanche, Jean, 'La Psychanalyse comme anti-herméneutique', in Jean Laplanche, *Entre séduction et inspiration: l'homme* (Paris: Presses Universitaires de France, 1999), pp. 243–62
— 'Psychoanalysis as Anti-Hermeneutics', trans. by Luke Thurston, *Radical Philosophy*, 79 (1996), 7–12
Laplanche, Jean, and J.-B. Pontalis, *Fantasme originaire. Fantasmes des origines. Origines du fantasme* (Paris: Hachette, 1985)
Laporte, Roger, 'Le Oui, Le Non, le Neutre', *Critique*, 229 (1966), 579–90

Leclaire, Serge, 'L'Inscription inconsciente: une autre mémoire', in Serge Leclaire, *Écrits pour la psychanalyse 1. Demeures de l'ailleurs. 1954–1993* (Paris: Seuil, 1996), pp. 177–86
— 'Unconscious Inscription: Another Memory', in *Psychoanalysis, Creativity, and Literature: A French-American Inquiry*, ed. by Alan Roland (New York: Columbia University Press, 1978), pp. 75–84

Leiris, Michel, 'Du temps de Lord Auch', *L'Arc*, 32 (1967), 6–15

Levinas, Emmanuel, *Le Temps et l'autre* (Montpellier: Fata Morgana, 1979)
— *Éthique et infini* (Paris: Fayard, 1982)
— *Ethics and Infinity: Conversations with Philippe Nemo*, trans. by Richard A. Cohen (Pittsburgh, PA: Duquesne University Press, 1985)
— *De l'évasion* (Montpellier: Fata Morgana, 1982 [1935])
— *On Escape*, trans. by Bettina Bergo (Stanford, CA: Stanford University Press, 2003)
— *De l'existence à l'existant* (Paris: Librairie Philosophique Vrin, 1993 [1947])
— 'La Réalité et son ombre' (1948), in Emmanuel Levinas, *Les Imprévus de l'histoire* (Montpellier: Fata Morgana, 1994), pp. 123–48
— 'Reality and its Shadow', trans. by Alphonso Lingis, in *The Levinas Reader*, ed. by Sean Hand (Oxford: Blackwell, 1989), pp. 129–43
— *Autrement qu'être ou Au-delà de l'essence* (Paris: Livre de Poche, 2004 [1974])
— *Sur Maurice Blanchot* (Montpellier: Fata Morgana, 2004 [1975])

Libertson, Joseph, 'Proximity and the Word: Blanchot and Bataille', *Substance*, 14 (1976), 35–49

Masson, André, 'Le Soc de la charrue', *Critique* 195/196 (1963), 701–05

May, Todd, 'Michel Foucault's Guide to Living', *Angelaki*, 11 (2006), 173–84

Merleau-Ponty, Maurice, *L'Œil et l'esprit*, in Maurice Merleau-Ponty, *Œuvres*, édition établie et préfacée par Claude Lefort (Paris: Gallimard, 2010 [1964]), pp. 1591–1628

Nancy, Jean-Luc, 'L'excrit', in Jean-Luc Nancy, *Une pensée finie* (Paris: Galilée, 1990), pp. 54–65
— 'L'Évidence du Film. Abbas Kiarostami / The Evidence of Film. Abbas Kiarostami', in Jean-Luc Nancy, *L'Évidence du Film. Abbas Kiarostami / The Evidence of Film. Abbas Kiarostami*, trans. by Christine Irizarry and Verena Andermatt Conley (Brussels: Gaevert, 2001), pp. 8–79
— 'Exscription', trans. by Katherine Lydon, *Yale French Studies*, 78 (1990), 47–65

— *Multiple Arts: The Muses II*, ed. by Simon Parks (Stanford, CA: Stanford University Press, 2006)
— *L'Adoration (Deconstruction du christianisme, 2)* (Paris: Galilée, 2010)
— *Adoration: The Deconstruction of Christianity II*, trans. by John McKeane (New York: Fordham University Press, 2013)
Pasolini, Pier Paolo, 'The Lost Interview' <https://mubi.com/notebook/posts/the-lost-pasolini-interview> [accessed 25 February 2022]
Paulhan, Jean, and Monique Saint-Hélier, *Correspondence, 1941–1955* (Paris: Gallimard, 1995)
Ragland-Sullivan, Ellie, *Jacques Lacan and the Philosophy of Psychoanalysis* (Urbana, IL: University of Illinois Press, 1986)
Rey, Jean-Michel, 'Le Signe aveugle', *L'Arc*, 44 (1967), 54–63
Ricœur, Paul, 'Guilt, Ethics and Religion', in *Talk of God*, Royal Institute of Philosophy Lectures, 2 (London: Macmillan, 1969), pp. 100–17; repr. in Paul Ricœur, *The Conflict of Interpretations: Essays in Hernemeutics*, ed. by Don Ihde (Evanston, IL: Northwestern University Press, 1974), pp. 425–39
— *Le Mal. Un défi à la philosophie et à la théologie* (Geneva: Labor et Fides, 2004)
— *Evil: A Challenge to Philosophy and Theology*, trans. by John Bowden (London: Continuum, 2007)
Ross, Alison, *The Aesthetic Paths of Philosophy: Presentation in Kant, Heidegger, Lacoue-Labarthe and Nancy* (Stanford, CA: Stanford University Press, 2007)
Scruton, Roger, *Beauty: A Very Short Introduction* (Oxford: Oxford University Press, 2011)
Sellars, John, 'An Ethics of the Event: Deleuze's Stoicism', *Angelaki*, 11 (2006), 157–71
Smith, Douglas, 'Beyond the Cave: Lascaux and the Prehistoric in Post-War French Culture', *French Studies*, 58 (2004), 219–32
Smock, Ann, 'Translator's Introduction', in Maurice Blanchot, *The Space of Literature*, intro. and trans. by Ann Smock (Lincoln, NE; London: University of Nebraska Press, 1982), pp. 1–15
Sollier, René de, 'L'Homme de Lascaux', *L'Arc*, 32 (1971), 58–62
Sontag, Susan, 'The Pornographic Imagination', in Susan Sontag, *Styles of Radical Will* (London: Penguin, 1966), pp. 35–73
— 'Against Interpretation', in Susan Sontag, *Against Interpretation and Other Essays* (London: Penguin, 2009), pp. 3–14
Steiner, George, *Language and Silence: Essays on Language, Literature, and the Inhuman* (New Haven, CT: Yale University Press, 1998)

Stoekl, Allan, 'Introduction', in Georges Bataille, *Visions of Excess: Selected Writings, 1927–1939*, ed. by Allan Stoekl, trans. by Allan Stoekl with Carl R. Lovitt and Donald M. Leslie, Jr. (Minneapolis, MN: University of Minnesota Press, 1985), pp. ix–xxv

Suleiman, Susan Rubin, 'Bataille in the Street: The Search for Virility in the 1930s', in *Bataille: Writing the Sacred*, ed. by Carolyn Bailey Gill (London: Routledge, 1995), pp. 26–45

— 'Transgression and the Avant-Garde: Bataille's *Histoire de l'œil*', in *On Bataille: Critical Essays*, ed. by Leslie Anne Boldt-Irons (Albany, NY: State University of New York Press, 1995), pp. 313–34

Surya, Michel, *Georges Bataille. La mort à l'œuvre* (Paris: Gallimard, 2012 [1992])

— *Georges Bataille: An Intellectual Biography*, trans. by Krzysztof Fijalkowski and Michael Richardson (London; New York: Verso, 2002)

Weil, Simone, *La Pesanteur et la grâce* (Paris: Plon, 1988 [1947])

— *Gravity and Grace*, trans. by Emma Crawford and Mario von der Ruhr (London and New York: Routledge, 1952)

Weiss, Alen S., 'Impossible Sovereignty: Between *The Will to Power* and *The Will to Chance*', *October 102*, 36 (1986), 128–46

Zizek, Slavoj, 'Ideology III: To Read Too Many Books is Harmful' <http://www.lacan.com/zizchemicalbeats.html> [accessed 18 February 2022]

Zupančič, Alenka, *Ethics of the Real: Kant and Lacan* (London; New York: Verso, 2000)

Index

absence 3, 12, 25, 40, 41, 49, 52, 53, 54, 55, 75, 78, 81, 82–83, 85, 88, 91, 148, 150, 155, 166, 189, 190, 227, 234
   of being 41, 54, 75
Adam 112
   Adamic myth 112, 225
allo–biography 67
alterity *see* otherness
analytic process, the 130, 137–43, 154, 155 n. 86, 156
annexes 57–58, 60–61
animality 213–20, 224, 225
art 4 n. 4, 71, 72 n. 3, 73–79, 83–85, 90–91, 102, 128, 132, 134, 198, 212–13, 215, 232
Artaud, Antonin 60–61, 64–65
   Le Théâtre et son double 65 n. 25
artwork, the 4 n. 3, 46 n. 25, 51, 71, 73, 75–76, 84, 85, 86–87, 88, 101, 171, 212
   origin of 73, 86, 131
authority 21, 32, 40, 41, 67, 88, 124, 173
autobiography *see* writing, autobiographical
autrui see other, the

base, the 20–22, 97, 197
Bataille, Georges 1–3, 5–13, 17–43, 47–50, 53–55, 57–58, 60, 62, 95–111, 113–14, 118–19, 121–24, 128, 129–30, 132–33, 167 n. 17, 193–221, 224, 225, 227–29, 231–35
   friendship with Maurice Blanchot 7, 9–10
   readings of 36–37
   works:
      'L'Anus solaire' 208
      Le Bleu du ciel 199, 200 n. 20
      'Coïncidences' 60 & n. 8, 61–62
      L'Érotisme 121, 197, 197 n. 12, 202–03, 209, 219–20
      L'Expérience intérieure 28–31, 33–34, 35, 36, 41–42, 64, 103, 167 n. 17, 209, 210 n. 51
      'Le Gros orteil' 18–19, 64
      Histoire de l'œil 60 nn. 7 & 8, 61, 62–64, 193–96
      L'Impossible 201
      Lascaux ou la naissance de l'art 196–97, 213–15, 217–19, 224

'Lettre à X' 33, 212
La Littérature et le mal 92,
   96–103, 104, 106–09,
   113–14, 121–24, 128,
   130, 132, 195
Madame Edwarda 35–36,
   201–03, 210, 214–15, 227
'Le Bas matérialisme et la
   gnose' 20–21
'Méthode de méditation'
   28, 34, 54 n. 48,
   128 n. 117
'Molloy's Silence' 204
'La Notion de dépense'
   26, 27–28
Sur Nietzsche 95–96
'La Valeur d'usage de
   D.A.F. de Sade' 23
Baudelaire, Charles 59, 97, 107,
   108, 110, 113–14, 118, 119,
   120, 122, 123, 186–87
Journaux Intimes 113
Les Fleurs du Mal 107
Beckett, Samuel 118, 186,
   204, 205–06
being 3, 8, 9, 10, 12, 24, 25, 33–34,
   35, 41, 46–47, 48, 50–53, 54,
   55, 75, 76, 77, 82, 83, 86, 88,
   89–90, 97, 98, 114–18, 121,
   123, 147–48, 150, 157 & n. 91,
   165, 166, 178, 182–83, 189–90,
   201–02, 216–17, 227, 228 n.
   102, 233, 234
of language 170–71
of the law 125–26
nature of 41
non–being/not being 53, 75,
   82, 83, 88, 168,
   189–90, 234
as presence 147, 166
as slippage 34, 35
in the world 46 n. 25, 53, 86,
   115, 165 n. 14, 233

Benjamin, Walter 25 n. 28,
   142–43, 173–74, 177–78
'The Storyteller' 142, 173–74,
   177–78
Blanchot, Maurice 1–3, 5–13, 32,
   39–55, 57–61, 64–67, 72–92,
   128–30, 132–33, 155–56, 161–68,
   171–91, 219, 228–29, 231–35
friendship with Georges
   Bataille 7, 9–10
works:
   'Le Chant des Sirènes.
      La rencontre de
      l'imaginaire' 88–90
   'Comment la
      littérature est–elle
      possible?' 43–44
   'Les Deux versions de
      l'imaginaire' 80–82
   L'Ecriture du désastre 66,
      184 n. 63
   L'Entretien infini 39–40, 67,
      76, 161 n. 1, 163, 164,
      166, 167, 168 & n. 19,
      171, 179–80, 181,
      183, 184–85, 187–89,
      190–91
   L'Espace littéraire 54, 72–73,
      76, 77–78, 85, 86 n. 40,
      91–92, 130, 132–33,
      162–63, 166, 168 & n. 18,
      185, 188
   'L'Expérience
      intérieure' 39–42
   'L'Expérience-limite' 39–40
   'La Lecture de
      Kafka' 186–87
   'L'Infini littéraire:
      L'Aleph' 179
   L'Instant de ma mort 66,
      173, 174, 175–77
   'Kafka et la littérature'
      44–45, 161–62, 167

'La Littérature et le droit à la mort' 46–52, 73
Le Livre à venir 179
La Part du feu 161
'Le Regard d'Orphée' 85–87
'(Une Scène primitive?)' 66
Thomas l'obscur 52 n. 45
Blixen, Karen (Isak Dinesen), *The Supper at Elsinore* 116 n. 78
body, the 23, 36, 49, 63, 65 & n. 25, 107, 142, 165, 194, 197, 199, 208–09, 214, 216–17
Borges, Jorge Luis 179, 180 & n. 51
Breton, André 8 n. 16, 18, 36, 37
Brontë, Emily 100, 102, 108, 110
Wuthering Heights 100, 102

capitalism 26–27
Cervantes, Miguel de, *Don Quixote* 180–81
child 108, 109, 110, 131, 133 & n. 9, 138, 146–47, 148–49, 152 n. 77
childhood 66, 108, 109, 110, 132–33, 147, 193, 194–95
communication 30–31, 35, 49, 211, 217, 234
corporeality *see* body, the
creation 27, 47, 59, 190, 203, 218–19
creativity 47, 59, 84, 86, 98–99, 107, 131–32, 144–45

Dada 18 & n. 4
death 48–49, 62, 64, 73, 75 n. 12, 87–88, 91–92, 106–07, 133, 156–57, 172 & n. 30, 173–74, 175–78, 185–87, 194 n. 4, 196, 201, 202, 204, 210, 228
'double death' 185

the impossibility of 176–77, 185–87
literature's right to 48, 73
by a thousand cuts 32 n. 48
le dehors see outside, the
denuding 197–98, 226, 227
desire 119, 137, 138, 139, 151 n. 72, 152, 157, 201–02, 204, 206
Dickens, Charles, *Great Expectations* 135–36
discourse 6, 7, 20, 22, 28, 29, 31, 42, 54, 141 n. 37, 152, 169, 170, 183, 189
'discourse of the Other' 150, 151 n. 72, 152
failure of 6
dissatisfaction 113–14, 118–20
Documents (journal) 17–18, 207
Dostoevsky, Fyodor, *The Brothers Karamazov* 110, 205 & n. 34
double, the 11–12, 145, 166, 169, 171, 180, 181, 193, 228–29, 234
doubleness 7, 12, 82, 90, 155, 162, 164, 178, 185, 188, 191, 198, 210, 234
doubling 145, 171, 178, 180, 185, 197
dreams 18 n. 8, 100, 116 n. 78, 136–37, 138–40
day-dreams 131–32
dream of knowledge, Freudian 133–35, 137
dualism 12, 20, 21, 71–72, 105
duality 12, 82, 114, 145, 150, 155, 169–70, 191
duplicity 12, 88, 90, 166, 169, 234

ego 148–50, 153, 155, 157
encounter 1–3, 6, 12–13, 29, 30, 85, 88–90, 203, 222, 233, 234
Eros 64, 196
erotic, the *see* eroticism

eroticism 29, 42, 60, 194 n. 4, 201, 209
escape 113, 114, 116–17
ethics 87, 93–96, 99, 100–01, 112, 127, 184
   of writing 91
Eurydice 53–54, 74, 85–86, 87, 91–92, 128
evil 96–114, 120–22, 127, 129, 205 n. 34
   fascination of 102–03, 109, 114
excess 3, 6, 7, 8, 12, 19, 22–27, 29, 30, 31, 32–33, 36, 37, 40, 41, 52, 55, 83, 96, 130, 151, 197, 201
   Bataillean 25–27, 36, 55
   of being 41, 52
   of existence 10, 23, 41
   of experience 2, 39
   of imagination 19
   of presence 13, 130, 203
   of reality/the real 19, 233
   of signification 29, 31
   of the subject 96
excrit see exscription
existence 2, 4 n. 3, 6, 8, 10, 12, 19–20, 22, 23, 31, 32–33, 37, 41, 46, 47, 49–50, 51, 52, 54, 67, 86, 87, 88, 91–92, 95, 97, 98, 100, 101, 113, 114–15, 120, 122, 123, 154–55, 165, 168, 170, 177, 186–88, 189, 196, 197, 202, 205 n. 34, 206, 212, 232–33, 234
   worldly 1, 2, 5, 7, 8, 229
Existentialism 31, 205–06
expenditure 3, 6, 12, 19, 24, 26–28, 32 n. 47, 36, 104, 106, 196
experience 2, 4, 6, 8, 9, 11, 19, 39–40, 42, 49, 53, 54, 59, 61, 72, 79, 87, 88, 90, 96, 103, 109–10, 133, 137, 138, 152 n. 77,
165 & n. 14, 171, 197, 199, 201, 210 & n. 51, 211, 221–22, 224
   inner 11, 28–37, 40–42, 43
   lived 18 n. 7, 64–65, 165
   originary 4 n. 5
exscription 10 n. 20, 19–20, 25, 31, 37, 42, 54, 211, 232, 234
eyes *see* vision

Fall, the 105, 112, 225, 226
fascination 80, 82, 132–33, 220, 221
   of evil 102–03, 109, 114
fiction 23, 60 n. 8, 61–64, 67, 73, 77–78, 127, 137–38, 149–50, 168, 198, 213, 228, 231–32
figuration 7, 31, 166, 213, 216–19, 232
Le Fils de Saoul, Le 87–88
First World War 142–43
form 3–4, 41, 57, 88, 206–07, 211, 228, 231
freedom 3, 4 & n. 3, 48, 73, 83, 96, 106, 108–13, 115, 123, 126, 185, 206, 223
   and evil 106, 108–11
Freud, Sigmund 130–42, 146, 152 n. 77, 154, 157 n. 91
   'Creative Writers and Daydreaming' 131–32
   'Dostoevsky and Parricide' 205 n. 34
   dream of knowledge *see* dream of knowledge, Freudian
   The Interpretation of Dreams 139–40

gaze, the 54, 74, 80–81, 156–57, 172 & n. 31, 211–12, 226–27
   of Orpheus 53–54, 87, 128
Gnosticism 20

God 5, 32, 35–36, 48, 63, 84, 109, 119–20, 168 n. 19, 183, 206, 210, 214, 225
good, the 96, 97, 101–02, 104–05, 106, 107–08, 110, 113, 114, 120, 121, 127
Greeks, the 147
  Greek miracle 196–97
  Greek truth 168 & n. 20

Hegel, Georg Wilhelm Friedrich 8 & n. 16, 10, 30–31, 32–33, 48, 55, 59, 92, 95, 103, 106, 154, 171, 196, 201–02, 204, 212, 213 & n. 60, 218, 221 & n. 82, 224
  negation 4 & n. 4, 82, 189
  negativity 4 n. 4, 33, 189, 190, 218, 221
  Phenomenology of the Spirit 33
Heidegger, Martin 4, 8, 10, 34, 47, 50, 51, 53, 74–75, 76–77, 84, 86 & n. 40, 111–12, 118, 147–48, 171, 172 & n. 30, 178, 181–82, 183 n. 61, 189, 190, 196, 201–02
  The Origin of the Work of Art 51, 76
Holbein, Hans the Younger, *The Ambassadors* 156–57
Husserl, Edmund 79, 165 & n. 14, 232
hypermorality 100–01, 108, 120, 122

il y a, the 7, 13, 51–55, 83, 86, 189–90, 232, 233
image, the 11, 13, 79 & n. 18, 87, 90–91, 92, 119, 129, 148–50, 155, 166, 216
  Blanchotian 11, 54, 55, 74, 77–84, 91, 92, 155, 161 n. 1, 166, 232
  Lacanian 155

imaginary, the 17, 77, 87, 91, 102, 166, 168 n. 19
  Lacanian 145, 148, 150–51, 153, 155
  Blanchotian 77, 79, 155–56
imagination, the 18, 19, 77–78, 79, 81–82, 84, 100, 155
impossibility *see* impossible, the
impossible, the 22, 42, 44–46, 109, 118, 119, 155, 156, 164, 172–73, 179, 185–86, 188, 189, 202, 211
  of death 176–77, 185–87
  of literature 44–46, 51
  of writing 33, 44–46, 72–73
inappropriable, the 2, 3, 8, 9, 10, 41
informe, the 206–08, 210–11
inscription 20, 83, 126
instant, the 13, 55, 92, 108, 118, 121–22, 128, 129, 199
interruption 28, 31, 86, 127, 137, 138–39, 141, 221, 224
intersubjectivity 165 n. 14

Kafka, Franz 72, 122, 124–28, 161, 167, 168, 185–87
  'Der Jäger Gracchus' 186 & n. 67
  Der Prozeß 124
  Die Verwandlung 186
  'Vor dem Gesetz' 124–28
Kant, Immanuel 3–4, 53, 79, 83–84, 99, 111, 112–13, 121, 127, 221–24
  aesthetic, category of 4 & n. 3
  notion of beauty 83–84
  notion of (re)presentation 3, 83–84
  Third Critique (*Critique of Judgement*) 4 & n. 3, 83–84
Kojève, Alexandre 8 & n. 16, 10, 32–33, 106, 151 n. 72, 212

Lacan, Jacques 136–37, 145–46, 147, 148–57, 233
  'La Chose freudienne' 136
  'Fonction et champ de la parole et du langage' 145
  'La Science et la vérité' 146
  'Le Séminaire sur la lettre volée' 151–52
  'Le Stade du miroir comme formateur de la function du Je' 149–50
language 24, 28, 31, 35, 51, 73, 84, 129, 132, 133, 145–46, 154, 162–63, 170–71, 189, 190, 208
  Bataille's relationship to 24, 37, 41, 54 n. 48, 55
  Blanchot's relationship to 41, 42–44, 48–50, 53, 83, 162–63, 190
  inadequacy of 29, 55, 79
  literary 48–50, 52, 77–78, 183–84
  as literary content 10–11, 29, 169–70
  relationship with the unconscious 146 n. 51, 150–51
Lascaux 196–97, 213–15, 217–18, 224, 225
laughter, in Bataillean thought 29, 34–35, 42, 49, 55, 128, 218
law, the 124–28
Leclaire, Serge 143–45
Levinas, Emmanuel 51, 52, 74–75, 79 & n. 18, 82–83, 86, 87, 94–95, 96, 165 & n. 15, 184, 186–87, 189–90
  Autrement qu'être ou Au-delà de l'essence 165 n. 14
  De l'évasion 114–18
  De l'existence à l'existant 52 n. 45, 86, 186–87
  'La Réalité et son ombre' 79 n. 18, 82–83
  Le Temps et l'autre 95
limitless, the 5, 40 & n. 3, 41, 196
literature
  and art 4 n. 4, 10, 51, 73, 76–79, 90–91, 128
  autobiographical approach to 57–67, 176
  biographical approach to 58–59, 60
  and childhood 132–33, 195
  and death 48–49, 73, 173–74, 175–76, 178
  encounter with the real 20, 54, 62–63, 67, 77–78, 91, 210, 211, 228–29, 231–33
  and evil 99–103, 106–08, 121–22
  failure of 128–29
  the impossibility of 44–46, 51, 72–73
  and life 178–81
  as a mode of being 42, 47, 127
  negative force of 48–51
  and psychoanalysis 130–33, 135–36, 141–44, 151–53, 155
  shift to writing 166–67
  as terror 43–44, 48
  as third space 73, 88, 91–92
loss 3, 26, 27, 28, 52, 92, 112, 138, 142, 144–45, 196
low, the *see* base, the

Mallarmé, Stéphane 28, 59, 75 n. 12, 77, 228
Manet, Edouard 10
  Olympia 227
Mann, Thomas 167
  Joseph und seine Brüder 167–68

mask, the 12, 13, 197, 198, 210–11, 214, 216, 217, 224, 228, 232, 234
masking 197–98, 210, 211, 213–14, 216, 217, 218, 224, 227, 228
materialism 8 n. 16, 20–21
materiality 43, 50, 51, 54, 73, 103, 189, 197, 205, 207, 208, 233
Melville, Herman, *Moby Dick* 89–90
Menard, Pierre 180 & n. 50
mimesis 8, 12, 25 n. 28, 71, 73, 74, 78, 211, 228
Modernism 10–11, 96–97, 101
morality 97–108, 118, 120, 122, 127, 167, 223
music/musician 24, 79, 88–89, 129

narration 89–90, 135, 141–43, 150 n. 68, 173–74, 179, 205
  Blanchot's theory of 173
narrative, the 8, 60, 66, 89, 125, 135–36, 141–42, 173–74, 175, 177, 178–79, 205
  narrated event 89, 135 n. 20
natural attitude, the 165 & n. 14, 232
nature 4, 84, 215, 217, 221–24
  beauty of 4 n. 3
  violence of 220–21
need, human 113, 116 n. 78, 117–18, 195 n. 8
negation 4 & n. 4, 11, 12, 13, 20, 40, 48–49, 50–51, 55, 73, 82, 189, 218–19, 232
negativity 4 n. 4, 8, 32–33, 39, 43–53, 162, 168 n. 19, 189, 190, 218
  unemployed (*négativé sans emploi*) 10, 13, 33, 40 n. 6, 42, 49, 53, 129, 212, 221

neuter (*neutre*), the 7, 12, 13, 58–59, 164, 165, 166, 183–84, 188–91, 232
Newton, Helmut, *Sie Kommen* 226–27
Nietzsche, Friedrich 4–5, 8, 21 n. 19, 40, 51, 66–67, 96, 97, 98, 100, 105–06, 114, 121, 196, 197, 233
  'How the True World Finally became a Fable' 4–5
non-knowledge 9, 30, 32 & n. 47, 33 n. 56, 39, 49
novel, the 49, 60, 66–67, 91, 135, 172, 175, 177–78, 200
nudity 197–98, 214, 225–28

Oedipus 35, 63 n. 19
One, the 181–84, 188, 191
operations, Batailléan 6 & n. 12, 8, 29, 31, 201, 204, 206–08, 218, 228
origin, the 6, 12, 25, 51, 52, 67, 73, 86–87, 90 & n. 46, 111, 112, 126, 127, 133, 134, 135–36, 145, 180, 194, 196, 213 n. 62, 215, 219, 233–34
  quest for 86, 134–35, 215
original, the 90–91, 134, 180, 234
originality 6, 21, 24, 25, 44, 80, 83, 180
Original Sin 105
Orpheus 53–54, 74, 85–88, 128, 234
other, the 22, 23, 34–35, 42, 88, 94–96, 150–51, 152, 165, 168, 182–83, 184, 224, 229
  Levinasian (*autrui*) 87, 94–95, 165 n. 15, 184, 190
otherness 107–08, 150–51, 153, 154, 182, 183, 184, 189–90, 232

outside, the (*le dehors*) 4, 19–20, 22, 29–30, 32, 39–40, 42, 52, 54, 91, 126, 128, 148, 149, 170, 187, 202

painting 79 & n. 18, 84–85, 91, 198–99, 203–04, 227 n. 102
Paris 119 n. 84, 214
  German occupation of 30
  Liberation of 35
Paulhan, Jean, *Les Fleurs de Tarbes* 43 & n. 17
Plato 3, 25, 66–67, 71–72, 98, 107, 147, 169 & n. 22, 208, 232
  Phaedo 67
  The Republic 3
  theory of ideal forms 3–4, 208
pleasure 113–14, 117–18, 132, 133, 137, 138–39, 196, 223
Poe, Edgar Allan, 'The Purloined Letter' 151–53
poetic, the 28–29, 31, 59, 73, 87, 118–20, 131–32, 190
poetry 27–28, 31–32, 50, 51, 118–19, 123
  and sacrifice 28
potlatch 26
presence 11, 12, 13, 25, 52 & n. 45, 54, 55, 64, 67, 75, 80, 83, 85, 88, 91, 92, 118, 123, 128, 129, 130, 137, 144, 162, 166, 189, 207, 227, 232, 233
  as being 34, 147, 166
  impossibility of 13
  problematization of 12, 41, 162
present, the 55, 64, 88, 98, 108, 109, 110, 111, 113, 118, 122–23, 205 n. 34
presentation 3–5, 11, 76, 83–84, 129, 169, 222 n. 83, 228
profane, the 215, 218, 219–21

psychoanalysis 63 n. 19, 130, 131–58, 228

Real, the 1–3, 5, 6, 7–8, 20, 57–58, 63, 67, 79, 82, 103, 117, 202, 212, 228, 233–35
  Lacanian 136, 137, 153–56, 202
  literary 1–2, 8, 215, 231
  relationship to writing 1–2, 20, 43, 54, 62–63, 67, 77–78, 91, 103, 130, 205, 210, 228, 231–33
reality 4, 5, 17, 18–19, 23, 29, 48–49, 53, 62–63, 73, 78, 81–83, 90 n. 46, 98–99, 115–16, 130, 131, 145, 150, 162, 168 n. 19, 183–84, 202, 204, 216
  return to 18–19
récit 58, 63, 89–90, 141 n. 37
relation 3, 7, 46, 47, 53, 80, 86, 94, 109, 135 n. 20, 137, 149–50, 154, 156, 172 n. 30, 177, 178–79, 181, 183–85, 188, 189, 190, 191, 216, 218, 219–20, 228–29, 232, 234
relationality 3, 73, 94, 158, 165 n. 15, 232
repetition 125, 138–39, 145, 153, 162, 190, 191, 210, 216–17
representation 2, 6, 76, 83–84, 89, 111, 143–44, 148, 150, 198, 210–11, 213–15, 216–18, 222 n. 83, 224, 229, 232, 233
  crisis of 143–44, 233
  failure of 221–24
return 51, 97, 133, 135, 138, 177, 178, 195–96, 218–19, 220, 228
  of animality 213, 217–18
  to childhood 132–33, 195
  to reality 18–19
Ricœur, Paul 111–13

Rodin, Auguste 91
  Balzac 91
  The Kiss 91
Romanticism 4 n. 3, 59, 75 & n. 12, 83–84, 114, 115–16, 232

sacred, the 23, 28, 215, 218–21
sacrifice 6, 27, 28, 29, 31, 35, 63 n. 18, 121, 219, 221 & n. 82
Sade, Marquis de 22–24, 48, 50, 107
Sartre, Jean-Paul 2, 8 n. 16, 43, 83, 107, 108–09, 118–19, 120, 122–23, 175
  L'Être et le néant 109
  L'Imaginaire 81–82
  La Nausée 174–75
  Qu'est-ce que la littérature? 48
self, the 30–31, 63 n. 18, 94–96, 148–50, 152, 155, 163, 165, 183, 184, 202–03, 209, 222–23
self-referentiality 47, 84–85, 89, 170, 178
self-representation 84–85, 171
sight *see* vision
silence 35, 52, 142–43, 204, 227
simulacrum, the 24–25, 37, 232, 234
Sirens, the 74, 88–89
slippage 32 n. 47, 34, 35, 36, 206, 208
slopes (*versants*) 50 & n. 39, 51, 73, 234
Socrates 67
space *see* spatiality
spatiality 11, 12, 41, 43, 51, 53, 73–74, 75, 77, 85, 88, 90 n. 46, 91–92, 127, 130, 136, 143, 144, 149, 169–70, 175, 185–86, 191, 217, 229, 234
speech 23, 50, 73, 130, 141, 145–46, 154, 169–72, 183, 189

speechlessness 143, 172, 189
story 61, 110, 141–42, 163, 171, 177–78, 181
storyteller, the 142, 143, 173, 177, 178
storytelling 142–43, 173, 175, 177–78
subject 2, 4, 10, 27, 30–31, 33, 53, 65–66, 83–85, 93–96, 99, 115–16, 130, 133, 148–52, 155–57, 165, 169–71, 183, 201, 203, 206, 222, 223, 233
subjectivity 30, 40, 65–66, 130, 148, 151, 161–62, 165 & n. 15, 176–77, 183–84, 201, 202–03, 206, 221–24, 233, 234, 235
sublime, the 221–24
Surrealism 17–18, 19, 20, 23, 103
Symbolic Order, Lacanian 148–54, 157
syncopation 129–30

temporality 97, 98, 99, 106, 108–09, 111–12, 118, 122, 126, 127, 130, 138 & n. 28, 141 n. 37, 153, 195, 205 n. 34, 218–19, 223
tension 25, 29, 31, 35–36, 37, 51, 73, 75, 88, 97, 102, 111, 143, 155, 210, 211, 214, 216, 219, 234
Thanatos 196
theory 137–38, 140, 146–48, 153, 154, 155
  of art 71, 74
  of ethics 93–94, 95, 96
  as fiction 137–38
  of the image 79–80
  psychoanalytic *see* psychoanalysis
time *see* temporality
touch 31, 80

transcendence 2, 6, 52, 54, 79, 87, 100, 123, 165, 184, 204–05, 218
   language as 190
truth, the 24, 25, 51, 67, 75, 84, 95, 136–37, 142, 145–46, 154, 157 n. 91, 168–70, 179–80, 183, 197–200, 201, 202, 203, 204, 210, 226, 227, 231
   of the body 197–98
   Greek 168–69
   of literature 75, 179, 199–200, 203–05
   narrative 136 & n. 24, 141–42
   in painting 198–99

Ulysses 74, 88–89
unconscious, the 139, 143–45, 146 n. 51, 150–52, 157 n. 91
unreal, the 39, 67, 81
unreality 23, 83

Velásquez, Diego Rodríguez de Silva y, *Las Meninas* 84–85
violence 40, 41, 152 n. 77, 209
   of laughter 128
   of nature 220–21
vision 54, 64, 80, 128, 147–48, 151, 153, 156–57, 193–95, 202–03, 214

Weil, Simone 101–02, 108, 120–21
   La Pesanteur et la grâce 101–02
Wilde, Oscar 72
work 32, 67, 113–14, 122, 162, 195 & n. 8, 196, 213, 218, 219
World War II 143, 176
writing
   autobiographical 57–67
   as contestation 42–43, 166–67, 183
   as death 174–79
   as downfall of subjectivity 161–71
   as exposure 2, 19–20, 40, 67
   and the impossible 22, 29, 33, 42, 44–46, 72–73
   and the outside 22–23, 29, 37, 42, 54

CPSIA information can be obtained
at www.ICGtesting.com
Printed in the USA
JSHW032243110123
36080JS00002B/2